AF505981

Japanese Public Opinion and the War on Terrorism

Japanese Public Opinion and the War on Terrorism

Edited by

Robert D. Eldridge
and
Paul Midford

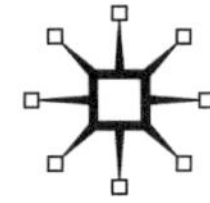

JAPANESE PUBLIC OPINION AND THE WAR ON TERRORISM
Copyright © Robert D. Eldridge and Paul Midford, 2008.

First published in 2008 by
PALGRAVE MACMILLAN®
in the US—a division of St. Martin's Press LLC,
175 Fifth Avenue, New York, NY 10010.

Where this book is distributed in the UK, Europe and the rest of the world,
this is by Palgrave Macmillan, a division of Macmillan Publishers Limited,
registered in England, company number 785998, of Houndmills,
Basingstoke, Hampshire RG21 6XS.

Palgrave Macmillan is the global academic imprint of the above companies
and has companies and representatives throughout the world.

Palgrave® and Macmillan® are registered trademarks in the United States,
the United Kingdom, Europe and other countries.

ISBN-13: 978–0–230–60643–2
ISBN-10: 0–230–60643–1

Library of Congress Cataloging-in-Publication Data

Japanese public opinion and the war on terrorism / edited by Robert D.
Eldridge and Paul Midford.
        p. cm.—(The Palgrave Macmillan series in international political
        communication)
    Includes bibliographical references and index.
    ISBN 0–230–60643–1
      1. Terrorism—Japan—Public opinion. 2. Public opinion—Japan.
    3. War on Terrorism, 2001—Public opinion. I. Eldridge, Robert D.
    II. Midford, Paul.

HV6433.J32J37 2008
973.931—dc22   2007051216

A catalogue record for this book is available from the British Library.

Design by Newgen Imaging Systems (P) Ltd., Chennai, India.

First edition: August 2008

10 9 8 7 6 5 4 3 2 1

Printed in the United States of America.

*Robert Eldridge wishes to dedicate this book to his mother,
Maureen Eldridge.*

*Paul Midford wishes to dedicate this book to his mother,
Carol E. Midford.*

Contents

Figures

Tables

CONTRIBUTORS

Chijiwa Yasuaki is currently a research fellow at the Graduate School of Law and Political Science, Kyoto University. He was a former visiting research associate at the Sigur Center George Washington University. He received his bachelor's degree in law at Hiroshima University, and his master's and doctorate in international public policy from Osaka University. His field of research includes Japanese political and diplomatic history, and his dissertation was entitled "Japan–United States Ambassadorial Diplomacy in the Postwar Period: A Comparative Historical Study on Their Roles." He has published several articles, including "Insights into Japan–U.S. Relations on the Eve of the Iraqi War: Dilemmas over 'Showing the Flag,'" *Asian Survey*, Vol. 45, No. 6 (November–December 2005), and others in Japanese language journals such as *Kokusai Seiji* (International Relations) and *Nihon Seiji Kenkyu* (Japanese Political Science).

Robert D. Eldridge is an associate professor of Japanese political and diplomatic history and U.S.–Japan relations at the School of International Public Policy, Osaka University, and a former scholar-in-residence at the headquarters of U.S. Marine Corps Forces, Pacific, at Camp Smith, Hawaii. He received his doctorate in political science from the Graduate School of Law, Kobe University. He has published extensively on the dynamics of the U.S.–Japan alliance and the Okinawa issue including *The Origins of the Bilateral Okinawa Problem: Okinawa in Postwar U.S.-Japan Relations, 1945–1952* (Garland, 2001) and (Osaka University Center for International Security Studies and Policy, 2004). He has recently translated the memoirs of Miyazawa Kiichi (*Secret Talks between Tokyo and Washington*, Lexington Books, 2007), and is completing a book on the return of Iwo Jima and the Bonin Islands to Japan in 1968.

Mark Hollstein is an associate professor of political science and Asian studies at Kansai Gaidai University in Osaka, Japan. He received his bachelor's degree in political science from the University of Utah, and his master's degree in journalism from the Columbia Graduate School of Journalism in New York. Before earning his PhD in political science from the University of Hawaii, he worked in both print and broadcast journalism. This included three years as a news producer at the New York bureau of TV Asahi, one of Japan's five major commercial television networks. He was a 1997–1999 recipient of the Crown Prince Akihito Scholarship, which he used to complete his PhD dissertation fieldwork in Okinawa, Japan. His dissertation was a discourse analysis of how Japanese national newspapers, local Okinawan newspapers, and American newspapers covered protests against the presence of American military bases in Okinawa in the mid-1990s.

Paul Midford is an associate professor in the Department of Political Science and Sociology, and director of the Japan Program at the Norwegian University for Science and Technology (NTNU) in Trondheim. Previously, he taught at Kwansei Gakuin University, Lafayette College, and Kanazawa University. He has published in *International Organization*, *Security Studies*, *Asian Survey*, *The Pacific Review*, and the *International Relations of the Asia-Pacific*. His most recent work is a chapter "Globalization and National Security: Is Japan Still an Island?" Chapter in Jonathan Kirshner, ed., *Globalization and National Security* (New York: Routledge, 2006), pp. 259–92. He is an associate editor at *Japan Forum*. Midford earned his PhD in political science from Columbia University.

Paul D. Scott is professor of modern Japanese and Chinese history, Asian Studies Program, Kansai Gaidai University. He serves on the Steering Committee of the Alliance for Reform and Democracy, and is a member of Transcend. He is also a board member of the Cambodia Education Project and serves as an advisor to Sam Rainsy. He is the project director for the Asia Democracy Index. His most recent publications include: *The Challenges of Democracy in Asia,* editor Hirakata City: The Intercultural Research Institute, Kansai Gaidai University, 2005; and the *Singapore Election Report* Singapore: The Alliance for Reform and Democracy in Asia, 2005 and the *Asia Democracy Index 2005* Singapore: Alliance for Reform and Democracy in Asia, 2005. In June 2006, Dr. Scott testified before the House Human Rights Caucus and in August that year, joined a democratic mission to Timor Leste. He received his PhD from the University of Virginia and was a graduate research student at the University of Tokyo.

Stephanie A. Weston, a resident of Japan for more than twenty years, is a professor of U.S.–Japan relations at the University of Fukuoka and Seinan Gakuin. Her most recent publications focus on the U.S.–Japan alliance including "Alliance in Transition: A New Strategic Partnership," *Fukuoka University Law Journal*, Vol. 47, No. 2 (September 2002); "The Clinton Legacy in Asia," *Current Politics and Economies of Asia*, Vol. 10, No. 4 (October 2002); and "The U.S.–Japan Alliance in the New Post Cold War," *Japanese Studies*, Vol. 24, No. 1 (May 2004). Weston previously was a foreign service officer with the State Department and served as the consular officer in charge of the consular and administrative sections at the U.S. Consulate in Fukuoka.

Acknowledgments

First and foremost, the editors and our fellow contributors wish to thank the Suntory Foundation for providing a grant to support the early stages and bulk of our research. Our study group received a Humanities and Social Science Grant (*Jinbun Shakai Kagaku Joseikin*) from the Foundation, located in Osaka, Japan, the region where most of the contributors are based, in the summer of 2003 and immediately began our research in an attempt to remedy the gaps in Japanese public opinion research, discussed in the introduction. Paul Midford wishes to thank the Japan Society for the Promotion of Science for funding a short-term research fellowship during June–August 2007, during which he conducted some final research related to chapters one and four.

Second, we would like to thank the various news agencies and polling services for allowing us to use their collected data. We would also like to thank the Japan Data Archive at the Roper Center, the University of Connecticut at Storrs, for providing us access and assisting Paul Midford during his visit to the Archive in March 2004. We would especially like to thank Roper Center associate director Lois Timms-Ferrara and archivist Cynthia Teixeira for extending a warm welcome and much assistance.

Third, we wish to thank the many knowledgeable individuals from all walks of Japanese society who agreed to be interviewed and otherwise shared their perceptions and insights about their organizations and social trends.

Fourth, we would like to thank our respective institutions for permitting us time to travel to conduct our interviews and research. We would also like to thank the Osaka School of International Public Policy especially for providing facilities for our sessions.

Fifth, we would like to thank the organizers of the American Political Science Association for allowing us to present our initial findings at the September 2004 conference in Chicago, which happened to be the 100th Annual Meeting. We are grateful to those who attended the session and made comments, including discussant Andrew Oros.

Sixth, the contributors would like to thank Kumagai Toshiki, formerly of the U.S. Consulate General, Osaka-Kobe, and currently professor at the Kyoto University of Foreign Studies, who provided much insights and advice in the early phases of this project.

Seventh, we would like to thank the East-West Center, Washington. Parts of Paul Midford's chapter on mass opinion (chapter one) and the Midford and Paul Scott chapter on political parties (chapter four) were originally published in *Policy Studies* 27 titled "Japanese Public Opinion and the War on Terrorism: Implications for Japan's Security Strategy," published by the East-West Center, Washington. For more information on the series and the original publication, please log on to the website www.eastwestcenter washington.org.

Finally, we thank Palgrave's senior editor Anthony "Toby" Wahl for supporting our project throughout and the staff at Palgrave, especially Emily Hue and Kristy Lilas, for seeing the project through to its completion.

Abbreviations

ANSWER	Act Now to Stop War and End Racism
ASDF	Air Self-Defense Force
CBO	Community-Based Organization
DPJ	Democratic Party of Japan
GSDF	Ground Self-Defense Force
ICT	Information and Communication Technology
IMFTE	International Military Tribunal, Far East
IO	International Organization
JANIC	Japan NGO Center for International Cooperation
JCP	Japan Communist Party
JDA	Japan Defense Agency
LDP	Liberal Democratic Party
MOD	Ministry of Defense (Japan)
MSDF	Maritime Self-Defense Force
NATO	North Atlantic Treaty Organization
NGDO	Nongovernmental Development Organization
NGO	Nongovernmental Organization
NPO	Nonprofit Organization
PDA	Popular Development Agencies
PILP	Public Interest Legal Persons
PKF	Peacekeeping Forces
QUANGO	Quasi-Autonomous Nongovernmental Organization (or National Governmental Organization)
SDF	Self-Defense Force
SDPJ	Social Democratic Party of Japan
UN	United Nations
VNPO	Voluntary Nonprofit Organization
WMD	Weapons of Mass Destruction

Introduction

Robert D. Eldridge and Paul Midford

WHAT IS PUBLIC OPINION AND WHY JAPAN?

Public opinion is an imprecise and often misused term. Who exactly is the "public"—the vocal minority, the silent majority, or both—and what is meant by "opinion"? Is opinion a stable attitude or simply a temporary view? If it is the latter, is this view based on imprecise information or sound reasoning? Is an opinion conditional? Is it temporary? Are opinions organized into coherent structures of attitude and belief, or are they jumbled and incoherent?

Because it is an imprecise term, it is also a convenient one—scholars, analysts, media, politicians, activists, and interest groups all use it with relative impunity. The contributors of this book were aware of these concerns, and indeed that is one of the reasons this study was organized.

An important question concerning *yoron*, or public opinion, then, becomes the degree to which it is accurately captured and assessed. Polls, particularly those conducted regularly, with a stable set of questions and scientifically sound methodology, can accurately track and gauge opinion, assuming the questions and methods are consistent. However, at the same time, all too often there is a strong tendency, whether intentional or not, to present leading questions that prompt the interviewee to unwittingly answer in a way that supports the views of the interviewer or agenda of the sponsor of the poll.

Assuming a poll is methodologically sound, the next question is the extent to which it should be listened to by policy makers and leaders at local and national levels. Many political leaders will argue that public opinion should be listened to, while others explain that public opinion is no more than one consideration out of many to reflect on when making a decision. In addition, the latter group will argue that public opinion changes and that it should be viewed over the longer range and not simply at one particular moment in time. Leaders, in other words, they say, should not and cannot be held hostage to a momentary national sentiment and lose sight of the greater picture, although they are sometimes inclined to ignore longer term public opinion as well. Koizumi Junichiro, Japan's prime minister from April 2001 until September 2006, belonged to this latter group.[1]

This book began as a project by a handful of American academics with long-term experience in Japan wishing to examine the seemingly dramatic changes in Japanese thinking on security issues following the terrorist attacks of 9/11 in the United States, its only alliance partner. Would Japan fail to "show the flag" again, repeating the situation seen after the Iraqi invasion of Kuwait and the start of the Gulf Crisis/War in 1990–1991, or had the evolution in thinking in the wake of the international criticism of Japan's nonparticipation in the Gulf Crisis/War led Japan to become an ally in every sense of the word with the United States? Moreover, is Japan's thinking in this regard influenced by the broader international community, or merely by its alliance with the United States, or does Japan tend to confuse the two? Did divergences exist between Japan and the United States, and between the Japanese public and its government? If so, how serious and permanent were they?

While both Japanese public and elite opinion were generally and genuinely supportive of the United States after the 9/11 attacks, divergences between Japan and the United States and between the public and the government started to be seen as soon as the United States began using force in Afghanistan in the fall of 2001. At first, the divergences on both levels were relatively modest. By the time of the Iraq War in March 2003, however, the divergences had become large between Japan and the United States and between the leadership and the public within both Japan and the United States. The United States was increasingly losing international support and understanding to the point that it was being seen as the cause of 9/11, rather than its victim. Five years after the 9/11 attacks, a broad survey conducted by the *Yomiuri Shimbun* (Japan), the *Korea Times* (South Korea), and the Gallup Group found that opinions in seven countries in the Asia–Pacific region toward the United States had declined in since 9/11.[2]

These trends were recognized early on by the Council on Foreign Relations' Independent Task Force on Public Diplomacy and pointed out in its September 2003 report, but to little avail.[3] Misdirection, confusion, and indifference continue to hinder U.S. public diplomacy with the result being the need to make up for not only lost time, but lost ground too.[4] The United States seems to have been steadily losing the battle for the hearts and minds of the people of the world.

As Americans living in Japan, we could not help but be concerned about the worsening image of the United States and thought a study of Japanese public opinion would assist in clarifying Japanese views on America's global war on terrorism, Japan's participation in it, and what this means for the bilateral relationship, and what it says more broadly about global perceptions of U.S. foreign policy, especially in Asia and among America's most developed and wealthy allies.

Japan was (and is) important to look at first because of these changes, but also because it is one of America's most important regional allies and an essential global partner. Despite its importance, particularly after the start of the George W. Bush administration, which included several prominent officials extremely knowledgeable about Japan, much of the debate on public diplomacy did not include traditional allies or regions less troubled by terrorism. U.S. policy was becoming myopic, and so was the analysis. Overlooking Japan was a case in point.

This study will explore an important yet understudied variable in democratic Japan: public opinion. Although it is a hotly discussed topic among Japan watchers on online list serves and other forums for debate, including those in policy circles, very little has been published in English regarding Japanese public opinion on security since the 1970s.[5] Such a study is especially relevant today, with international public opinion regarding the war on terrorism, the use of military force, and attitudes toward the United States grabbing headlines and generating large multinational comparative opinion surveys—surveys that often omit Japan.[6] Thus, this study not only sheds light on how public opinion affects Japan's security strategy, it also offers insights into how Japanese public opinion toward the war on terrorism diverges or converges with that found elsewhere.

In addition to using opinion polls and other publicly available data, we have examined public opinion at key junctures during the first several years after 9/11, which correspond to the years of the Koizumi administration, using a variety of angles and approaches including looking at mass opinion, intellectual and elite opinion, television news discourse, editorial framing, the role of political parties and public opinion, and NGOs/NPOs and public opinion. These methods are explained in full later. In short, we believe they are informative and original, as well as highlight the same conclusions, discussed in the following paragraphs.

ELITIST AND PLURALIST APPROACHES TO PUBLIC OPINION

The study of public opinion can be largely divided into essentially two schools: the elitists and the pluralists. The elitists argue that public opinion is often unstable, uninformed, moody, and even incoherent.[7] Public opinion, according to the famous findings of Philip E. Converse, is composed of "non-attitudes."[8] Public opinion is, in short, a factor that if allowed to be influential, threatens the rational, consistent, and coherent foreign policy of any democracy. If public opinion is moody, unstable, and often incoherent, the good news for elitists is that public opinion is also malleable and able to be manipulated to the point that it usually does not threaten to become influential.[9]

Pluralists, on the other hand, view public opinion as stable and composed of rational and coherent attitudes.[10] "The Rational Public," according to Benjamin I. Page and Robert Y. Shapiro, because it is a collective phenomenon of large numbers, possesses certain "emergent properties" that gives it something approaching "wisdom."[11] In other words, public opinion in this view is more than the sum of its parts. In accessing policies or reacting to events, individuals sometimes make random errors. However, at the level of collective opinion these random errors generally cancel each other out, causing collective opinions to have greater coherence and stability, if not wisdom, than that generally found at the individual level.

In the twentieth-century American study of public opinion, the elitist view predominated from at least the time of Walter Lippmann's landmark works, *Public Opinion*, published in 1922, and *The Phantom Public*, published in 1925,[12] until sometime in the 1960s. The Vietnam War encouraged the rise of the pluralist school, as pluralists came to believe that collective mass opinion toward the war ended up being more coherent and even rational than elite opinion.[13]

Not surprisingly, this debate between elitists and pluralists is heard not only in the United States and Europe, but in Japan as well. Miyatake Michiko describes in detail the origins and contemporary uses of the concept of public opinion in Japan, and the numerous Japanese terminology with it—*seiron, seron*, and *yoron*—as well as the respective *kanji*, or Chinese characters, used when writing many words in Japanese.[14] Miyatake traces the idea back as far as the year 1415, but notes the expression "public opinion" became more commonly used in the political sense only at the end of the Tokugawa Shogunate and early years of the Meiji Restoration in the late 1860s.[15] There were variances, however, in how public opinion was being used. One view saw public opinion, however irrational it might be at times, as giving justification for political decisions, while the other saw public opinion simply as the summation of feelings at the time in a community (popular sentiments, talk of the town). Those adhering to the former perspective tended to use the *kanji* that implied the elitist view and read them as "yoron," while the latter, pluralist school used a slightly different *kanji* and read it as "seiron" or "seron." In the postwar reforms of the Japanese language and *kanji* usage, the two sets of *kanji* have been dropped in favor of one. Today, "yoron" is the most common reading of the wording, but "seron" is also heard. In either case, most often any difference in reading is done without an awareness of the origins of its use.[16]

Regardless of the term used, in Japan the elitist view has tended to predominate, even in Western studies of Japanese politics.[17] When a foreign observer, for example, suggests that political parties can and should follow public opinion, it is not uncommon to hear policy elites dismiss such an idea as "mobocracy" or *shugu seiji*.[18] However, the elitist view has not gone unchallenged by scholars with a more pluralist orientation.[19]

This book's focus on Japanese public opinion toward the war on terrorism offers a good opportunity to test the competing predictions of the elitists and the pluralists, even though the elitists can be said to have the "home-court advantage," as the predominant paradigm. This means if pluralist predictions about public opinion, namely that it will be stable, coherent, and influential in the medium to long term, if not always in the short term, turns out to be confirmed by this study, then the pluralist perspective will emerge with greatly enhanced credibility and the elitist perspective will emerge with greatly reduced credibility.[20] In this sense as well, the findings of this volume have significance for other democracies beyond Japan, including the study of public opinion in Europe and the United States.

The testing of elitist versus pluralist perspectives on public opinion also has implications for how elites should integrate public opinion into policy-making. If the elite model emerges with enhanced credibility, then elites should seek to lead, mold, or at least, ignore public opinion. Generally, for elitists, the less independent influence public opinion wields over foreign policy, the better. On the other hand, the pluralist model suggests that elites should lead during short-term contingencies, but otherwise educate public opinion, and then step back, listen, and finally incorporate public opinion when making policy.

In the contemporary context of Japanese politics, this debate takes on additional significance. The tenure of Koizumi, one of Japan's most influential prime ministers in the postwar era, ended in September 2006, raising anew questions about the relationship between public opinion and elites. An exceptionally stubborn and skilled politician, Koizumi claimed to lead rather than follow public opinion. Public opinion, in his view, would inevitably endorse his policies. "People who were once against the U.S.–Japan Security Treaty and UN peace-keeping operations are now in favor of them. The deployment to Iraq will be just the same."[21] Later, Koizumi advised his successor, Prime Minister Abe Shinzo, "Don't worry about the [cabinet] support rate...It is important to have insensitivity."[22]

Since this volume covers the response of Japan and its public opinion to the war on terrorism during the Koizumi administration, it gives an insight into how influential elites can be when they are at their height of power. This is another reason for concluding that the elitist perspective has the "home-court" advantage in this study: if Koizumi cannot have his way with policy because of opposition from public opinion, it is hard to imagine how any other politician could hope to do so for the foreseeable future.

Beyond the question of whether politicians are influenced by mass opinion or vice versa (or neither) is the question of how other elites, such as scholars, the media, and activists, relate to mass opinion. To what extent do the media—both print and television—act to mold public opinion, or, to what extent do they reflect mass opinion? How influential are scholars and activists in influencing mass opinion, the media, or politicians? What is the role of the Internet in accessing and disseminating information? Can local communities, such as the base communities in Okinawa, impact mass opinion, politicians, or other elites nationwide? In sum, should we think of these other actors as extensions of mass opinion, of elites, or as independent actors that influence policy, if not mass opinion itself?

Overall, we find that mass opinion, while subject to a limited degree of elite molding, is nonetheless an important policy influence in democratic Japan. Although the events of 9/11 and the subsequent war on terrorism shook Japan, and although ruling political elites, led by Koizumi and "his team," sought to expand Japan's military role overseas, public opinion set limits that prevented Japan's military role from exceeding incremental and slow expansion.[23] Most importantly, public opinion prevented this slow and incremental expansion from approaching direct involvement in combat. On the other hand, much more important changes occurred domestically as public opinion increasingly accepted an expansion of the state's role in preparing to counter attacks on Japan from terrorists or more conventional threats. Given Koizumi's exceptional political skills, these findings suggest that normally public opinion will have even greater influence. Overall, elites have some leeway to lead during short-term contingencies and then to "educate" the public. For this to happen, accurate information and open debate, originating not only with politicians and the government, but also from a competitive marketplace of ideas in which there is serious competition between various forms of media, is essential. After attempting to educate, elites need to listen, and then incorporate public opinion into policy-making. Otherwise, they risk pursuing unsustainable, if not politically counterproductive, policies.

Structure of the Book

The book is divided into seven chapters, not including this introduction and a concluding chapter. In chapter one, "Japanese Mass Opinion toward the War on Terrorism," Paul Midford examines the measurable responses of Japanese mass opinion to Tokyo's participation in the war on terrorism through publicly available media and government-sponsored opinion polls. It focuses on the dispatch of Self-Defense Forces' (SDF) naval vessels to the Indian Ocean in fall 2001, their continued operations there, and the dispatch of SDF troops to Iraq in 2004. Integral to this concern is an analysis of mass public opinion toward American foreign policy and the utility of using military force. Beyond these foci lies the larger issue of whether 9/11 and the American "war on terrorism" have provoked radical change, gradual evolution, or reinforced preexisting beliefs about the efficacy of using force in international politics. This chapter concludes that Japanese public opinion is gradually shedding antimilitarist distrust of the state, a trend that reveals a set of attitudes corresponding to a form of defensive realism. Although the 9/11 attacks and the war on terrorism have brought limited innovation in Japanese defense policy, they have done little to speed up the evolution away from antimilitarist distrust.

Chapter two, written by Stephanie A. Weston and titled "Framing the Japanese Homeland Security Debate: Mass Media and Public Opinion," examines the editorials of the three largest mainstream Japanese newspapers—the *Asahi Shimbun*, *Yomiuri Shimbun*, and *Mainichi Shimbun*. Her purpose is to assess the debate on the evolving nature of Japanese homeland security following 9/11 and using the concept of "framing" to highlight how the media tend to frame the debate. Finally, she analyzes how these dynamics impact on both U.S.–Japan relations as well as on the future of Japanese homeland security.

In chapter three, "Japan's Insider and Outside Media Discourse about the SDF Dispatch to Iraq," Mark Hollstein goes one level deeper by exploring the ability of the Japanese government to shape public opinion through the use of the *kisha* (reporters) club system. Many media analysts within and outside of Japan are highly critical of this system, which encourages reporters from competing news organizations to form cooperative working relationships with each other and their government sources. Hollstein uses discourse analysis of newspaper and television reports about a specific event—the dispatch of the advance team of the Japan SDF to Iraq in January 2004—to test whether these "insider" *kisha* club reporters truly create homogenous stories that favor government interpretations, as many of these critics assert.

In the next coauthored chapter titled "Japanese Political Parties Face Public Opinion: Leading, Responding, or Ignoring?" Midford and Paul D. Scott examine how political parties deal with public opinion: do they attempt to shape public opinion, respond to it, or ignore it? Their chapter considers several hypotheses about when political parties will respond to public opinion, and when they will attempt to reshape or ignore it. They find that political parties are most likely to respond to public opinion when clear and stable opinion majorities form, and when the ruling and opposition sides take opposing stands, or when the ruling side worries that a stable opposing opinion majority in one area may endanger higher priority policy initiatives in other issue areas. Most commonly, political parties, especially the ruling side, respond to a stable opposing opinion majority by watering down their policy proposals until the opposing majority becomes unstable or retreats to plurality status. In other words, they seek the indifference point of public opinion, the limit of policy ambition that does not provoke a stable opposing opinion majority.

In chapter five, "Japanese Intellectuals and Public Opinion in the War on Terrorism," project organizer Robert D. Eldridge and Chijiwa Yasuaki look at another group who influence public opinion, scholars, academics, critics, and commentators. Specifically, it explores the opinions on the 9/11 terrorist attacks and the war on terrorism expressed by Japanese intellectuals and the manner in which they attempted to express these views for the general public by reviewing the discussions in monthly intellectual periodicals and academic journals. The chapter suggests that the initial interpretation of 9/11 became a sort of prism for evaluating events afterward, such as the Afghanistan War, the Iraq War, and Japan's participation in both. The authors looked primarily at the debates appearing in the following leading journals (from oldest to most recent): *Chuo Koron, Gendai, Bungei Shunju, Sekai, Ushio, Shokun!, Seiron,* and *Ronza,* and several other smaller journals, such as *Kokusai Anzen Hosho* (International Security Studies), *Kokusaiho Gaiko Zasshi* (Journal of International Law and Diplomacy), and *Gaiko Forum.* Several hundred articles were examined and analyzed.

Chapter six, by Scott, examines the role of NGOs in the debate surrounding the Iraq War and its aftermath, and is subtitled "Mobilizing Public Opinion and the War in Iraq." The war in Iraq was an opportunity for Japan's NGOs to mobilize and demonstrate against the decisions of the Koizumi government. The outbreak of the war was preceded by a long period of sanctions imposed after the Gulf War and a period of intense diplomatic activity in the months before the ground attack. This long time frame allowed both Japan's NGOs as well as the international community to engage in debate and discussion. Scott examines both the scope of activity and its effect on shaping and framing the debate and the limits of the Japanese NGO community today.

In the final chapter of the book, prior to the conclusions, Eldridge looks at public opinion in a community that hosts U.S. bases, Okinawa, which for all intensive purposes became the frontline in the public perceptions in Japan about the war on terrorism and the concerns about entanglement in it due to Japan's alliance with the United States. The historically large presence of U.S. forces and their current involvement, both direct and indirect, in military operations related to the war on terrorism have been viewed with mixed feelings in Okinawa, both because of the generally pacifist orientation of the residents of the prefecture and the inconveniences associated with the heavy concentration of bases in the prefecture. These feelings, due to Okinawa's unique situation, are stronger than in other parts of Japan, a fact highlighted in the unambiguous antiwar editorial policies of the two local newspapers. This chapter compares Okinawan opinion toward U.S. bases and the U.S.–Japan alliance before and after the 9/11 terrorist attacks and the Iraq War, as well as with opinion trends on the Japanese mainland. It draws on opinion polls and commentary by the local Okinawan media, and on extensive interviews conducted by the author in Okinawa.

Notes

1. Throughout the book, the names of Japanese individuals will be written according to Japanese cultural practice, i.e., family name first.
2. "Survey: U.S. Image in Asia Deteriorating," *Daily Yomuiri*, September 10, 2006.
3. Peter G. Peterson, *Finding America's Voice: A Strategy for Reinvigorating U.S. Public Diplomacy: Report of an Independent Task Force Sponsored by the Council on Foreign Relations* (New York: Council on Foreign Relations, 2003).
4. For recent reviews of public diplomacy, see Stephen Johnson, Helle C. Dale, and Patrick Cronin, *Strengthening U.S. Public Diplomacy Requires Organization, Coordination, and Strategy,* Heritage Foundation Backgrounder No. 1875, August 5, 2005, http://www.heritage.org/Research/NationalSecurity/bg1875.cfm (accessed September 2006), and Lionel Beehner, Perceptions of U.S. Public Diplomacy, Council on Foreign Relations Backgrounder, September 29, 2005, http://www.cfr.org/publication/8934/perceptions_of_us_public_diplomacy.html?breadcrumb=default (accessed September 2006). The State Department's Advisory Commission on Public Diplomacy (http://www.state.gov/r/adcompd/) should be helping to set the agenda and introduce reforms, but instead appears to be more like a cheerleader than a coach.
5. A major exception is Davis B. Bobrow, "Japan in the World: Opinion from Defeat to Success," *The Journal of Conflict Resolution*, Vol. 33, No. 4 (December 1989), pp. 571–604. Another partial exception is Everett Carl Ladd and Karlyn H. Bowman, *Public Opinion in America and Japan: How We See Each Other and Ourselves* (Washington D.C.: American Enterprise Institute Press, 1996), chapter 3. Notable studies from the 1970s include Douglas H. Mendel, Jr., "Public Views of the Japanese Defense System," in James H. Buck ed., *The Modern Japanese Military System*

(Beverly Hills: Sage, 1975), pp. 149–80; "Japanese Views of the American Alliance in the Seventies," *Public Opinion Quarterly*, Vol. 35, No. 4 (Winter 1971–72), pp. 521–38; and "Japanese Defense in the 1970s: The Public View," *Asian Survey*, Vol. 10 (December 1971–72), pp. 1046–69.

6. See, e.g., Andrew Kohut and Bruce Stokes, *America against the World : How We Are Different and Why We Are Disliked* (New York: Times Books 2006).

7. In addition to the landmark works by Lippmann cited here, major works in the elitist tradition include Gabriel Almond, *The American People and Foreign Policy* (New York: Praeger, 1950); "Public Opinion and National Security," *Public Opinion Quarterly*, Vol. 20, No. 2 (1956), pp. 371–8; Thomas A. Bailey, *The Man in the Street: The Impact of American Public Opinion on Foreign Policy* (New York: Macmillan, 1948); George F. Kennan, *American Diplomacy, 1900–1950* (Chicago: University of Chicago Press, 1951); and Michael Crozier, Samuel P. Huntington, and Joji Watanuki, *The Crisis of Democracy: Report on the Governability of the Democracies to the Trilateral Commission* (New York: New York University Press, 1975).

8. Phillip E. Converse, "Attitudes and Non-Attitudes: Continuation of a Dialogue," in Edward R. Tufte ed., *Analysis of Social Problems* (Reading, Mass.: Addison-Wesley, 1962); and Converse, "The Nature of Belief Systems in Mass Publics," in David Apter ed., *Ideology and Discontent* (New York: Wiley, 1964), pp. 206–61.

9. The classic study supporting the elitists' conclusion that public opinion does not affect policy is by Warren E. Miller and Donald E. Stokes, "Constituency Influence in Congress," *American Political Science Review*, Vol. 57, No. 1 (March 1963), pp. 45–6. Also see Michael Margolis and Gary Mauser (eds.), *Manipulating Public Opinion: Essays on Public Opinion as a Dependent Variable* (Belmont, Calif.: Wadsworth, 1989); Benjamin Ginsberg, *The Captive Public: How Mass Opinion Promotes State Power* (New York: Basic Books, 1986).

10. Major pluralist works include Sidney Verba, Richard A. Brody, Edwin B. Parker, Norman H. Nie, Nelson W. Polsby, Paul Ekman, and Gordon S. Black, "Public Opinion and the War in Vietnam," *American Political Science Review*, Vol. 61, pp. 317–33; John E. Mueller, *War, Presidents and Public Opinion* (New York: Wiley, 1973); Ole R. Holsti, "Public Opinion and Foreign Policy: Challenges to the Almond–Lippmann Consensus," *International Studies Quarterly*, Vol. 36, No. 4 (December 1992), pp. 440–5; Miroslav Nincic, "A Sensible Public: New Perspectives on Popular Opinion and Foreign Policy," *Journal of Conflict Resolution*, Vol. 36, No. 4 (December 1992), pp. 772–89; Bruce W. Jentleson, "The Pretty Prudent Public: Post Post-Vietnam American Opinion on the Use of Military Force," *International Studies Quarterly*, Vol. 36, No. 1 (March 1992), pp. 49–74.

11. Benjamin I. Page and Robert Y. Shapiro, *The Rational Public: Fifty Years of Trends in Americans' Policy Preferences* (Chicago: Chicago University Press, 1992).

12. Walter Lippmann, *Public Opinion* (New York: Macmillan, 1922); and *The Phantom Public* (New York: Harcourt, Brace, 1925).

13. Jentleson, "The Pretty Prudent Public." They also showed that public opinion, although not always influential in the short-run, decisively influenced policy toward the Vietnam War over the medium to long-term. More recently, Ninic has demonstrated a tendency by the public to manipulate and try to control elites by playing a game of "the politics of opposites." Miroslav

Nincic, "The United States, the Soviet Union, and the Politics of Opposites," *World Politics*, Vol. 40, No. 4 (July 1988) pp. 452–75.

14. Miyatake Michiko, "Seron/Yoron Gainen no Seisei (The Birth of the Concept of Public Opinion)," in Tsuganesawa Toshihiro and Sato Takumi, eds., *Koho, Kokoku, Puropaganda* (Public Relations, Advertising, and Propaganda) (Kyoto: Minerva, 2003), pp. 56–74. Also see Okada Naoyuki, Sato Takumi, Nishihira Shigeki, and Miyatake Michiko, *Yoron Kenkyu to Seron Chosa* (Opinion Research and Public Opinion Polls) (Tokyo: Shinyosha, 2007).

15. Miyatake, "Seron/Yoron Gainen no Seisei," p. 59.

16. Ibid., p. 70.

17. Donald Hellmann, *Japanese Foreign Policy and Domestic Politics* (Berkeley: University of California Press, 1969); Chalmers Johnson, *Japan: Who Governs? In The Rise of the Developmental State* (New York: W.W. Norton & Company, 1995); Glenn D. Hook, *Militarisation and Demilitarisation in Contemporary Japan* (New York: Routledge, 1996); and Sheldon Garon, *Molding Japanese Minds: The State in Everyday Life* (Princeton: Princeton University Press, 1997).

18. A former secretary to a member of the Upper House used this expression when Midford suggested that it is natural for political parties to follow public opinion. Similarly, in an interview Midford conducted, a Japanese middle-level career diplomat saw public opinion toward foreign opinion as being composed primarily of non-attitudes: "foreign policy issues simply do not register." This diplomat further volunteered that in his personal opinion this was a very unfortunate situation, and he would be happier with a more opinionated public, even if this meant that the Foreign Ministry would have to change policy from time to time to accommodate such a public. Personal interview dated March 18, 1994.

19. Leading pluralist works on Japanese foreign policy include Akio Watanabe, "Japanese Public Opinion and Foreign Affairs: 1964–73," in Robert Scalapino, ed., *Foreign Policy of Modern Japan* (Berkeley: University of California Press, 1977), pp. 105–45; and Martin Weinstein, *Japan's Postwar Defense Policy, 1947–1968* (New York: Columbia University Press, 1971). For a balanced view of these two tendencies in Japanese conceptions of public opinion, see Miyatake, "Seron/Yoron Gainen no Seisei."

20. Since the elitist perspective is a priori more credible, the opposite is not true: if elitist predictions are confirmed, this will strengthen elitist credibility and reduce pluralist credibility, but to a lesser extent. This logic follows from the "crucial case-study" model of Arend Lijphart. See "Comparative Politics and the Comparative Method," *American Political Science Review*, Vol. 65, No. 3 (September 1971), pp. 158–77.

21. "Seiken 1000 Nichi Koizumigo no Tenki (At 1000 Days of the Administration, a Turning Point in Koizumi Language)," *Asahi Shimbun*, January 20, 2004.

22. "Koizumi Tells Abe Cabinet 'be insensitive,'" *Asahi Shimbun*, February 22, 2007.

23. For more on the Koizumi administration, see Iijima Isao, *Koizumi Kantei no Hiroku* (A Secret History of Prime Minister Koizumi's Office) (Tokyo: Nihon Keizai Shimbunsha, 2006); and Tomohito Shinoda, *Koizumi Diplomacy: Japan's Kantei Approach to Foreign and Defense Affairs* (Seattle: University of Washington Press, 2007).

CHAPTER 1

Japanese Mass Opinion toward the War on Terrorism

Paul Midford

INTRODUCTION

This chapter examines the responses of Japanese mass opinion to Tokyo's participation in the American-led "War on Terror." It focuses on the dispatch of the Maritime Self-Defense Force (MSDF) ships to the Indian Ocean in the fall of 2001, their continued operations there, and the dispatch of the Ground Self-Defense Force (GSDF) and Air Self-Defense Force (ASDF) to Iraq in 2003–2004. Secondary foci include views of the threat posed by international terrorism and opinions about American foreign policy.

While addressing these issues, this chapter considers whether the war on terror and especially the events of 9/11 have changed, encouraged gradual evolution, or reinforced preexisting Japanese beliefs about the efficacy of using force. It finds that Japanese public opinion is gradually evolving away from rigid and ideological pacifism and toward a view best captured by the concept of "defensive realism." For the sake of placing Japanese public opinion in comparative perspective, this chapter analyzes comparable data on American and German public opinion. Germany appears to be a plausible defensive realist peer while American opinion shows greater faith in the utility of military force, suggesting closer proximity to what will be described as "offensive realism."

For data, this chapter utilizes publicly available media and government-sponsored opinion polls. However, this chapter suffers from at least two methodological problems that challenge any researcher interested in Japanese public opinion. The first problem is what this writer calls "question instability." Although Japanese opinion does at times appear to shift wildly, and is often dismissed as changeable and fickle, more often than not these changes reflect too frequent variations in question wording and sources. These changes not only make opinion look more unstable than it really is, but also complicate any attempt to accumulate multiple data points into a single table or graph. Second, Japanese polling agencies are notoriously unwilling to make raw data sets (cross-tabs, etc.) publicly available, preferring to limit released data to top-line results, and occasionally scattered cross-tab results. Nevertheless, this chapter does make use of several data sets released by the *Nihon Keizai Shimbun* to the Japan Data Archive at the Roper Center and obtained by the author.

The remainder of this chapter consists of three sections. The following section identifies several major currents in Japanese mass opinion regarding the use of force and relates them to broader theories about the utility of military force. The third section presents detailed hypotheses regarding perceptions about the utility of military force and a wealth of polling data supporting these hypotheses. The final section considers the policy implications of the gradual shift in Japanese mass opinion away from pacifist beliefs and toward those of defensive realism.

Anti-Militarism, Defensive Realism, and Offensive Realism

Although this chapter uses the term "pacifism," at its base, Japanese beliefs about the military and military force originate less from a pacifist worldview than from what has been called a "culture of antimilitarism."[1] Because of a widespread belief that the Japanese military hijacked the Japanese state in the 1930s and led it into a devastating and irrational war, distrust of the military and the Japanese state's ability to assert civilian control and wisely wield the sword has been deep-seated. A spokesperson of the Japan Socialist Party (JSP), speaking against Japan's plan to begin sending the Self-Defense Forces (SDF) overseas in 1992 to participate in UN peacekeeping, summarized this view when she claimed, "once the SDF is allowed to go abroad, there will be no limits as to what it will do, as the experience of the Pacific War has shown."[2]

Around this core of distrust in the Japanese military grew several broader attitudes.[3] First, there was the belief that all wars are equally unjustified and counterproductive; offensive and defensive wars cannot therefore be distinguished. Second, some desired to see Japan pursue, as the Socialist Party once advocated, unarmed neutrality. Third, a lightly armed Japan was believed the best way to discourage others from targeting or attacking Japan, as it would then pose no threat to them. This view is perhaps best captured in the phrase of Takemura Masayoshi, a leading centrist politician of the mid-1990s, who advocated "a small but bright and shining Japan (*chisakutomo kirari to hikaru koku nihon*)" that would avoid provoking others to target it.[4] This view also implied that the more Japan armed itself or involved itself with supporting U.S. military power, the more likely it was to provoke military responses from other nations (the so-called *makikomareru kyofu*, or fear of entrapment). Finally, dispatching the Japanese military overseas for any purpose was believed likely to provoke other nations, especially those in

East Asia with memories of Japan's invasion of occupation. This was coupled with skepticism about the ability of the Japanese state to exercise civilian control over the military, especially in the case of overseas deployments.

It is important to note, however, that in other aspects, Japan's "pacifism" and antimilitarism departs from that found elsewhere. For example, unlike Germany or Europe more generally, pacifism in Japan coexists with high support for the death penalty. Nonetheless, declining pacifism has corresponded to increasing support for the death penalty in Japan: support increased from 56.9 percent in 1975 to 81.4 percent in 2004.[5] This fact reinforces the idea that Japan's supposed pacifism was less based upon a belief that violence has no constructive role to play in human affairs, and more upon mistrust of the Japanese state's ability to wield the sword.

Another caveat is that some of the attitudes in Japanese postwar public opinion are not altogether inconsistent with defensive realism. Most notably, the idea that a lightly armed Japan that avoided bellicose or aggressive behavior would avoid provoking others to see Tokyo as a threat is consistent with a recognition of the security dilemma,[6] and the tendency of other states to balance against those viewed as harboring aggressive intentions.[7] Given the historical legacy of Japan's invasion and brutal occupation of much of Asia up to 1945, many Japanese policy makers as well as the public at large recognized that full rearmament risked provoking other Asian states to counterbalance Japan, economically as much as militarily.[8] Nonetheless, the solution proposed by many Japanese, namely lightly armed neutrality, went well beyond what defensive realism would suggest. Most importantly, this view betrayed an unwillingness to see that military weakness, or a lack of deterrent capability, may provoke others to exploit the state just as surely as over-armament or aggressive behavior may provoke others to counterbalance the state.[9]

Although antimilitarist mistrust never exerted uncontested dominance, it did exert great influence during the Cold War. Since at least the beginning of the 1990s, however, antimilitarist mistrust of the state has gradually receded, revealing public attitudes consistent with defensive realism. Although defensive and offensive realism are schools of thought within academic realism, and have not before[10] been applied to the study of belief structures in mass opinion, this chapter argues that defensive and offensive realism provide significant analytical leverage (descriptive inference) regarding foreign policy related beliefs.

Defensive realism asserts that defensive military postures are usually optimal for achieving security. The contrasting form of realism, offensive realism, holds that offensive military action often contributes to security.[11] The difference between these two positions stems in part from differing views about the balance of offensive versus defensive military technology, but also from differing views about other variables related to the efficacy of offensive versus defensive military action, such as the presence or absence of first-move advantages and the cumulativity of resources (i.e., the degree to which conquest pays).[12]

Defensive realists contend that military technology and related variables favor the defense, and consequently assert that the state should pursue a defensive military doctrine. By contrast, John Mearsheimer, the acknowledged dean of offensive realism, summarizes the view of this school by claiming "the international system creates powerful incentives for aggression."[13] Underlying this view is the belief that the balance of military technology and related factors favor the offense. Although cast in terms of military technology and related factors such as the ease of conquest, for the purposes of analyzing the belief structures of mass opinion, this chapter will use the closely related, but more general, concept of utility. The author therefore defines defensive realism as the belief that the utility of military power is limited to national defense in the face of imminent threats. By contrast, offensive realism can be seen as corresponding to the belief that offensive military power has utility for pursuing a wide range of state interests beyond defense of the homeland.[14]

What has been labeled as Japan's "Reluctant Realism"[15] consists of several beliefs that represent a marked change from the pacifist and antimilitarist beliefs discussed earlier and a convergence with defensive realism. First, wars can be distinguished according to whether they are for the sake of national defense against an actual or imminent threat versus offensive wars for other purposes; the former are justified, the later are not. As discussed later, Japanese opinion reacted very differently to the invasion of Afghanistan, which was seen by many as an inevitable act of self-defense by the United States, than it did to the invasion of Iraq. Second, war is an ever-present possibility; therefore, Japan must prepare for this possibility.[16] By voting to enact a legal framework for dealing with foreign attack in 2003, the approximately 80 percent of Diet members that so voted thereby signaled acceptance of this essential tenet of realism. Third, a growing section of Japanese public opinion holds beliefs that correspond to a "defense dominant" view of military force. In other words, military power has value for national defense, but not for much else. As demonstrated later, Japanese public opinion expresses skepticism about the utility of military force for fighting terrorism, countering the proliferation of weapons of mass destruction or promoting democracy. Finally, coexisting with this belief is high and stable support for the dispatch of the SDF overseas for humanitarian and reconstruction projects. This reflects support for the "internationalization" of what many Japanese have regarded the SDF as being: a disaster relief organization. Ironically, support for SDF overseas dispatches reflects the belief that nonmilitary solutions have the highest utility for conflict resolution and reducing terrorism.

Overall, this chapter argues that the 9/11 attacks and the ensuing American-led "war on terrorism," although important shocks for Japan, did not fundamentally alter Japan's worldview. Specifically, 9/11 and the war on terrorism at most contributed to modestly and temporarily accelerating the evolutionary shift of Japanese public opinion toward defensive realist beliefs. In other words, the data shows that there has been no dramatic shift in mass opinion. Japanese *policy*, however, has changed more than opinion, opening up a gap between opinion and policy, the public and political leaders. This is especially evident regarding the Iraq War. (Similar evidence is found in chapter five concerning opinion makers and intellectuals.) This gap now constrains policy, and as discussed in the following paragraphs, may continue to do so by limiting the extent of Japanese military involvement in international security.

One caveat is in order: the conclusions drawn here about Japanese public opinion reflect opinion at the aggregate level of opinion as measured by opinion polls. The chapter does not claim that all or even most Japanese hold beliefs that approximate "defensive realist" views. Rather, Japanese opinion is composed of distinguishable groups: pacifists who are in decline yet continue to exert influence, a small group of hawks who are relatively sanguine about the utility of military force, and centrists. It is the *aggregated* views of all these groups that this chapter claims approximates defensive realism. This caveat will become obvious in the following section, which presents detailed polling data on how Japanese view the utility of military force.

HYPOTHESES AND POLLING DATA

Hypothesis #1: Rather than opposing all wars, the Japanese public now distinguishes between wars justified for national defense against an imminent threat versus wars fought for other purposes.

When asked whether they supported American preparations to use military force against terrorist organizations in Afghanistan in a Yomiuri Shimbun poll conducted between September 24 and 25, 2001, 44.1 percent of Japanese respondents (60 percent of whom were men) supported such preparations while 26.7 percent opposed. And while 28.9 percent answered that they could not say one way or another, 0.3 percent were unable to give any answer. By party, approximately 60 percent of Liberal Democratic Party (LDP) supporters favored such preparations, as did nearly 50 percent of Democratic Party of Japan (DPJ) supporters. On the other hand, among New Komeito (Clean Government Party), Social Democratic Party of Japan (SDPJ), and Japan Communist Party (JCP) supporters, opposition outweighed those favoring action.[17]

By contrast, Japanese opinion about the prospect of attacking Iraq was, from the beginning, overwhelmingly critical. Although the size of the lopsided majority opposing the Iraq War waxed and waned over the months, it almost never failed to achieve absolute majority status. As the results in table 1.1 suggest, the reasons for the waxing and waning of opposition were thus: the return of UN weapons inspectors and U.S. cooperation with the United Nations might have temporarily increased support for the eventual prospect of an attack on Iraq in December 2002. However, by December 2003, as it became clear that the United States was planning to attack soon without UN authorization or the completion of weapons inspections, public support in Japan fell again.

Table 1.2, which for comparative reasons includes public opinion figures from Germany, reveals that the start of the war in Iraq coincided with a

Table 1.1 Prospect of a U.S. attack on Iraq (all figures in percentages)

	Aug 02		December 02	January 03
	Japan	U.S.	Japan	Japan
Support	14	57	26	20
Oppose	77	32	65	69

Source: *Asahi Shimbun*, September 3, 2002, and January 27, 2003.

Table 1.2 (a) Japanese opinion regarding the wars in Iraq and Afghanistan; (b) public opinion in Germany regarding the wars (all figures in percentages)

(a)

Iraq War	*Mar. 20–21, 03*	*Mar. 29–30, 03*	*Apr. 19–20, 03*
Support war	31	27	29
Oppose war	59	65	63

Afghan War	*Oct. 01*	*Nov. 01*
Support war	46	46
Oppose war	43	46

(b)

Iraq War	
Do not invade Iraq	28
Only invade with UN approval and support of allies	56
Invade even if they have to do it alone (Pew 2002 poll)	12
The Iraq War cannot be legitimized (March 2003 poll)	81

Afghan War	
Support war	61
Oppose war	31

Sources: *Asahi Shimbun*, March 22, 2003, p. 4; and March 24, 2003, p. 4. *Der Spiegel*, May 18, 2002, as cited by Peter Rudolf, "Mutual Perceptions," presentation prepared for AICGS Conference on "German–American Relations One Year After September 11," Washington, D.C., September 10, 2002; The Chicago Council on Foreign Relations and The German Marshall of the United States, "Europeans See the World as Americans Do, But Critical of U.S. Foreign Policy," *World Views* (September 4, 2002), p. 2.

relative increase in support for war. Yet, even during the first week, support noticeably eroded as men and LDP supporters became increasingly opposed to the war.[18] In contrast to a pacifist rejection of all wars as unjustified, Japanese public opinion showed understanding for the U.S. attack on the Taliban regime in Afghanistan. Although support for this war did not achieve a clear majority, it achieved a tie with opponents of the war. By contrast, opponents of the Iraq War commanded a clear majority approaching two-thirds of respondents.

An October 2001 *Yomiuri Shimbun* poll provides even stronger evidence of reluctant defensive realism in Japanese mass opinion. When asked their opinion about the U.S. attack on Afghanistan, 23.5 percent of respondents claimed attacking Afghanistan was "appropriate," while 14.9 percent claimed the attack was "unacceptable." However, the *Yomiuri* poll also gave respondents the option of answering "there was no alternative" to attacking Afghanistan. A clear majority of 59.5 percent, likely including both respondents who would have answered "approve" or "disapprove" in the *Asahi* poll listed in table 1.2, chose this answer (2.4 percent chose "don't know" or did not answer).[19] In many ways this answer is emblematic of the reluctant defensive realism discussed in this chapter: a recognition that the U.S. attack on Afghanistan was a necessary act of defense in response to the 9/11 attacks, yet also a simultaneous reluctance to approve of war. Nonetheless, Japanese respondents appear to be drawing distinctions between distasteful wars that are nonetheless necessary and those that are both distasteful and ineffective.

Table 1.3 suggests that eighteen months after the initial invasion of Iraq, the view of the Iraq War as having been unnecessary and unjustified had grown to embrace more than two-thirds of the Japanese public. Japanese public opinion exceeded Canadian opinion and approached French opinion in its opposition to the war.

Table 1.4 reveals that 15 percent of the Japanese public had been convinced the Saddam Hussein regime was indeed a threat, perhaps because of the then widespread belief that Iraq possessed Weapons of Mass Destruction (WMD) stockpiles (see later). Iraq's consistent violations of UN resolutions and the need for solidarity with its only ally, the United States, figured as far less important reasons for Japanese supporters of the war. The bottom

Table 1.3 "Was the war in Iraq justified?" (all figures in percentages)

	Japan	*ROK*	*Canada*	*France*
It was justified	16	11	24	18
It was a mistake	71	85	67	77

Source: *Asahi Shimbun*, October 18, 2004, p. 8.

Table 1.4 Reasons for supporting and opposing the U.S. invasion of Iraq (Mar. 20–21; all figures in percentages)

Supporting	
Because Iraq flagrantly violated UN resolutions	8
Because the Hussein regime was a danger	15
Because America is an ally	6
Opposing	
Because there was not a new UN resolution	8
Because it lacked a legitimate reason for the war this time	12
Because of opposition to war	39

Source: *Asahi Shimbun*, March 20, 21, and 23, 2003.

half of the table provides a good measure of the continued sway of pacifism in Japan. The U.S. invasion was opposed by 39 percent of Japanese simply because they oppose war, a figure not much lower than the total percentage of Japanese opposed to the war in Afghanistan (see earlier). By comparison, the 12 percent that choose the option of opposing the war because there was no legitimate reason for war at the time signaled a willingness to accept potentially legitimate reasons for going to war, thus distinguishing them from pacifists. Arguably, this group comes closest to defensive realist thinking. The 8 percent who opposed the war because of the absence of a new UN resolution also signaled a willingness to support war under some circumstances, and therefore are also reasonably close (albeit perhaps more legalistically inclined) to a defensive realist position.

The results in table 1.5 indicate that Prime Minister Koizumi Junichiro's public support for the war was more popular than the war itself: 36 percent of respondents supported Koizumi's position. North Korea appears to be one reason; even among those who supported Koizumi's statement of support for the war in Iraq, only 2 percent thought U.S. assertions were persuasive. By contrast, the perceived need for U.S. cooperation and support on the North Korea issue loomed large among supporters of Koizumi's statement, suggesting mistrust of U.S. alliance commitments and fear of abandonment. By implication, however, the wide majority who opposed the war did not see the North Korean threat, or the fear of abandonment of the United States, as reasons to endorse Koizumi's support for the Iraq War. Moreover, when all respondents were asked how important North Korea was as a factor in evaluating Koizumi's statement of support for the U.S. war effort, 67 percent said this was a very (29 percent) or somewhat (38 percent) important factor in their evaluation.[20] This high number (about 1.5 times the rate of support for Koizumi's statement) means that many opponents of Koizumi's statement considered North Korea an important reason when choosing opposition. Fear of encouraging an American preventive strike against North Korean nuclear facilities and entrapment in an ensuing war might have been behind North Korea's appearance as a reason to oppose Koizumi's statement. Certainly, polling data elsewhere in this chapter suggests Japanese fear of entrapment by the United States and deep skepticism about American use of force.

Table 1.5 Reasons for supporting Koizumi's statement supporting the invasion of Iraq (of the 36 percent who stated support in a Mar. 29–30, *Asahi Shimbun* poll; all figures in percentages)

Because U.S. assertions were persuasive	2
Because the United States is an ally	12
Because U.S. cooperation is needed on the North Korean problem	21

Source: Asahi Shimbun, April 1, 2003.

Hypothesis #2: The Japanese public now recognizes war is an ever-present possibility, and therefore supports preparations to repel a possible attack.

In August 1999, a year after North Korea had test-fired a long-range Taepodong missile over northern Honshu, a *Nihon Keizai Shimbun* poll asked: "There is an opinion that laws should be made to prepare Japan for an attack by foreign forces. Do you think Japan should consider creating such laws or are they not necessary?" In response, 76 percent contended that "Japan should consider enacting such laws," whereas 14 percent answered that this was not necessary, and 10 percent answered "do not know" or did not answer.[21] Thus, this poll suggests that Japanese overwhelmingly recognize war as an ever-present possibility under anarchy, and, therefore, that military preparations to meet this contingency have positive utility. A July 1999 *Yomiuri Shimbun* poll tested this proposition against the cost of some loss of civil liberties. This poll asked: "There is an opinion that a law should be passed to make it easier for the Self-Defense forces to initiate military actions in case Japan is attacked by a foreign force, even if it means civil rights are somewhat restricted. Do you agree or disagree?" In response, 46 percent agreed that such a law should be passed even at the cost of some civil liberties, 24 percent disagreed, and 25 percent responded that "it was difficult to say" (5 percent had no response).[22] While the results of this poll showed much greater ambivalence about enacting emergency legislation if it means a loss of civil liberties, a plurality nonetheless supported the enactment of such legislation. Given that Japanese antimilitarism is first and foremost about mistrusting the state, this result suggests a significant retreat from antimilitarist distrust. By enacting such legislation (albeit belatedly) in 2003, the approximately 80 percent of Diet members who so voted signaled their acceptance of the essential tenet of realism that war is an ever-present possibility that must be prepared for.

Hypothesis #3: Military force has utility for national defense, but not for much else.

Although table 1.6 frames the question in terms of legitimacy, not utility, to this author's knowledge it is the closest any polling question in Japan has come to asking directly about the utility of military force. It is reasonable to assume, albeit with some uncertainty, that most respondents would tend to link utility with legitimacy. With this caveat in mind, table 1.6 supports the main claim of this chapter, namely that Japanese public opinion has become defensive realist. With the partial exception of preventing genocide in another country, solid majorities oppose going to war to promote human rights in other countries or going to war when another country is suspected of harboring terrorist suspects. By contrast, 78.1 percent of Japanese believe that going to war when attacked is legitimate.

This pattern supports the defensive realist hypothesis presented earlier: Japanese see military force as having value for national defense, but not for much else. Offensive military power is not seen as having much value for promoting objectives ranging from promoting human rights, suppressing

Table 1.6 Legitimate reasons for going to war (all figures in percentages)

	Legitimate	Somewhat legitimate	Not very legitimate	Not legitimate
Prevent human rights abuses in other countries	8.8	32.9	33.0	20.3
Prevent genocide in another country	13.9	36.8	25.0	18.8
When another country is suspected of harboring terrorists	7.6	29.8	34.8	22.5
When attacked	47.8	30.3	7.9	9.0

Source: Data and question wording obtained from International Christian University–Washington State University Survey on Attitudes and Global Engagement (SAGE) Poll, accessible at www.wsu.edu/pols/sage/data.htm Japanese survey question number 16.

terrorism, or WMD proliferation. The only partial exception is that offensive military action in direct response to an attack is seen as relatively justified. The response of Japanese public opinion to the invasion of Afghanistan supports this interpretation, although opinion was more or less evenly divided about this attack. Also, as discussed later, Japanese opinion was skeptical about the utility of this attack for suppressing terrorist attacks. This reflects the drawback of asking about legitimate reasons for going to war without specifying the country initiating the war. As other polling data in this chapter indicate, specifying Japan as the initiator of war, or even the United States, significantly reduces support for war.

Corollary 1: Military force has low utility for combating terrorism.

Most Japanese supported the war on terrorism well into 2002, but this support apparently reflected support for the war in Afghanistan as a legitimate act of national defense. Cross-national polling results from the Pew Foundation in 2002 found that 61 percent of Japanese respondents supported the war on terrorism, versus 32 percent who opposed. Similar, if somewhat more supportive, results were found in Germany: 70 percent supported the war on terror in 2002 versus 25 percent who opposed. However, German support for the war on terrorism had fallen to 60 percent by May 2003, and 55 percent (versus 43 percent who opposed) by March 2004 (Japan was not included in the 2003 and 2004 Pew polls),[23] a trend apparently reflecting the unpopularity of the Iraq War. Japanese support for the war on terrorism, however, did not reflect a belief in the utility of military force for combating terrorism.

When asked directly about the effectiveness of military action for combating terrorism, however, Japanese generally express skepticism. An October 2001 *Asahi Shimbun* poll asked whether the U.S. military attack on Afghanistan will be effective in preventing future terrorist attacks. In response, 36 percent answered that the U.S. attack will be "effective," versus 49 percent who answered it would not, and 15 percent who answered "don't

Table 1.7 Results of a November 2001 *Yomiuri Shimbun* poll asking how effective military force would be at routing out terrorism (all figures in percentages)

	Japan	United States
Very effective	9.5	30.7
Somewhat effective	21.1	56.9
Aggregate effective	*30.6*	*87.6*
Little effect or no effect	33.3	8.3
No effect	24.1	3.7
Aggregate no effect	*57.4*	*12.0*
DK/NA	12.0	0.4

Source: Yomiuri Shimbunsha Seron Choosabu, *Nihon no Seron*, pp. 343, 345–6.

know" or did not answer at all.[24] This suggest a large plurality bordering on a majority thought the U.S. invasion of Afghanistan would not be effective in preventing future terrorist attacks despite the comparably favorable view of this war in Japan. Similarly, table 1.7 indicates that Japanese are far more skeptical of the effectiveness of military force in routing out terrorism than are Americans, with over 85 percent of American respondents believing two months after the 9/11 attacks that military force would be effective, versus slightly more than 30 percent of Japanese who thought so. By comparison, a majority of Japanese, 57.4 percent, thought military force would have no effect in suppressing terrorism.

An *Asahi Shimbun* poll conducted in late August 2002 found continued Japanese skepticism about the utility of military force for routing out terrorism, and a continued gap with Americans on this question, although the gap closed somewhat as Americans became slightly less sanguine about the impact of military force. Although 72 percent of Japanese respondents evaluated highly (22 percent) or somewhat (50 percent) the new government in Afghanistan, only 37 percent thought that the application of U.S. military force in that country would reduce the incidence of terrorism, versus 71 percent of Americans who thought so.[25]

These results support the hypothesis that Japanese opinion does not see military force as an effective means for combating terrorism. The October 2004 poll presented in table 1.8 suggests that Japanese respondents are more skeptical than British respondents or even Korean respondents. Japanese respondents were also more skeptical than Canadian respondents, 51 percent of whom answered that Iraq occupation and invasion contributed to the war on terror, but less skeptical than French, Spanish, or Mexican respondents: 80, 73, and 74 percent of these respondents, respectively, answered that the Iraq invasion and war had not contributed to the war on terror (Germany and the United States were not included in this poll).[26]

Corollary 2: Military force has low utility for halting the proliferation of WMD.

Table 1.8 Results of an October 2004 cross-national poll that *Asahi Shimbun* participated in, asking whether the "Iraq occupation (War) contributed to the war on terrorism?" (all figures in percentages)

	Japan	*ROK*	*United Kingdom*
Contributes very much	6	18	32
Contributes somewhat	36	30	20
Aggregate contributes	*42*	*58*	*52*
Does not contribute	43	37	21
Does not contribute at all	11	11	19
Aggregate does not contribute	*54*	*48*	*40*

Source: *Asahi Shimbun*, October 18, 2004, p. 9.

Table 1.9 Results of an April 2003 *Yomiuri Shimbun* poll asking about the effectiveness of the Iraq War in reducing the WMD proliferation threat (all figures in percentages)

WMD proliferation will lessen	16.5
Will have no effect	57.8
WMD proliferation threat will increase	15.4

Source: *Yomiuri Shimbun*, April 21, 2003, p. 2.

Table 1.10 Results of a poll conducted by *Asahi Shimbun* asking: America invaded Iraq because that nation was developing/possessing WMD. Do you believe this was a legitimate reason for the invasion? (all figures in percentages)

	Jun. 03	*Jul. 03*	*Feb. 04*	*Mar. 04*
I think so	29	25	22	19
I do not think so	57	60	65	66
DK/NA	14	15	n.a.	n.a.

Sources: *Asahi Shimbun*, July 24, 2003, and March 17, 2004, p. 4.

Tables 1.9 and 1.10 suggest that Japanese mass opinion has from the beginning been skeptical about the legitimacy and utility of using military force to prevent the proliferation of WMD. The gradual increase over time in the view that the alleged possession of WMD was not a legitimate or sufficient reason for invading Iraq no doubt reflects the failure to find WMD. Nonetheless, the lopsided majority citing this as an illegitimate reason as far back as June 2003 suggests that most Japanese never saw suppressing WMD proliferation as a legitimate reason for attacking Iraq, even if Iraq had in fact been in possession of these weapons.

Corollary 3: There is little support in Japan for using military force to promote democracy.

The evidence supporting this corollary is mostly negative: the lack of polling questions on this question. Given that the failure to find WMD led the

Bush administration to subsequently place greater emphasis on democracy promotion as a reason for invading Iraq, the fact that Japanese pollsters have not asked Japanese whether they support the use of force to promote democracy is telling.[27] This omission suggests that the claim that military force should be used to promote democracy is beyond the pale of debate in Japan. Japanese pollsters have asked a related question, however: "Is Iraq's reconstruction positively proceeding?" In March 2004, a mere 15 percent thought Iraq's reconstruction was proceeding positively, versus 74 percent who did not.[28] By 2004, as democracy promotion increasingly replaced counter-WMD and counterterrorism as the primary justification for the U.S. invasion of Iraq, the *Asahi Shimbun* asked respondents how they evaluated U.S. policy toward Iraq. In February 2004, 21 percent of respondents positively evaluated U.S. policy in Iraq; by April this number had fallen to 12 percent. By contrast, 63 percent negatively evaluated U.S. Iraq policy in February 2004; the number of those disapproving had increased to 71 percent by April 2004.[29]

Corollary 4: America's use of force for reasons that are viewed with skepticism has contributed to growing distrust of the United States among Japanese.

When asked about America's post-9/11 security policy almost one year after the attacks, Japanese reactions were less than supportive. An *Asahi Shimbun* poll conducted in late August 2002 found that only 23 percent of respondents believed America's post-9/11 policies had had a favorable impact on global security, versus 50 percent who believed these policies had had a negative impact.[30]

Table 1.11 shows that eighteen months after the initial invasion of Iraq, a majority of Japanese continued to believe that America's "actions" did not contribute to world peace, although the margin had narrowed significantly as those with the positive view almost doubled, while those with a negative view grew only slightly. Comparing the results from Table 1.11 with the 2002 *Asahi* poll discussed above should be done cautiously, however, since different question wording might have influenced the outcome. Respondents

Table 1.11 Results of an *Asahi Shimbun* poll asking if America's actions contribute to world peace (all figures in percentages)

	Japan	*ROK*	*Canada*
Greatly	5	3	13
Somewhat	39	44	33
Aggregate agree	*44*	*47*	*46*
Disagree somewhat	39	42	27
Emphatically disagree	14	7	25
Aggregate disagree	*53*	*49*	*52*

Source: *Asahi Shimbun*, October 18, 2004, p. 8.

might have a more critical view of "American policies" than of "American actions since 9/11." The former might imply U.S. foreign policy, while the later could implicate a broader set of actions, including non-governmental actions.

Table 1.12 shows a significant decline in the willingness of Japanese to trust, in a general context, America. In the immediate aftermath of the 9/11 attacks, and despite the U.S. invasion of Afghanistan, trust in the United States peaked, with an absolute (if small) majority claiming to trust the United States. This effect, albeit diminished, continued into 2002. However, by 2003, mistrust had clearly surpassed that found in December 2000, the last pre-9/11 poll by the *Yomiuri Shimbun* to ask this question. Unlike the December 2000 poll, a plurality expressed distrust in the United States. This trend continued and deepened significantly in 2004, with a big jump in the percentage of Japanese respondents claiming to distrust the United States, and a continued slow decline in the number claiming to trust the United States. Consequently, an absolute majority claimed to distrust the United States. The timing of the 2003 and 2004 results suggests the influence of the Iraq War in increasing mistrust of the United States. These results also provide side evidence supporting the point made above, namely that Japanese public opinion was relatively understanding of the war in Afghanistan, but highly critical of the invasion of Iraq. In other words, Japanese mass opinion distinguished these two wars as justified and unjustified respectively, and this judgment affected their propensity to trust the United States. In 2005 the percentage of respondents distrusting the United States leveled off and declined slightly in intensity. Nonetheless, the percentage of those distrusting the United States also continued to decline slightly in numbers and intensity. Overall, however, the 2005 results reflect great continuity with the 2004 numbers, and suggest that the majority of Japanese will continue to distrust the United States as long as its war in Iraq continues.

Table 1.13 reports the results of a cross-national poll from October 2004 that asked respondents whether their view of America had changed in the

Table 1.12 *Yomiuri Shimbun* poll: Do you trust America? Do you distrust America? (all figures in percentages)

	2000	*2001*	*2002*	*2003*	*2004*	*2005*
Trust very much	7.8	15.2	8.4	8.0	8.9	8.2
Trust somewhat	36.7	35.7	40.4	32.5	28.9	28.4
Aggregate trust	*44.5*	*50.9*	*48.4*	*40.5*	*37.8*	*36.3*
Distrust somewhat	30.3	26.1	30.0	34.5	38.6	39.7
Distrust very much	11.5	8.9	9.1	10.4	14.1	12.8
Aggregate distrust	*41.8*	*35.0*	*39.1*	*44.9*	*52.7*	*52.5*
No answer	6.4	14.1	12.1	14.7	9.4	10.9

Sources: *Yomiuri Shimbun*, December 29, 2000; November 30, 2001; December 5, 2002; December 12, 2003; December 16, 2004; December 15, 2005.

past three years. Overwhelmingly, by a margin of 74 percent to 17 percent, Japanese respondents reported that their view of America had changed for the worse. The majority claiming their view had worsened clearly exceeded majorities reaching the same conclusion in South Korea and the United Kingdom, while only slightly exceeding this majority in France.

Hypothesis #4: Overseas dispatches of the SDF for humanitarian and reconstruction projects enjoy strong and growing support.

Corollary 1: Support for overseas dispatches of the SDF is based upon the perception of the SDF as a domestic disaster relief organization and support for the idea of internationalizing these operations.

As table 1.14 makes clear, Japanese citizens view the SDF as first and foremost a disaster relief organization, and only secondarily as a military tasked with ensuring national security. More respondents mentioned disaster relief as the reason for the SDF's existence than those citing "ensuring national security." Making an international contribution tied or exceeded "ensuring domestic order" as the third most important role for the SDF. Since the SDF's international "contribution" has mostly consisted of humanitarian

Table 1.13 Has your view of America changed over the past three years? (all figures in percentages)

	Japan	ROK	United Kingdom	France
It has improved	2	2	3	2
It has somewhat improved	15	23	11	12
Aggregate improved	*17*	*25*	*14*	*14*
Has not changed	5	—	33	13
It has somewhat worsened	53	49	27	39
It has greatly worsened	21	18	18	31
Aggregate worsened	*74*	*67*	*45*	*70*

Source: *Asahi Shimbun*, October 18, 2004, p. 9.

Table 1.14 Perceptions of SDF roles (multiple answers allowed; all figures in percentages)

	Ensuring national security	Ensuring domestic order	Disaster relief	International contribution	Support civilian activities
Reason for existence	59.0	24.3	67.1	25.1	7.6
Secondary role	19.1	11.8	87.2	35.5	17.7
Future role	44.7	20.4	67.5	36.1	9.0

Source: Poll conducted by the public affairs office of the prime minister's office, January 2000, as carried in Boei Nenkan Kanko Kaihen, *Boei Nenkan 2001*, p. 190.

relief and reconstruction activities, support for the SDF's "international contribution" can be seen as a proxy indicator of support for making this domestic relief organization go international.

Already before the first Gulf crisis and war (1990–1991), the issue of dispatching Japanese personnel overseas had been slowly welling to the surface in Japanese politics. This question appeared in an opinion poll sponsored by the prime minister's office in October 1986, at the time of the Nakasone Yasuhiro administration. Respondents were asked whether Japan should cooperate with UN peacekeeping operations in disputed areas such as the Middle East or Cyprus by dispatching nationals and equipment and extending financial aid within the limits of domestic legislation. Of the respondents, 39.2 percent said Japan should do so, versus 25.3 percent who replied to the contrary, and 34.6 percent who were unsure. Although not asked specifically about the participation of the SDF in peacekeeping, the willingness of a plurality to consider dispatching personnel to conflict zones (and the uncertainty of another third) suggests that as early as 1986 over two-thirds of Japanese were relatively open to this prospect.[31] Table 1.15 reveals consistently growing support for SDF participation in disaster relief activities overseas. Between 1991 and 2000 support for international disaster relief operations grew from a slim majority to an overwhelming majority while opposition collapsed, as the Japanese public increasingly recognized the distinction between overseas deployments for humanitarian and reconstruction activities (*kaigai haken*) versus deployments for the sake of using military force (*kaigai hahei*). The domestic disaster relief corps had successfully gone international.

Corollary 2: Overseas dispatches for participation in UN peacekeeping enjoy public support because they are associated with disaster relief and reconstruction missions.

SDF participation in peacekeeping has, in practice, largely consisted of operations closely resembling humanitarian relief and reconstruction missions:

Table 1.15 Support for SDF participation in disaster relief operations overseas (all figures in percentages)

	Agree/agree somewhat	*Can't say/DK*	*Disagree/ disagree somewhat*
Feb. 91	54.2	15.3	30.4
Jan. 94	61.6	16.4	21.9
Feb. 97	78.0	10.1	11.9
Jan. 00	86.3	8.3	5.4

Source: Poll conducted by the public affairs office of the prime minister's office, January 2000, as carried in Boei Nenkan Kanko Kaihen, *Boei Nenkan 2001*, p. 191.

purifying water and providing medical assistance to civilians, rebuilding roads and schools, and so on. Of course, given the relatively high regard in which Japanese mass opinion has held the UN, the association of these overseas deployments with the UN is another reason for popular support. Nonetheless, this chapter argues that the key variable is the association of these deployments with humanitarian or disaster relief type missions. As shown later, SDF participation in UN peacekeeping missions involving the use of force has not enjoyed support, while purely humanitarian and disaster relief SDF deployments overseas, which have been outside of a UN framework, have enjoyed strong popular support.

Before the lifting of the so-called PKF freeze in December 2001,[32] SDF participation in peacekeeping was legally limited to missions corresponding to humanitarian and disaster relief. This freeze itself reflected mass opposition to participation in operations, even those sanctioned by the UN, which hinted at the use of military force. Even after the lifting of the PKF freeze, SDF participation in peacekeeping has continued to consist mostly of humanitarian and reconstruction missions (with a few exceptions in East Timor). Both the Japanese government and the media coverage of SDF involvement in peacekeeping operations have consistently stressed the disaster relief and reconstruction aspects. So interchangeable has peacekeeping become with international disaster relief efforts that even government pollsters frequently mix the two. Polls conducted by the prime minister's office that ask Japanese about the SDF's "international contribution" define this as "participation in and cooperation with UN peacekeeping and international emergency relief."[33] Moreover, as discussed later, rising support for Japanese participation in peacekeeping has paralleled (albeit at a slightly lower level) support for participation in international disaster relief missions.

Immediately after Japan enacted its peacekeeping law in June 1992, a July *Asahi Shimbun* poll found the public evenly split on whether the law was a positive development or not. This poll asked: "The PKO cooperation bill was just enacted by the Diet. Do you think the enactment of this law is a positive development? Do you think it is not a positive development?" In response, 36 percent evaluated this as a "positive development," while another 36 percent evaluated it as "not a positive development, and 28 percent answered otherwise or not at all."[34] By mid-September 1992, following the initial deployment of SDF troops overseas for a peacekeeping mission (Cambodia), a subsequent *Asahi* poll found growing support. This poll asked: "The SDF has been dispatched overseas for UN peacekeeping operations in Cambodia, in other words, for PKO. Do you agree with this? Do you oppose this?" In response, 52 percent agreed, 36 percent opposed, and 12 percent answered otherwise or not at all.[35]

By May 1994, a *Yomiuri Shimbun* poll found that 70.5 percent of Japanese supported SDF participation in UN peacekeeping.[36] Table 1.16 presents the results of a prime minister's office poll question asked four times over the course of ten years, demonstrating consistently rising support for SDF participation in UN peacekeeping.

Table 1.16 Poll Question asking respondents if they agree or disagree with SDF participation in future UN peacekeeping operations (all figures in percentages)

	Agree/agree somewhat	Can't say/DK	Disagree/disagree somewhat
Feb. 91	45.5	16.6	37.9
Jan. 94	48.4	21	30.6
Feb. 97	64	22.4	13.6
Jan. 00	79.5	11.9	8.7

Source: Poll conducted by the public affairs office of the prime minister's office, January 2000, as carried in Boei Nenkan Kanko Kaihen, *Boei Nenkan 2001*, p. 191.

Table 1.17 Regarding the SDF operations in the future, what areas do you think it should prioritize? (multiple answers allowed; all figures in percentages)

Deterring an attack from another nation	45.1
International peace cooperation work such as UN peacekeeping operations	53.8
Domestic and international disaster relief operations	71.0
Dealing with a missile attack	27.9
Dealing with terrorists and guerillas	43.1
Dealing with mystery or spy ships	35.7
Emergency evacuation and transportation of Japanese nationals from foreign countries after conflict, etc., breaks out there	33.9
Other	0.4
Nothing especially	3.6
No answer	0.7

Source: *Yomiuri Shimbun*, June 3, 2004, p. 24, question 10.

A *Yomiuri Shimbun* poll conducted May 22–23, 2004, timed to coincide with the fiftieth anniversary of the SDF's formal establishment, asked a wide range of questions about the SDF, and especially about overseas deployments. Despite the accumulated weight of the 9/11 attacks, and the subsequent invasions of Afghanistan and Iraq, perceptions of the SDF's role continued to show great continuity with the Cold War and the post–Cold War decade of the 1990s.

As depicted in table 1.17, a question regarding the areas in which the SDF could make the most important contributions (multiple answers allowed) had the following responses: 71.0 percent of respondents identified national and international disaster relief activities,[37] thus building on Cold War era and 1990s perceptions of the SDF's most popular role. Also reflecting a legacy from the 1990s, 53.8 percent of respondents supported participation in "UN peacekeeping activities and other international peace-cooperation work" whereas 45.1 percent saw the SDF as playing an important role by deterring attacks from other nations. By contrast, responding to the new threat of terrorism came in fourth, with 43.1 percent of respondents identifying "dealing with terror and guerrilla" threats as an important role for the SDF. This finding reinforces other polling results suggesting that the Japanese public remains relatively skeptical about the utility of military force in combating terrorism. Another "new threat," "dealing with suspicious ships," came in fifth at 35.7 percent, a clear reference to a series of intrusions into Japanese waters by ships linked to North Korea. It should be noted, however, that the MSDF shares responsibility for dealing with spy ships with the Maritime Safety Agency, which plays the role of first responder, and this may account in part for the smaller numbers of respondents identifying this as a primary mission for the MSDF.[38] Of the respondents, 33.9 percent identified "the emergency evacuation of Japanese nationals from foreign countries where conflicts, etc., have erupted" as an important mission for the SDF. Dealing with another new threat, namely ballistic missiles, did not register very highly: only 27.9 percent said this should be an important SDF mission. Other missions were named by 0.4 percent whereas 3.6 percent answered the SDF has no particularly important missions, and 0.7 percent did not answer.

However, the *Yomiuri* poll revealed opinion instability as small changes in wording produced significant shifts in opinion. Recounting the 1992 enactment of Japan's PKO law, and how under this law the SDF has conducted various "international cooperation" and "international assistance" activities, another question, reproduced in table 1.18, asked what sorts of activities the SDF should engage in when sent overseas (multiple answers allowed). In comparison with the question discussed in the previous paragraph, an even larger majority, 78.4 percent, said that the SDF should conduct disaster relief operations. The majority who had said in the previous question that the SDF should participate in UN peacekeeping operations shrank to a minority of 41.8 percent in response to this question.

Table 1.18 Results of a poll conducted by *Yomiuri Shimbun* asking: "Since the enactment of the 1992 UN peacekeeping operations cooperation law, otherwise known as the PKO cooperation law, the SDF has gone overseas to participate in various forms of international cooperation and assistance. If the SDF participates in overseas activities, what sorts of activities do you think they should perform?" (multiple answers allowed; all figures in percentages)

Emergency relief operations in the event of a natural disaster	78.4
PKO operations based upon a UN resolution after a conflict has ended	41.8
Even outside of PKO, humanitarian relief operations such as those the GSDF is performing in Iraq	39.1
Participation in a multilateral army based upon a UN resolution	15.9
Other	0.1
There is no need to participate in overseas operations	4.9
No answer	2.6

Source: *Yomiuri Shimbun*, June 3, 2004, p. 24, question 6.

Differences in question wording might account for this discrepancy; the PKO option given for this question stated "perform peacekeeping operations following the end of a conflict and based upon a UN resolution," whereas the question discussed earlier referred to "international peace cooperation work such as UN peacekeeping operations (PKO), etc." One may speculate that the inclusion of the term "after a conflict ends" suppressed support by linking an SDF deployment to recent, if not current, combat. On the other hand, the inclusion of the term "international peace-cooperation work" raised the level of support in the question introduced in table 1.17. This suggests that support for SDF participation in peacekeeping operations assumes a detachment from combat or even conflict, reinforcing the conclusion that Japanese are not as enthusiastic about the SDF's overseas involvement in peace enforcement as they are in peacekeeping operations with little or no implication of conflict.[39] The results in table 1.18 also indicate that only 15.9 percent supported SDF participation in a multilateral army based upon a UN resolution, while 39.1 percent of Japanese supported SDF humanitarian relief activities outside of PKO "like those being conducted by the GSDF in Iraq." This last result appears substantially different from that found in another question in the same *Yomiuri* poll, which asked respondents whether they supported the government's decision to dispatch the SDF to Iraq humanitarian and reconstruction support. In response to this question, 18.4 percent strongly supported and 40.6 percent somewhat supported, for an aggregate support level of 59 percent. By contrast, 15 percent strongly opposed and 22.9 percent somewhat opposed the Iraq dispatch, for an aggregate opposition total of 37.9 percent.

Corollary 3: Overseas dispatches that imply the use or involvement in the use of force do not enjoy popular support.

Growing public support for overseas dispatches of the SDF for noncombat purposes such as humanitarian and disaster relief and reconstruction missions appears to reflect a growing realization that overseas dispatches of the SDF do not have to involve the use of force, and that the SDF can play the same disaster relief and rebuilding role overseas that it has long played in Japan. In this sense, the Japanese government's strategy of promoting the distinction between these two types of deployments (*kaigai haken*, or noncombat deployment, versus *kaigai hahei*, or overseas combat deployment) was successful. Although public opposition to noncombat overseas SDF deployments therefore steadily eroded, a new and formidable barrier emerged at the threshold of overseas combat, and to a lesser extent, anything that smacked of military operations. Thus, the same May 1994 *Yomiuri Shimbun* poll that found a large majority favoring SDF participation in UN peacekeeping operations also found that a slightly larger majority of Japanese, 71.6 percent, opposed expanding SDF participation into peacekeeping operations involving the use of force.[40]

In the wake of the 9/11 attacks, Prime Minister Koizumi introduced legislation enabling him to dispatch the SDF (especially the MSDF and ASDF) to so-called *hisento chiiki*, or noncombat zones, in the vicinity of Afghanistan to provide logistical support for U.S. military operations and humanitarian relief for displaced refugees. The dispatch of the MSDF to provide rear-area support for U.S. military operations in Afghanistan was the first such SDF dispatch. Since this deployment created the new precedent of a noncombat dispatch in support of another state's military operations, it was a significant step toward tackling the taboo on overseas deployments for military purposes, and engaging in the self-imposed restriction on exercising collective self-defense. As such, it failed to attract clear and consistent support from the Japanese electorate. A late-September *Asahi Shimbun* poll asked respondents whether they supported Prime Minister Koizumi's proposal for a new law enabling the SDF to provide "rear area support for the American military." In response, 42 percent expressed approval while 46 percent expressed disapproval.[41] After the Anti-Terrorism Special Measures law had been approved, a subsequent *Asahi Shimbun* poll in November 2001 asked respondents if they supported the dispatch of MSDF destroyers to the Indian Ocean based upon this act. In response, 44 percent expressed support while 48 percent expressed opposition.[42]

In between public opposition to the SDF engaging in combat overseas and support for overseas noncombat disaster relief, humanitarian, and reconstruction missions, Japanese public opinion was at best ambivalent about SDF rear-area support missions for U.S. military operations in Afghanistan. The earlier cited *Asahi* polls reveal a Japanese public divided to negative about noncombat support for U.S. military operations in Afghanistan.

Table 1.19 suggests that once dispatched, the SDF was able to build a modicum of public support for its role of providing rear-area logistical support for U.S. military operations in Afghanistan. This increase in support may reflect the demonstration effect of the MSDF peacefully and professionally resupplying the U.S. military while not repeating any behavior associated with the prewar Imperial Japanese military. However, this support also reflects the increasing isolation of this mission from actual support of combat. In contrast to the results in table 1.18, which reflected Japanese

Table 1.19 Results of polls conducted by *Asahi Shimbun* asking: "In the wake of the simultaneous terror attacks in America, the Japanese government enacted legislation and dispatched SDF naval vessels to the Indian Ocean to supply the American military with fuel and provisions. Do you favorably evaluate these Japanese responses? Do you negatively evaluate them?" (all figures in percentages)

	Aug. 02	*Jul. 03*
Favorably evaluate	50	49
Negatively evaluate	41	37
Other/don't know	9	14

Sources: *Asahi Shimbun*, September 3, 2002, and July 22, 2003.

views while combat was ongoing, by August 2002, high-intensity combat in Afghanistan was long over. Moreover, resupplying U.S. and other allied ships in the Indian Ocean had little connection with continuing counter-insurgency operations in that country. This pattern largely held when this question was repeated in July 2003.

The same July 2003 *Asahi* poll asked whether the respondents favored extending the SDF Indian Ocean dispatch for two more years when the Special Anti-Terror Law was scheduled to either expire or come up for a single two-year renewal in November 2003. Although a large plurality favorably evaluated the overall dispatch in table 1.19, when asked about whether this mission should be extended, only 32 percent said yes, versus 55 percent who opposed extending this mission and 13 percent who answered other or don't know.[43] In other words, despite the favorable evaluation of the mission itself a lopsided majority opposed extending the MSDF's Indian Ocean dispatch. In part, this result may reflect a recognition that the SDF's support of the U.S. military was no longer needed with the end of large-scale hostilities in Afghanistan. However, it appears to even more clearly reflect ambivalence, if not opposition, to overseas deployments that are implicated, even indirectly, in the use of force. Growing skepticism about U.S. foreign policy certainly appears to be another reason.

Corollary 4: The Japanese public has been ambivalent to negative about the Iraq dispatch because it is a humanitarian relief and reconstruction mission in close proximity to combat.

As early as April 2003, a *Yomiuri Shimbun* poll asked respondents about what Japan could do for Iraqi reconstruction. In response, 9.8 percent said Japan should only contribute financially, 14.1 percent said it should only contribute personnel, 61.2 percent said it should contribute both, and 10.7 percent said it should not contribute anything at all; 75.1 percent in total said Japan should contribute personnel. Of this 75 percent who supported a personnel contribution, 17.5 percent said only civil servants and private individuals should be sent, 14.2 percent said only the SDF should be sent, and 65.9 percent said civil servants, private individuals, and the SDF should be sent; a total of 80.1 percent of those who said personnel should be sent (or about 60 percent of all respondents) thought the SDF should be sent.[44]

Table 1.20 Response to a *Nihon Keizai Shimbun* poll asking: "The government and ruling parties, in order to dispatch the SDF to Iraq for reconstruction assistance, have proposed a new bill. What do you think about this new bill?" (all figures in percentages)

	Support	*Oppose*	*DK/NA*
Overall	43	41	16
Men	55	35	9
Women	33	46	21

Source: *Nihon Keizai Shimbun* polling, June 2003, obtained from the Roper Center Japan Data Archive.

Table 1.21 Results of a poll asking: "The Japanese government has hammered out a policy for dispatching the SDF to Iraq. Do you support the SDF's dispatch? Are you opposed?" (all figures in percentages)

	Jun. 03	*Jul. 03*
Support	46	33
Oppose	43	55
Other, no answer	11	12
To those who answered "Support," Why do you feel this way?		
Because relations with the United States are important	6	6
Because it means making an international contribution	29	17
Because we need to support the SDF	8	8
Because Iraq has become safe	2	1
Other, no answer	1	1
To those who answered "Oppose," Why do you feel this way?		
Because the demand for the dispatch comes from America	4	7
Because this conflicts with the Constitution	8	9
Because non-SDF support is sufficient	13	12
Because Iraq is still dangerous	16	25
Other, no answer	2	2

Sources: Asahi Shimbun, June 30, 2003, July 22, 2003, and July 23, 2003. Polling questions come from *Asahi Shimbun*, July 23, 2003, p. 4.

Table 1.22 Results of a *Nihon Keizai Shimbun* poll asking: "The Iraq Reconstruction Support law has been enacted and the government has a plan to dispatch troops this fall. What do you think about this?" (all figures in percentages)

	Support	*Oppose*	*DK/NA*
Overall	28	52	20
Men	38	47	14
Women	19	55	26

Source: Nihon Keizai Shimbun poll, August 2003; data obtained from the Roper Center Japan Data Archive.

A mid July 2003 *Yomiuri Shimbun* poll found a plurality opposing dispatch. Asked whether they supported the dispatch of the SDF to Iraq to provide "humanitarian and reconstruction assistance to the Iraqi people" and to provide "rear area support for the U.S., British and other armies' efforts to maintain law and order," 30.5 percent expressed support versus 24.2 percent who expressed opposition, and a relatively large 43.5 percent who were unsure (1.9 percent did not answer).[45] *Asahi Shimbun* polls conducted in late June and mid July 2003 recorded a shift from a small plurality supporting dispatch to the emergence of a clear opposing opinion majority (see table 1.21). An August *Nihon Keizai Shimbun* poll (see table 1.22), taken after the Iraq Reconstruction Special Measures bill authorizing SDF dispatch had been enacted found that the opposing opinion majority continued to dwarf the minority supporting dispatch by almost the same margin as that found in *Asahi's* July 2003 survey. Again, women were significantly more opposed than men, although a men opposed dispatch by a large plurality."

In an *Asahi Shimbun* poll conducted approximately ten days before the Lower House election on November 9, 2003, when asked which issue would most influence their choice of candidate and party, a mere 4 percent of respondents answered that it was the Iraq problem. By comparison, 6 percent listed reform of the public roads (expressway) corporations, 43 percent pension reform, and 45 percent economic policy. In short, Iraq was not a significant influence on voting behavior in this election.[46] This result appears to reflect the fact that the LDP ran away from this issue during the election campaign, issuing vague statements about when, under what circumstances, or whether troops would actually be dispatched to Iraq. The opposition Democratic Party's concentration on domestic economic issues also probably drove down the salience of Iraq.

A *Yomiuri Shimbun* poll in mid-December 2003 asked respondents whether they supported the immediate dispatch of the SDF to Iraq for humanitarian and reconstruction assistance, or only after the stabilization of the security situation. Of the respondents, 17.8 percent answered as soon as possible, 48.2 percent as soon as the security situation stabilized, while 29.8 percent answered that there was no need to dispatch the SDF (4.2 percent had no answer). The plurality answer on this question appears consistent with the view of the SDF as a disaster relief organization that only deploys to noncombat zones. Koizumi's justification for dispatching the SDF to Iraq was unconvincing to an overwhelming majority of Japanese. Of the respondents, 85.7 percent answered that Koizumi had not provided a sufficient explanation (needed to provide a better explanation) for dispatching the SDF to Iraq, versus 10.7 percent who did not think so (and 3.6 percent who did not answer).[47] A mid-December *Nihon Keizai Shimbun* poll revealed that a clear majority of Japanese opposed the Koizumi Cabinet's plan to dispatch the SDF to Iraq. Overall, 52 percent opposed the plan, versus 33 percent who supported it and 15 percent who were unsure. Men were more supportive with 44 percent in favor, versus 47 percent against, while 57 percent of women opposed and mere 24 percent supported.[48]

Nonetheless, opposition to the dispatch declined somewhat as the GSDF was dispatched to Samawah in southern Iraq. An *Asahi Shimbun* poll conducted in February and again in March 2004 found support for dispatch growing from 42 to 44 percent, while opposition registered at 41 percent in February and 48 percent in March.[49] This decline in opposition appears to reflect the public's favorable reaction to the SDF's noncombat humanitarian reconstruction mission, its most popular domestic mission.

Majority opposition to the SDF playing a military role in Iraq reemerged in June 2004, when Koizumi, after meeting with Bush, announced that the

SDF force deployed to Iraq would continue its deployment there, and based upon a recently passed UN Security Council resolution, would participate in a multilateral force. An *Asahi Shimbun* poll conducted between June 19 and 20 asked interviewees whether they supported the SDF's participation in this multilateral force. In response, 31 percent said they approved while 58 percent expressed opposition. When those expressing opposition were asked why, 25 percent (percent values reflect percentage shares of all respondents) selected the danger of using military force, 17 percent said because the Diet had not debated the issue, and 14 percent because America forced this decision on Japan. Supporters selected the existence of a new UN resolution, 7 percent, the usefulness of SDF work in reconstructing Iraq, 15 percent, and the importance of relations with the United States, 7 percent. These findings again underscore the sensitivity of Japanese voters to any hint that the SDF might participate in the use of force overseas,[50] even though the actual change was more legal than substantive.

The perception that the United States had coerced Japan, or that Koizumi had used this excuse (foreign pressure, or *gaiatsu*) as a sly tactic to get approval for the SDF's participation in the multinational force became evident when the *Asahi Shimbun* asked respondents whether they considered it problematic that Koizumi had informed Bush of the decision to join the multilateral army before discussing this in Japan. In response, 69 percent found this problematic versus 21 percent who did not.[51] The issue of the SDF joining the multilateral army and Koizumi's way of handling this issue became one of two top issues (along with pension reform) in the July (2004) Upper House election, contributing to the LDP's stinging defeat.[52] This result suggests that the prospect of the SDF using force overseas remains a potent issue with the potential to mobilize voters.

Corollary 5: Support for SDF overseas dispatches for humanitarian and reconstruction missions reflects the belief that nonmilitary solutions have the highest utility for conflict resolution and tamping down terrorism.

Although there is no polling data directly relevant to this corollary, it follows logically from the corollaries and data already presented. Japanese support SDF overseas dispatches for humanitarian and rebuilding missions while simultaneously expressing skepticism about the utility of military force for combating terrorism or WMD proliferation. Taken together, these results suggest that the Japanese public views nonmilitary approaches to these forms of conflict as more effective. And since SDF operations in Iraq, East Timor, Cambodia, and elsewhere have all entailed nonmilitary reconstruction and humanitarian relief operations, this leads to the ironic conclusion that the Japanese public supports SDF overseas dispatches precisely because they believe in the superiority of nonmilitary solutions for conflict resolution.

Hypothesis #5: Concern about Japan's economy reduces, not increases, support for a more activist foreign policy involving overseas deployments of the SDF.

Many observers suggest that a decline in economic performance and stagnation can cause, or has already, Japanese to become more nationalistic. In other words, Japan's postwar political order was legitimated by high-speed economic growth; the end of this growth would undermine this legitimacy and perhaps spark a resurgence of nationalism. Since the early 1990s many analysts have claimed to see a link between economic stagnation and a supposed rise of neo-nationalism in Japan.[53]

Contrary to the expectations of many observers, tables 1.23 and 1.24 suggest a negative correlation between worries about the economy and support for a more assertive Japanese role in international security. Table 1.23 shows that those with a pessimistic view of the economy are far more likely to oppose the Iraq dispatch, while those with a favorable view of the economy are more likely to support the dispatch. Likewise, Table 1.24 suggests that those who list economic security as top priorities, such as employment policy, pension, and welfare, are somewhat more likely than average Japanese

Table 1.23 December 2003 *Nihon Keizai Shimbun* poll: View of economy versus Iraq dispatch (all figures in percentages; numbers in brackets denote overall support and opposition rates for the Iraq dispatch)

	Economic conditions			*Iraq dispatch*		
	Overall	*Male*	*Female*	*Support (33)*	*Oppose (52)*	*DK/NA (15)*
Getting better	13	17	9	59	36	5
Not getting better yet	57	58	56	37	56	7
Will get worse	19	16	20	19	75	6
No answer	11	8	14	n.a.	n.a.	n.a.

Sources: Nihon Keizai Shimbun polling, obtained from the Roper Center Japan Data Archive. Also see Nihon Keizai Shimbun, December 22, 2003.

Table 1.24 December 2003 *Nihon Keizai Shimbun* poll: Policy priority versus Iraq dispatch (all figures in percentages)

(a) Listed as policy priority	*Support Iraq dispatch*	*Oppose*	*DK/NA*
Overall	33	52	15
1. Administrative reform	45	47	7
2. IT policy	41	54	5
3. Education reform	39	55	6

(b) Listed as policy priority	*Oppose Iraq dispatch*	*Support*	*DK/NA*
1. Employment policy	60	35	5
1. Diplomacy, security	60	35	5
2. Pension, welfare, and so on	59	34	7
2. Tax reform	59	35	7

Source: Nihon Keizai Shimbun polling, obtained from the Roper Center Japan Data Archive. Nihon Keizai Shimbun, December 22, 2003.

voters to oppose the Iraq dispatch. By contrast, those interested in promoting economic change through reforms also appear to be more sanguine about the dispatch of the SDF to Iraq.[54]

Hypothesis #6: Greater concern about a potential North Korean threat has not produced significant or sudden change in how Japanese public opinion evaluates security issues.

The data presented earlier demonstrates that Japanese mass opinion on security issues is gradually evolving, not radically shifting. Although opinion is becoming more "realist" in the sense that military force is increasingly seen as necessary to guard national independence, deep skepticism remains about offensive uses of military force. This gradual evolution toward defensive realism has occurred during, and to some extent despite, rising concern about a potential North Korean threat. North Korea's test of a Taepodong missile that flew over northern Japan in August 1998, subsequent and well-publicized incursions into Japanese waters in 1999 and 2001 by North-Korea-linked suspicious vessels, and confirmation in 2002 that North Korean agents had indeed infiltrated Japan in the 1970s and 1980s and abducted numerous Japanese citizens undoubtedly contributed to the gradual shift toward defensive realism. Nonetheless, the shift was evolutionary, not revolutionary. Moreover, at the time of this writing, there is no evidence that Japanese public opinion has come to support military options for dealing with the North Korean threat except as a defensive response to an attack. In this sense, Japanese public opinion responds to the North Korean threat in the same way that it responds to the use of force in Iraq and elsewhere.

Corollary 1: Japanese public opinion favors a negotiated settlement with North Korea.

As table 1.25 reveals, the public overwhelmingly supported Koizumi's attempts at summit diplomacy with North Korean leader Kim Jong-Il, although his second visit to Pyongyang proved significantly less popular than his first. Nonetheless, a *Yomiuri Shimbun* poll conducted at the time of Koizumi's less popular second visit found an overwhelming 84.1 percent

Table 1.25 *Asahi Shimbun* polls: "How do you view Koizumi's meeting with Chairman Kim Jung-il in Pyongyang?" (all figures in percentages)

	Sept. 02	*May 04*
Support	37	21
Somewhat support	44	46
Aggregate support	*81*	*67*
Somewhat oppose	12	19
Oppose	4	12
Aggregate oppose	*16*	*31*
DK/NA	3	2

Sources: Asahi Shimbun, September 3, 2002, and May 23, 2004.

of Japanese supporting the establishment of diplomatic relations with North Korea as soon as possible (30.3 percent), or in good time (53.8 percent). By contrast a mere 10.9 percent thought there was no need for diplomatic relations to be established.[55] This last number likely approximates the outer limit of the small minority of Japanese who favor a military solution to Japan's problems with North Korea, especially forcible regime change. The overwhelming majority, by favoring the establishment of diplomatic relations, appear to favor resolving bilateral problems diplomatically.

An *Asahi Shimbun* poll conducted in December 2004 asked respondents whether they favored Prime Minister Koizumi's incremental and cautious approach to the question of imposing economic sanctions on North Korea, and in response a plurality of 48 percent said they favored this cautious approach, versus 40 percent who opposed. Those who opposed Koizumi's visit to Pyongyang, or opposed normalization all together, constitute the base from which one might be able to build support for a preemptive attack on North Korea. Beyond this 20–30 percent, it is simply implausible to argue that one could simultaneously favor diplomatic normalization with Pyongyang while also supporting a preemptive first strike.

Corollary 2: There is no evidence that significant numbers of Japanese would favor a preemptive attack on North Korea.

Here, the evidence is entirely negative in form: the fact that Japanese pollsters have not asked respondents whether they would support an attack on North Korea. Given that pollsters must be sensitive to both currents in public opinion and policy debates, their failure to ask this question can be taken as evidence that the question of conducting a preventive attack on North Korea remains beyond the pale.

CONCLUSIONS

The findings of this chapter support an evolutionary view of Japanese public opinion and clearly call into question "revolutionary" views that see a series of recent shocks as transforming Japanese public opinion on security issues. Despite the shocks of the 1998 North Korean missile launch over Japan, incursions into Japanese waters by North-Korean-connected suspicious ships, the impact of revelations about North Korea's abductions of Japanese nationals, the shock of the 9/11 terrorist attacks, U.S. invasions of Afghanistan and Iraq, and China's rise as a military power, Japan has so far witnessed only gradual evolution away from antimilitarist attitudes about war and the use of force. The shift has been toward what this chapter characterizes as defensive realist views about the utility of military force. Japanese are moving away from an undifferentiated view of all wars as wrong and unjustified toward making distinctions between wars based upon whether the resort to force is in response to an attack or an eminent threat to homeland defense, as opposed to other reasons.

The very different responses to the war in Afghanistan, where public opinion was relatively understanding, versus the Iraq War, where lopsided majorities have consistently opposed the war, well captures this trend. Simply put, Japanese public opinion remains skeptical about the utility of military force for purposes other than national defense, such as for fighting terrorism, preventing WMD proliferation, or promoting democracy. Nonmilitary solutions are believed to be more effective for achieving these goals. Ironically, to the extent that the deployment of GSDF troops to Southern Iraq achieved limited and conditional public support, this reflects support for the nonmilitary humanitarian and reconstruction missions being conducted by the SDF there.

The growing dominance of defensive realist views among the Japanese public has long-term implications for Japan's evolving security strategy, its alliance with the United States, and U.S. policy makers. First, Japan will continue to gradually reduce the constraints on, and increase the capabilities of, its armed forces for conducting operations related to territorial defense. Second, as a consequence, Japan's defense dependence upon the United States will, in many areas, gradually decrease. Third, Tokyo is unlikely to agree to play a large military role, such as joint combat operations with U.S. forces or stand-alone security and stabilization missions, in operations such as Iraq that are far from Japan and involve missions not directly linked to territorial defense. The most Japan will likely commit to for the time being are humanitarian and reconstruction missions similar to those in Iraq.

Fourth, because of the perceived lack of success, and more crucially a perceived lack of legitimacy, in the Iraq mission, Japan will likely become more selective and less willing to involve its military in any way in future U.S. invasions of other nations; even humanitarian and reconstruction missions will be a harder sell. As demonstrated by this study, the Iraq deployment has become a negative example that the Japanese public, and by extension decision-makers, will seek to avoid repeating in the future. Rather than being a stepping stone that sets a precedent for a further expansion in Japan's overseas military role, as Koizumi and his advisers had intended, the Iraq deployment has ended up defining the limits for overseas SDF operations, limits that will not likely be breached for many years to come. Many Washington policy makers and observers have come to expect that Japan's adoption of a more realist grand strategy and its deployments to the Indian Ocean and Iraq indicate that in the near future Japan will provide even greater support for U.S. military operations in areas far from Japanese shores. They will be disappointed.[56]

NOTES

1. Thomas U. Berger, "From Sword to Chrysanthemum: Japan's Culture of Anti-Militarism," *International Security,* Vol. 17, No. 4 (Spring 1993), pp. 119–50; and Berger, *Cultures of Antimilitarism: National Security in Germany and Japan* (Baltimore: Johns Hopkins University Press, 1998).
2. Kwan Weng Kin, "South-East Asia 'Not Against Japanese Peace Troops Plan,'" *The Straits Times,* May 28, 1992. Many politicians on the Right also shared this mistrust of the Japanese military and the prospects for controlling

it. Gotoda Masaharu, former Cabinet chief secretary for Prime Minister Nakasone, who passed away in September 2005, was a leading example. See Masaharu Gotoda, "Kaigai Hahei no Boron wo Haisu (Stopping the Debate on Sending the SDF Abroad)," *Gekkan Asahi* (December 1990), pp. 40–6.

3. Peter J. Katzenstein, *Cultural Norms and National Security: Police and Military in Postwar Japan* (Ithaca: Cornell University Press, 1996); and "Same War—Different Views: Germany, Japan, and Counterterrorism," *International Organization*, Vol. 57, No. 4 (Fall 2003), pp. 731–60.

4. Takemura Masayoshi, *Chisakutomo Kirari to Hikaru Koku Nihon* (A Small But Bright and Shining Japan) (Tokyo: Kobunsha, 1994).

5. *Asahi Shimbun*, February 20, 2005.

6. Robert Jervis, "Cooperation under the Security Dilemma," *World Politics*, Vol. 30, No. 3 (January 1978), pp. 167–214.

7. This idea stems from an important strand of defensive realism known as balance of threat theory. See Stephan Walt, *Origins of Alliance* (Ithaca: Cornell University Press, 1987).

8. Paul Midford, "The Logic of Reassurance and Japan's Grand Strategy," *Security Studies*, Vol. 11, No. 3 (Spring 2002), pp. 1–43.

9. Arguably, revelations about North Korean abductions of Japanese civilians from coastal regions of Japan drove home to many Japanese the lesson that a failure to secure national territory or deter threats can lead to others targeting the state and its citizens. The August 1998 North Korean missile test over Northern Japan also contributed to the realization that Japan might be targeted by others.

10. One exception is Paul Midford, *Japanese Public Opinion and the War on Terrorism: Implications for Japan's Security Strategy*, Policy Study #27 (Washington, D.C.: East-West Center Washington office, 2006).

11. Jack Snyder, *Myths of Empire: Domestic Politics and International Ambition* (Ithaca: Cornell University Press, 1991), p. 12.

12. See Stephen van Evera, *Causes of War* (Ithaca: Cornell University Press, 1999).

13. John Mearsheimer, "Back to the Future: Instability in Europe after the Cold War," *International Security*, No. 15 (Summer 1990), pp. 5–56.

14. The limits of this range of interests are not defined here, but they are potentially limitless. Although the utility of defensive versus offensive military action comes close to capturing the divide between defensive and offensive realists, this should not be taken as meaning that offensive realists actually support the use of military power for a wide range of objectives, such as promoting democracy, eradicating terrorism, or preventing weapons proliferation.

15. Michael Green, *Japan's Reluctant Realism* (New York: Palgrave Macmillan, 2001).

16. To be sure, this assumption is common to both defensive and offensive realism.

17. Yomiuri Shimbunsha Seron Chosabu, *Nihon no Seron* (Tokyo: Koubundo, 2002), pp. 338–9, 344–5.

18. *Asahi Shimbun*, March 22, 2003, and March 24, 2003.

19. Yomiuri Shimbunsha Seron Chosabu, *Nihon no Seron*, pp. 341–2, 344–6.

20. *Asahi Shimbun*, April 1, 2003. All numbers are percentages.

21. *Nihon Keizai Shimbun*, August 22, 1999, as carried by JPOLL, the Japanese Public Opinion Database, Roper Center, University of Connecticut, at

http://roperweb.ropercenter.uconn.edu/cgi-bin/hsrun.exe/Roperweb/JPOLL/.

22. *Yomiuri Shimbun*, July 20, 1999, as carried by JPOLL, the Japanese Public Opinion Database, Roper Center, University of Connecticut, at http://roperweb.ropercenter.uconn.edu/cgi-bin/hsrun.exe/Roperweb/JPOLL/.

23. The Pew Research Center for the People and the Press, *A Year after Iraq War: Mistrust of America in Europe Ever Higher, Muslim Anger Persists* (March 2004), pp. 3, 17, accessible at www.people-press.org.

24. *Asahi Shimbun*, October 16, 2001.

25. "Iraku Kogeki, Nihon de 'Hantai' 77% Bei ha 'Sansei' 57% (77% of Japanese Oppose Attack on Iraq, 57% of Americans Oppose Attack)," *Asahi Shimbun*, September 3, 2002. All numbers are percentages.

26. *Asahi Shimbun*, October 15, 2004, and October 18, 2004.

27. This is all the more striking since the Bush administration has cited postwar Japan as a prime example of the successful use of military force to promote democracy.

28. *Asahi Shimbun*, March 17, 2004.

29. *Asahi Shimbun*, April 17, 2004.

30. "Iraku Kogeki."

31. Prime Minister's Office, "Public Opinion Survey on Diplomacy" (Tokyo: Foreign Press Center, March 1987), p. 13. Shin Joho Center conducted the survey, with a sample of 3,000, and an effective response of 2,385 (79.5 percent). Accessed from the Japan Data Archive, Roper Center, University of Connecticut.

32. PKF, an acronym unique to Japan, stands for "Peacekeeping Forces" (*heiwaijigun*), and denotes mainline operations such as monitoring compliance with a cease-fire; being stationed in and patrolling a buffer zone; weapons' inspection; collection or storage of abandoned weapons; assistance in prisoners-of-war exchanges among the parties to a dispute; and assistance in designating cease-fire lines. These operations were thought to imply involvement in military operations.

33. Boei Nenkan Kankokai, ed. *Boei Nenkan 2001 Nenban*, p. 191.

34. *Asahi Shimbun*, July 13, 1992.

35. *Asahi Shimbun*, September 28, 1992.

36. Yasuhiro Takeda, "Redefining Japan's National Security," *Business Times*, August 27, 1994, p. 1.

37. The very wording of the option, "foreign and domestic" (*kokunaigai*) disasters, suggests the breakdown of any meaningful distinction between the two areas of operation.

38. Indeed, in a December 2001 incident involving the interception (and subsequent sinking under unclear circumstances) of a North Korean spy ship, the MSA had exclusive responsibility.

39. *Yomiuri Shimbun*, June 3, 2004.

40. Takeda, "Redefining Japan's National Security."

41. *Asahi Shimbun*, October 1, 2001.

42. *Asahi Shimbun*, November 27, 2001.

43. *Asahi Shimbun*, July 22, 2003.

44. *Yomiuri Shimbun*, April 21, 2003. All numbers are percentages.

45. "Koizumi Naikaku Shiji (Support for Koizumi Cabinet)," *Yomiuri Shimbun*, July 15, 2003. All numbers are percentages.

46. *Asahi Shimbun*, November 2, 2003.
47. "Koizumi Naikaku, Seito Seijiritsu no Chosa Kekka (Results of Support for Koizumi Cabinet and Political Parties)," *Yomiuri Shimbun*, December 16, 2003.
48. *Nihon Keizai Shimbun*, December 22, 2003.
49. *Asahi Shimbun*, March 17, 2004, p. 4.
50. *Asahi Shimbun*, June 22, 2004.
51. Ibid.
52. The LDP's defeat was much bigger in terms of votes than seats, due to substantial malapportionment in Japan's upper house. According to one estimate, had the same voting patterns held for a lower house election, the LDP would have ended up with 160 seats versus 233 for the Democrats. In other words, this would have marked the end of LDP/Komei rule. See Peter Morgan, "LDP on the Way to Extinction?" *Japan Weekly HSBC*, July 16, 2004, pp. 1–5, available at www.research.hsbc.com.
53. The classic argument concerning the relationship between economic growth, political legitimacy, and nationalism in Japan is Chalmers Johnson, *Japan: Who Governs? In The Rise of the Developmental State* (New York: W.W. Norton & Company, 1995), pp. 45–50.
54. The author also obtained comparable data for *Nihon Keizai Shimbun* polls that included the same questions and were conducted in June and August 2003. This data was also obtained from the Japan Public Opinion Data Archive at the Roper Center, University of Connecticut. The results from these two polls were very similar to the results for the December poll depicted in tables 1.26 and 1.27. For the sake of reducing production expenses, the author has deleted four tables depicting this data from the final version of this chapter.
55. *Yomiuri Shimbun*, May 23, 2004.
56. Political developments in mid-2007, especially the LDP's massive defeat in an upper house election in July appear to confirm this prediction, which the author first wrote in 2005, and subsequently published in 2006 in Paul Midford, *Japanese Public Opinion and the War on Terrorism: Implications for Japan's Security Strategy*, Policy Study #27.

CHAPTER 2

Framing the Japanese Homeland Security Debate: Mass Media and Public Opinion

Stephanie A. Weston

INTRODUCTION

From 9/11 to the present, terrorist attacks around the world, including in Asia, continue to deepen the Japanese people's sense of vulnerability in the face of asymmetrical threats. The twenty-four Japanese victims of 9/11, the killing of Japanese nationals in Iraq, and the dispatch of the Self-Defense Forces (SDF) to join the international effort against terrorism have made the war on terrorism a not-so-distant reality to many Japanese. Both China's increasing economic and military powers as well as North Korea's development of missiles, nuclear capacity, and employment of spy ships have added to Japanese citizens' homeland security anxieties.

In order to better understand these insecurities and assess the evolving nature of the debate on homeland security post-9/11, this chapter examines 694 editorials from the three largest mainstream Japanese newspapers—the *Asahi Shimbun*, *Yomiuri Shimbun*, and *Mainichi Shimbun*. The author then explores the impact of these dynamics on both U.S.–Japan relations as well as on the future of Japanese homeland security from September 11, 2001, until early 2004. The survey covered this period because it includes 9/11, the attacks on Afghanistan and Iraq, new Japanese legislation related to homeland security and antiterrorism, the killing of two Japanese diplomats in Iraq, and finally the initial dispatch of more than one thousand Ground Self-Defense troops to Iraq for humanitarian assistance and reconstruction assistance.

FRAMING JAPANESE HOMELAND SECURITY

Numerous definitions exist for "framing," a key concept in mass media theory. However, for the purposes of this study, the author uses the definition employed by Robert M. Entman: "to frame is to select some aspects of a perceived reality, make them more salient in communicating text, in such a way to promote a particular problem, definition, causal interpretation, moral evaluation and or treatment recommendation."[1] In addition, the decision of which frames to use was partially based on two references about framing and the news media. One is by Patti M. Valkenburg, Holli A. Semetko, and Claes H. De Vreese, which refers to four different frames—"conflict, human interest, responsibility and economic cost."[2] An article by Price, Tewksbury, and Powers refers to three new values—"conflict, human interest and consequence" in news reporting.[3]

Based on these interpretations of framing and the kinds of topics addressed by the editorials surveyed, this author selected frames such as national interest, cost/consequence, threat, responsibility, and human interest as classifiers for this data. The threat frame was further subdivided into North Korean, Chinese, Iraqi, and Japanese[4] threats. The cost category included any kind of cost or consequence in addition to economic costs. Beyond economic cost, "the consequence frame can be taken to mean effect in a broader sense."[5]

Any editorial could contain more than one frame. Consequently, some articles are referenced more than once. Some editorials were not cited in the main text if the point was not repeated by other editorials. However, some of these editorials served as reference or background information. All of the editorials surveyed, whether cited in the chapter or not, are listed completely in a separate appendix at the end of this chapter.

The meanings of the frames are as follows:

National interest—This frame emphasizes actions taken for the benefit of the national good, country, or citizens.

Cost/consequence—This frame, called the "economic consequences" frame by Valkenburg, Sametko, and Vreese, "presents an event, problem, or issue in terms of economic consequences it will have on an individual group, institution, region or country."[6] This definition is enlarged, as previously mentioned, to include any kind of negative effect.

Threat—This frame not only emphasizes threat basically "as a function of military power, offensive capability, geographic proximity and aggressive intentions"[7] but it also looks at perceptions of threat. The perception of threat in this case, paraphrasing Robert Jervis, "equals one state perceiving the other states' intentions as being more aggressive than those intentions actually are."[8]

Responsibility—This frame "presents an issue or a problem in such a way to attribute responsibility for causing or solving a problem to the government or to an individual's story or an emotional angle to the presentation of an event, issue or problem."[9]

Human interest—This frame "brings an individual's story or an emotional angle to the presentation of an event, issue or problem."[10]

In this chapter, the frames for each newspaper are listed according to frequency.

Besides the concept of framing, this analysis also refers to Japanese homeland security. The basic principles of Japan's security policy define two objectives of Japan's homeland security—*hondo boei* or *kokudo boei* in Japanese (but with a connotation usually implying state-to-state relations). Specifically, these are "to prevent any threats from reaching Japan or repel it; and improve international security environment so as to reduce the chances that any threat will reach Japan. Japan will achieve these objectives by an integrated combination of three approaches: Japan's own efforts, cooperation with the ally and cooperation with the international community."[11] The Department of Defense, however, has a broader definition for homeland security—"the preparation for, prevention of, defense against, and response to threats and aggressions directed towards U.S. territory, sovereignty, domestic population, and infrastructure; as well as crisis management, consequence management, and other domestic civil support."[12] In this chapter, the broader homeland security definition is used and applied to Japan.

The key search words for the surveyed database were "shasetsu," or editorial, "yoron" (also pronounced as *seron*[13]), or public opinion. When surveying the respective databases, editorials were selected by their related title to this study. If there was any doubt about its title, the editorial was checked before downloading. After editorials or opinion polls were selected and downloaded, a content analysis eliminated those without any direct connection to homeland security. Of particular interest were editorials concerning Japan's contingency legislation, counterterrorism laws and treaties, homeland defense infrastructure, missile defense, satellite surveillance, expanded roles for the Self-Defense Forces, external threat and the U.S.–Japan alliance.

Although the author uses mass media terminology to frame her review of Japanese national newspapers and polls, the intent is to reach some substantive conclusions about the purport of this data for policy makers concerning U.S.–Japan relations and Japanese homeland security versus a theoretical contribution to the mass theory of framing. Given this background, the author first analyzes how the three biggest Japanese national newspapers framed homeland security in their editorials as well as selected polls. In the conclusion, the author will address how those dynamics impact U.S.–Japan relations and future Japanese homeland security.

JAPANESE HOMELAND SECURITY
AND *ASAHI SHIMBUN*

Asahi Shimbun, established in 1879, has an approximate circulation of eight million copies for its morning edition. And its English version is associated with the *International Herald Tribune*. Of the three surveyed newspapers in this study, it is the most liberal. Often critical of official government policies, the *Asahi Shimbun* is often also characterized as anti-U.S. It emphasizes the role of "disarmament, peace, human rights and democracy."[14] In the 1970s as well, *Asahi Shimbun*, *Yomiuri Shimbun*, and *Mainichi Shimbun* were the three major dailies. At that time, they resembled each other in content, but *Yomiuri* changed its editorial policies by becoming more conservative. *Asahi*, on the other hand, according to political scientist Ofer Feldman and an expert on the Japanese media, continued its "leftist flavor on issues such as the imperial system, the U.S.–Japan alliance and the SDF. It also has an intellectual and serious tone."[15] *Mainichi Shimbun* has maintained a liberal stance. Today, in general, *Asahi* and *Mainichi* editorials tend to be more reflective of opposition views including those of the largest opposition party, the Democratic Party of Japan, as well as other smaller leftist parties. Alternatively, *Yomiuri Shimbun* editorials are more reflective of the ruling Liberal Democratic Party's brand of conservatism, and, to a lesser extent, its coalition partner, the Clean Government (New Komeito), which has traditionally acted as a brake on the LDP both prior to and after forming the coalition in 1999.

Given this comparative background, the following is an analysis of 210 *Asahi Shimbun* editorials from September 11, 2001, to February 29, 2004, related to homeland security and the five frames in this study. *Asahi* editorials were framed in the following order—(i) threat; (ii) responsibility; (iii) human interest; (iv) cost/consequence; and (v) national interest.

Threat Frame

After 9/11, major threats related to homeland security, as viewed by *Asahi* editorials surveyed, included North Korea, Iraq, and the consequences of U.S. unilateral action against terrorism. *Asahi Shimbun* editorials, like those of *Mainichi Shimbun* and *Yomiuri Shimbun* concerning homeland security, commented largely on the North Korean threat followed by the Chinese threat. Also discussed was how Japan's attempts to strengthen its homeland security could be seen as a threat by nearby countries.

Eleven *Asahi Shimbun* editorials specifically emphasized the fact that North Korea is a direct threat to Japanese security as well as to regional security.[16] The abduction issue along with missiles, suspicious ships, and nuclear development, all factors involving North Korea, were considered important threats to Japanese security. Seventeen editorials referred to North Korea's "brinkmanship diplomacy." Others also reflected possible threat scenarios involving North Korea. Fourteen other editorials, however, emphasized bilateral to multilateral negotiation, engagement, diplomacy rather than the use of any kind of force to resolve the impasse, and North Korea's violations of various international agreements.

Although the Koizumi Junichiro administration implemented many changes in the name of security, little consensus existed between the Ministry of Foreign Affairs bureaucrats and Koizumi's team over how to handle the North Korean threat. MOFA officials pushed for dialogue and honoring promises (in the case of the abduction issue, the promise of returning to North Korea the Japanese abductees who were temporarily allowed to visit Japan) in spite of North Korean brinkmanship. Koizumi emphasized "economic sanctions and thorough preparations in military terms."[17]

There was a split in threat perception as well between the ruling coalition and the opposition. This was evidenced in many articles that spelt out opposition opinions over the rushed passage of the emergency laws and the delay in passing laws for the protection of citizens' rights and property during a contingency.

There are different threat perceptions held as well by the parties involved in the Six Party Talks concerning North Korea.[18] One editorial argued that both Japan and United States stress dialogue and pressure, with the latter being more of a hardliner.[19] Another pointed out that South Korea and China emphasize more dialogue.[20] Various editorials, however, discussed South Korea, Japan, and the United States trying to find a way to deal with the North Korea threat in spite of three countries' differences in approaches.[21] Involving China and Russia in the process was considered to be essential, too.[22]

Although the Chinese threat in *Asahi* editorials was not played up as much as that of North Korea, some *Asahi Shimbun* editorials expressed a sense of uneasiness about China's growing economic and military power. At the same time, there was recognition of China's influential role in the talks with North Korea. Despite the normalization of their relations in 1972, the Sino-Japanese relationship remains ambivalent at best. Shortly after 9/11, there were numerous incidents that further hurt relations. These included the forcible removal of North Korean asylum seekers by Chinese authorities who had entered the grounds of the Japanese consulate general in Shengyang, Prime Minister Koizumi's repeated visits to Yasukuni shrine and ensuing protests from South Korea and China, the Taiwan referendum before its presidential elections, rising criminal incidents of Chinese nationals in Japan, and court cases involving weapons abandoned by Japan in China during World War II.[23]

From a different perspective, there were also various *Asahi Shimbun* editorials about how Japanese homeland security policies in turn could be perceived as a threat by surrounding countries. Although, Japan is increasing its security measures for homeland defense including missile development and the launching of reconnaissance satellites, some *Asahi Shimbun* editorials indicated that simultaneously these actions could also cause perceptions of threat if these defensive intentions were misinterpreted by surrounding nations.[24] Prime Minister Koizumi's visits to Yasukuni shrine and the negative perceptions of neighboring countries were also emphasized.[25] Some editorials further emphasized that discussion about Japan possibly engaging in a preemptive strike if threatened could also cause anxieties in the region or trigger a war.[26]

A smaller percentage addressed homeland security infrastructure issues. Infrastructure problems included the revamping of nuclear power facilities and adequate inspection, tightening domestic security, cost and perceptions concerning the launch of reconnaissance satellites as well as Japan's involvement in missile defense. Finally, to a much lesser degree *Asahi Shimbun* editorials discussed the issue of Iraq's WMD. Although many editorials surveyed recognize the threat to international security that Iraq represents in general, they also hoped that the conflict would be resolved through diplomatic means rather than through the use of force. One editorial was not convinced that the "importance of the alliance is sufficient to explain Japan's support for war on Iraq."[27]

Responsibility Frame

After the threat frame, the responsibility frame was used frequently to discuss the Japanese government's responsibility as it relates to the enactment of laws and policies including a clear explanation of them to the general public. There was anxiety or concern, for example, about the possible abuse of powers by the government, including the SDF, if not checked by appropriate legislation or civilian control.[28] *Asahi Shimbun* editorials also called for a stronger Japan within the alliance as well as in the global community. For example, eleven editorials concerning negotiations with North Korea commented on the importance of Japan's regional responsibilities or contributions, including the Pyongyang Declaration,[29] toward peace and stability in Northeast Asia. Still other editorials, using the responsibility frame, pointed out what the government further needed to do in order to enhance domestic infrastructure for homeland defense.[30] These suggested initiatives included measures for "guarding U.S. military bases; tighter immigration controls; broader cooperation among law enforcement and investigative organs; exchanging of accurate and relevant information among foreign investigative agencies; carrying out crisis management for biological and chemical attacks as well as operating a unified SDF command."[31]

Human Interest Frame

Among the *Asahi Shimbun* editorials surveyed, the human interest frame was the third most frequently used. Balancing enhanced security measures with the protection of civil rights to fight terrorism was a recurring theme. With every new piece of legislation, whether it was the Anti-Terror Law, the emergency laws, the Law Concerning the Special Measures on Humanitarian Assistance (Iraq), Secrecy Amendments to the Self-Defense Forces Laws, or the International Convention for the Suppression of the Financing of Terrorism, eleven editorials expressed concern about human rights, human security, or civil liberties being restricted or infringed. There was an emphasis by twelve other *Asahi* editorials concerning the Japanese government's responsibility to get at the truth about the abductees' situation and break the stalemate on this issue.

Cost/Consequence Frame

The fourth most emphasized frame by *Asahi Shimbun* editorials was that of cost/consequence. The consequences of supporting the U.S. war on terrorism, especially in Iraq, were analyzed in terms of financial cost, access to oil, and threat to the Japanese homeland. One editorial, for example, stated

"The U.S. military operates on a global scale to counter threats at all times. It's time to think about what degree Japan should provide assistance to the U.S. in exchange for protecting the nation's security and the cost of effectiveness of such cooperation."[32] Another editorial expressed concern that Japan could become a target of terrorism because of its support of the U.S. war on terrorism. Since 9/11, Japan has received several threats allegedly from Al Qaeda. Japanese diplomats were killed in connection with Japan's support of U.S. action in Iraq. For the same reasons, shots were fired at the Japanese Embassy in Baghdad in November of 2003.

National Interest Frame

The least used frame by *Asahi Shimbun* editorials was national interest. The question of whether to support the U.S. alliance in the war on terrorism was a national interest concern.[33] Various articles also linked explicitly or implicitly the need for Japan to support the United States in return for U.S. support if a contingency arises in North Korea.[34] Another editorial stated alternatively, "In explaining his support for the Iraq campaign, PM Junichiro Koizumi keeps referring to the U.S. military might as deterrence against North Korea."[35] Japan's involvement in Iraq was also linked to the former's national interest in Middle East oil.[36]

Homeland Security and the *Mainichi Shimbun*

The *Mainichi Shimbun*, originally called *Tokyo Nichi-Nichi Shimbun*, was founded in Osaka in 1872. In 1944, the *Tokyo Nichi-Nichi Shimbun* merged with the *Osaka Mainichi Shimbun* to become the *Mainichi Shimbun*. *Mainichi*, which is considered to be a liberal newspaper left of center but not as liberal as the *Asahi Shimbun*, has a reported morning edition circulation of approximately four million. Its market share of Japanese readers is third behind that of the *Yomiuri*, the largest, and the *Asahi Shimbun*. The *Mainichi Shimbun*, like the *Asahi Shimbun*, tends to focus on issues such as "disarmament, peace, human rights and democracy."[37]

The following is an analysis of 219 *Mainichi Shimbun* editorials from September 11, 2001, to February 29, 2004, related to homeland security and the five frames in this study. *Mainichi* editorials framed homeland security in the following order: (i) threat; (ii) responsibility; (iii) human interest; (iv) national interest; and (v) cost/consequence. The order of surveyed *Mainichi Shimbun* editorial frames was very similar to that of *Asahi Shimbun* editorials. Threat, responsibility, and human interest frames for surveyed editorials ranked one, two, and three, respectively. However, the cost/consequence frame for surveyed editorials ranked fourth for the *Asahi Shimbun* versus fifth for *Mainichi*. At the same time, the national interest frame ranked fifth for surveyed *Asahi* editorials but fourth for *Mainichi* editorials.

Threat Frame

After 9/11, the reporting on issues related to homeland security was high. Many *Mainichi Shimbun* editorials also showed a concern for the protection of human rights as well as the strengthening of homeland security infrastructure. In addition, as with surveyed *Asahi Shimbun* editorials, the largest number of *Mainichi* editorials dealing with threat referred to the North Korean problem involving its nuclear weapons and missile development, the abductees issue, "brinkmanship diplomacy," lack of sincerity, and increasing self-isolation.[38] Other *Mainichi Shimbun* editorials also viewed North Korea's abduction of Japanese nationals as a violation of Japanese sovereignty, a human rights problem, and/or a criminal act.

One *Mainichi Shimbun* editorial pointed out gaps in Japanese homeland security concerning North Korea, namely, illegal smuggling activities in counterfeit currency, drugs, and missile components by the North Korean ship *Mangyonpon*.[39] Besides questions of defense-related infrastructure for dealing with the North Korean threat, some *Mainichi* editorials, as did those of the *Asahi*, pointed out a split inside the Koizumi administration involving hardliners versus doves over the correct approach to North Korea. In addition, some editorials emphasized the historical significance of Koizumi's visit to North Korea but cautioned against Japan's rushing to negotiate without conditions.[40] The possible positive as well as negative impacts of Koizumi's visit to North Korea for regional stability and peace were also discussed.[41] As expressed by some *Mainichi Shimbun* editorials, there was a large concern as well over the differences in approach among the five parties involved in negotiations with North Korea. In addition, ten *Mainichi* editorials, like various *Asahi Shimbun* editorials, also stressed bilateral as well as multilateral channels to resolve the North Korean problem.

There was some discussion about the Chinese threat. However, there was more of a focus on maintaining good relations between Japan and China versus escalating tensions between the two countries over their numerous disagreements. The Iraq threat as it relates to Japanese homeland security was not addressed directly. The idea of a "Japan threat" was barely discussed compared to surveyed *Asahi Shimbun* editorials' much more in-depth discussion of this aspect.

Responsibility Frame

Some *Mainichi Shimbun* editorials emphasized keeping a balance between the alliance and international cooperation with the war on terrorism. Other editorials emphasized the importance of alliance behind Japan's decision to support the United States in the attacks on Afghanistan and Iraq.[42] At the same time, still other *Mainichi Shimbun* editorials pointed out the government's responsibility to debate more openly with the public about its policies regarding SDF logistical support.[43] Four other *Mainichi* editorials also indicated the need for a more autonomous Japanese foreign policy including on the war on terrorism. One editorial pointed out, for example, "Besides the U.S.–Japan relationship, Japan should build stronger ties with its neighbors."[44] There was also concern about the effects of following perceived American unilateralism.[45]

Many *Mainichi* editorials looked critically at Japan's emergency laws. Criticisms included the government not deciding on a clear policy about terrorism and suspicious ships or enacting legislation at the same time to protect its citizens. Concern was also expressed about the ability to maintain enough civilian control.[46] There was worry expressed in one editorial as well about either the U.S. military or the SDF taking "supra legal action" because the emergency laws have not specified clearly enough its limitations.[47] Japan's responsibility to the abductees was also underlined by *Mainichi*'s editorials.

Human Interest Frame

Like many *Asahi Shimbun* and *Yomiuri Shimbun* (introduced later) editorials, *Mainichi Shimbun* editorials often used the human interest frame to principally discuss the abductee issue and North Korea. The abductions were equated to "state-sponsored terrorism" and a criminal act.[48] Six *Mainichi* editorials emphasized clearly the importance of resolving the abductee issue before Japan could reopen negotiations to normalize relations with North Korea. At the same time, some editorials indicated that Japan needed to clear up the past concerning its "colonization of the Korean peninsula."[49] Other editorials detailed the history behind the abductions, including the participation of the Red Army in the kidnappings.[50] Finally, some *Mainichi Shimbun* editorials focused on the need for emergency laws to protect citizens' rights.[51]

National Interest Frame

Mainichi Shimbun editorials did not use the national interest frame often. The idea of Japan supporting the alliance in terms of national interest was not really emphasized as it was in *Asahi Shimbun* editorials. One editorial instead asked the opposite question: "If the SDF were not dispatched to Iraq, would it really damage Japan's national interest?"[52] A few *Mainichi Shimbun* editorials mentioned how Japan decided to place priority on its alliance with the United States regarding North Korea and Iraq instead of the kind of international contribution it has made in the war on terrorism.[53]

Cost/Consequence Frame

In terms of cost analysis, there were very few *Mainichi Shimbun* editorials that discussed the consequences of Japanese foreign policy as it relates to homeland security. Two *Mainichi Shimbun* editorials touched on the impact of a prolonged war with Iraq on the world economy.[54] Yet other editorials pointed out that the SDF could possibly be targeted in Iraq.[55] Another editorial discussed the possible conflict between the SDF's potential role in Iraq and Japan's constitutional limitations concerning the use of force.[56]

Japanese Homeland Security and the *Yomiuri Shimbun*

According to its corporate profile, the *Yomiuri Shimbun*, founded in 1874, is "Japan's oldest and the world's biggest commercial newspaper with 10 million copies." It is also the most conservative of the three newspapers surveyed for this study. The following is an analysis of 265 *Yomiuri Shimbun* editorials over the same period mentioned ealier and related to homeland security and the five frames in this study. The number of *Yomiuri Shimbun* editorials surveyed was slightly larger than those for the *Asahi* or *Mainichi*. *Yomiuri Shimbun* editorials framed homeland security in the following order: (i) threat; (ii) responsibility; (iii) national interest; (iv) cost/consequence; and (v) human interest. Compared to surveyed *Asahi Shimbun* editorials or those of the *Mainichi Shimbun*, surveyed *Yomiuri Shimbun* editorials emphasized more the responsibility and national interest frames. For surveyed *Yomuiri Shimbun* editorials, the national interest frame ranked third compared to fifth for surveyed *Asahi Shimbun* editorials and fourth for *Mainichi Shimbun*. For surveyed *Yomiuri Shimbun* editorials, the human interest frame ranked fifth versus third for surveyed *Asahi Shimbun* and *Mainichi Shimbun* editorials, respectively.

Threat Frame

For all three newspapers, threat was the largest frame. One *Yomiuri Shimbun* editorial importantly pointed out that it is naïve to think there is no connection between terror and Japan.[57] Another editorial stated, "it cannot accept the thinking which says [all is alright if] only Japan is safe." Yet another pointed out that many Japanese were victims of 9/11.[58] Still another *Yomiuri Shimbun* editorial further argued "if Japan doesn't send the SDF for logistical support related to the attack on Afghanistan, Japan will be seen as soft on terrorism."[59] One *Yomiuri* editorial mentioned that "terrorist organizations could attack worldwide including Japan."[60]

Another general issue addressed by *Yomiuri Shimbun* editorials concerning threat was Japan's preparedness to handle it. Japan passed, for example, the emergency laws for contingencies. However, many editorials criticized this legislation for still being based on Cold War concerns rather than the asymmetrical threats of the twenty-first century. Subsequently, Japan has passed other legislation that deal with the new threats as well as the protection of citizens' rights.[61]

Japan's multilateral efforts to control threats in the region, including terror and the proliferation of WMD, were also discussed.[62] On the other hand, Japan's legal constraints concerning collective defense and homeland security were also examined. Six editorials urged a change in the government's interpretation of collective defense as it relates to the Constitution. Some *Yomiuri Shimbun* editorials asked to close the gap between the Constitution and the reality concerning collective defense as well as other security issues, namely, the identity mission of the SDF, given the changing international situation.[63] Five *Yomiuri Shimbun* editorials linked the issue of collective defense to the development of joint missile defense with the United States.

For all three newspapers, the largest threat was North Korea. Fifty-one different *Yomiuri* editorials during the survey period pointed out that North Korea is a direct problem or threat to Japanese security or violates its sovereignty because of its possible production of nuclear weapons and/or targeting of Japan with missiles and spy ships. Twenty other *Yomiuri Shimbun* editorials, for example, discussed how North Korea is perceived as a deceitful, "insincere," "immoral," "lawless," "unreasonable" rogue nation, perpetrator of national terrorism, "military dictatorship, non-constructive member of international society, which also lacks common sense." North Korean actions concerning the reprocessing of nuclear materials or possible development of nuclear weapons and/or missile testing were viewed by four *Yomiuri Shimbun* editorials as a "breach of trust" of previous agreements and/or official statements. Various *Yomiuri Shimbun* editorials also maintained that North Korea is continually engaged in "brinkmanship diplomacy," for example, with its announcement concerning the abductees; its confirmation of the spy ships; its claimed reprocessing of plutonium in spite of various international agreements; and its having instigated tensions or confrontation between itself and South Korea. Thirteen *Yomiuri Shimbun* editorials maintained this kind of diplomacy is a "card" to negotiate economic assistance or other benefits. Eighteen editorials emphasized that international cooperation is also needed to get North Korea to abandon its weapons of mass destruction. Seventeen other *Yomiuri Shimbun* editorials viewed the strengthening of relations among the actors in the region through bilateral and multilateral engagement as another way to pressure North Korea. Some *Yomiuri Shimbun* editorials emphasized that "encircling North Korea through an international net was one way to make a breakthrough in negotiations."[64] Another eight *Yomiuri* editorials stressed the role of the United States at the center of negotiations or the strengthening the U.S.–Japan alliance in order to put pressure on North Korea. Concern was expressed in eight *Yomiuri* editorials about the differences in positions among the United States, Japan, South Korea, and China concerning the North Korean threat.

After North Korea, eight *Yomiuri Shimbun* editorials emphasized the possible threat of China's military power. Two editorials pointed out that Japan has to also face the gap between U.S.–China relations and U.S.–Japan alliance versus China relations.[65] In spite of these challenges, in other surveyed editorials, Japan and China are urged to work together.[66]

Iraq was not emphasized as a big threat. However, the threat concerning Iraq and homeland security was addressed on two different levels.[67] One was the global war on terrorism. The other was the link between Japanese support for its ally's attack on Iraq and a contingency with North Korea.

One *Yomiuri Shimbun* editorial mentioned "as the U.S. turns towards Iraq and North Korea, the possibility of North Korean terrorist action can not be ignored."[68] Finally, surveyed *Yomiuri Shimbun* editorials were not really focused on Japanese homeland security policies as a possible threat to the region.

Responsibility Frame

The responsibility frame of *Yomiuri Shimbun* editorials concerning homeland security was quite strong. There are clear messages about responsibility to the alliance, the international community, and the nation for a secure region and global order. Six *Yomiuri Shimbun* editorials, for example, emphasized Japanese international responsibility to fight terror and/or address the North Korean, Afghanistan, and Iraq issues. At the same time, although Japan's support as an ally for the U.S war on terrorism was stressed,[69] so was its responsibility to speak frankly with the United States about strategy or differences of opinion.[70] Various editorials, however, were critical of Japan's *heiwa boke*, or "peace-induced stupor," concerning threat.[71] There was also an emphasis on throwing off the restraints or getting rid of obstacles for fuller Japanese participation in the international community by the SDF. Like *Asahi Shimbun* and *Mainichi Shimbun* editorials, at least fourteen *Yomiuri Shimbun* editorials similarly advised how Japanese homeland security could be improved. Eight of these same *Yomiuri Shimbun* editorials also stressed the need for a spy law and swift passage of the emergency laws and other laws related to the fight on terrorism and homeland defense. There was also a call by some *Yomiuri Shimbun* editorials for broader legislation or policy for the SDF to handle asymmetrical threats.[72]

National Interest Frame

Thirteen *Yomiuri Shimbun* editorials viewed Japan's involvement in the fight against the ongoing war on terrorism after 9/11 as being important for the alliance, regional stability, and/or the international community. Fifteen *Yomiuri* editorials also saw the alliance as "a matter of national interest or regional/global security and or essential to Japanese foreign policy." There was often discussion as well concerning the need to support the U.S. attack on Iraq, for example, because of a possible contingency with North Korea. Many editorials were critical of the stance of the opposition parties, especially that of the DPJ, on constitutional revision, new legislation related to homeland security issues, and Japan's support of the U.S. attack on Iraq. One editorial mentioned that "just talking about peace" is not enough. The same article implied that the DPJ has not grasped the idea of "national interest." If this is so, the editorial stated, "the party is not fit to lead the nation."[73]

Two *Yomiuri* editorials expressed concern that the DPJ's position on Iraq would weaken the alliance and impact negatively on Japan's national interest.[74] Other surveyed *Yomiuri* editorials from a national interest viewpoint discussed how Japan's interpretation of collective defense hampers SDF's international contributions as well as better homeland security.[75] Finally, five *Yomiuri Shimbun* editorials linked Japan's national interest to oil interests and the war on terrorism.

Cost/Consequence Frame

Compared to the national interest and responsibility frames, the cost frame is utilized sparingly to refer to the impact of terrorism or the war on terrorism on Japan's and/or the global economy. Concern was expressed about the negative impact of 9/11 on the global economy and/or the U.S. and Japanese economies in nineteen different editorials. There was not much discussion about the cost of strengthening homeland defense infrastructure.

Human Interest Frame

Finally, the human interest frame, least used by the *Yomiuri Shimbun* editorials surveyed, mostly centered on the abductee issue and North Korea. For example, the abduction of Japanese nationals was recognized as a crime or, in some editorials, as an "unprecedented" state-sponsored criminal act.[76] In addition, various editorials concerning the emergency laws emphasized the importance of protecting citizens' rights as well as civilian control.[77] Finally, the abduction of Japanese nationals was recognized as a crime.[78]

TOWARD STRONGER JAPANESE HOMELAND SECURITY

Since 9/11, the world has entered into a "post post Cold War"[79] era characterized by increasing asymmetrical threats. Old paradigms concerning national security were changed to address the war on terrorism and other transnational threats. Incidents such as 9/11 and the subsequent terrorist attacks have heightened Japanese awareness of a less secure world.

Given the new asymmetrical threats, namely, rising terrorism, proliferation of WMD, possible aggression by North Korea, and Japanese's rising sense of vulnerability, it became easier for the Koizumi administration to expand Japan's defense posture internationally and domestically through incremental legislation, public statements, and concrete policies. Moreover, the framing of homeland security by the three newspapers shows that the government importantly has a clearer mandate than before to move ahead with homeland security concerning Japanese national territory. At the same time, public concern also exists, as reflected strongly in *Asahi Shimbun* and *Mainichi Shimbun* editorials, about Japanese government's infringement of civil rights in the pursuit of this security.

In general, Japan's crisis management response has greatly accelerated since the first Gulf War. The speed with which the Koizumi administration was able to push through the Anti-Terrorism Special Measures Law and subsequent related homeland security legislation is noticeable. Soon after 9/11, in line with making Japan strong for homeland security, the government, for example, established the Emergency Anti-Terrorism Headquarters inside the cabinet office and emergency response measures in order to cooperate with the United States as well as protect people of Japan. The LDP also established an Anti-Terrorism Headquarters within party head offices.

Under the Koizumi administration as well, the emergency laws, which are principally for handling contingencies or possible external threats or attack, were finally adopted in 2003, some twenty-five years after the initial research on these issues began by the then LDP government. These laws were further supplemented by seven additional related laws that were adopted in 2004.[80] Among the latter laws is one that will further strengthen the cooperation between the SDF and the U.S. military in the event of a contingency.[81] Another created a special bureau to protect the rights and property of citizens in the event of a contingency.[82]

In the Mid-Term Defense Program (2001–2005),[83] the Japanese Defense Agency (JDA) placed emphasis as well on the "rationalization" and "efficiency" of Japan's defense in the following areas:

> guerilla-commando attacks; disaster-relief; warning and surveillance capability; information capability; education and training; accident prevention and safety measures; human basis to support defense capability; technological research and development; aircraft with in-flight refueling capability and transport capability which can be used for international cooperation activities; ballistic missile defense; procurement and acquisition reforms; defense production and technological base; evacuation of Japanese nationals overseas; intelligence capability; transport capability and mobility, night time operational capability; search and rescue; sustainability and survivability; facilities; and greater harmony with areas surrounding bases.[84]

The new National Defense Program Guideline (NDPG; 2004) further builds on these trends and enlarges Japan's vision concerning homeland defense.[85] Specifically, the NDPG shifts Japan's Basic Defense Force Concept from deterrent effect-oriented defense capabilities to a response-oriented one to meet new contingencies in the twenty-first century. The guidelines also fostered turning the Defense Agency into the now Defense Ministry. It also emphasized the realignment of U.S. forces in Japan for a more effective alliance.

Besides the SDF, the National Police Agency, the Department of Justice, the Cabinet Office, and the JDA are redefining their policies to deal with asymmetrical threats. For example, amendments were made to the SDF and the Japan Coast Guard Laws in order to handle suspicious ships. The Police Law also was amended "so that the National Policy Agency can directly instruct prefectural police in the case of possible nuclear, biological, or chemical attacks." The government has also "compiled a manual to strengthen cooperation among the ministries and agencies." In addition, as of 2003, antiterror units run by special police under the Ministry of Justice have been established in eight prefectures.

In August of 2004, Japan also reorganized the Headquarters for Promotion of Measures against Transnational Organized Crime and Other Relative Issues into the Headquarters for Promotion of Measures against Transnational Organized Crime, Other Relative Issues and International Terrorism. This office later adopted in December of the same year the Action Plan for Prevention of Terrorism, which included sixteen measures and three others for further study.[86] Several concrete actions for Japanese homeland security have already been taken as described earlier and as detailed in the previously mentioned Action Plan.[87]

Although these efforts, policies, and initiatives are all positive steps forward, there is still room to improve Japanese homeland security's soft and hard infrastructure even further. The soft infrastructure issues involve human resources, government and public relations as well as policy and operational issues. The hard infrastructure issues involve future development of missile defense, "upgrading military technology and increasing Japan's capacity to protect its sea lanes."[88]

While the Japanese government continues to move ahead with new policies for homeland defense involving the alliance and/or the SDF, there exists a gap between the public's opinions and the broader picture of homeland security. There is a lack of clear explanation by the government concerning its security policies. For example, the Japanese government needs to explain to its citizens how SDF's international cooperation is linked to Japan's overall national security. Closing this gap will make it easier for the central government to further break old taboos concerning Japan's national security policy including revision of Article 9, changing the identity of the SDF, and upgrading the nature of Japan's international cooperation concerning conflict and asymmetrical threats.

This gap was evident through the survey of editorials conducted for this study. It was also confirmed by The Council on Security and Defense Capabilities report titled *Kuni to Kokumin no Anzen he no Kyoi oyobi Kore ni Taisuru Taio ni tsuite* (Japan's Vision for Future Security and Defense Capabilities) in October 2004.[89] The Council emphasizes integrated security strategies through the combination of the three approaches mentioned earlier regarding the revision of Japan's Basic Defense Force Concept. The Council also advocated "government pursuit of a Multi-Functional Flexible Defense Force" that can perform multiple functions (responding to terrorist attacks and ballistic missiles, and international cooperation) through flexible operation of the defense forces. Clearly, increased information gathering, deeper cooperation among various related ministries/agencies as well as quick crisis management are needed for enhanced Japanese homeland security.

Another problem area is human intelligence to prevent terrorism before it happens. Here, various problems also exist. Although the SDF has the Defense Intelligence Headquarters, it still needs to strengthen its intelligence gathering through people. A positive measure for this is the Ground

Self-Defense Force's decision to create a new "Central Intelligence Unit," comprised of senior officers and nineteen hundred others as intelligence specialists.[90] In addition, as the Council urged, "the amendment of the National Security Council of Japan Law will also help to integrate and reinforce security policy at an administrative level that transcends the hierarchy among ministries and departments and to rework National Security Council practices."[91]

The issue of how to maintain a balance as well between human rights and homeland security has not been resolved legally or logistically. This dilemma is exemplified by an incident involving the JDA a few years ago. Specifically, the JDA "kept a list of people who sought information under the Information Disclosure Act. The list recorded the birth date, occupation and even the names of the organization they belonged to. It was a clear abuse of those citizens' privacy and the system of information disclosure."[92]

Countermeasures for cyber terror are another problem. According to a National Police Agency Survey of company and cyber terror countermeasures, "80 percent said they were inadequately prepared and only 2 percent had prepared manuals."[93] The 2003 Japan Defense Report also "mentions a new approach is needed for handling cyber, nuclear, biological, chemical, terrorist and missile attacks."[94]

Japan's Headquarters for Promotion of Measures against Transnational Organized Crime Other Relative Issues, and International Terrorism proposed three homeland security initiatives requiring further study. These are "legislation on basic policy for terrorism prevention measures; a system to designate terrorists and terrorist organizations and a way to regulate terrorist related transactions among residents in Japan."[95]

Finally, the Council on Security and Defense Capabilities also suggested the revision of the present Japanese defense policy based on outdated Cold War concepts. Specifically, the report recommends a new Integrated Security Strategy,[96] which involves enhancing the SDF roles and capabilities, to handle new threats to the Japanese homeland, and/or to the global environment. These perspectives, since the initial survey for this chapter, have now been incorporated in the Mid-Term Defense Program (FY 2005–2009). Since the initial survey for this chapter, these perspectives have been incorporated now in the Mid-Term Defense Program (FY 2005–2008).[97] However, the Government of Japan's efforts to carry out these goals must continue in the new millennium.

U.S.–Japan Alliance and Global Terrorism after 9/11

An *Asahi Shimbun* editorial, ironically dated September 11, 2001, stated that "Japan should seek ways to extricate itself from too heavy a reliance on its alliance with the U.S. while preserving the presence of the U.S. in the Asia Pacific region."[98] However, 9/11 has tied Japan even closer to the alliance. Japan has shown its strong support for the U.S. war on terrorism post-9/11 through legislation, bilateral meetings, economic support, policies, public statements, and the dispatch of the SDF for logistical support and humanitarian assistance. It has also emphasized the importance of the U.S.–Japan alliance as a pillar of its homeland defense.

Indeed, U.S.–Japan relations after 9/11 have grown closer in the face of new transnational threats. The deepening alliance between the United States and its most important Asian ally at this time can partially be attributed to the various threat issues raised by the editorials surveyed, including the Korean peninsula problem, frictions and uncertainty with China, terrorism, and the protection of the Japanese homeland. It can also be linked to an earlier transformation of the alliance due to the political, socioeconomic, and security upheavals after the end of the Cold War.

For Japan, the alliance means not only benefits but also costs. Underneath the strong vote of confidence for the alliance, for example, there is anxiety over abandonment if Japan opposes U.S. policies in its war on terrorism. One *Yomiuri Shimbun* editorial states the idea that "Under the U.S.–Japan Security and Cooperation Treaty, the U.S. has a duty to protect Japan" and "even if Japan did not support the U.S. attack on Iraq, it would be incorrect to argue that this would fail to work against the alliance." The editor goes on to say, "history is full of broken alliances."[99]

Another cost involves a growing perception of a Japanese threat in the region due to Japan's increased defense capacity and expansion of SDF parameters, as well as political rhetoric bordering on nationalism. While the United States welcomed increased Japanese support for its war on terrorism, Japan's failure to resolve remaining historical frictions with its Asian neighbors only aggravates the perception of Japan's being a source of regional instability. Another cost involves Japan becoming a target for terrorism because of its support of U.S. counterterrorism policies. Already terrorist attacks in Madrid and London as well as incidents involving Japanese nationals in Iraq show how realistic a scenario this is. Finally, another cost, as discussed by different surveyed editorials, entails economic backlash related to access to Middle East oil and a growing burden on Japanese and/or global economies.

FUTURE DIRECTIONS

With the landslide Lower House elections on September 10, 2005, voters placed their support behind Koizumi. This support can partially be contributed to Koizumi's charisma, his strong efforts to reform the Liberal Democratic Party, his push for postal privatization, and the weakness of the largest opposition party or the Democratic Party of Japan. This snap election, which garnered two-thirds of the seats in the Lower House for the LDP and its coalition partner Komeito, created a cushion for U.S.–Japan relations on which to further build its already expanding alliance for global and regional prosperity, security, and democracy. President George W. Bush and Prime

Minister Koizumi's close relationship and similar conservative agendas have been institutionalized through joint agreements, including the "U.S.–Japan Roadmap for Realignment Implementation" (May 2006) and the "Japan–U.S. Alliance of the New Century" (June 2006), and further strengthens this direction of the alliance, a direction that has continued under Koizumi's successor, Abe Shinzo, who took over in late September 2006.[100]

By looking at mainstream Japanese newspaper editorials and public opinion polls, the author attempted to grasp the dynamics of a key period in the evolution of Japanese homeland security debate and the implications of this for U.S.–Japan relations as well as for Japan's defense of the alliance, a direction that has continued under Koizumi's successors, Abe Shinzo (9/06–9/07) and Fukuda Yasuo (9/07–present). Based on the opinions expressed by both the public and experts, it is clear Japan must continue to improve its homeland security in this new era. Presently, Japan is restructuring its homeland security to include missile defense, surveillance satellites, and expanded roles for the SDF domestically and internationally. At the same time, however, Japan must be careful to reassure its neighbors that it is still carrying out "defensive" defense (otherwise known as "exclusive defense") or else it might face stronger challenges from its neighbors in the future.

The United States and Japan, as well, must pay closer attention to the gap between government policies on global terrorism and public understanding and support for the war on terrorism as well as the protection of their respective homelands. Both nations must also confront growing public concern over long-term domestic issues including social welfare, economic revitalization, as well as socioeconomic equality.

From a global perspective concerning homeland security and the international community, changing Japan's national security stance from that of "bystander" to a member of international society actively contributing to global order is still one of Japan's biggest challenges in the twenty-first century. During this process, Japan faces the challenge of balancing its domestic priorities, development of autonomous foreign policies, and its historic commitment to the United States . In order to truly become a strong country in the area of homeland security, Japan must also overcome these and other challenges, such as constitutional reform, infrastructural problems, resolution of historical issues with Asian neighbors, and the creation of a political and popular consensus for this direction.

Beyond the defense of its own borders, the Council on Security and Defense Capabilities has also linked Japan's contributions through the SDF to the international security environment to its national security interest. On the positive side, Japan is already actively involved in international cooperative efforts to fight terrorism in such organizations or groups as the G-8, APEC, ASEAN and the U.N., the U.S.–Japan alliance, the TCOG (Trilateral Coordination and Oversight Group),[101] and the Six Party Talks. Japan has ratified all twelve of the UN related antiterror treaties. Moreover, Japan is involved in capacity-building assistance to fight terrorism, principally in Asian countries. It is clear that while strengthening its homeland security as well as the U.S.–Japan alliance, Japan joins other members of the international community who, in spite of varying degrees of positive to negative support for their homeland security policies, are struggling to comprehend the new security paradigm including global terrorism after 9/11. Since completing the analysis of my original database, events such as North Korea's firing of seven missiles into the Japan Sea in July of 2006 (and its testing of a nuclear weapon in October 2006) to a foiled terrorist plot in August of 2006 to blow up several planes leaving Heathrow airport for the United States, only reconfirm the need for the international community to strengthen its cooperation, while adapting quickly to different kinds of asymmetrical threats.

APPENDIX 1   FRAMING THE JAPANESE HOMELAND SECURITY DEBATE: COMPARATIVE ANALYSIS OF THREE JAPANESE MAINSTREAM NEWSPAPERS

Database: 694 Editorials.

	Yomiuri Shimbun (Est. 1874)	*Asahi Shimbun* (Est. 1879)	*Mainichi Shimbun* (Est. 1944 [predecessor est. 1872])
Circulation morning edition only	10,042,075	8,093,885	3,974,559
Political orientation	Conservative	Liberal left	Liberal/left of center
Framing order *	1. Threat a) North Korea b) China c) Iraq —Terror impact on Japan —National preparedness to handle threat —Constitutional revision —Collective security	1. Threat a) North Korea b) China c) Japan —Homeland security —Infrastructure issues —Iraq	1. Threat a) North Korea b) China c) Japan
	2. Responsibility —Alliance, international community, and the nation to secure regional and global order —Critical of Japan's "peace-induced stupor" attitude —Improve homeland defense	2. Responsibility —United States only protector —Government and laws —Regional responsibility —Government responsibility to enhance domestic security infrastructure	2. Responsibility —Balancing U.S.–Japan alliance and cooperation with war on terror —Critical of Japan's emergency laws regarding protection of citizens as well as civilian control

Continued

Appendix I   Continued

	Yomiuri Shimbun (Est. 1874)	Asahi Shimbun (Est. 1879)	Mainichi Shimbun (Est. 1944 [predecessor est. 1872])
	3. Human interest —Abduction of Japanese nationals a crime —Protection of citizens' rights —Civilian control	3. Human interest —Balancing security and protection of civil rights	3. Human interest —Abductees issues —Protection of citizens rights
	4. Cost/consequence —Global economy —Domestic economy	4. Cost/consequence —Support for U.S. war on terrorism, costs-financial, access to oil, threat to Japanese homeland	4. Cost/consequence —Iraq War and world economy —SDF possible target in Iraq —SDF role in Iraq and Japan's constitutional limitations
	5. National interest —Important for alliance, regional stability, and community —Japanese support for Iraq attack for later U.S. support for possible North Korea contingency —Critical of positions of opposition parties regarding constitutional revision, legislation related to homeland security issues, and Japanese support of U.S. Iraq attack —Middle East oil and war on terror	5. National interest —Japanese support for Iraq attack for later U.S. support for possible North Korea contingency —Middle East oil	5. National interest —Critical of priority on U.S. alliance over Japanese international contribution to the war on terror

* There are five frames used in this analysis—threat, responsibility, national interest, human interest, and cost/consequence. For the purposes of the chart, the three top threats seen by each newspaper are also ranked. The major threats seen commonly by all three newspapers were North Korea and China. However, other threats included Iraq and Japan itself. The Japan threat was due to its expanded security policies including a stronger alliance with the United States and enhanced SDF responsibilities, especially overseas.

APPENDIX 2   TRANSLATION OF EDITORIAL TITLES
Yomiuri Shimbun

1. 2001/09/18   9/11 Push for Urgent Legislation for International Cooperation
2. 2001/09/20   No Inward-Looking Debate for International Antiterrorism Efforts
3. 2001/09/21   Antiterrorism Coalition: Speed up to Legislate SDF Dispatch
4. 2001/09/22   U.S.–Japan Summit: Deepen Strategy Talk to Exterminate Terrorism
5. 2001/09/27   U.S.–Japan Summit: Convert Determination to Fight against Terrorism into Action
6. 2001/09/28   Koizumi's Policy Speech: Urges Ruling and Opposite Parties to Share Crisis Awareness
7. 2001/09/28   New Logistical Support Law: Placing Importance on the International Coalition's Effectiveness
8. 2001/10/03   Revision of U.S. Defense: Better Preparation for "New Threat"
9. 2001/10/03   Terrorism and Air Security: Government Support Focuses on Air Route Protection
10. 2001/10/05   What Kinds of International Antiterrorism Measures would a Democratic Party of Japan Administration Take?
11. 2001/10/06   "International Responsibility" should be the Center of the Debate on Antiterrorism Special Measures Bill
12. 2001/10/08   G 7 Joint Declaration: Daring Move against Terrorism is Urgent
13. 2001/10/09   Military Action Begins: International Consensus is to Exterminate Terrorism
14. 2001/10/09   Japan's Role: The Enactment of Bill on Antiterrorism Measures is Urgent
15. 2001/10/10   Brace for Retaliatory Terror Strikes
16. 2001/10/10   Japan–China Summit: Ask China to Overcome "Tensions"
17. 2001/10/11   Antiterrorism Special Measures Bill: Establish it Prior to APEC Meeting
18. 2001/10/13   Antiterrorism Special Measures Bill: Arbitrary Amendment will Impair the Bill
19. 2001/10/16   Bioterrorism: Orderly Handling by all Possible Measures
20. 2001/10/16   Japan–Korea Summit: Seeking "Normal Country" Relationship
21. 2001/10/17   Antiterrorism Special Measures Bill: Democratic Party of Japan's Opposition Belittles "International Responsibility"
22. 2001/10/20   New Round: Start Negotiations to Stop World Recession
23. 2001/10/21   APEC: Time to Test Japan's Diplomatic Power
24. 2001/10/21   Will Tough Ground Battles against Terrorism Bring Results?
25. 2001/10/22   APEC Closes: Will Antiterrorism Change U.S.–China Relations?
26. 2001/10/23   ODA to China: Fundamental Scale and Substance Natural
27. 2001/10/25   Prime Minister Koizumi Administration at 6 Months: Still no Vision for Economic Revitalization
28. 2001/10/27   Bioterrorism: Severe Punishment for Rampant Copycat Crimes
29. 2001/10/31   Antiterrorism Treaty: Push for Ratification to Strengthen International Cooperation

30. 2001/11/01   Japan Diplomacy: Replacement of Foreign Minister is the only Way to Recover its Function
31. 2001/11/02   Global Recession: Japanese Economy Needs A Major Shift
32. 2001/11/06   Rice Aid to North Korea: Not The Right Time for it without Conditions
33. 2001/11/08   A Broad Cut in U.S. Interest Rate: Reflects a Sense of Crisis Concerning an Economic Slump Due to Terrorist Attack
34. 2001/11/09   SDF Dispatch: What is Wrong about Aegis?
35. 2001/11/10   Minus Growth: Quickly Advance Stimulus Measures for the Economy
36. 2001/11/13   Air Industry Integration: Survival Strategy should have Accountability
37. 2001/11/17   Cyber Terror: Strengthen Critical Infrastructure Protection
38. 2001/12/02   Dispatch of Self-Defense Forces: Approval by Democratic Party of Japan is a Big Step Forward
39. 2001/12/15   Withdrawal from The Antiballistic Missile Treaty: Can Order of Nuclear Disarmament Be Maintained?
40. 2001/12/18   Midair Refueling Plane: Building New Era Defense System is Urgent
41. 2001/12/23   Suspicious Vessel Sunk: Is this kind of Response Sufficient to Stop Terrorism?
42. 2001/12/24   Abduction Issue: North Korea's Stance is Unjustifiable
43. 2001/12/29   Looking Back on Japan 2001: Social Stability Still Being Disturbed
44. 2002/01/01   Challenge for Japan after a Terrorist Attack : Take All Possible Measures to Avoid Panic
45. 2002/01/03   Overcoming Danger: Fighting Terrorism is the New Era's Challenge for New International Order
46. 2002/01/04   Overcoming Danger: On The Road towards Economic Recovery, Utilize 9/11 Experience
47. 2002/01/07   Overcoming Danger: Rush to Rebuild Peace and Prosperity, Outlining Political Responsibility
48. 2002/01/08   Overcoming Danger: Reform of Security Consciousness Needed for Threat Confrontation
49. 2002/01/22   Suspicious Vessel: Don't hesitate to Salvage it
50. 2002/01/22   Bush Administration at One Year: Questioning Leadership Capacity for Economic Recovery
51. 2002/01/26   Contingency Legislation: Preparing Broadly for Diversified Threat
52. 2002/01/26   Chinese Diplomacy: Must Act as a "Responsible Country"
53. 2002/01/27   Japan–Korea Exchange Year: Will it Build a Basis for Mature Relationship?
54. 2002/02/06   Transfer of *Futenma* Base: Push to Realize it while Respecting Local Citizens
55. 2002/02/15   President Bush's Round of Visits: Antiterrorism Cooperation with China, Japan, and South Korea is on the Agenda
56. 2002/02/19   Japan–U.S. Summit: Recovery from Economy Crisis is the Way to Strengthen the Alliance
57. 2002/02/26   Investigation of the Suspicious Vessel: Only Salvaging will Elicit the Truth
58. 2002/03/11   Cooperation for Antiterrorism: Exercising the Right of Collective Self-Defense

59. 2002/03/13 Abduction Issue: New Testimony Reveals North Korea's Deception
60. 2002/03/14 Suspicious Vessel: Critical to Salvage it without Making A Fuss
61. 2002/03/18 Stopping Terrorist Financing: Rush to Ratify Treaty for International Cooperation
62. 2002/03/21 Contingency Legislation: Let's Prepare with "International Standard" as the Basis
63. 2002/03/23 Japan–Korea Summit: Overcoming the Policy Gap over North Korea
64. 2002/03/23 Expressing Concerns about U.S. Unilateralism is Necessary
65. 2002/03/24 Abducted Japanese Issue: Maintain a Resolute Attitude for Future Breakthrough
66. 2002/04/05 General Public Poll on the Constitution: Time for Political Support of Voices Seeking Amendment
67. 2002/04/13 Japan–China Summit: Maintain a Resolute Attitude toward North Korea
68. 2002/04/14 Letters from Readers over the Past 50 years (15): Social Party Leader Asanuma Stabbed Dead, Many People want Terrorism to be Driven Out
69. 2002/04/14 Japan–Southeast Asia: Rush to Build Cooperative Relationship in a New Era
70. 2002/04/16 Japan–China Economic Relations: To Promote Mutually Complementary Relationship Quit "Assistance"
71. 2002/04/17 Emergency Defense Bills: Use as Foothold for Broad Preparations
72. 2002/05/01 Japan–North Korea Meeting: No Progress without Clarification of Abduction Issue
73. 2002/05/02 PM Koizumi's Round of Visits: Challenges Remain for Asian Community Framework
74. 2002/05/03 Constitution Day: Demand for Establishment of Security Sense
75. 2002/05/09 Investigation of a Suspicious Vessel: Need for Salvage Increases
76. 2002/05/11 Asylum Attempt in *Shenyang*: South Korean Papers Criticize Japanese Response
77. 2002/05/11 Contingency Legislation Deliberation: Don't Repeat Futile "Theological Argument"
78. 2002/05/11 "Media Review": Lack of "Contingency Legislation" Abnormal, Role, People Enlightenment
79. 2002/05/15 Thirtieth Anniversary Reversion of Okinawa: Share the Heavy Burden of U.S. Bases
80. 2002/05/17 Support for Antiterrorism: Extension of 6 Months Proves Determination to Carry Out International Duty
81. 2002/05/24 American Terrorism Report: International Cooperation is the Way to Contain Terrorism
82. 2002/05/25 Media Review: Japan–China Media Coverage should Focus on Global Trends Instead of Face Saving
83. 2002/06/04 Japan Defense Agency List: Rush to Disclose Organization Involvement, Wipe Out Distrust
84. 2002/06/11 Put an End to Nuclear Statement Problem: Speed up Deliberations on Contingency Legislation
85. 2002/06/13 Countermeasures for Airport Security: Strengthening Groundwork for Stopping Terrorism

86. 2002/06/21 Japan Defense Agency List: Correcting Loose Rules to Recover Trust
87. 2002/06/30 Exchange of Gun Fire between North and South Korea: Heightened Tensions on the Peninsula Again
88. 2002/07/02 Japan–Korea Summit: More than Ever Ties are Needed against North Korea
89. 2002/07/11 *Yodo* Hijacker Returns Home: Has he Become a Nuisance to North Korea?
90. 2002/07/14 Contingency Legislation: Make Way for its Establishment at the Next Diet
91. 2002/07/19 Radioactive Waste: Pave the Way for its Future Disposal
92. 2002/07/30 Transfer of *Futenma* Base: Aim for Early Start of Consensus-Based Construction
93. 2002/07/30 Democratic Party of Japan: Will the Party Come Together on its Constitutional Report?
94. 2002/08/02 Abductors Wanted: Ask North Korea to Turn Them Over
95. 2002/08/03 Defense of Japan White Paper: Create the Conditions for Defense Posture Great Change
96. 2002/08/06 Open North Korea–South Korea Talks: Substance of North Korea Peace Offensive is Questioned
97. 2002/08/15 End of War Anniversary: Humble Desire for Revision of History
98. 2002/08/16 South and North Korea's Summit: Still no Promise of Tensions Relief
99. 2002/08/20 Abduction Incidents: Don't Allow North Korea to Delay the Inevitable
100. 2002/08/26 Russia–North Korea Summit: Russian Card Weakens its Effectiveness
101. 2002/08/27 Japan–North Korea Talks: Progress on the Abduction Issue Premise of the Talks' Continuation
102. 2002/08/29 Japan–U.S. Strategic Talks: Powerful Diplomatic Framework Needed to Build Trust
103. 2002/08/31 P.M. Koizumi's Visit to North Korea: Will his Determination to Develop the Situation be Successful?
104. 2002/08/31 International Politics Groaning Underneath: Down to Earth Perspective needed to Observe U.S. Moves
105. 2002/09/04 Suspicious Vessel: Political Consideration of North Korea, Useless
106. 2002/09/14 Bush Speech: Imposition of tough warning on Iraq
107. 2002/09/15 PM Koizumi Visit to North Korea: Rational Disagreement is an Option
108. 2002/09/17 South Korea hopes Japan-North Korea Summit has [Good Influence on Korean Peninsula]
109. 2002/09/18 Japan-North Korea Leaders Summit: Will North keep Pyongyang Declaration in Good Faith?
110. 2002/09/19 Clarification of Abduction Incidents: Don't Repeat "Snuggle Up Diplomacy"
111. 2002/09/20 Abductees Information: Useless Cover Up Amplifies Distrust
112. 2002/09/23 30th Anniversary Normalization of Sino-Japan Diplomatic Relations: Build Honest Communication

113. 2002/09/27 30th anniversary Normalization of Sino-Japan Diplomatic Relations: Will China be able to get rid of the "China Threat"?
114. 2002/09/30 North Korea's Covert Operations Boats: "Training" Can't Be an Excuse
115. 2002/10/02 Nuclear Plant Inspection: Rational Rulemaking Needed
116. 2002/10/03 Abduction Survey Results: Increasing and Deepening Doubts Concerning North Korea Explanation
117. 2002/10/07 U.S.–North Korea High-Level Consultations: No Other Option for North Korea Except Continued Dialogues
118. 2002/10/10 Reopening of Japan–North Korea Negotiations: No Need to Rush Normalization of Relations
119. 2002/10/11 Party Head *Doi* Apology: Can't Erase History Surrounding Abductions
120. 2002/10/14 Bali Tragedy: Need to Counter Weak Antiterrorism Environment
121. 2002/10/16 5 Abductees Return Home: Only One Step toward Full-Scale Clarification of the Issue
122. 2002/10/17 Contingency/Personal Information Protection Bills: What about the Consensus "to Pass Them at Extraordinary Diet"?
123. 2002/10/18 North Korea Nuclear Development: Don't allow Defection from International Society
124. 2002/10/22 North Korea Nuclear Development: Pursuit of Immediate Cessation by International Cooperation
125. 2002/10/25 Abductees: Government should Ensure their Permanent Return to Japan
126. 2002/10/27 Terrorists Seized a Theater: Russian Government Showed Firmness by Breaking Them Down
127. 2002/10/28 North Korea Nuclear Development: Japan, U.S., and South Korea Urge an Immediate Halt
128. 2002/10/29 APEC Declaration: Japan's Responsibility Heavier Due to its "North Korea" Policy
129. 2002/10/31 Reopening of Japan–North Korea Negotiation: Sticking to Principles Recognized as Necessity
130. 2002/11/12 Amendment of Contingency Bills: Time for Opposition Party to Show Responsibility
131. 2002/11/13 Abductees: Investigation of Remains Strengthens Doubts Concerning [North Korea]
132. 2002/11/16 KEDO Declaration: North Korea should Take Warning Seriously
133. 2002/11/23 Japan–North Korea Negotiations: Security Perspective Indispensable
134. 2002/11/25 Department of Homeland Security: Immense Bureaucracy Shows Determination to Stop Terrorism
135. 2002/11/28 North Korea Negotiations: Japan No Reason for Early Normalization
136. 2002/11/30 Serial Terror Attacks: Halt Spread of Terrorism by Strengthening International Cooperation
137. 2002/12/05 Aegis Dispatched: Departure from "Peace Addiction"

167.	2003/03/24	Iraq War: Don't be Lazy Regarding International Terrorism Caution
168.	2003/03/25	Response to Iraq War: Evaluated as Correct Decision by Public Poll
169.	2003/03/28	Iraq War: Japan Pressed to Reconsider U.N.-Based Diplomacy
170.	2003/03/30	(Support of U.S. Iraq Attack): Courageous Koizumi Statement
171.	2003/03/31	New Round: Don't Get Involved in Iraq Conflict
172.	2003/04/02	Public Poll on Constitution: "Threat" Increases Security Concern
173.	2003/04/03	Japan's Defense: Let's Think about Response to North Korea Missiles
174.	2003/04/04	Iraq War: U.S.–England Historical Decision Correct, Let's Reconfirm Meaning of U.S.–Japan Alliance
175.	2003/04/06	Iraq Attack: Pros and Cons
176.	2003/04/08	Japan–China Foreign Minister Meeting: Cooperation Possible concerning North Korea Nuclear Problem?
177.	2003/04/12	North Korea Nuclear Development: Can We Contain it with Multilateral Talks?
178.	2003/04/17	Abduction Condemnatory Resolution: International Recognition of North Korea's Injustice
179.	2003/04/18	U.S.–China–North Korea Consultations: Iraq War Impacts North Korea
180.	2003/04/20	U.S.–China–North Korea Consultations: Brinkmanship Card No Longer Useful
181.	2003/04/23	Relaxation of Weapons Standard: Main Political Parties in Agreement
182.	2003/04/24	Response to Abductees Incident: Foreign Ministry's Nature Yet to be Changed
183.	2003/04/29	Contingency Legislation: Through Amendment Consultations, Let's Create One Quickly
184.	2003/05/01	South Korea–North Korea Cabinet Meeting: Limit to Ineffective Conciliation Policy for Nuclear Development
185.	2003/05/02	Koizumi Visits Europe: Approach Necessary regarding U.S.–Europe Split
186.	2003/05/03	Constitution Day: Revise Deceptive Interpretation Harmful to "National Interest"
187.	2003/05/14	Amendment of Contingency Bill: State Consensus to Close Gap
188.	2003/05/15	Saudi Terror: More than Ever International Ties Needed
189.	2003/05/16	U.S.–South Korea Summit: Gap Remains Concerning North Korea Nuclear Development
190.	2003/05/23	North Korea Nuclear Development: Preparations for Sanctions Indispensable
191.	2003/05/25	Japan–U.S. Summit: North Korea, Iraq Tests Strength of Alliance
192.	2003/06/03	Encircling North Korea: International Resolve for Pressure Stance
193.	2003/06/07	Three Contingency Related Bills Passed: Needed Framework for a Law Governed Country

221. 2003/11/15   Iraq Situation: Constructive Debate Needed for Self-Defense Forces Dispatch
222. 2003/11/16   (North Korea) Security Guarantee: Giving Priority to U.S.–Japan Alliance Natural
223. 2003/11/19   KEDO: North Korea blamed for Halting Light Water Reactor Construction
224. 2003/11/20   Koizumi Coalition Administration: Responsible Policy Implementation Wipes Out Concerns
225. 2003/11/22   Turkey Terror: International Society should not Flinch
226. 2003/11/25   WMD: Push Quickly for Prohibited Related Materials Encirclement
227. 2003/11/27   Iraq Support: Let's Increasingly Strengthen Understanding of Self-Defense Forces Dispatch
228. 2003/11/28   Iraq Nuclear Allegation: Not Proved to be Innocent
229. 2003/12/03   SDF Dispatch: Stick to Fundamental Iraq Support
230. 2003/12/04   U.S. Forces Overseas Realignment: Premise, Maintain Restraining Power in Asia
231. 2003/12/04   Self-Defense Forces Dispatch: Self-Realization Regarding Responsibility Necessary
232. 2003/12/10   Self-Defense Forces Dispatch: National Spirit Test
233. 2003/12/16   Hussein's Detention: Possible Momentum for Public Order Improvement?
234. 2003/12/19   Self-Defense Forces Dispatch: New Duty for International Peace Cooperation
235. 2003/12/19   Enola Gay: Never Total Agreement about Historical Perspective
236. 2003/12/20   Missile Defense: Preparation for Serious North Korean Threat
237. 2003/12/22   Six-Party Talks: North Korea should Take Seriously Libya's Nuclear Relinquishment
238. 2003/12/26   Self-Defense Forces Dispatch: Let's Send Them Out as "National Representatives"
239. 2003/12/28   2003 Review: Taking Helm toward "Normal Country"
240. 2003/12/29   2003 World Review: North Korea–Iraq Long Way to Finding a Solution
241. 2004/01/01   Citizens' Calm Mind Set Basis for Japan's Revitalization Heavy Decision for Japan's 100-Year Plan
242. 2004/01/04   Year of Decision: Time for Action to Take on Turning Point
243. 2004/01/05   Year of Decision: Without Extermination of Terrorism, No Peace; Critical Stage for Iraq Recovery
244. 2004/01/09   Year of Decision: Outline to Recover Public Order Urgent Duty to Reverse Vulnerable Society
245. 2004/01/10   Abduction Issue: North Korea's Obvious Shake-Up Strategy
246. 2004/01/13   Citizens Voters Law: Quickly Push for Environment to Reform Constitution
247. 2004/01/15   Proposal for Constitutional Amendment: Epoch-Making Step by the Main Opposition Party
248. 2004/01/16   Arms Embargo Principles: Revision Proposal Worthy of Consideration
249. 2004/01/20   Close of Ordinary Diet: Desire to Deepen Debate Regarding Iraq and the Constitution

Mainichi Newspaper

15. 2001/10/02   New Law for Logistical Support: Diet Participation to be Made Clear
16. 2001/10/03   Restructuring U.S. Defense: Forced to Change the Way of Thinking
17. 2001/10/04   Discovery of Terror Evidence: Explanation Needs to convince Local Citizens
18. 2001/10/05   Prime Minister Visits China and South Korea: Let's Deepen Mutual Understanding of Counterterrorism Measures
19. 2001/10/05   Seajack: Carry Out Cooperation for International Investigation Networking
20. 2001/10/06   Support Antiterrorism Law: Not Going to War
21. 2001/10/07   Terror and Refugees: Let's Show Flag through Humanitarian Assistance
22. 2001/10/09   Air Attack on Taliban: International Coalition, Burden Sharing to Prepare for Long War
23. 2001/10/10   Sino-Japan Summit: From Antagonism to Cooperation against Terrorism
24. 2001/10/11   9/11: What has Changed in this One Month
25. 2001/10/14   Contingency and Media: Not Exceeding the Limits Even during Emergency Time
26. 2001/10/14   Support Antiterrorism Law: Unrealistic Debate Not Good
27. 2001/10/17   Support Antiterrorism Law: In the House of Councilors for Another Amendment Concerning (Advance Approval)
28. 2001/10/19   Self-Defense Forces Law Revision: Make What is the Defense Secret Becomes Clearer
29. 2001/10/19   Anthrax Terror: Let's Face it Calmly and Firmly
30. 2001/10/24   Japanese Values: Big Strategic Contribution by Continued Support of U.S. Military
31. 2001/10/27   International Terror Countermeasures: Don't Give them Even the Smallest Chance
32. 2001/11/01   Terror and Freedom: In Order to Protect Open Society
33. 2001/11/17   Basic Plan: No More than Just One Terrorism Countermeasure
34. 2001/11/26   Let's Think About the Constitution/20 Citizens Duty: Will National Defense Change National Perception?
35. 2001/12/20   Doubts Regarding Abduction: Halting Investigation is Betrayal
36. 2001/12/23   Suspicious Ship Chase: Firm Attitude Understandable
37. 2001/12/27   Armed Suspicious Ship: Protect Marine Safety through International Cooperation
38. 2001/12/29   *Futenma* Transfer: Stationed Marines; Let's Debate Directly
39. 2002/01/03   "Building Great Country Take-Off Year": North Korea's Three Papers' Editorial
40. 2002/01/04   Polish New Diplomacy Skills: For Recognition of (Cooperation and Competition)
41. 2002/01/12   Report on U.S. Nuclear Strategy: Don't See Outline for Nuclear Reduction
42. 2002/01/22   Bush Administration at 1 Year: Don't Forget Consideration and Cooperation
43. 2002/02/06   Contingency Legislation: Show What it Does Concretely
44. 2002/02/17   Bush Visits Japan: Talk Clearly about Japan's Position

105. 2002/10/31   Japan–North Korea Negotiations: North Korea Should Keep Pyongyang Declaration
106. 2002/11/04   General Association of Korean Residents in Japan: Their Reflections on Abduction Incident Needed
107. 2002/11/05   Let's Think about Constitution House of Representatives' Interim Report/2: Self-Defense Forces Debate on National Security Image
108. 2002/11/06   Sino-Japan–South Korea Meeting: Good if Held More Frequently
109. 2002/11/14   Self-Defense Forces Dispatch: Debate in Diet on Extension–Increase
110. 2002/11/16   Japan–North Korea Negotiations: Time to Stick to Principles Seriously
111. 2002/11/18   Let's think about the Constitution: House of Representatives' Interim Report/3: International Cooperation, Balance between Self-control and Restriction
112. 2002/11/20   Japan–North Korea Issue: Create a Special Diet Committee to Debate
113. 2002/11/29   Diplomatic Strategy Meeting: PM Leadership Requires Great Wisdom
114. 2002/12/14   North Korea: Such a Trick Doesn't Work Anymore
115. 2002/12/17   Three Months after Pyongyang Declaration: Put a Brake Very Soon on Worsening Relations
116. 2002/12/19   Missile Defense: Too Early to Enter the Disposition and Development Stages
117. 2002/12/20   Roh Moo-Hyun Elected: Take over Future-Oriented Japan–South Korea Relationship Policy
118. 2002/12/24   North Korea Nuclear Development: Restore Removed Seals to Original State
119. 2003/01/03   North Korea: Asked Japan to Abandon following U.S. Policy
120. 2003/01/05   Determination to Solve Difficult Problems: Rush to Improve Sino-Japan Relationship
121. 2003/01/09   Japan–U.S.–South Korea Consultations: Urge North Korea to Dialogue
122. 2003/01/15   Prime Minister visits *Yasukuni*: Action Lacking Consideration
123. 2003/01/16   Next South Korea President: Meeting with Foreign Minister Kawaguchi to Start Full-Scale Diplomacy
124. 2003/01/16   Investigation on Abduction Incident: Police Should Stand above Politics
125. 2003/01/17   Foreign Minister Kawaguchi Visits South Korea: Dialogue with North Korea without Bending Principles
126. 2003/01/28   *Monju* Decision: Revise Entirely Inspection System
127. 2003/02/14   UNSC Entrusted: North Korea Nuclear Development Makes the World its Enemy
128. 2003/02/20   Japan Speech at UN: Hope for Koizumi's own Words
129. 2003/02/21   Iraq and North Korea: United UNSC is in Japan's National Interest
130. 2003/02/25   South Korea New Administration: New Sunshine Policy with International Perspective

131. 2003/02/26   Japan–South Korea Summit: Realized More Frequent Meetings for Closer Relationship
132. 2003/02/28   Reopening Graphite Reactor: Stop Using Dangerous Card
133. 2003/03/04   Crisis Awareness: Remote Iraq, Urgent North Korea
134. 2003/03/06   Iraq Problem: Did Prime Minister Turn his Back on Public Opinion?
135. 2003/03/08   North Korea: Stop Dangerous Military Provocation
136. 2003/03/12   Iraq Problem: Convince United States and England toward Cooperation
137. 2003/03/19   Support for Prime Minister: Can't Speak about that Reason?
138. 2003/03/21   Iraq Hostilities Opening: End Destruction as Soon as Possible and Don't Make it Unilateral War
139. 2003/03/22   Strong America Running Ahead: How Do We Resolve this Difficult Issue?
140. 2003/03/29   Surveillance Satellites: For New Resolution Regarding Peaceful Use of Space Needed
141. 2003/04/02   Reform of Foreign Ministry: Can't Confront Drastic World Trends
142. 2003/04/02   Japan's Economic Policies: Initially, Calm Decision Regarding War Situation
143. 2003/04/06   Sino-Japan Relations: Pave the Way for Recovery of Leaders Visits
144. 2003/04/07   North Korea: Talks, Only Option
145. 2003/04/08   Tactics to Take Complete Control of the Capital: Quickly Finish Procedures for Ending the War
146. 2003/04/11   Crushing Hussein Administration: Rush Reconstruction and Recovery of Peace
147. 2003/04/12   North Korea Nuclear Development: China and Russia are Responsible to Convince North Korea
148. 2003/04/18   U.S.–China–North Korea Talks: Connect to Multilateral Framework
149. 2003/04/19   Three Contingency Bills: Debate along with Civilians Protection Legislation
150. 2003/04/22   Reopening Nuclear Plant: Explanation Needed to Wipe out Distrust
151. 2003/04/26   North Korea Nuclear Possession: Inviting by Itself Sanctions Foolish Action
152. 2003/05/01   Democratic Party of Japan Contingency Proposal: Stick to Civilian Protection in Amendment Discussion
153. 2003/05/03   Constitution Day: Departure from Onlooker Mannerism. How did Japan Respond to (Iraq) War?
154. 2003/05/08   For Japan: North Korean Threat Seen in Double Exposure
155. 2003/05/12   U.S.–South Korea Summit: Harden the Encirclement Net against Nuclear Proliferation
156. 2003/05/14   Contingency Bill Amendment: More Debate with Political Leadership
157. 2003/05/16   U.S.–South Korea Summit: North Korea, Be Aware of your Isolation
158. 2003/05/23   Japan–U.S. Summit: For Both Alliance and International Cooperation

159. 2003/05/25 Japan–U.S. Summit: North Korea should Understand the Meaning of Pressure
160. 2003/05/28 Support Antiterrorism Law: Should not be Delayed
161. 2003/06/01 Sino-Japan Summit: Let's Deepen Cooperation on North Korea Issue
162. 2003/06/05 South Korean President Visits Japan: Let's Mature (Future Directions)
163. 2003/06/06 *Manbyon* in Port: Inspect Strictly the Doubt
164. 2003/06/07 Passage of Three Contingency Bills: Flesh Out Arguments Now
165. 2003/06/08 Japan–South Korea Summit: Let's Make an Effort to Narrow Perspectives Gap
166. 2003/06/10 Iraq Special Measures Law: Make Rationale for Self-Defense Forces Clear
167. 2003/06/14 Iraq Special Measures Bill: Ambiguous from a Common Sense Viewpoint
168. 2003/06/15 Break the Impasse with Five Countries' Talks
169. 2003/06/17 North Korea Vessels: Let's Carry out Calmly Security Inspection
170. 2003/06/20 North Korea: Listen to Asian Voices
171. 2003/07/08 Iraq Special Measures Bill: In the House Councilors, Close the Gap Between Government and Public Opinion
172. 2003/07/15 North Korea Nuclear Development: China's Heavy Responsibility to Stop Wild Action
173. 2003/07/27 Iraq Special Measures Law: Serious Consideration Needed Concerning Self-Defense Forces Dispatch
174. 2003/08/02 Abduction Victims: Return their Children Home Now
175. 2003/08/02 Six-Party Talks: Harden Coalition to Contain Nuclear Development
176. 2003/08/21 Iraq Bomber Terror: Resume UNSC Discussion for Public Order Recovery
177. 2003/08/27 Six-Party Talks: North Korea's Relinquishment of Nuclear Development is the Entire Premise
178. 2003/08/28 UN Disarmament Conference: Nuclear Powers should Stand at Forefront of Nonproliferation Efforts
179. 2003/08/30 Six-Party Talks: A Long Process Started
180. 2003/08/31 Abduction Issue: Heavy Prime Minister Responsibility to Find Solution
181. 2003/09/08 Missile Defense: Debate Defense Policy from Basics
182. 2003/09/11 Two Years Since 9/11: International Cooperation Equals Antiterrorism Power
183. 2003/09/17 A Year Since Pyongyang Declaration: North Korea should not Forget "Pending Issues"
184. 2003/10/04 Extension of Antiterrorism Special Measures Law: Questions Remain Regarding Irresponsible Deliberation
185. 2003/10/08 Japan–China–South Korea Joint Declaration: Connect with East Asia Stability
186. 2003/10/10 Asia Diplomacy: Japan's Influence too Weak
187. 2003/10/17 Iraq Support: Explain More about Japan's Role
188. 2003/10/21 North Korea's Security Guarantee: 5 Countries Should Unify Based on U.S. Proposal

189. 2003/10/22 Dispatch to Iraq within the Year: Don't Leave Everything to Self-Defense Forces
190. 2003/10/31 Shifting Politics: Iraq Problem Debate Self-Defense Forces Dispatch without Reservation
191. 2003/11/01 Six-Party Talks: Still Can't be Optimistic
192. 2003/11/16 U.S. Pentagon Chief visits Japan: Did We Tell Him about the Difficulties Concerning Dispatch?
193. 2003/12/02 Self-Defense Forces Dispatch: Answer to the 80% Concerned Citizens' Concerns
194. 2003/12/04 Self-Defense Forces Dispatch: Has Public Consensus been Formed?
195. 2003/12/10 Self-Defense Forces Dispatch: Reconstruction, Only Mission
196. 2003/12/16 Self-Defense Forces Dispatch Debate: Don't Leave Constitutional Doubt
197. 2003/12/17 Six-Party Talks
198. 2003/12/19 Missile Defense: Introduction Decision by Improper Procedures
199. 2003/12/21 Right Wing Terror Incident: Thorough Investigation of Background Needed
200. 2003/12/22 Revision of Defense Capacity: Listen to Public Opinion
201. 2003/12/27 Advanced Team of Air Self-Defense Forces Dispatched: Stick to Humanitarian Recovery Assistance Cause
202. 2003/12/31 This One Year: [Koizumi Reform] Loses Steam, System to Allow Diversity Essential
203. 2004/01/03 Super Power Lacking Virtue? Reaffirmation of Soft Power
204. 2004/01/07 Iraq's Debts Reduction: Keep the Paris Club Framework
205. 2004/01/15 Abduction Issue: Start Intergovernmental Negotiation to Return Abductees' Children to Japan
206. 2004/01/16 Self-Defense Forces and Media: Government's Media Coverage Restriction Out of Line
207. 2004/01/18 Six-Party Talks: North Korea Shouldn't Stick to Wrong Choice
208. 2004/01/19 Three Arms Embargo Principles: Don' Shake Peaceful Country Philosophy
209. 2004/01/21 U.S. President Election: America and the World Linked by Iraq
210. 2004/01/23 North Korea Sanctions Bill: For Negotiation Progress through Pressure Card
211. 2004/01/27 Command for Main Forces Dispatch: Don't Abandon Pacifism Principle, Diplomatic Effort for UN Leadership Essential
212. 2004/02/04 Reopening of Six-Party Talks
213. 2004/02/05 *Monju* Reform: Does the Government Have Confidence in its Approval?
214. 2004/02/07 Outflow of Nuclear Weapons Technology: Was it Thorough Investigation Conducted?
215. 2004/02/10 Iraq Dispatch Approved: After Dispatch, Diet Responsibility Heavy
216. 2004/02/14 *Futenma* Return: Seize an Opportunity to Break the Deadlock
217. 2004/02/24 Six-Party Talks: Stick to Cooperation among 5 Countries
218. 2004/02/25 UN and Japan: Rush Reform with International Cooperation as Axis
219. 2004/02/29 Six-Party Talks: Not to Give in on the Nuclear Development Renunciation Principle

The Asahi Newspaper

1.	2001/09/11	Foreign Security Policy must Address Flaws in Peace Treaty
2.	2001/09/13	Terrorist Aggression an Attack on the World Community
3.	2001/10/05	Koizumi Sticks to the Script When his own Words Matter
4.	2001/10/06	Japan Needs to Join the World on Choking off Terrorist Funds
5.	2001/10/12	Security-Enhancing Measures Must not Jeopardize Freedoms
6.	2001/10/16	Nation Must Be Prepared with Bioterrorism Defense
7.	2001/10/17	Don't Rush SDF Law Changes as an Opportunity for Secrecy
8.	2001/10/25	SDF Law Secrecy Provisions Far Too Broad in Amendment
9.	2001/10/29	The Realities Have Changed, So Must Japan's ODA to China
10.	2001/10/31	Japan Need not be in a Hurry to Show its Will to Send SDF
11.	2001/11/27	Compromise would Benefit Biological Weapons Protocol
12.	2001/12/01	Safeguards of Human Rights should Precede Cyber Treaty
13.	2001/12/20	Cool-Headed Approach Right in North Korean Abduction Case
14.	2001/12/25	Verify Legitimacy of Actions in Sinking of Suspicious Ship
15.	2002/01/09	How should Japan Approach the United States, the Sole Superpower?
16.	2002/01/16	Worthwhile Cooperation Plan Emerges from Koizumi's Trip
17.	2002/02/18	Time for Empty Slogans is Past as Bush Arrives on Japan Visit
18.	2002/02/21	Koizumi should have Chosen Words to Bush with More Care
19.	2002/02/23	Restructure Trilateral Relations to Rekindle North Korea Talks
20.	2002/03/07	China Facing Challenges of Free Trade and Social Stability
21.	2002/03/14	Redoubled Efforts Needed to Resolve Suspected Abductions
22.	2002/03/25	Pyongyang Must Back Words with Action over Abductions
23.	2002/03/29	No Need to Rush to Develop Law for Military Contingency
24.	2002/04/18	Emergency Bills Too Vague; Thorough Debate Necessary
25.	2002/04/23	Why Does Koizumi Insist on Inflammatory *Yasukuni* Visits?
26.	2002/04/29	Fifty Years after San Francisco, Japan–U.S. Ties Need Fresh Look
27.	2002/04/30	(Untitled)/Yoichi Funabashi @Tokyo
28.	2002/05/04	Discuss Constitutional Issues to Advance Will of the People
29.	2002/05/16	Calm Down and Seek Solution with a Cool Head
30.	2002/05/23	Military Emergency Bills
31.	2002/05/25	World Cup Security Must Still Let Fans Have Fun
32.	2002/05/27	Time to Review the Inspection System
33.	2002/05/30	A Skeptical Public Must be Told the Whole Truth
34.	2002/06/04	Changes to Protect the People Must be Included
35.	2002/06/05	Fukuda's "Background" Remarks were Out of Line
36.	2002/06/07	Laws should Not Stifle Aid to Developing Nations
37.	2002/06/10	One Pitiful Diet Session
38.	2002/07/30	Government should Present Broader Pictures
39.	2002/08/03	Specific Action Will Go Down Better Than Words
40.	2002/08/05	The Document Underscores the Need for Change
41.	2002/08/20	Capable Inspectors are Vital to Ensuring Safety
42.	2002/08/28	Japan Needs a Broader Diplomatic Strategy Base
43.	2002/09/02	Koizumi must be Prepared to Take a Diplomatic Risk
44.	2002/09/04	Most Japanese Oppose Attack on Iraq
45.	2002/09/12	Time, Unfortunately, has not Narrowed the Gaps
46.	2002/09/12	Pursue Dialogue to Spur Change in North Korea

208. 2004/02/14   Cool Heads are Needed for Cross-Strait Stability
209. 2004/02/16   Tokyo–Pyongyang Talks: Push for a Breakthrough on
                  Abductions Issue
210. 2004/02/25   North Korea Needs to Realize it's Running Out of Time

NOTES

1. Robert M. Entman, "Framing: Toward Clarification of a Fractured Paradigm," *Journal of Communication*, Vol. 43, No. 4 (Winter 1993), pp. 52–8.
2. Patti M. Valkenburg, Holli A. Semetko, and Claes H. De Vreese, "The Effects of News Frames on Readers' Thoughts and Recall," *Communication Research*, Vol. 26, No. 5 (October 1999), p. 551.
3. Vincent Price, David Tewksbury, and Elizabeth Powers, "Switching Trains of Thought: The Impact of News Frames on Readers' Cognitive Responses," *Communication Research*, Vol. 24, No. 5 (October 1997), p. 2.
4. By "Japanese threat," the frame refers to how Japan's efforts to increase its capabilities can be viewed as a threat by its neighbors.
5. Ibid.
6. Valkenburg et al., "The Effects of News Frames," p. 551.
7. Stephen W. Walt as quoted in David L. Rousseau, et al., "Identity and Threat Perception—An Experimental Analysis," Paper for American Political Science Association 8/01, "http://www.albany.edu/rockefeller/pos/faculty_2/rousseau%20UAlbany/papers/APSA2001id.PDF (accessed August 2007).
8. Robert Jervis, "Hypothesis on Misperception," *World Politics*, Vol. 20. No. 3 (April 1968), pp. 454–79.
9. Valkenburg et al., "The Effects of News Frames," p. 551.
10. Ibid.
11. Japan Defense Agency, *Defense of Japan 2006* (Tokyo: Japan Defense Agency, 2006), p. 103.
12. Steven J. Tomisek, "Homeland Security—The New Role for Defense," *Strategic Forum*, No. 189 (2002), p. 4 (available at: http://www.ndu.edu/inss/strforum/SF189/sf189.htm, accessed February 2004).
13. See the discussion in the introduction to this volume.
14. Arai Naoyuki, *Sengo Journalism Danmen* (A View of Postwar Journalism) (Tokyo: Soshisha, 1984), p. 228.
15. Ofer Feldman, *Politics and the News Media in Japan* (Ann Arbor: University of Michigan Press, 1993), p. 11.
16. The eleven editorials were dated December 25, 2001; September 12, 2002; September 20, 2002; October 19, 2002; November 7, 2002; November 18, 2002; December 10, 2002; February 15, 2003; March 17, 2003; April 28, 2003; and January 6, 2004.
17. *Asahi Shimbun* ed., May 30, 2003.
18. *Asahi Shimbun* ed., January 24, 2003.
19. *Asahi Shimbun* ed., January 31, 2003; February 19, 2003; and December 27, 2003.
20. *Asahi Shimbun* ed., June 11, 2003.
21. *Asahi Shimbun* ed., December 20, 2001; June 11, 2003; June 21, 2003; and July 8, 2003.

22. *Asahi Shimbun* ed., February 18, 2002; January 1, 2003; January 10, 2003; and May 17, 2003.

23. *Asahi Shimbun* ed., September 30, 2002; April 23, 2002; April 30, 2002; May 16, 2002; December 26, 2002; January 14, 2003; October 2, 2003; and February 14, 2004.

24. *Asahi Shimbun* ed., January 6, 2004; November 4, 2002; March 31, 2003; May 3, 2003; May 13, 2003; July 31, 2003; and December 9, 2003.

25. *Asahi Shimbun* ed., September 2, 2002, and January 6, 2004.

26. *Asahi Shimbun* ed., March 31, 2003; June 10, 2003; and June 26, 2003.

27. *Asahi Shimbun* ed., February 21, 2003.

28. *Asahi Shimbun* ed., October 17, 2001; December 31, 2002; and May 13, 2003.

29. The Pyongyang Declaration sets out the "principles of normalization between North Korea and Japan including settling Japan's past with North Korean compliance with international laws, resolution of the abduction problem and a moratorium on missile firing."

30 *Asahi Shimbun* ed., March 29, 2002; May 27, 2002; August 29, 2002; and November 29, 2002.

31. *Asahi Shimbun* ed., September 13, 2001; October 12, 2001; October 16, 2001; and December 31, 2002.

32. *Asahi Shimbun* ed., December 22, 2003.

33. *Asahi Shimbun* ed., April 29, 2002; July 12, 2003; March 20, 2003; and January 27, 2004.

34. *Asahi Shimbun* ed., January 25, 2003; March 7, 2003; and January 1, 2004.

35. *Asahi Shimbun* ed., March 27, 2003.

36. *Asahi Shimbun* ed., September 16, 2002, and February 21, 2003.

37. Arai, *Sengo Journalism Danmen*, p. 229.

38. *Mainichi Shimbun* ed., February 14, 2002; September 18, 2002; October 23, 2002; October 28, 2002; December 17, 2002; December 24, 2002; February 14, 2003; April 7, 2003; April 12, 2003; August 2, 2003; September 12, 2002; and February 24, 2004.

39. *Mainichi Shimbun* ed., June 6, 2003.

40. *Mainichi Shimbun* ed., August 31, 2002.

41. *Mainichi Shimbun* ed., September 11, 2002, and September 16, 2002.

42. *Mainichi Shimbun* ed., June 10, 2003; June 14, 2003; and December 10, 2003.

43. *Mainichi Shimbun* ed., October 17, 2003; October 31, 2003; and November 16, 2003.

44. *Mainichi Shimbun* ed., April 30, 2002.

45. *Mainichi Shimbun* ed., June 25, 2002, and August 29, 2002.

46. *Mainichi Shimbun* ed., May 24, 2002; May 14, 2003; May 1, 2003; April 19, 2003; and June 7, 2003.

47. *Mainichi Shimbun* ed., May 24, 2002.

48. *Mainichi Shimbun* ed., September 24, 2002, and September 28, 2002.

49. *Mainichi Shimbun* ed., January 3, 2003, and September 17, 2003.

50. *Mainichi Shimbun* ed., July 11, 2002, and September 27, 2002.

51. *Mainichi Shimbun* ed., March 21, 2002; May 13, 2002; and May 31, 2002.

52 *Mainichi Shimbun* ed., December 4, 2003.

53. *Mainichi Shimbun* ed., March 19, 2003; May 8, 2003; and December 31, 2003.

54. *Mainichi Shimbun* ed., March 22, 2003, and April 2, 2003.

55. *Mainichi Shimbun* ed., December 4, 2003; December 16, 2003; December 27, 2003.
56. *Mainichi Shimbun* ed., December 16, 2003.
57. *Yomiuri Shimbun* ed., March 24, 2003.
58. *Yomiuri Shimbun* ed., May 17, 2002.
59. *Yomiuri Shimbun* ed., October 6, 2001.
60. *Yomiuri Shimbun* ed., October 9, 2001.
61. The laws are the following: *Buryoku Kogeki Jitai nado ni okeru Kokumin no Hogo no tame no Sochi ni Kansuru Ho, Buryoku Jitai nado ni okeru Tokutei Kokyo Shisetsu nado no Riyo ni Kansuru Ho, Kokusai Jindo Ho no Judai na Ihan Koi no Shobatsu ni Kansuru Ho, Buryoku Kogeki Jitai ni okeru Gaikoku gun Yohin nado Kaijo Yusoo no Kisei ni kansuru Ho, Buryoku Kogeki Jitai ni okeru Horyo nado no toritsukai, Jietai Ho no Ichibu wo Kaisei Suru Ho,* and *Buryoku Kogeki Jitai ni okeru Amerika Gasshuu Koku no Guntai no Kodo ni Tomonai Ware Ware ga Jisshi Suru Sochi no Ho.*
62. *Yomiuri Shimbun* ed., May 25, 2002, and November 25, 2003.
63. *Yomiuri Shimbun* ed., December 18, 2001; January 1, 2002; January 7, 2002; and July 30, 2002.
64. *Yomiuri Shimbun* ed., November 28, 2002; August 17, 2003; October 15, 2003; January 10, 2004; and February 5, 2004.
65. *Yomiuri Shimbun* ed., April 16, 2002, and May 25, 2002.
66. *Yomiuri Shimbun* ed., October 9, 2001; October 10, 2001; and September 23, 2002.
67. *Yomiuri Shimbun* ed., March 25, 2003, and May 2, 2003.
68. *Yomiuri Shimbun* ed., March 24, 2003.
69. *Yomiuri Shimbun* ed., October 3, 2001, October 21, 2001; and February 7, 2003.
70. *Yomiuri Shimbun* ed., October 10, 2001.
71. *Yomiuri Shimbun* ed., December 5, 2002; February 22, 2002; and May 14, 2003.
72. *Yomiuri Shimbun* ed., January 26, 2002; March 21, 2002; January 23, 2003.
73. *Yomiuri Shimbun* ed., March 19, 2003.
74. *Yomiuri Shimbun* ed., March 22, 2003, and March 25, 2003.
75. *Yomiuri Shimbun* ed., September 18, 2001; September 20, 2001; March 11, 2002; and January 16, 2004.
76. *Yomiuri Shimbun* ed., September 18, 2002; November 28, 2002; December 5, 2002; and August 29, 2003.
77. *Yomiuri Shimbun* ed., March 21, 2002; April 29, 2003; May 11, 2002; and May 15, 2003.
78. *Yomiuri Shimbun* ed., September 18, 2002; November 28, 2002; December 5, 2002; and August 29, 2003.
79. Ralph Cossa, "Toward a Post Post Cold War World," *PacNet Newsletter*, No. 44 (October 12, 2001), 1–6, http://www.csis.org/media/csis/pubs/pac0141.pdf (accessed August 2007).
80. See note 61.
81. *Asahi Shimbun* ed., February 26, 2004.
82. Prime Minister's Office 2004, "Kokumin Hogo Hosei Seibi Honbu Kosei (Composition of Membership of Kokumin Hogo Hosei Honbu)," http://www.kantei.go.jp/jp/singi/hogohousei/kousei.html (accessed August 2007).

83. The Mid-Term Defense Program includes specific guidelines for Japan's defense capability to be carried out based on the National Defense Program Outline.

84. Japan Defense Agency, *Defense of Japan 2001 White Paper*, pp. 1–2, http://www.mod.go.jp/e/publications/wp2001/chapter3/section1.html (accessed April 2004).

85. See the NDPG at http://www.kantei.go.jp/foreign/policy/2004/1210taikou_e.html.

86. The sixteen measures are "firmer measures to stop terrorists at the border; entry restriction to terrorists; mandatory advanced submission of crew and passenger list by airplane/vessel captain; denial of entry of terrorists by using the International Criminal Police Organization's database on lost and stolen passports; mandatory check of passengers' passports by air and sea carriers; assistance to foreign governments to improve travel document examination capacity; through identification of foreign guests by hotels and inns; establishment of system to control pathogenic microorganisms potentially used for bioterrorism; tightened control over explosive-related material potentially used for bomb attacks; tightened import control through designation of explosives as prohibited goods for import; measures to fully implement FATF (Financial Action Task Force); tightening of security measures for important facilities at emergencies; firmer counter-terrorism measures at airports and nuclear facilities; stronger protection over nuclear material; firmer anti-highjack measures through introduction of sky marshal program; and reinforcement of terrorism-related intelligence capacity" (MOFA, 2005).

87. MOFA, 2005, pp. 17–22, http://www.mofa.go.jp/policy/terrorism/action.pdf (accessed April 2004).

88. Council of Defense Strategic Studies, *2003–2004 Report on Defense and Strategic Studies* (Tokyo: NIDS, 2003), pp. 64–71, http://www.nids.go.jp/english/dissemination/other/studyreport/e2003.html. The National Institute of Defense Studies (*Boei Kenkyusho*), or NIDS, in Tokyo has been hosting the Council of Defense Strategic Studies (*Boei Senryaku Kenkyu Kaigi*), a group made up of scholars and experts outside of government to forecast the future global strategic environment and the appropriate defense strategy of Japan since 1999.

89. The Council on Security and Defense Responsibilities, established on April 2004, was chaired by Hiroshi Araki, advisor of Tokyo Electric Power Company. "It was established with the purpose of gathering opinions from the experts in security and economy areas under the supervision of Prime Minister Koizumi to conduct comprehensive review with broad perspectives on the holistic governmental efforts for future security and defense posture." See Japan Defense Agency, *Defense of Japan 2006*, p. 97. One of the key members of the committee, Dr. Iokibe Makoto, became president of the National Defense Academy in August 2006.

90. "GSDF to create Central Intelligence Unit to boost Information Gathering for International Missions," *Yomiuri Shimbun*, December 31, 2006.

91. Ibid.

92. *Asahi Shimbun* ed., May 30, 2002.

93. *Yomiuri Shimbun* ed., November 17, 2001.

94. *Asahi Shimbun* ed., August 6, 2003.

95. MOFA, 2005, pp. 15–16.

96. "Integrated Security Strategy has two major goals. The first is to prevent direct threat from reaching Japan and in the event that it does reach Japan to minimize the damage. The second goal is to reduce the changes of threats rising in various parts of the world with the aim of preventing such a direct threat from reaching Japan or affecting the interests of Japanese expatriates or corporations overseas." See the Council on Security and Defense Capabilities, *Japan's Vision for Future Security and Defense Capabilities*, 2004, p. 5.

97. See http://www.mod.go.jp/e/publ/w_paper/pdf/2005/2.pdf (accessed August 2007).

98. *Asahi Shimbun* ed., September 11, 2001.

99. *Yomiuri Shimbun* ed., April 11, 2003.

100. As readers will know, a joint statement by President Bush and Prime Minister Koizumi announced a new U.S.–Japan Alliance of Global Cooperation for the twenty-first century. It emphasized the common values and interests of the United States and Japan as well as the alliance's bilateral political, security, and economic cooperation. This statement also reaffirms the importance of agreements made for the transformation and realignment of the U.S.–Japan alliance made by the U.S.–Japan Security Consultative Committee on October 29, 2005. The document released on May 1, 2006, by the SCC "finalized recommendations for realignment of U.S. forces in Japan and related Japan Self Defense Forces."

101. TCOG was created in April 1999 to coordinate policies between Japan, the United States, and South Korea.

CHAPTER 3

Japan's Insider and Outsider Media Discourse about the SDF Dispatch to Iraq

Mark Hollstein

INTRODUCTION

As the U.S.-led military coalition prepared to invade Iraq in March 2003, opinion polls in Japan showed large public opposition to the war. This sentiment was in stark opposition to the policies of the Japanese government that had pledged billions of dollars in support of the operation and was considering sending its Self-Defense Forces (SDF) to help rebuild the war-torn country. However, by early 2004, when the SDF was poised to enter Iraq, Japanese public opinion had begun to shift to a more positive stance toward the dispatch of troops to Iraq, and a humanitarian role for the Japanese military in Iraq.

One possible explanation for this shift in public opinion was the role of the *kisha* (reporters) club newsgathering system in Japan. This system is widely believed to give the government substantial influence over how reporters frame news stories,[1] and therefore over how government policy is perceived by the public. *Kisha* clubs are exclusive associations of reporters from major competing news organizations who share a workspace within the government entity they are covering. *Kisha* club reporters develop close working relationships with their government sources, who provide them with a variety of perks and privileges. They also enter into cooperative agreements with each other to regulate the gathering and release of information. According to many critics, this creates homogenous, government-friendly reports in the major media on most important issues. Because of their exclusive and close relationship with the government sources they cover, the *kisha* club news organizations can be thought of as the "insider media."

This system undoubtedly has a detrimental influence on the free flow of information in Japan. However, most analysts of the Japanese mass media assign too much power to the *kisha* clubs and the government's ability to influence them. At the same time, too little attention is paid to non-*kisha* club sources, "outsider media," available to Japanese news consumers.

In this chapter, the degree to which these insider and outsider media have covered one key event in Japan's involvement in Iraq—the Japanese SDF's advance contingent's deployment into the Southern Iraqi city of Samawah—is examined. This event marked the first time since World War II that Japanese troops entered a country still at war. The author uses discourse analysis of three days of reports about the SDF from three newspapers and three television programs to test the degree to which the insider and outsider news reporting follow different news frames. Analysis of three days of reporting offers only a snapshot of how this complicated issue has been reported. However, it is enough to demonstrate the degree to which these various kinds of media responded to the Japanese government's efforts to influence how reporters framed the event.

COMPETING FRAMES: PACIFIST NATION VERSUS NORMAL NATION

In 1947, a new constitution, written largely by the United States, went into effect in Japan. The American goal was to transform its vanquished World War II foe into a stable democracy that no longer possessed the means or will to war. The documents the Americans helped create is often referred to as Japan's "pacifist constitution" because of its war-renouncing Article 9, which decrees "land, sea, and air forces, as well as other war potential, will never be maintained." However, even before the American-led occupation of Japan had come to an end in April 1952, the United States was already focusing on the new Communist threat and was beginning to see Japan as a potentially important ally in the developing Cold War. As a result of the outbreak of the Korean War in June 1950 and the dispatch of U.S. garrison forces in Japan to the Korean peninsula, MacArthur ordered in July that year the creation of the Japan National Police Reserve and Japan Coast Guard, which would form the foundation of Japan's de facto military known today as the SDF.[2] Today the SDF is divided into three services: an army, known as the Ground Self-Defense Force (GSDF); a navy, the Maritime Self-Defense Force (MSDF); and an air force, known as the Air Self-Defense Force (ASDF).

In 1955 the Liberal Democratic Party (LDP) was formed and quickly became the majority party in government. With the exception of an eleven-month hiatus in the early 1990s when an anti-LDP coalition seized control, it has retained uninterrupted control of the Japanese political process to the present day. Guided by American pressure and its own conservative ideology, the LDP has repeatedly reinterpreted the meaning of Article 9 to allow for the expansion of the role of the SDF. However, the process has been slow, as each step toward full-scale rearming has been met by strong resistance from the public and opposition parties. As a result, the SDF today is one of the most mightily armed, yet legally constrained, militaries in the world.

The story of the SDF and Japan's current military dilemma is one of two competing worldviews or frames. The first is what the author has termed the "Pacifist Nation Frame." This nomenclature is used to denote the mindset of those who have embraced Japan's U.S.-drafted pacifist constitution. It is not meant to imply that everyone who views the world in this way possesses the kind of fear and hatred of all things military that is often ascribed to "pacifists" or "antimilitarists." In fact, it is possible to support the role of the SDF in guarding Japanese borders and, at the same time, to strongly defend the language of Article 9 that renounces both "war as a means of settling international disputes" and "the right of the belligerency of the state." Competing with this is what the author calls the "Normal Nation Frame." This is the paradigm of those who believe Article 9, as it is currently worded, is an anachronistic holdover from the early postwar period and a hindrance to Japan's ability to carry out its international obligations and fully integrate into the modern world.

People who see the world in terms of the Pacifist Nation Frame believe Article 9 has been an important factor in creating and maintaining friendly relations with Japan's neighbors and former victims of Japanese aggression in Asia. They view any expansion of the mission of the SDF as a dangerous step backward toward the kind of nationalism and militarism that proved disastrous prior to World War II. At the very least, it could be perceived as such a step by neighbor nations, thereby destabilizing security in the region. The Pacifist Nation Frame views expansion of military power as a turn away from Japanese values of soft power through economic integration, which Japan has pursued to great success in the postwar period, and toward an American view of the world as ordered by force and military power. Those of this mindset believe that giving in to American pressures to rearm puts Japan in danger of becoming a pawn in American military adventurism and geopolitics, and could lead Japan to become involved in a war it did not want. Thomas Berger of Boston University explains that this frame was engendered by more than just guilt over Japan's militaristic past. It stemmed largely from a sense of dual victimization.

> One the one hand [Japanese] felt victimized by the United States, a country they felt had waged war against them with a ruthlessness and racially motivated hatred that culminated in the dropping of the atomic bombs on Hiroshima and Nagasaki. On the other hand they felt victimized by their own government and especially the military leadership that had dragged them into a hopeless war that could not be won, but that the military men refused to give up regardless of the horrific suffering that had been inflicted upon the nation.[3]

In its early and most extreme form, the Pacifist Nation Frame demanded unarmed neutrality (*hibuso churitsu*). Large numbers of people opposed the creation of the SDF. They also opposed the first U.S.–Japan security treaty, signed in September 1951, which allowed American bases to remain in Japan after the return of Japanese sovereignty, and the revised and expanded U.S.–Japan security treaty of 1960. While the revised treaty rectified major problems the Japanese public had with the previous treaty, liberals were troubled by broad language in the text, which recognized that Japan and the United States had a "common concern in maintaining peace and security in the Far East (Article 6)." Today, even many on the far Left accept the need for a limited SDF role to protect Japanese territory, but they continue to resist expansion of SDF powers, especially expansions that place the SDF in a potential military role on foreign soil.[4] Similarly, these same people, as well as those closer to the center, worried about the Defense Agency becoming a ministry in early 2007 due to fears of its ability to exercise civilian control, and also due to the ability of the Japanese government to exercise control over it.[5]

Conservative Japanese, including the current leadership of the LDP, frame rearmament in opposite terms. For them, the expansion of the SDF is a matter of Japan becoming a "normal nation," one that is an equal partner with the United States and capable of fulfilling international responsibilities in all the same ways that other nations can. This requires having a military that can be used not just for *individual* self-defense, but also for military alliances in pursuit of *collective* self-defense and the enforcement of international agreements. True partnership with the United States can only come by expanded SDF powers. Conservatives find their constitutional justification in the document's preamble, which declares,

> We believe that no nation is responsible to itself alone, but that laws of political morality are universal; and that obedience to such laws is incumbent upon all nations who would sustain their own sovereignty and justify their sovereign relationship with other nations. We, the Japanese people, pledge our national honor to accomplish these high ideals and purposes with all our resources.

The basic themes of the two competing roles have been summed up in table 3.1.

In recent years conservatives have been making steady advances in expanding the SDF's mission. Japan supported the 1991 Gulf War with thirteen billion dollars in financial aid, and dispatched MSDF minesweepers to the region after the conflict to assist in clean-up operations. However, citing constitutional limitations, Japan declined to commit troops or personnel to the actual war. Despite the legitimacy of this argument, the Japanese government and people were dismayed by worldwide criticism leveled at their inability to be more than an automated teller machine. The criticism made it easier for the Japanese government to generate public acceptance for the International Peace Cooperation Law (*kokusai heiwa kyoryokuho*) enacted in 1992. This law allowed Japan to send SDF personnel to provide non-combat assistance to UN peacekeeping operations assuming there was a complete cessation of hostilities in the country and both sides in the dispute consented to SDF deployment, among other conditions. As a result of this law, Japan has participated in peacekeeping, humanitarian relief operations, and election-monitoring in countries such as Angola, Cambodia, Mozambique, El Salvador, East Timor, Bosnia, and Herzegovina, as well as ceasefire-monitoring in the Golan Heights.

Table 3.1 Major themes of the *Pacifist Nation Frame* and the *Normal Nation Frame* regarding the expansion of the SDF's international role

The Pacifist Nation Frame	The Normal Nation Frame
• Violates Article 9 of the Constitution	• Enables Japan to fulfill the international mandate set out in the Constitution's preamble
• Should never involve sending troops to war zones	• Must allow for significant human contribution to international activities
• Should correspond to defense of Japanese territory only	• Should allow for collective self-defense
• Is a step backward toward excessive nationalism and the reliance on military power to pursue national interests	• Is progress away from postwar fears and toward modern understandings of national responsibilities
• Decreases sovereignty as Japan is drawn away from its own antimilitaristic values and into conflicts that are not vital to its own security	• Decreases dependence on the United States and thus increases sovereignty
• Places Japan in danger of being a pawn in U.S. military adventurism	• Helps make Japan an equal partner with the United States
• Places Japan in conflict with other nations	• Enhances Japan's prestige and respect in the international community
• Increase fear of Japan among Asian neighbors	

In April 1996, Japan and the United States reaffirmed their commitment to military cooperation in a joint declaration and the two countries began reviewing the Guidelines for Defense Cooperation, first worked out in the late 1970s without much development. The review of the 1978 guidelines was completed in September 1997, and the legislation enabling their implementation was enacted in 1999 in Japan. On November 2, 2001, the Japanese Diet responded to the 9/11 terrorist attacks on the United States by enacting the Antiterrorism Special Measures Law (*Tero Taisaku Tokubetsu Sochiho*). This new law was used to send MSDF to assist in the American-led war against the Taliban regime in Afghanistan by refueling and resupplying coalition ships in the Indian Ocean.

However, this does not mean that the Japanese public has abandoned the Pacifist Nation Frame. A poll taken by the *Asahi Shimbun*, one of Japan's five major national daily newspapers, immediately after the March 2003 U.S.-led invasion of Iraq found that 65 percent of Japanese did not support the war.[6] Despite this opposition, the LDP-led government pledged five billion dollars in grants and loans to help finance the operation. The dispatch of troops was made possible by the Special Measures Law for Iraq passed on July 29, 2003, which allowed the SDF to engage in humanitarian activities in the country despite the lack of a UN mandate or the end of hostilities in the country. On December 9, 2003, the cabinet of Prime Minister Koizumi Junichiro, formed in April 2001, approved the dispatch of SDF forces to the relatively secure city of Samawah in southern Iraq. The mission would be humanitarian, not military, and would focus on infrastructure projects, such as rebuilding the city's water purification system. A contingent of soldiers from the Netherlands was already providing military security for the city and would help protect Japanese troops (they were later replaced by Australian troops). An advance contingent of Japanese Ground Self-Defense members arrived in Samawah on January 19, 2004, becoming the first Japanese troops since the end of World War II to enter a war zone. The first troops to form the main contingent of Japanese forces in Iraq arrived in Samawah on February 9, 2004. As required by the July law, the Japanese parliament retroactively voted on it, approving the dispatch on February 10, 2004.

An opinion poll published November 25, 2004, by the *Sankei Shimbun*—widely recognized as the most conservative and pro-LDP of the five large national newspapers—found 88 percent of respondents dissatisfied with the government's explanation of why it had pledged to send troops to Iraq. Of the respondents, 45 percent were opposed to any dispatch of troops to Iraq and an additional 43 percent said Japanese troops should stay home until Iraq was stable.[7] An opinion poll published December 1, 2003, by the *Mainichi Shimbun* mirrored these results closely, finding more than 80 percent of Japanese opposed to or cautious about the government's plan to send troops into an insecure Iraq. The poll showed that 43 percent believed SDF troops should not go at all and another 40 percent said they should not go until the security situation had improved. Support for Koizumi and his cabinet also dropped 14 percentage points to 42 percent and the disapproval rating increased by 11 points to 37 percent from the previous October.[8]

By mid-January 2004, public opinion had begun to shift. A poll by the *Asahi Shimbun* on January 19, 2004, showed a 40-percent approval of and 48-percent opposition to the troop deployment in Iraq.[9] A poll by the *Mainichi Shimbun* on January 26 showed opposition and approval even at 47 percent each.[10] By the middle of April, a poll by the *Yomiuri Shimbun* found that support for the troop dispatch had exceeded opposition for the first time with 60 percent of respondents backing the deployment.[11] The increase in support came despite, or perhaps because of, the kidnapping of three Japanese civilians in Iraq by Islamic militants. The kidnappers threatened to kill the hostages if the Japanese troops were not removed. Although the Koizumi government refused to give in to the kidnappers' demands, the hostages were eventually released unharmed (amid reports that the kidnappers had been bought off). This same poll showed 74 percent of respondents approving of how the government handled the hostage crisis.[12] Indeed, the tone of the public debate suggested the three antiwar activists were irresponsible and at fault for being in Iraq in the first place.

THE INSIDER *KISHA* CLUB SYSTEM AND NEWS FRAMING

Commenting on polls showing even support and opposition to the SDF deployment to Iraq, Tanifuji Etsushi, a professor of political communication at Waseda University, has explained that the results may demonstrate a "for the flag effect" as images of the troops departing for the Middle East created a burst of patriotism.[13] Whether that support could be maintained depended on the government's ability to "draw up a story" that would convince the Japanese people of the need for the foreign deployment, he said.[14] The fact that public support has survived well beyond the initial stage of deployment may signal that such a story, or frame, has been created and accepted by the public. Critics of the Japanese mass media claim that the system affords the Japanese government exceptional power to influence the frames journalists adopt for their stories—in this case, to persuade reporters to adopt the Normal Nation Frame over the Pacifist Nation Frame when reporting on the dispatch of troops to Iraq.

In Japan, there exist more than one thousand *kisha* clubs—four hundred in Tokyo alone—that are attached to various government offices, political parties, key economic organizations, local government offices, courthouses, police headquarters, and so on.[15] *Kisha* clubs are organizations for cooperative newsgathering formed by reporters from competing news organizations who are covering the same government body. The government body designates a space within its facilities for its *kisha* club. The clubroom then becomes the principal workplace for the reporters from various competing news organizations. Ofer Feldman, professor of political psychology and political processes at Doshisha University, says this workspace

> serves as the "club," the base and operation room for the reporter to gather, confirm, organize, and write all the news that emanates from a certain location; to receive briefings, handouts, press releases, and other communication; and to interact with their information sources…Each club has anywhere from a dozen to three hundred or more reporters, depending on the nature of the agency and its importance.[16]

Club members receive a variety of resources and favors from their government sources. Political science professor Laurie Anne Freeman an associate professor of political science at the University of California Santa Barbara explains that these favors include:

> Physical space for the club (the *kisha shitsu*), desks, tables, chairs, bookshelves, telephones and payment for outside calls. Frequently, television sets, subscriptions to popular magazines, and parking spaces or exemption from parking restrictions, are also provided. Free photocopies, fax machines, and copies of each of the papers' morning editions are other common items as are mahjongg, *Shogi*, and *Igo*, popular games journalists rely on to wile away the time between scheduled events.[17]

The most important privilege *kisha* club reporters receive is exclusive access to government information. Government officials will only give press releases, interviews, and briefings to club members. *Kisha* club journalists protect this special access by requiring club members to share any and all information they receive from independent research or interviews with the club as a whole. In this way, individual initiative is stifled, but club members are protected from being scooped up by their competition.

As Freeman notes, a common club practice is to embargo certain news from release until a decided date to make sure all reporters have time to fully analyze the information and that no news organization is first with the information. Such rules are commonly called "blackboard agreements" because embargoed topics and release dates are posted on the club's blackboard.[18] Sometimes club members from competing organizations will even divide the labor of reading government reports among themselves to reduce the workload.[19] During embargo periods some government entities hold study classes through their public relations offices to help reporters understand the government's position on the issue.[20] Reporters who violate embargoes and other rules can be suspended or expelled from the club by their fellow journalists, and a number of off-the-record interviews with reporters by this author confirm this.

Each club is particular to the government institution it covers and creates its own bylaws. However, all clubs recognize the Nihon Shimbun Kyokai (NSK), the Japan Newspaper Editors and Publishers Association, as their guiding organization and claim to adhere to the NSK's guidelines for club operation. In principle, membership in the *kisha* clubs is open to "NSK members and journalists and non-NSK member media organizations of similar standing."[21] As of October 2004 the NSK claimed 144 members, 108 daily newspapers, 4 news agencies, and 32 broadcasters.[22] NSK membership is open to newspapers with a circulation of ten thousand or more.[23] However, freelance journalists, religious newspapers, and magazines are excluded.[24] Since 1993, the NSK guidelines have recommended that the clubs also be open to foreign media organizations, but organizations owned by foreign governments (such as the British Broadcasting Company, or BBS, and the *China Daily*) are excluded.[25,26]

In practice, the number of news organizations represented in the clubs is but a small fraction of NSK members. As Freeman points out, membership in the NSK is a requirement but alone is not sufficient for *kisha* club membership. Each club limits its own membership as it sees fit. "Only the major fifteen to twenty mainstream Japanese news organizations participate as regular club members in many of the clubs in Tokyo," she says.[27] What is more, even in the few very large *kisha* clubs, such as the National Diet club, which hosts hundreds of reporters, "the establishment of rules and enforcement of sanctions are the responsibility of a much smaller group of companies—those having voting rights in the clubs general committees."[28]

This means the *kisha* club system is dominated by reporters from Japan's public broadcasting corporation, the Nihon Hoso Kyokai (NHK), and the five major commercial media conglomerates, Yomiuri, Asahi, Mainichi, Sankei, and Nikkei (Nihon Keizai) groups, each of which controls a major national daily newspaper with a morning and evening edition, and a television network. NHK is commercial-free and funded by viewer fees. However, content must be approved by a government-appointed Board of Governors, which is comprised largely of business leaders and educators. The Diet must also approve NHK's operating budget. The big five are the Yomiuri group, which controls the *Yomiuri Shimbun* newspaper, with a combined morning and evening circulation of 14.1 million[29] and the Nippon Terebi television network; the Asahi group, which controls the *Asahi Shimbun* newspaper with 12.2 million combined morning and evening circulation[30] and the Terebi Asahi television network; the Mainichi group, which controls the *Mainichi Shimbun* newspaper with 5.6 million combined circulation[31] and the Tokyo Hōsō television network; the Sankei group, which controls the *Sankei Shimbun* newspaper with a combined circulation of 2.6 million[32] and Fuji Terebi; and the Nikkei group, which controls the *Nihon Keizai Shimbun* with a combined circulation of 4.6 million[33] and the Terebi Tokyo television network.

Freeman refers to this monopoly of official information by *kisha* clubs dominated by a handful of companies as an "information cartel." This is because they consist of

> rules and relationships guiding press relations with their sources and with each other that serve to limit the types of news that gets reported and the number and makeup of those who do the reporting. By reinforcing close ties with official sources while restricting competition among journalists, the Japanese press primarily responds to an agenda of political discourse that has already been set.[34]

Shibayama Tetsuya, a former Asahi Shimbun reporter who now works as a professional media analyst says the problem of journalists following official frames is compounded by a Japanese cultural tendency to defer to authority. Throughout Japanese history, he says, the government has always been superior to the people. Before the war, the Constitution gave power to the emperor, who delegated his authority to the government. The people were considered the "children of the emperor." The Meiji Era slogan *kanson minpi*, or respect the bureaucrats and look down upon the people, was very much an extension of that thinking. The postwar Constitution gives the people the power, but many are still unwilling to challenge authority.[35]

> A lot of reporters see their democratic duty as providing government information to the people in an understandable way. And, if the government does something wrong that angers the people, it is [the media's] duty to report that anger to the government. They see this as the meaning of democracy. The American case is more that the people and the government are equals. Here it is not that kind of relationship.[36]

"In America," continues Shibayama, "if the press sets the agenda, the government will respond. In Japan, it's the other way around. The central government sets the agenda."[37]

Japanese reporters themselves tend to downplay the influence of the clubs on news content. Fujita Hiroshi has worked as a reporter for both Japanese and American news agencies and now teaches journalism at Sophia University in Tokyo. He says, "I don't think the organization of, or the existence of *kisha* clubs, has anything to do with, or barely anything to do with, editorial policy. The editorial policy, the opinion or viewpoint of the news organization is not influenced by the *kisha* clubs or the relationship of the news organization and the *kisha* clubs." "However," he goes on:

> If you are talking about the handling of information, then there is something to say for the power of the *kisha* club system. The flow of information is greatly influenced by that system. Because most *kisha* clubs are attached to the central government offices such as the *Okurasho* (now, Zaimusho) [Ministry or Finance], *Gaimusho* [Ministry of Foreign Affairs], or other offices, these offices do become the main sources of the information that newspapers and television stations carry. They provide information though news announcements, background briefings, or press conferences that reporters can't get in any other way. They become a very simple way for the government to control information.[38]

What is more, Fujita says, "Reporters are not bound by the *kisha* clubs. They don't have to rely on the information that government officials offer at briefings and press conferences. They can do their own digging or develop other sources." He says when he was a member of the Ministry of Foreign Affairs *kisha* club he found that other club members, even those from his own organization, did not like to share ideas or information with him. "I found I could get more useful information on my own," he says.[39]

Dutch reporter and long-time observer of Japan Karl van Wolferen sees their tendency to encourage reporter laziness as the main problem with the *kisha* club system. Within the *kisha* club, he says, "There is hardly any incentive for individual journalists to investigate anything by themselves, and no reward at all for presenting a case in a manner that contradicts the conclusions of their colleagues."[40] He agrees that the Japanese newspapers "appear to play an adversarial role in the System." However, he says the press's "almost consistent 'anti-establishment' attitude is quite superficial."[41] The newspapers never really "take on" the system, he says. They will occasionally rage at some of its elements, but are rarely consistent for more than a few weeks. And the rage is often to the benefit of competing elements. Most important, they make no attempt to analyze the system, to provide a critical frame of reference enabling readers to ask questions concerning the system's essential nature and the direction in which it is taking them.[42]

About 104 members of the then-Defense Agency *kisha* club provided reports on the SDF advance contingent in Samawah. In the week leading up to the advance contingent deployment, the weekly magazine *Shūkan Shincho* reported that Defense Agency *kisha* club reporters received a crash course in war zone safety at a GSDF base in Hokkaido. Non-*kisha* club reporters were not barred from covering the SDF in Iraq, but they were not allowed to take part in the advance training, the magazine said.[43] The article, titled "Once Again, 'Announcements from Imperial Central Command' ("'Daihonei Happyō' Futatabi")," suggests that the government is attempting to gain the same kind of control over news reports on the military that it had during World war II.[44]

THE OUTSIDER NON-*KISHA* CLUB MEDIA

While the *kisha* club media have garnered significant attention from Japanese media and political analysts, they represent just a fraction of the media that could have an influence on Japanese public opinion. In fact, it is often the outside, non-*kisha* club media where much important information first appears. As mentioned earlier, reporters for sports newspapers, partisan newspapers, religious newspapers, and magazines of all varieties are excluded from *kisha* clubs. Many reporters for television tabloid shows also work outside of the *kisha* clubs and their rules. *Los Angeles Times* reporter Maggie Farley covered Asia for the American media for ten years. She has also worked for Fuji Television in Tokyo. She calls these media "an outside press corps that, while not completely free of the constraints that limit the insider journalists is less affected by them. Thus it is responsible for most of the investigative reporting in Japan—and much of the scandal coverage."[45]

While many of these media are independent of the major media conglomerates, independence is not a requirement for outsider status. In fact, each of the five media groups produces at least one weekly magazine that is outside of the *kisha club system*. The big three, *Yomiuri*, *Asahi*, and *Mainichi*, also produce tabloid newspapers that focus on sports but also cover major political or economic news. As Fujita notes, reporters for the mainstream newspapers will often leak or sell the news that they cannot report because of *kisha* club agreements or rules to the weekly magazines, both those within their corporate groups and those that are independent. This is especially true of political scandal stories: "[Mainstream newspapers] allow the weekly magazine to test the water, to see what the public and government reaction will be," he says.[46] Okadome Yasunori, chief editor of the now-defunct weekly magazine *Uwasa no Shinso* (The Truth behind the Rumors) told the English language *Japan Times* that between 30 and 40 percent of the information in his magazine came from leaks by *kisha* club reporters who for the reasons mentioned earlier could not publish the information in the mainstream press. In addition, mainstream reporters write under pen names in these weekly magazines.[47]

While the big five networks and their affiliates control nearly all of Japan's television news, each network airs a number of "infotainment" programs that also enjoy a degree of freedom from the *kisha* club system. These programs come in various forms, including nightly one-hour news and commentary programs, early morning news variety programs, afternoon "wide shows" (so known because of their widely ranging topics), weekend news and entertainment roundup shows, and Sunday morning news analysis and interview programs.

Such programs are a relatively new phenomenon, coming into their own with the premier of TV Asahi's nightly one-hour-and-fifteen-minute news and commentary program, *News Station,* in the mid-1980s. Before *News Station,* NHK held a virtual monopoly on primetime news. The success of *News Station* led the way for TV Asahi and the other networks to experiment with the news genre leading to today's proliferation of infotainment programs. *News Station* began in October 1985 with the philosophy that news should be interesting and understandable to anyone, even a junior high school student (graduation of which marks the end of compulsory education in Japan). It quickly began pulling average audiences of more than twenty million viewers.[48] By the time it ended its eighteen-year run in March 2004, it had become the most popular news program in Japan. *News Station*'s host Kume Hiroshi was a popular music show host before taking up the anchor chair. Former *News Station* reporter Kyoko Altman observed, "Lacking a background in journalism, Kume ignored conventional rules and taboos."[49] Ellis Krauss, who teaches at the Graduate School of International Relations and Pacific Studies at the University of California, San Diego, explains that *News Station* had its own forty-member staff, including reporters who were independent of the two-hundred-member Asahi News Division and therefore the *kisha* club system. He quotes a *News Station* insider who explained that "The program uses the raw news data that TV Asahi's regular news staff gathers, including that gathered at reporters' [*kisha*] clubs, but also often adds its own angle and sends out its own reporters on special assignments and to gather supplementary material."[50]

News Station's independence often earned it the government's ire. Some ranking members of government tried to pressure companies to stop advertising on the program.[51] Members of the LDP refused to appear on or be interviewed for the program from November 2003 until February 2004 as punishment for what it considered biased reporting about the November 2003 House of Representatives general election.

METHODOLOGY

With the background presented hitherto, this chapter will now examine how several *kisha* club dependent news organizations and non-*kisha* club news sources covered stories related to the SDF deployment in Iraq from January 19 to 21, 2004. The news during this period included the entrance of the SDF advance contingent into Iraq, the departure of the first group of ASDF members to Kuwait in preparation for entering Iraq, the opening of 2004 general session of the Diet and Prime Minister Koizumi's policy address in which he outlined his case for sending SDF troops to Iraq, and a series of suicide bomb attacks in Iraq.

The intent of this study is to determine the degree to which the themes of the Normal Nation Frame—favored by the government and therefore presumably the *kisha* clubs and their reporters—were dominant in reports, and the degree to which the Pacifist Nation Frame was present in news stories.

The reports of two television news programs with close connections to *kisha* clubs were examined. These were NHK's flagship evening news show *News 7*, which airs from 7:00 to 7:30 p.m. seven days a week, and TBS's national evening news *News Forest (News no Mori)*, which aired from 4:55 to 5:25 p.m. Monday through Friday (this program is now know as *Evening Five*). The third program analyzed was TV Asahi's one-hour-and-fifteen-minute program *News Station*, which largely operated outside of the *kisha* club system. *News Station* aired from 9:54 to 11:10 weekday evenings.

The three newspapers studied were Japan's two largest and most influential newspapers, the *Yomiuri Shimbun* and the *Asahi Shimbun*, and one daily sports newspaper, *Nikkan Sports*. The *Asahi Shimbun* and *Yomiuri Shimbun* are important members of nearly all national *kisha clubs*. Both newspapers average about thirty-two pages each day, not including an eight-page evening edition. The *Yomiuri Shimbun* is generally considered to be right-of-center on issues regarding defense. The *Asahi Shimbun* has the reputation of being left-of-center on such issues. The *Nikkan Sports* is published by the Asahi corporate group, but is not a member of any governmental press club. It averages about twenty-four pages a day and has a daily circulation of about 972,000.[52] As its name suggests, it devotes most of its space to sports news. However, it does include political stories on its "society" (*shakai*) page, which is usually page twenty-one or twenty-two. It also runs non-sports stories with large headlines on its front page if they are significantly important. A daily sports newspaper was chosen over another possible "outsider" media, such as weekly magazines, in order to make possible a day-for-day comparison with the major mainstream dailies.

Television reports were coded for the number of seconds in which positive, negative, and neutral information was provided in four categories: government positions; SDF activities; security in Samawah; and nongovernment opinions. Newspaper reports were coded for the amount of square inches devoted to the same categories. These categories were chosen after an initial survey of the dominant themes in Japanese news discourse about the SDF in Iraq and for their ability to demonstrate the influence of government frames.

In the case of "government positions," any stated justification for the SDF deployment, or statement of support for the deployment by government officials was coded positive, as was any description of an official's position by a reporter. Any statement or description of a government official's opposition to the deployment, or his or her rebuttal of the government's rationales for the SDF deployment was coded negative. Any dispassionate discussion of the political process involved in the SDF deployment was coded neutral.

With regard to the "SDF in Iraq," any description of the SDF as relaxed, happy, or providing needed assistance to Iraqis was coded positive. Any comments that cast the SDF activities as being unnecessary or of the SDF as being in danger or endangering others was coded negative. Any dispassionate report about SDF activities was coded neutral. For example, descriptions of SDF members laughing, smiling, and taking souvenir pictures were coded positive. Descriptions of heavy protection being provided to the SDF by Dutch troops in Samawah or of defensive attitudes or postures were coded negative. Descriptions of SDF living conditions or daily routine that did not seem out of the ordinary for military personnel were coded neutral.

In the case of "Samawah security," comments by Samawah citizens welcoming the SDF or expressing appreciation to the Japanese were coded positive. Any discussion of unrest, demonstrations, violence, or conditions that had the potential to cause unrest such as high unemployment or the high cost of consumer goods were coded negative. Stories that dealt with disruptive problems that could potentially be solved by the SDF were nonetheless coded negative if the story provided no direct discussion of efforts or plans by the SDF to address the problems. This was done to avoid being overly subjective in deciding which problems were "good problems" for the SDF and which were "bad problems." Descriptions of Samawah City and its environment that did not indicate either trouble or welcome for the SDF were coded neutral.

The "nongovernment opinions" category includes comments made by any discussant on a television show or newspaper editorial writer who was not a Japanese government official. It also includes comments by foreign media or foreign government officials.

Coverage of Iraq Issues

On Monday, January 19, 2004, NHK *News 7* dedicated eleven minutes and forty-eight seconds of its thirty-minute program (39 percent of the broadcast) to news about Iraq including the GSDF's move across the border into Iraq and the opening of the Diet and Koizumi's policy speech that focused largely on the SDF deployment. The following day it dedicated seven minutes and thirty-seven seconds (25 percent of its program) to news about the GSDF advance contingent's first day gathering information in Samawah, and the departure of the first group of ASDF to Kuwait where they would prepare to enter Iraq. TBS's *News Forest* dedicated a comparable twelve minutes and fifty-four seconds (43 percent of its airtime) to the same stories on that Monday and five minutes and fifty-nine seconds (20 percent) to the Ground and Air SDF on Tuesday. TV Asahi's *News Station* provided about twice as much time to the issues on both days, resulting in comparable percentages of airtime. On Monday it gave 42 percent of its program (thirty minutes and twelve seconds) to Iraq including the SDF advance contingent and Koizumi's speech. On Tuesday, it dedicated 28 percent of its airtime (nineteen minutes and two seconds) to the SDF deployment and other Iraq issues.

From January 19 to 21, 2003, the *Asahi Shimbun* ran thirty-one articles about Iraq and the SDF deployment to Samawah including five front-page stories. The *Yomiuri* ran fourteen stories, four of which were on the front page. While at first glance this looks like significantly more coverage by the *Asahi Shimbun,* in fact the *Asahi* stories tended to be much shorter than the

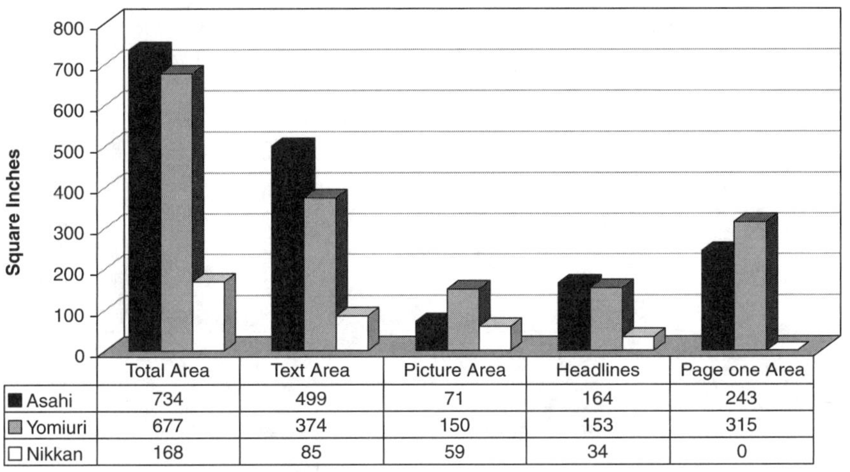

	Total Area	Text Area	Picture Area	Headlines	Page one Area
■ Asahi	734	499	71	164	243
▨ Yomiuri	677	374	150	153	315
☐ Nikkan	168	85	59	34	0

Figure 3.1 Newspaper coverage of SDF in Iraq by square inches.

Yomiuri Shimbun stories. In terms of total area devoted to these stories, the Asahi gave 724 square inches to these topics, 499 square inches of which was story text. The *Yomiuri Shimbun* dedicated 677 square inches to Iraq and the SDF in Iraq—about 8 percent less than the *Asahi*—of which 374 square inches were story text, 25 percent less than the *Asahi*. *Nikkan Sports* provided significantly less information, just six stories, none of them on the front page, totaling 168 square inches, only 23 percent of the total *Asahi* coverage. Figure 3.1 shows the total area each newspaper devoted to Iraq and the SDF deployment, and how much of that area was used for story text, pictures, headlines, and front-page stories.

Coverage of SDF Activities

All three television programs made the activities of the SDF their top story during the January 19–20 (2004) time frame. Figure 3.2 shows that all three stations devoted the most time, in almost identical percentages of total airtime, to neutral explanations of the SDF's daily activities.

Nonetheless, there were important differences in how the stories were framed. *News 7*'s report contained nearly no mention of the potential danger in which SDF troops worked. Both *News Forest* and *News Station* made danger a central theme in their reports. This suggests that NHK favors the Normal Nation Frame while the commercial networks are more willing to employ the Pacifist Nation Frame. While facing danger is certainly what a normal nation does, downplaying the potentially disastrous consequences of the SDF dispatch works to mask the radical change the mission represents—the SDF may have been sent into a war zone but all is well, the people welcome them. People who see the world from the Pacifist Nation Frame are

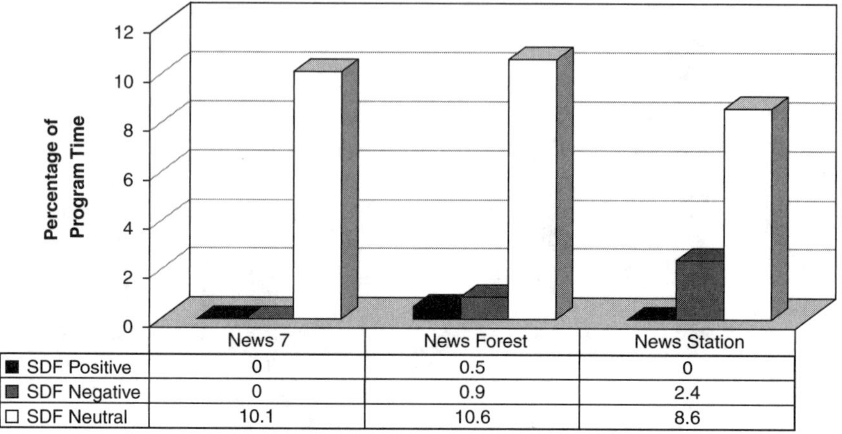

	News 7	News Forest	News Station
■ SDF Positive	0	0.5	0
■ SDF Negative	0	0.9	2.4
□ SDF Neutral	10.1	10.6	8.6

Figure 3.2 TV coverage of SDF activities in Iraq by percentage of program time.

more likely to point out that the dispatch represents a radical change that is fraught with new dangers, uncertainty, and possible catastrophe.

This difference can be clearly seen in the way in which the three programs framed the SDF advance contingent's move across the border into Iraq. NHK *News 7* began its one-minute opening montage of its Monday, January 19, 2004, broadcast with video of the GSDF crossing the Kuwait–Iraq border. This was immediately followed by video of Koizumi proclaiming to the newly convened Diet, "If we consider that Japan's peace and prosperity are part of the world's peace and security, then we must fulfill our responsibility to the international community through action." This juxtaposition framed the SDF move across the border in terms of international duty, a key Normal Nation Frame. The anchorman welcomed viewers by telling them the advance contingent of the GSDF has been sent to Iraq to begin "humanitarian assistance." This helped suggest that the mission is a logical next step for the SDF, and that expanding SDF activities will bring greater respect and prestige to Japan.

Neither *News Forest* nor *News Station* mentioned humanitarian assistance in their story lead-ins. Instead, both programs framed the story as Japan's first post–World War II step into a war zone. Reporters for both programs made repeated reference to the fact that the SDF needed to be protected by Dutch troops, a fact mentioned only once by *News 7.* The two programs also repeatedly drew their viewer's attention to the weapons being carried by SDF members, their bulletproof vests, helmets, and the mounted machine guns on their vehicles. Both programs commented on the tense mood of the SDF members, something *News 7* never mentioned. The overall effect was to focus viewer attention on the risks of moving beyond the formerly accepted limits imposed on the SDF by the Pacifist Constitution.

News Station began its Monday broadcast with anchorman Kume creating the image of Japanese troops going to war. Hiroshi Kume opened his program with an English phrase "boots on the ground"; he said,

"Japanese ground forces (*chijo butai*) [he did not call them Self-Defense Forces] wearing the rising sun have taken their first steps into Iraq." *News Station*'s reporter in Iraq repeated the phrase, as he reported on the SDF at the Kuwait–Iraq border. "The first of the convoy has crossed the border, it is now a 'boots-on-the-ground' situation," he said.

In its reports over the three-day study period, *News Station* inserted an element of conflict or danger into even some of the most mundane aspects of SDF activities. The reporter said a local man "seemed nervous" responding to a question about water cleanliness from SDF advance team commander Colonel Sato Masahisa, because the commander was carrying a large rifle. As they visited local government officials, members of the advance contingent and their Dutch armed escorts drove at high speed through the city, alarming some residents and causing others to look suspiciously at the SDF contingent, the *News Station* reporter said.

Figure 3.3 shows the amount of area each of the three newspapers studied dedicated to positive, negative, and neutral descriptions of SDF activities in Iraq.

Negative comments about the SDF in all three newspapers centered on a few observations of the nervousness evident on the faces of the SDF soldiers, the fact that they needed Dutch protection, and their defensive equipment and postures. However, unlike the TV programs, none of the newspapers made danger a central theme of their reporting. Nor did they focus on positive images. The *Asahi Shimbun* provided no positive descriptions of SDF activities. The *Yomiuri Shimbun* included one positive comment by a Dutch commander who said he was happy to see the SDF because they were better equipped than the Dutch to provide much needed services, such as water purification, to the people of Samawah.[53] The most positive view of the SDF came from the *Nikkan Sports,* which included a brief description

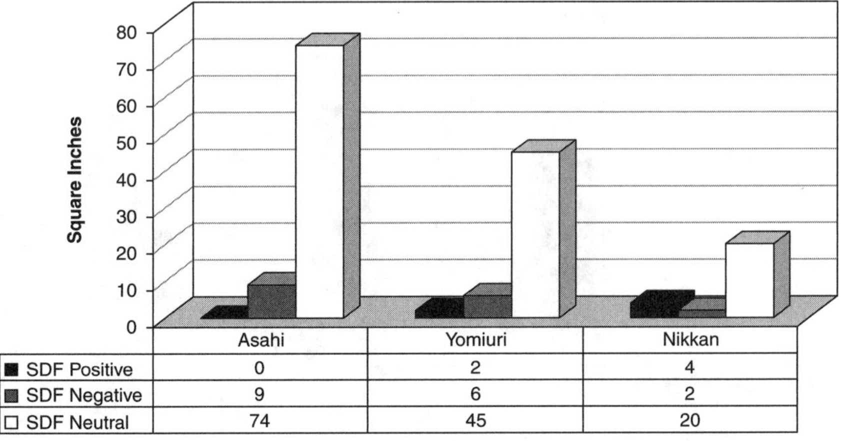

	Asahi	Yomiuri	Nikkan
■ SDF Positive	0	2	4
■ SDF Negative	9	6	2
☐ SDF Neutral	74	45	20

Figure 3.3 Newspaper coverage of all aspects of SDF forces in Iraq by square inches.

of the SDF's three-step plan for aiding Samawah: step one, humanitarian assistance; step two, rebuild the public infrastructure; and step three, encourage economic revival.[54]

Coverage of Samawah

Figure 3.4 shows that *News Station* and *News Forest* emphasized danger in their reports about conditions in Samawah more often than did *News 7*. What is more, very little of what *News Station* reported about Samawah could be categorized as neutral.

The first two minutes of *News 7*'s Monday, January 19th report was dedicated to video of the SDF contingent crossing the Kuwait–Iraq border and explanation of its route to Samawah. This was followed by a report on the security situation in Samawah. The NHK reporter told viewers that some people seemed unaware that the SDF advance contingent was entering their city that day. However, along the road into the city, some people had hung signs welcoming the troops. The report then cut to video taken earlier in the day of an elderly resident of Samawah who says emphatically, "Our city is safe and secure! We welcome our friends, the Japanese!" The reporter describes how crowds of Samawah residents approached the NHK news team wanting to shake their hands and asking if they had a job for them.

The reporter's only negative comment about Samawah on this first day was that "in a city where unemployment is a crisis, we felt the expectation of jobs coming with the SDF contingent was a little too high." Explanation of the mission of the SDF was necessary, the reporter said. On the second day, the program did give forty-five seconds to a negative report on protesters outside the CPA office in Samawah. Approximately five hundred demonstrators were demanding direct elections to choose a new local government, the reporter explained. Yet even when reporting this negative-coded event, the implication

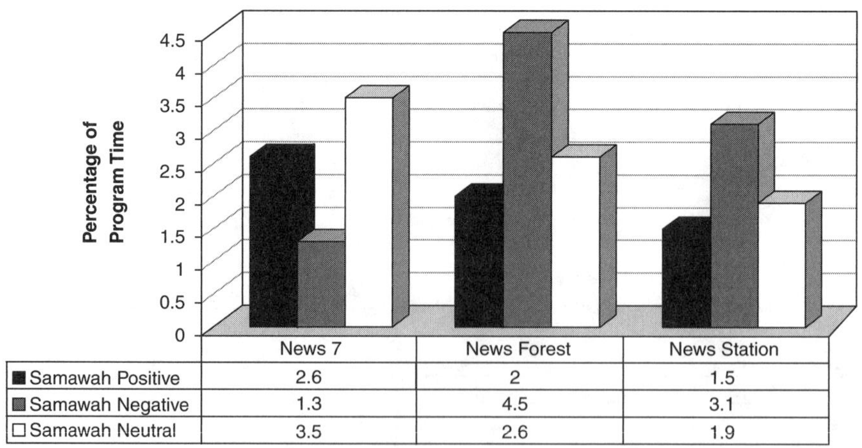

	News 7	News Forest	News Station
■ Samawah Positive	2.6	2	1.5
▨ Samawah Negative	1.3	4.5	3.1
☐ Samawah Neutral	3.5	2.6	1.9

Figure 3.4 TV coverage of Samawah security by percentage of program time.

was that the protestors were impatient for more of what the Americans and their allies had claimed to be bringing them—democracy.

New Forest also spent the first two minutes of its report on Monday showing video of the troops crossing the Iraq border, describing the makeup of the contingent and reviewing their arrival in Kuwait, and life at U.S. Camp Virginia there. However, it then cut to a minute-and-a-half of reports on four terrorist attacks against coalition targets in four Iraq cities the day before. The images were graphic with bodies lying lifeless in pools of blood, wounded men writhing in pain, coalition tanks and soldiers moving quickly into position shouting at civilians, and mangled and burning wreckage of automobiles used as improvised bombs. The reporter returned to the issue of the SDF by saying, "This is the situation into which Japanese troops are stepping."

News Forest also interviewed Samawah residents, but the comments selected for airing were less supportive of the arrival of the SDF. "We would rather have Japanese companies coming," an older man tells the reporter. "Samawah is secure, we don't need Japanese help that way," says a younger man. "Japan built us a hospital in the past. We want more facilities like that." The anchor in Tokyo asks the reporter in Samawah, "There have been severe terrorist attacks all over Iraq. Is Samawah really safe?" The reporter responds that he asked a Dutch soldier that same question. "We'll protect [the SDF] in our camp when they arrive, but then they will have to provide their own security," the Dutch soldier is shown saying. The comment does not leave viewers with a picture of the SDF's advance team secure in its new Iraqi environment.

The following evening *News Forest* concluded its report on Iraq with an even more ominous statement, "We have a new piece of information on the security situation here," the reporter says. "At a security committee meeting on Monday it was announced that the security situation is quickly deteriorating and it is possible that a terrorist attack could be attempted soon after the main contingent of SDF forces deploy to Samawah."

News Station also asked Samawah residents if their city was safe. But the reporter phrased the question much differently than did reporters for the other programs. "Isn't Samawah dangerous?" the *News Station* reporter asks a local man. "No," the man says, "There is nothing dangerous. It's safe. Nothing is going to happen." The reporter then characterized the situation himself. "He says it is safe, but the unemployment rate is more than 70 percent, and there have been demonstrations one after the other." Video of a demonstration is then played with a subtitle telling viewers "On the third of this month a demonstration of 5,000 people turned violent and two people were killed." The reporter then asks a Dutch soldier if he has any advice for the SDF advance contingent. "Don't trust these people," the soldier says in English, "they seem nice, but you can't trust them." *News Station* also covered the five hundred protesters outside the CPA office on Tuesday. However, whereas NHK had emphasized the protesters desire for democracy, *News Station* focused on armed Dutch troops rushing to secure the situation as SDF members looked on from a distance.

Though both *News Forest* and *News Station* reports focused on danger, neither program provided a context for understanding that danger within the Pacifist Nation Frame. The closest either show comes to providing such analysis was at the end of *News Station*'s Monday report on all issues about Iraq. In his closing thoughts, anchor Kume reads aloud Article 2 section 3 of the Special Measures Law for Iraq. "The SDF support activities for achieving security shall be implemented in the areas where combat is not taking place and is not expected to take place throughout the period during which activities are to be conducted there." Turning to invited guest commentator, Hagitani Jun of the *Asahi Shimbun* editorial board, Kume asks, "It says this, but on the 18th a car packed with 500kg of explosives exploded near the main gate of the CPA headquarters in Baghdad killing 22 people. This is a country where attacks continue to happen one after another, how can this not be considered a combat zone?" Hagitani responds,

> What you are saying is that this is the first time in the postwar period that the SDF have been dispatched to a country that is still at war, there are many possible situations, they could be drawn into conflict, captured or injured and you are hoping they can conduct their humanitarian activities without that happening, that is why your opinion carries weight.

This is a weak expression of the Pacifist Nation Frame theme that an expanded military role for the SDF could draw the country into conflicts that are not vital to its own security.[55] Neither *News 7* nor *News Station* provided a true philosophical basis for understanding why the peril faced by the SDF was important beyond a personal concern for the well-being of the men of the advance contingent.

Looking at the reporting on Samawah by the three newspapers, next, the coverage is summed up in figure 3.5.

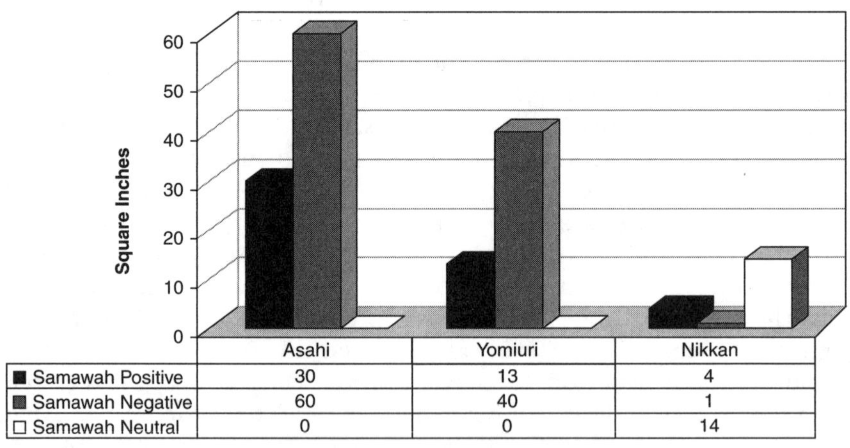

	Asahi	Yomiuri	Nikkan
■ Samawah Positive	30	13	4
■ Samawah Negative	60	40	1
□ Samawah Neutral	0	0	14

Figure 3.5 Newspaper coverage of Samawah security by square inches.

Although the *Asahi Shimbun* again provides more coverage of Samawah than the *Yomiuri Shimbun*, the two newspapers appear to have similar ratios of high negative reporting to lower positive reporting. However, there are important differences in the kind of negative reporting that each paper practiced. Much of the *Asahi Shimbun*'s negative reporting is found in a single story "Choosing a Base Site is First Problem,"[56] which ran on page thirty-one on January 21. The story describes the area around Samawah as a dangerous terrain littered with mines and unexploded bombs left over from both the Gulf War and the recent U.S. invasion. In other words, it is American military action that has made the area unsafe. The story also explains that the Japanese forces were having difficulty negotiating with the Samawah people for use of their land.[57] The *Yomiuri Shimbun*'s negative reporting also came largely from a single story, "Samawah Thirsts for Clean Water."[58] In contrast to the *Asahi* story, the problems in Samawah are described by the *Yomiuri* as being the result of years of neglect by the government of Saddam Hussein.[59] In fact, had this story included discussion of SDF efforts or plans to alleviate the water problem it would have been coded positive for the category of SDF activities in Iraq. However, since it dealt only with the potentially disruptive water condition, it had to be coded negative for the category of Samawah security to remain consistent with the coding system. It is not until the last sentence of this article that the SDF are mentioned. A thirty-eight-year-old Samawah resident says he is pleased the Japanese have arrived but hopes they will fix the roads before taking on the water supply problem. "Even if we have water, without roads we cannot transport it,"[60] he says.

Once again it was the *Nikkan Sports* newspaper that had the most positive reporting about the city of Samawah. In the story "'Self-Defense Force' Not Understood by Samawah People,"[61] the newspaper describes the amazement of the Samawah people at the peaceful nature of the SDF members. The story says the people, who have hung banners around the city welcoming the Japanese troops, have been surprised to learn that the SDF is not supposed to engage in military activities and to see that many members do not even carry weapons.[62] This could be read as an endorsement of the special nonaggressive nature of the SDF. However, here again, the real effect of such reporting is to undermine the Pacifist Nation Frame by obscuring the realities of the major change that is taking place in the SDF role and threats that come with such change.

Coverage of Government Positions on SDF Deployment

While government comments about the SDF deployment were scattered throughout reports on the three days studied, most came in stories about the opening day of the 2004 Diet session on January 19 and a Diet question-and-answer period on January 21 in which Prime Minister Koizumi defended his decision to send troops to Iraq against complaints from opposition party leaders. The percentage of airtime dedicated to the category "government positions" is illustrated in figure 3.6.

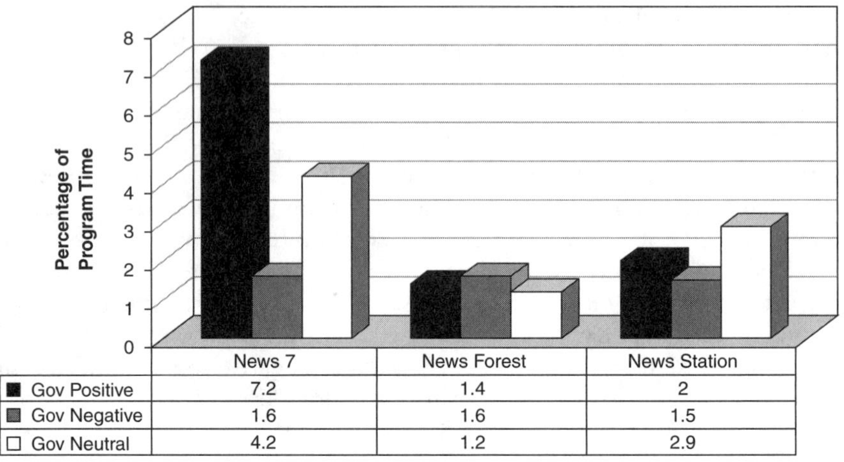

	News 7	News Forest	News Station
Gov Positive	7.2	1.4	2
Gov Negative	1.6	1.6	1.5
Gov Neutral	4.2	1.2	2.9

Figure 3.6 TV coverage of government positions on SDF deployment to Iraq by percentage of program time.

Over the three days studied, NHK's *News 7* devoted a greater percentage of its program to government explanations of its policy in Iraq than did the other two programs. In fact, the station's report on the prime minister's policy speech provided space for nearly all of the Normal Nation themes outlined earlier. *News 7* was the only one of the three TV programs analyzed to spend more time on the opening of the Diet (6:22 minutes) than on the SDF activities that day (5:16 minutes). More than a third of its Diet report (2:28 seconds) was dedicated to Koizumi's explanations for deploying the SDF. The report began with a quote from Koizumi in which he advances the international duty theme and the significant human contribution themes or the Normal Nation Frame. "Peace cannot come by calling for it in words alone," he says, "Japan must fulfill its responsibility to the international community through action." The Normal Nation themes of duty, action, normalcy, constitutionality, international respect, and honor are emphasized in a subsequent quote, "It is a matter of course," he says, "for a country to act to overcome difficulties. This [SDF deployment to Iraq] will help Japan earn an honored place in the world as called for in the preamble of the constitution," he says. The possibility that the deployment might anger Japan's neighbors is not mentioned in the *News 7* report. In his summation of Koizumi's speech, the reporter again mentions the reference to the preamble of the Constitution but the reporter does not compare this argument to arguments based on Article 9. The Normal Nation theme of progress away from fears of the past is also emphasized. The reporter tells us that in other recent speeches Koizumi has drawn parallels between his decision to send SDF troops to Iraq and Japan's decision in the final days of the Edo Period (1603–1853) to end some two hundred years of isolation and rejoin the world community.

In stark contrast to the time allotted to Normal Nation themes, NHK devoted only twenty-two seconds to opposition parties. The Diet reporter noted that opposition parties "questioned the thinking" of the ruling party in deploying the SDF to Iraq without explaining their particular concerns. He also told viewers the opposition parties felt the ruling parties "had not fully fulfilled their obligation to explain" the deployment. Neither comment is a forceful critique of the deployment. This is followed by a quote from Democratic Party of Japan leader Kan Naoto who hints at Pacifist Nation themes but does not state them clearly. "For Japan to send its military to another nation's territory, especially when a de facto state of war exists in that country, has very deep meaning," he says, but he does not explain what that meaning is. The prime minister flatters the public rather than explaining the issue clearly, he says. He concludes by calling Koizumi Japan's "worst prime minister." These twenty-two seconds provide the appearance of harsh criticism when, in fact, none of the Pacifist Nation arguments is presented directly.

It was not until January 21 that NHK provided any airtime to meaningful criticism of the deployment. In its lead story on the prime minister's question-and-answer period with lawmakers, the NHK anchor framed the back and forth comments between Democratic Party leader Kan and the prime minister as an opportunity for Koizumi to explain the legality of the deployment. The report begins with Kan claiming that the Constitution forbids troops to be sent abroad for military purposes, to which Koizumi replies the SDF are on a humanitarian mission and not military one. Kan argues back that the prime minister is trying to have it two ways at once by claiming the troops are on a humanitarian mission while assigning them to part of a coalition of forces that are at war. Koizumi replies that it has never been suggested that the Japanese troops would be treated as military personnel with duties like those of the American and British troops. What is more, the Special Measures Law for Iraq settles any constitutional questions about the deployment. Kan's statements count for forty-four seconds of the three-minute report. Koizumi's replies take up sixty seconds. In the remaining one minute and sixteen seconds the reporter reiterates the prime minister's position without additional analysis of the constitutional issue. The report clearly focuses on the prime minister's ability to deflect complaints about the constitutionality of the deployment.

As figure 3.6 shows, it is the insider commercial network News Forest that again provided the most room for anti-deployment statements. It gave one minute and thirty-six seconds of the program to the opening of the Diet on January 19. Of this time, only seventeen seconds were devoted to Koizumi's policy speech. The report included the prime minister's comment that words alone are not enough to fulfill international responsibility, which was followed by more than a minute (sixty-seven seconds) of comments from lawmakers opposed to the deployment. The same quote from Democratic Party leader Kan that NHK used is repeated but was cut before the "worst prime minister" jab. Chairman of the Japanese Communist Party Shii Kazuo faulted the LDP for lack of explanation. The report also included comments from two former LDP secretaries general, Koga Makoto and Kato Koichi, who opposed their own party's decision on deployment. However, here again, none of the lawmaker comments clearly explained any of the Pacifist Nation themes.

News Forest's report on the question-and-answer session was featured less prominently than NHK's report on the same subject. It was half as long as NHK's story (one minute and thirty seconds) and tacked on to the end of its report on the advance contingent in Samawah. However, it was framed in such a way as to provide more importance to the issue itself and to Kan's criticism. The reporter introduced the story as a clash over the constitutionality of the deployment rather than as a chance for Koizumi to justify the deployment, as NHK had done. A longer version of Kan's remarks were used, which including the very strong criticism that Koizumi had lost his right to be prime minister by violating the Constitution and should resign. Koizumi is shown responding that the forces are humanitarian and therefore constitutional, and then obstinately refusing a second lawmaker's demand for clarification. "I know you are not satisfied with this answer, but I have already answered this question. You can ask me again in some other committee," he says. The reporter concludes that the atmosphere in the Diet was strained, but offers no analysis of the constitutionality issue.

As is clear from figure 3.6, TV Asahi's *News Station* provided slightly more time, to proponents of the deployment than to opposition positions during the three days of coverage. However, *News Station* actually went much farther than even TBS in framing the opening of the Diet and the question-and-answer period in terms of controversy and clashing worldviews.

Anchorman Kume introduced the first day of the Diet story with a vague call for citizen involvement in the issue.[63] "The 150-day general session of the Diet was called to order today," he said. "The rationale for sending troops into a war zone and the response of lawmakers, who receive their authority from the citizenry, will be the most important topic."

Before addressing Koizumi's policy speech and rationale for the SDF deployment, the program aired thirty seconds of lawmakers outside the Diet in traditional Japanese costume, the wearing of which is an opening day tradition. The camera lingered on former LDP president and Prime Minister Mori Yoshiro—a politician most noted for his political gaffes—as he asks another lawmaker if his kimono makes him look like a sumo grand champion. An additional eight seconds were then allotted the speaker of the house calling on the body to accept the resignation of an LDP lawmaker involved in scandal. The program continued to set a negative light on the LDP and Koizumi's policy speech by turning first to comments from the head of the Communist Party, the Social Democratic Party, and the Democratic Party. As ominous music pulsated in the background, comments from dissident LDP members, Koga, Kato, and images of anti-mainstream LDP faction leaders Eto Takami and Kamei Shizuka were presented with quick cuts and dramatic camera angles. This was followed by LDP secretary general Abe

Shinzo's remarks to the LDP faithful at the party's recent convention calling for member unity on the SDF deployment to Iraq, a call that rings hollow given the preceding juxtaposition of dissenter views. Into this picture of discontent are inserted Koizumi's appeals to international duty and the need to back up words with actions. "If we provide material contribution but leave human contribution to other countries," he says, "we cannot say that we are carrying out our obligations as a member of the international community." Several of the same Koizumi quotes used by the NHK and TBS programs also appear in the *News Station* story. However, such comments have a much different context than in the *News 7* report or even the *News Forest* report. More criticism follows the quotes from Koizumi's speech. Social Democratic Party leader Fukushima Mizuho calls Koizumi's explanation for troop deployment an "empty argument." Kan describes Koizumi as "very dangerous." Sandwiched between negative comments, Koizumi's appeal for support of the SDF a deployment to Iraq is treated with skepticism.

News Station's report on Kan and Koizumi's constitutionality debate during the question-and-answer period was slightly shorter than NHK's (two minutes and eleven seconds) and focused on the conflict between the two party leaders rather than on the issue itself. Quick cuts of the two men's comments (including Kan's call for Koizumi's resignation) were separated by the clang of a boxing-ring bell and round-card graphics. The issue of the constitutionality of the SDF deployment is never commented on or analyzed in a serious way.

In short, government justification for the deployment of the SDF to Iraq gets significantly different treatment by the three television programs. The public network, NHK, provides much more airtime for Koizumi and his supporters than for opposition leaders, and frames reports to favor Normal Nation Frame themes. The other insider (*kisha* club dependant) program, TBS's *News Forest*, actually provides more time for comments from opposition leaders. However, as with NHK's reports, the opposition comments fail to employ or explain Pacifist Nation Frame themes. One exception is the issue constitutionality, which is introduced but not explained or analyzed in a meaningful way. TV Asahi's *News Station* provided more airtime to proponents of the deployment, but tended to frame such comments in ways that questioned their validity. Yet even in its ominous and sometimes mocking reports on the deployment, this program never provided theoretical context or analysis any of the Pacifist Nation Fame themes.

Figure 3.7 shows that the newspapers were more reluctant to provide negative government opinions, and instead opted for neutral descriptions of the political process.

The *Asahi Shimbun* was the only newspaper to present any significant comments from government officials. However, like the television reporting, the *Asahi* tended to give ruling party officials space to present arguments from the Normal Nation Frame while supplying only vaguely stated criticism from opposition party leaders. In an article titled "At 1000 Days of the Administration, a Turning Point in Koizumi Language" (*Seiken 1000*

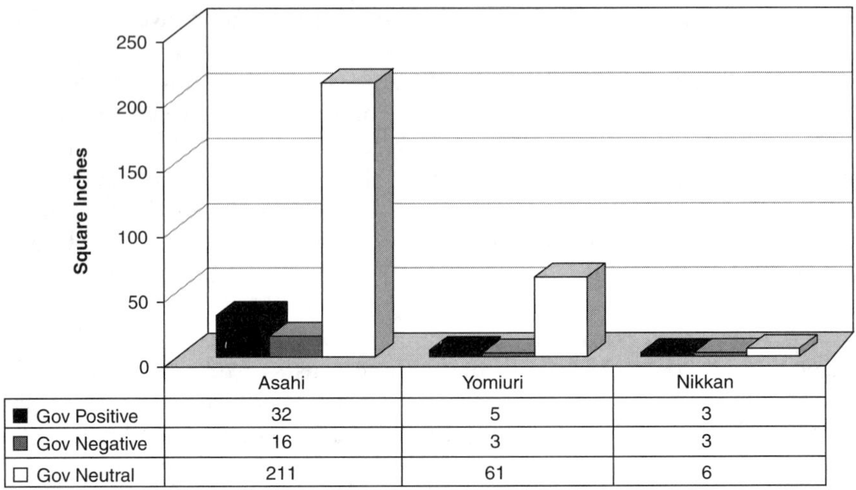

	Asahi	Yomiuri	Nikkan
■ Gov Positive	32	5	3
▨ Gov Negative	16	3	3
☐ Gov Neutral	211	61	6

Figure 3.7 Newspaper coverage of government positions on SDF deployment to Iraq by square inches.

Nichi Koizumigo no Tenki), which ran on January 20, the newspaper quoted from Koizumi's speech to the Diet that the SDF deployment to Iraq would bring honor and respect to Japan for fulfilling its international obligations.[64] Meeting with reporters after the speech, Koizumi is quoted as saying, "People who were against the U.S.–Japan Security Treaty and UN peace-keeping operations in the past are now in favor of them. The deployment to Iraq will be just the same."[65]

On January 20, the *Yomiuri Shimbun* ran two stories that included government comments on the deployment. The first, "Using 'Iraq Support' as a Façade, Economic Management Also Insufficient," quotes Democratic Party leader Kan's comment that deployment of the SDF to a war zone "has very deep meaning."[66] In a second story, "Secretary General Abe Looks Ahead to Exercising Constitutional Interpretation,"[67] Abe explains that he believes it is possible to interpret Article 9 to allow for collective self-defense. The story did not explain why or how he felt such an interpretation was possible.

Inclusion of Nongovernment Commentary

Figure 3.8 shows that neither NHK *News 7* nor TBS *News Forest* provided any non-Japanese government commentary or opinions on the SDF deployment to Iraq. However, over the three days surveyed, TV Asahi's *News Station* aired five minutes and forty seconds of personal opinion by the anchor, Kume, guest commentators, anti-deployment demonstrators, foreign government officials, and reporters. Most of the comments (2:51 minutes) could be categorized as negative. The remainder (2:41 minutes) was neutral in tone. There were no positive attitudes expressed by any non-Japanese official on either day.

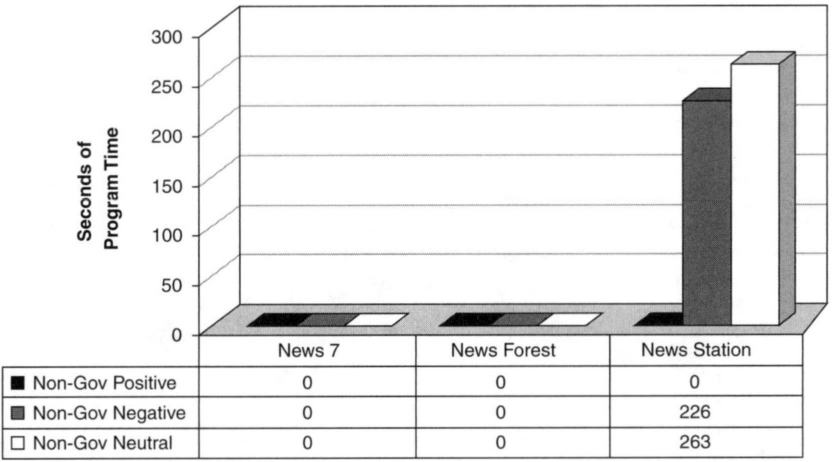

	News 7	News Forest	News Station
■ Non-Gov Positive	0	0	0
▨ Non-Gov Negative	0	0	226
☐ Non-Gov Neutral	0	0	263

Figure 3.8 TV inclusions of nongovernment comments on SDF deployment to Iraq by seconds of program time.

On Tuesday, January 20, *News Station* included one minute and twelve seconds of comments by the Arab language Al Jazeera news agency, as well as Chinese and North Korean mass media. A subtitled Al Jazeera commentator said Koizumi was taking a big political risk with this "turn away from the policy of [limited] defense only that had guided Japan since the end of World War II." She predicted that the main contingent of GSDF would not be sent if there was an attack on the advance contingent. A large two-page spread on the SDF advance team in the *Beijing Morning Post* was shown and summarized by the *News Station* reporter. The articles accused Japan of "breaking its constitutional promise not to send troops to war zones," the reporter said. North Korea radio was quoted as saying, "The deployment of a large armed force to Iraq by the reactionary Japanese has begun." Although it was not clearly stated, the Pacifist Nation Frame fear of angering Japan's neighbors with expanded SDF roles is suggested by the inclusion of such comments.

Of the three programs, only *News Station* included in its reports any mention of anti-deployment demonstrations within Japan. Twenty seconds were given to protesters in the Okinawa Prefecture capital city of Naha.[68] The reporter noted that protesters were demanding the return of the advance contingent and the end of plans to deploy ground troops to Samawah. But she did not explain why.

At the end of reports on Iraq issues on Tuesday, Kume offered his harshest criticism of the deployment. "This is the first time that the SDF has been deployed without a UN mandate and the first time to a war zone. Of course, there needs to be a first time for everything, but to have the Dutch military defending the Japanese troops, to have one military defending another military, defies common sense," he says. Turning to invited commentator, *Asahi Shimbun* editorial board member Shimizu Tateki, he asks, "Could this be about anything except politics?" Shimizu counters Kume's directness with a

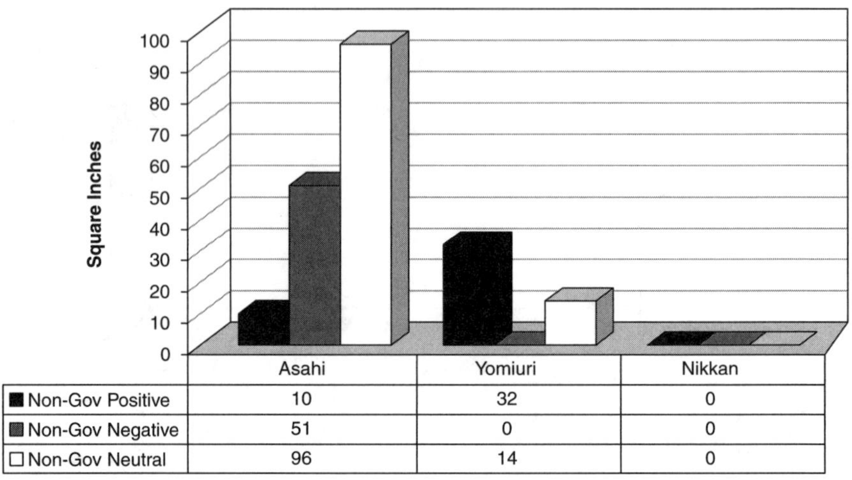

	Asahi	Yomiuri	Nikkan
■ Non-Gov Positive	10	32	0
■ Non-Gov Negative	51	0	0
□ Non-Gov Neutral	96	14	0

Figure 3.9 Newspaper inclusions of nongovernment comments on SDF deployment to Iraq by square inches.

more neutral comment expressing hope that during the 150 days of the Diet session, lawmakers will fully explain why the deployment is necessary. Taken together, the tone is critical, and yet, the antigovernment comments are not supported with any philosophical context.

In the *Asahi Shimbun* and the *Yomiuri Shimbun*, it was the newspapers' own editorials that made up the bulk of the non-Japanese government opinion provided. *Nikkan Sports*'s reporting did not include any nongovernment comments. It is in these editorials that the *Asahi* and the *Yomiuri* newspapers differ from each other most. This difference in editorial direction is shown in figure 3.9.

In its January 21, 2004, editorial titled "America Should Not Dislike Compromise" (*Beikoku ha Joho wo Itona*), the *Asahi Shimbun* strongly criticizes George W. Bush for failing to anticipate the ethnic and religious problems that would hinder elections and the transfer of power back to Iraqis after the war. It called on him to compromise and work with the Iraqi people and the UN to create the conditions necessary for reconstruction and nation-building to occur.[69] In contrast, the *Yomiuri* editorial on January 19 titled "American Military Pressure Inspires Softening,"[70] praised Bush as a strong leader whose decisive action has made the world safer. It is because of Bush and the Iraq War that rogue nations such as Libya, North Korea, and Syria are beginning to change their ways, it said.

CONCLUSION

The study shows that the *Asahi Shimbun* provided more news about SDF deployment to Iraq than did the *Yomiuri Shimbun*. However, both newspapers consistently chose neutral reporting over information that could be categorized as negative or positive. Both newspapers also provided more positive government opinions than negative. What is more, the ratio of positive to negative information in the two papers was comparable in most categories. The non-*kisha* club newspaper *Nikkan Sports* provided far less news on Iraq and the SDF and did not mirror the other two newspapers in ratio of negative to positive reporting. This could indicate that the *kisha* club system does indeed have a homogenizing effect on the print media.

On the other hand, there were some important differences in some of the stories in the two *kisha* club newspapers. For example, both newspapers provided more negative than positive reports on SDF activities, and a more negative than positive picture of Samawah. This suggests that they were not simply following government frames. There were also differences in the kind of negative reporting in both newspapers. For example, an *Asahi* report on Samawah focused on problems caused by the American invasion and earlier Gulf War. The *Yomiuri* focused on problems caused by Saddam Hussein's neglect of the area. The two newspapers were also significantly different in the category of nongovernment opinion. The *Asahi* editorial criticized President Bush for lack of foresight while the *Yomiuri* praised him for action that has caused rogue nations to reconsider their ways. It is also interesting that *Nikkan Sports*, the newspaper freest to challenge the Japanese government, actually provided the most positive view of the SDF activities.

As for television reporting, the study showed a great deal more diversity than evident in the print media. There was significant difference in the way the two *kisha* club dependent programs *News 7* and *News Forest* covered the first deployment of Japanese troops abroad without a UN mandate, and to a region where violence has not ceased. NHK's *News 7* did indeed mirror government positions. It depicted Samawah, the site of SDF activity in Iraq, as a secure city that welcomed Japanese troops. It downplayed problems in the city that could lead to unrest and minimized the danger that SDF troops faced. The NHK program also allotted generous space for Prime Minister Koizumi and other LDP officials to present their rationale for deploying troops to Iraq. Themes of the Normal Nation Frame were clearly stated. These included the argument that the deployment of SDF forces to Iraq is important for Japan to meet its international responsibility, fosters national independence and fulfills the admonition of the constitution for Japan to become an active member of the world community, satisfies the need for Japan to make a human contribution to solving international problems, and enhances Japanese prestige within the world community. Very little time was given to critics of deployment and the comments that were included lacked substance.

News Forest gave more time to government critics of the SDF deployment than to supporters. Some Normal Nation Frame themes were presented but were not guiding elements in the reports. *News Forest* also focused on dangers in Samawah to a much greater extent than did NHK. The clear difference between how these two programs framed their stories suggests that the *kisha* club's influence on content is not as great as is often argued. It is most likely that NHK mirrors government frames because of its role as a public television network rather than because of *kisha* club relationships or rules.

However, *News Forest*'s does not place its focus on danger into a philosophical context. The reports never directly discuss a reversion to militarism or growing nationalism in Japan. They did not deal with the question of whether the SDF deployment represents subservience to or equality with the United States or if it would anger Japan's neighbors.

News Station went the furthest in presenting some of these Pacifist Nation Frame issues. It clearly framed the SDF advance contingent's activities in Iraq in military, rather than humanitarian, terms. It focused on danger, potential unrest, and the weaponry and protective gear of the contingent. It even adopted militaristic terminology for referring to the deployment—"boots-on-the-ground." What is more, anchor Kume directly expressed skepticism about the motives for deployment, "could this be about anything other than politics." He suggested that placing the SDF in a position of being guarded by the Dutch "defied common sense." Time was allotted to relay the criticism from the Al Jazeera news agency and North Korean and Chinese media sources that accused Japan of breaking its constitutional promise of defense only. SDF leaders in Iraq were criticized directly for failing in their duty to keep the media informed. In other words, Pacifist Nation Frame themes were *suggested* by *News Station* more clearly than in either of the two *kisha* club dependent programs. Independence from the clubs might well have played a role in this apparent freedom to criticize.

However, here again the criticism was implied without being put into context or clearly explained, either by a reporter or by anchorman Kume. Van Wolferen's analysis of Japanese media—that they "appear to play an adversarial role in the System" but actually take a "very superficial" adversarial attitude—seems an appropriate criticism of both *News Forest* and *News Station*'s reporting on this issue. Through all their efforts to negatively positioning Koizumi's policy speech to the Diet, it is the prime minister's comments that most clearly provide viewers with a philosophy or frame to explain the SDF deployment.

A longer study period is necessary to determine whether this is a consistent tendency of these programs. However, it is interesting that so little of the opposition philosophy is explained when editors of both programs considered the news important enough for a major portion of their program airtime. Part of the blame for the lack of clarity in opposition position undoubtedly lies with opposition leaders who do not make their cases convincingly. However, in the end, it may not be the influence of the *kisha* clubs, fear of reprisal, or close government–reporter relationships that keep opposition messages out of the Japanese media. A lack of journalistic mission or sense of responsibility to balance and explain competing ideologies may lie at the heart of the government's ability to use the media to articulate its positions and advance its frames.

Notes

1. For more on framing, see the discussion in chapter two.
2. Sheila A. Smith, "The Evolution of Military Cooperation in the U.S.–Japan Alliance," in Michael J. Green and Patrick Cronin, eds., *The U.S.–Japan Alliance: Past, Present, and Future* (New York: Council on Foreign Relations Press, 1999), pp. 71–2.
3. Thomas U. Berger, "Alliance Politics and Japan's Postwar Culture of Antimilitarism," in Green and Cronin, *The U.S.–Japan Alliance*, p. 192.
4. At its 22nd Party Congress in November 24, 2000, the Japanese Communist Party reasserted its basic belief that the Self-Defense Forces are unconstitutional, while acknowledging for the first time that "if an unexpected emergency [such] as violation of our national sovereignty or major disaster occurs, the existing Self-Defense Forces would be used to ensure the security of the people. Government has due responsibility to defend the constitutional principles by using all possible means." See the JCP website at http://www.jcp.or.jp/english/22nd_congress_reso.html (September 2007).
5. For a timely study of the question of civilian control in Japan, see Musashi Katsuhiro, "Reisengo Nihon no Anzen Hosho Seisaku no Seiritsu Katei ni Okeru Shibirian Kontorooru no Kenkyu (A Study of Civilian Control in the Legislative Process for Japanese Security Policy in the Post Cold War)," Doctoral Dissertation, Osaka School of International Public Policy (Osaka University, 2007).
6. "Irakusen 'Fushiji' 65% (65% 'Disapprove' of Iraq War)," *Asahi Shimbun*, March 31, 2003.
7. "Seifu no Setusmei 'Busoku' 88% (Government Explanations 'Not Satisfactory' 88 %)," *Sankei Shimbun*, November 23, 2003.
8. "Koizumi Naikaku 'Shiji'" 42% ('Support' for Koizumi Cabinet 42%)," *Mainichi Shimbun*, December 1, 2003.
9. "Sansei Fue 40% Hantai 48% (Approval Increases to 40% Opposed 48%)," *Asahi Shimbun*, January 19, 2004.
10. "Sanpi 47% de Narabu (Approval and Disapproval Even at 47%)," *Mainichi Shimbun*, January 26, 2004.
11. "Seifu no Taio 'Hyoka' 74% ('Approval' of Government Response 74%)," *Yomiuri Shimbun*, April 20, 2004.
12. Ibid.
13. Yoshida, Reiji, "Koizumi's Career Could be Biggest Casualty of Iraq Dispatch," *Japan Times*, February 12, 2004.
14. Ibid.
15. Ofer Feldman, *Politics and the News Media in Japan* (Ann Arbor: University of Michigan Press, 1993), p. 70.
16. Ibid., p. 69.
17. Laurie Anne Freeman, *Closing the Shop: Information Cartels and Japan's Mass Media* (Princeton, New Jersey: Princeton University Press, 2000), p. 80.
18. Ibid., p. 103.
19. Ibid., p. 119.
20. Ibid., p. 104.
21. "Kisha Club Guidelines," Nihon Shimbun Kyōkai (The Japan Editors and Publishers Association), http://www.pressnet.or.jp/english/ (accessed November 2007).

22. "Organization and Activities of Nihon Shimbun Kyōkai," Nihon Shimbun Kyōkai (The Japan Editors and Publishers Association), http://www.pressnet.or.jp/english/member/list.htm (accessed March 2006).

23. "Organization and Activities of Nihon Shimbun Kyōkai."

24. Freeman, *Closing*, p. 89.

25. Ibid., p. 97.

26. "Kisha Club Guidelines."

27. Freeman, *Closing*, p. 89.

28. Ibid.

29. "Member News Organizations: Tokyo District," Nihon Shimbun Kyōkai (The Japan Editors and Publishers Association), http://www.pressnet.or.jp/english/ (accessed March 2006).

30. Ibid.

31. Ibid.

32. Ibid.

33. Ibid.

34. Freeman, *Closing*, p. 4.

35. Shibayama Tetsuya. Interviewed by author, July 10, 1999.

36. Ibid.

37. Ibid.

38. Fujita Hiroshi. Interviewed by author, December 10, 1998.

39. Ibid.

40. Karl van Wolferen, *The Enigma of Japanese Power* (New York: Alfred A. Knopf, 1989), p. 95.

41. Ibid., p. 93.

42. Ibid.

43. "'Daihonei Happyo' Futatabi (Once again, 'Announcements from Imperial Central Command')," *Shukan Shincho*, January 21, 2004, pp. 9–10.

44. For a story on a supposed agreement Japanese media were asked to make with SDF in Iraq, see "'Daihonei' to Kakusha Ankeeto ('Imperial Headquarters Reports' and the Survey for Various [media] Companies)," *Shukan Kinyobi*, http://www.kinyobi.co.jp/uramadoEntries/kaze/37 (accessed November 7, 2007). And, "Kore 'Zantei Tachiiri Shuzai Shinseisho' da (This is the Application for Temporary Entering and Reporting)," *Shukan Kinyobi*, http://www.kinyobi.co.jp/uramadoEntries/kaze/37 (accessed November 7, 2007).

45. Maggie Farley, "Japan's Press and the Politics of Scandal," in Susan J. Pharr and Ellis S. Krauss, eds., *Media and Politics in Japan* (Honolulu: University of Hawaii Press, 1996), p. 140.

46. Fukuda interview.

47. "Magazine Muckrakers Where Major Media Won't Make Waves," *Japan Times*, November 11, 2002.

48. Kristin Kyoko Altman, "Television and Political Turmoil: Japan's Summer of 1993," in Pharr and Krauss, *Media and Politics in Japan*, p. 170.

49. Ibid., p. 171.

50. Ellis Krauss, *Broadcasting Politics in Japan: NHK and Television News* (Ithaca, NY: Cornell University Press, 2000), p. 221.

51. Altman, "Television and Political Turmoil," p. 171.

52. Member News Organizations: Tokyo District.

53. "Tairetsu Kinpaku no Kokkyogoe (Troops Cross the Tense Border)," *Yomiuri Shimbun*, January 20, 2004.
54. "Samawah Shimin ni Rikai Sarenai 'Jieitai' ('Self-Defense Force' Not Understood by Samawah People)," *Nikkan Sports*, January 21, 2004.
55. The possibility of being drawn into a conflict that is not vital to the interests of one's own country is a concern even for those who view the world through the Normal Nation Frame. However, for those who favor the Pacifist Nation Frame, this possibility is more than a concern; it is a central justification and a defining element of their worldview. Here Hagitani is not just expressing a concern but is clearly warning the Japanese people of the dangers implicit in allowing the SDF to take on roles that are closer to those of a real military, such as entering war zones.
56. "Shukueichi Erabi Mazu Nandai (Choosing a Base Site is First Problem)," *Asahi Shimbun*, January 21, 2004.
57. "Shukueichi Erabi Mazu Nandai."
58. "Kyusui Katsubo Suru Samawah (Samawah Thirsts for Clean Water)," *Yomiuri Shimbun*, January 20, 2004.
59. "Kyusui Katsubō Suru Samawah."
60. Ibid.
61. "Samawah Shimin ni Rikai Sarenai 'Jieitai'."
62. Ibid.
63. For more on citizens' movements, see chapters six and seven.
64. "Seiken 1000 Nichi Koizumigo no Tenki (At 1000 days of the Administration, a Turning Point in Koizumi Language)," *Asahi Shimbun*, January 20, 2004.
65. Ibid.
66. "'Iraq Shien' Zenmen ni Keizai Unei dewa Fuman (Using 'Iraq Support' as a Façade, Economic Management Also Insufficient)," *Yomiuri Shimbun*, January 20, 2004.
67. "Kempo Kaishaku de no Koshi Abe Kanjicho Maemuki (General Secretary Abe Looks Ahead to Exercising Constitutional Interpretation)," *Yomiuri Shimbun*, January 20, 2004.
68. For more on the Okinawan protests, see chapter seven.
69. "Beikokuha Jyoho wo Itona (America Should Not Dislike Compromise)," *Asahi Shimbun*, January 21, 2004.
70. "Nanka wo Unagashita Beikoku no Gunjiteki Atsuryoku (American Military Pressure Inspires Softening)," *Yomiuri Shimbun*, January 19, 2004.

CHAPTER 4

Japanese Political Parties Face Public Opinion: Leading, Responding, or Ignoring?

Paul Midford and Paul D. Scott

INTRODUCTION

Does Japanese public opinion influence political parties and ultimately shape foreign policy? It is common to dismiss the influence of public opinion in Japan. In contrast to American debates between elitists[1] and pluralists,[2] with respect to Japan the elitist view has dominated. Public opinion is often claimed to have had little influence on Japanese foreign policy, and public opinion is often seen as subject to elite molding.[3]

By contrast, this chapter argues that public opinion wields significant influence on political parties, and therefore on foreign policy. Namely, public opinion acts as a crucial constraint on policy formation. This is not to say that elites and the state do not influence public attitudes regarding foreign policy. Elite influence over mass opinion, when it occurs, is nonetheless gradual. In areas where the position of the elites conflicts with basic underlying public attitudes, however, its impact is largely ineffective. For example, as discussed elsewhere in this volume, elite efforts to build support for the Iraq War and a military role there for Japanese troops have failed to sway the public.

Elite influence over Japanese public opinion has been most effective at promoting the gradual erosion of antimilitarist mistrust of the Japanese state's ability to wield the sword. Here, a clear pattern of gradual and rational reassurance is evident, in which the state and elites gradually demonstrate to the public the state's capacity to successfully control and manage a greater and wider range and scope of military activities without experiencing a reversion to 1930s militarism, when civilian control broke down, and military leaders hijacked the nation to engaging in, first, a quagmire in China and then a hopeless war against the United States,

Great Britain, and the Netherlands.[4] This reassurance strategy, which is the domestic analogue of a foreign reassurance strategy[5] aimed at neighboring Asian nations, has thus entailed a gradual step-by-step expansion of Japan's military role over the course of more than fifty years. In this respect public opinion has proven to be a soft and somewhat malleable constraint, one that slows down security policy change, but does not necessarily stop it.

Peter Woolley's study of the gradual expansion in the roles and missions of the Maritime Self-Defense Forces offers an excellent description of this process.[6] Woolley shows a consistent pattern: a plan for expanded naval operations is put forth, this generates domestic controversy, but eventually the mission is accepted and slips into obscurity as the Maritime Self-Defense Force (MSDF) incrementally grows into its new mission with professionalism and without incident. In this way, the Japanese state reassures public opinion, and Asian nations, that the MSDF [and other branches of the Self-Defense Forces (SDF)] can assume greater security roles without triggering a return to 1930s style militarism. Woolley goes so far as to argue that "public opinion was just as likely to have reflected the development of missions by the JSDF as it was to have limited the JSDF."[7] In this view, the impact of public opinion, if any, is to slow policy change.

However, other underlying beliefs, most notably beliefs about the utility of offensive versus defensive military force, have proven much more resistant to elite efforts to induce opinion change. In these areas public opinion has proven to be a hard constraint on policy change. Thus, elite efforts to gain public acceptance for the Japanese military moving beyond noncombat overseas missions to embrace combat missions have not been successful. This lack of public acceptance in turn has prevented Japanese elites from enacting policies that would move SDF activities beyond noncombat missions into low intensity combat, security, and patrol missions. Although there is much speculation about Japan ending its ban on the exercise of the right of collective defense,[8] as discussed later, there are few indications that it will engage in joint combat operations with U.S. forces in areas far from Japan anytime in the foreseeable future.[9]

FACTORS AFFECTING POLICY OUTCOMES AND THE ROLE OF PUBLIC OPINION

When and how does public opinion affect policy outcomes? This chapter argues that the following factors determine the impact of opinion majorities on policy outcomes.

When large and stable opinion majorities exist.   When opinion majorities are well over 50 percent, persist, and are not much affected by changes in survey question wording, these majorities will have the greatest impact on policy. Smaller opinion majorities or pluralities, or those that are changeable in the face of new question wording or short-term developments will not do much to constrain policy makers.

Large and stable opinion majorities will impact policy in several ways: by emboldening and mobilizing politicians supported by stable opinion majorities, restraining, immobilizing, or demoralizing politicians opposed by stable opinion majorities. These dynamics often operate at the interparty level, but just as often in Japan, they operate at the intra-party level, especially within the faction-ridden Liberal Democratic Party (LDP).[10]

When there is political competition.   Many observers view Japan as a nation with a seemingly oxymoronic "one-party dominant democracy" where the LDP has ruled almost continuously since 1955.[11] According to this view, there is little political competition in Japan. Yet, the reality of LDP dominance is frequently exaggerated. LDP rule has often been precarious, based upon extremely narrow majorities, as was the case in the 1970s. Indeed, the LDP has not won a majority of the popular vote in any lower house election since 1963. Moreover, since 1989, the LDP has not controlled the Upper House (the House of Councilors) of the National Diet, effectively preventing the LDP from passing normal legislation on its own.[12] This reality, reinforced by a decline in the LDP's core voter base, its inability to obtain an outright majority in most recent lower house elections (2005 being a notable exception), and its increasing reliance on support from its coalition partner of the last decade, Komeito, for electing LDP candidates, suggests a much more competitive political environment than the convenient image of a one-party dominant democracy would suggest, one in which the LDP constantly struggles to hang on to power. Under such conditions, it cannot easily ignore stable opinion majorities.

More importantly, the mislabel of one-party dominance masks the crucial role played by political competition within the LDP, battles that have important policy implications. Through most of its history the LDP has been more a collection of competing factions than a coherent political party.[13] Although factions have not normally held consistent policy positions and are organized by personal loyalties and interests, policy positions have at times influenced competition among them. Crucially, the tendency for factions to polarize around so-called mainstream (*shuryuha*) and anti-mainstream (*hanshuryuha*) groupings has often involved differences over policy. Indeed, the alternation of these two groups in power has sometimes had effects on policy comparable to those stemming from a change of party. To take the most recent example, the change of mainstream and anti-mainstream sides between the premiership of Obuchi Keizo and that of Koizumi Junichiro (via the transitional figure of Mori Yoshiro's one-year administration between April 2000 and April 2001) had far-ranging policy implications for domestic and foreign policies. In this way, the LDP was simultaneously able to play the role of both ruling and opposition party.[14] Most clearly illustrating this was the fact that until the mid-1990s, Japan's multi-seat constituency system, by encouraging rival LDP factions to run candidates against each other in the same districts, gave voters the opportunity to vote against the mainstream factions controlling the government while still voting for the LDP (i.e., by voting for anti-mainstream LDP candidates).

This combination of the LDP's precarious, if long, hold on power, combined with fierce internal competition within the LDP and its key coalition partner, Komeito, has meant that political competition is the rule rather than the exception in Japanese politics. Nonetheless, political competition is a variable, not a constant. As discussed later, during periods when political competition has appeared to wane, such as when the main opposition party stumbles, the government has shown greater willingness to defy opinion majorities.

When a united Diet opposition also has the support of a stable opinion majority. If the LDP can coax one or more opposition parties, especially the Democratic Party of Japan (DPJ), the largest opposition party (formed in 1996), to support its positions, it can usually pursue these policies with little concern for public opinion. To take an example from another parliamentary democracy, British prime minister Tony Blair had little reason to worry about public opposition to the Iraq War since the other major party, the Conservatives, also supported the war. On the other hand, when the opposition unites against a policy, and has the support of a stable opinion majority, it has the opportunity to exploit this opposition to gain at the expense of the ruling coalition. As Kurt Gaubatz argues, it is not public opinion itself, but the potential for it to be exploited by the opposition that motivates the ruling side to concern itself with electoral backlash, especially when an election is near.[15]

When the ruling coalition is divided and leaders worry about the consequences for other priorities by defying a stable opinion majority. Even when the opposition is not united, if important pieces of legislation, especially those in the same or a related issue area, are coming up for Diet consideration, coalition leaders have to worry about an opinion backlash derailing these other bills. This is especially true when the presence of a stable opinion majority coincides with divisions within the ruling coalition. As discussed later, the Koizumi administration's desire to beef up SDF deployments in the Indian Ocean in the first half of 2002 in support of U.S. and coalition military operations in Afghanistan were restrained by an even greater desire to see the quick enactment of an Emergency Legal Framework (*Buryoku kogeki jitai taisho kanren san ho*) for responding to armed attack on Japanese territory. Opponents within the LDP and Komeito exploited this situation to block beefed-up deployments.

Ironically, the desire of the LDP to revise the constitution renders opinion majorities more influential for Japan today than at anytime in the postwar era. Because constitutional revision is a long and difficult process requiring a two-thirds majority of the Diet plus a majority vote in a national plebiscite (the bill for which remains undrafted), the LDP faces an especially strong incentive not to defy stable opinion majorities. Bucking such majorities on security issues significantly increases the risk that constitutional reforms, especially those pertaining to Article 9, will fail to achieve a two-thirds majority in the Diet or will fail to achieve a simple majority in a national referendum.

When consensus democracy norms and institutions are present.   Consensus democracy norms encourage the view that simple majority votes are insufficiently broad to have democratic legitimacy. These norms therefore encourage super-majorities well beyond 50 percent plus one simple majority.[16] These norms enhance the role of public opinion, especially the views of vocal minorities and their representatives in the Diet. Peter J. Katzenstein sees Japan "as a non-majoritarian political community," where "minorities have considerable veto power"[17] Similarly, Thomas Rohlen argues "the Japanese preference is to avoid majority rule."[18] "The public need not unanimously approve of policies," according to Davis Bobrow, but "the great majority has to find them acceptable" with "the avoidance, or at least isolation, of dissent."[19] Akio Watanabe observes that the "ideal mode of decision making for the Japanese is one in which as many people as possible are duly consulted and not a single dissentient voice remains at the time of the final decision."[20]

Consequently, the LDP has often found it advantageous to avoid ramming legislation through the Diet even when it has had a single-party parliamentary majority. Instead, as T.J. Pempel notes, cabinets have often followed "the norm of cross-party consensus building. Usually, the LDP [tried] to ensure support for its proposals by at least one, and often more, opposition parties,"[21] or what is sometimes known as a strategy of "partial coalition" with at least one opposition party.[22]

On national security issues in particular, there is often a strong incentive for the ruling side to reach out to the opposition in order to achieve a wide consensus. For example, in 2003, Prime Minister Koizumi, despite having a secure majority for enacting landmark Emergency Legal Framework legislation, nonetheless chose to reach out to the opposition DPJ. In exchange for the Democrats' support, Koizumi agreed to several DPJ amendments to the bill. This compromise reflects the political advantages of obtaining a super-majority, a great consensus in other words, in Japan, especially as concerns security issues. Such dynamics clearly discourage a majority party from attempting to ram legislation through the Diet against the will of a united opposition backed up by a stable opinion majority.

The result.   What this all suggests is that policies are crafted to avoid provoking the opposition of a stable opinion majority. For all these reasons, the ruling side actively tailors policies that avoid provoking the emergence of stable opposing opinion majorities. Using polls and other means, the government attempts to anticipate the reaction of voters. According to Watanabe, "Policy means accommodation before anything else. What is most required of political leaders...is not the power to decide but the power to compromise."[23] As Bobrow puts it, "A party alert to electoral support," the LDP "will go to some pains to avoid defying public opinion...Polls enter into 'defiance avoiding' because...[ruling politicians]...have reasons to avoid bold, visible actions that run counter to them."[24]

When the ruling side wishes to push policies it is aware are unpopular, including those related to defense, it may go as far as to aim for voters' indifference point, where support and opposition is evenly divided, or where an unstable plurality or even a slim majority opposes a policy. Japanese cabinets avoid policies that go beyond this, and when a clear opposing majority emerges, they generally back down.

THE KOIZUMI PHENOMENON: THE USE AND ABUSE OF PUBLIC OPINION

The election of Koizumi as president of Japan's ruling LDP in April 2001, was seen by numerous observers as a turning point in both postwar as well as post-bubble Japanese politics. Koizumi was the seventh prime minister since the LDP lost its initial hold on power in 1993 (after thirty-eight years as the ruling party), and the fourth from the LDP. Although the LDP regained control in 1994 and had its party president Hashimoto Ryutaro installed as prime minister by early 1996, the Japanese public was again tired of the LDP old guard by 2001.

The unexpected death of Prime Minister Obuchi Keizo from a stroke in the spring of 2000 cast a further pallor over the LDP and the nation, as did the highly debatable way in which Mori Yoshirō was chosen as Obuchi's successor. Moreover, although he was once dubbed "cold pizza" by a foreign analyst (which caught on with the media), Obuchi had managed to generate respect for his fairness, willingness to consider outside opinions, and for his efforts at strengthening relations with Japan's neighbors. Mori, while personable, had lacked important political skills for crises. His public approval rating shrank to single digits as his administration went from misstep to misstatement and the economy remained mired in stagnation and the banking system teetered on the edge of crisis.

Koizumi's selection was a shock since pundits and insiders alike assumed that like most previous LDP leadership election contests, the outcome would be decided by backroom negotiations among the heads of the main party factions. On the surface, Koizumi stood little chance of being elected, as his support among LDP factions in the Diet was meager compared with that of former Prime Minister Hashimoto. On the other hand, Hashimoto's victory, as the candidate of the largest LDP faction, was regarded as a virtual fait accompli. The only thing needed, it was widely assumed, was the formality of actual vote counting.[25]

In the weeks prior to the election, Koizumi understood that he could not win it through the normal party faction process. Fortunately for him, this traditional process did not apply in 2001, as the LDP prefectural chapters were in full revolt and demanding a greater voice for themselves and ordinary party members in the selection process. The result was an open primary vote for party members. Although Hashimoto attempted to control party members' votes through traditional interest groups such as the Postmasters Association (*Taiju*), the LDP's 3.2 million members proved themselves to be more independent than in the past. As a result Koizumi swept about 90 percent of primary ballots, thereby carrying 123 of the 141 delegate votes representing the LDP's 47 prefectural branches. The local chapters and rank and file members were motivated by a palpable fear of impending defeat in the July 2001 Upper House elections, with Mori's approval ratings extremely low. With news of Koizumi's overwhelming primary victory, it was hard for LDP Diet representatives to refuse to back Koizumi, even though factional political strength among Diet members strongly favored Hashimoto. Among the 346 LDP legislators in Japan's two houses of parliament, Koizumi won 175 votes versus 140 for Hashimoto; a third candidate, Aso Taro, received 31 votes. Overall, Koizumi won an outright majority of 298 of the total 484 votes cast for LDP president.[26]

Koizumi succeeded in securing an overwhelming majority of the primary vote by making three deft tactical moves: (i) he resigned from his own faction; (ii) he called for broad cross-factional LDP support; and, (iii) he appealed directly to mass opinion and local party leaders. He promised drastic and painful economic austerity policies and renounced feel-good pump-priming pork-barrel politics. He also promised to reform, if not destroy, the LDP.[27] The public was captivated because Koizumi was not only stating the obvious, but was doing so in a political culture where direct attacks are considered certain to fail, if not backfire. Honesty and courage made him even more appealing as a candidate.

Koizumi could afford being blunt for a number of reasons. On the economic front, massive government public-works spending to pump-prime the economy over the course of a decade had not moved the economy into strong sustained growth. Public debt soared to over six trillion dollars and as a result Japan was being compared to Argentina. Japan's economy had consistently failed to live up to its potential since its real estate asset bubble had burst at the beginning of the 1990s. As a result, a consensus in favor of deep economic restructuring had taken root by the time of Koizumi's election.[28]

There was also policy paralysis within the LDP. As Japan's government debt increased, many wondered if drastic measures might not be considered to lower the ratio. These drastic measures would allow the Japanese economy to become more open. This was anathema to many sectors. Small shopkeepers and medium-sized businesses called for increased bailouts and farmers counted on protectionist and continued price support measures.[29]

Koizumi's victory helped to break the institutional log-jam and policy paralysis that Japan found itself in 2001. After Koizumi had swept the overwhelming majority of LDP primary voters, the LDP establishment reluctantly and belatedly decided to back him. Tanaka Makiko added her own charisma to Koizumi's reformist agenda and became a visible and vocal supporter (to the point where she was later said to have been the birthmother of the Koizumi administration). The two largest newspapers, the *Yomiuri Shimbun* and the *Asahi Shimbun*, both portrayed Koizumi as the only candidate seriously proposing solutions to the Japanese government's debt crisis and the looming failure of the banking system. Hayami Masaru, the governor of the Bank of Japan, went so far as to criticize existing government policies, and took the unusual step of openly backing reform.[30]

The media quickly portrayed Koizumi as a rebel, conveniently ignoring the fact that he spent his entire political life as a representative of the LDP. More attention was given to his good looks, wavy salt-and-pepper (and generally unkempt) hair, taste for rock music, and divorcee status. He seemed such a change from the aged factional LDP leaders that Koizumi's style became his substance. Dubbed the "Lion," Koizumi seemed youthful and current; he was the first prime minister to profess a liking for rock music. Public disillusionment and LDP desperation in April 2001 allowed Koizumi to glide in on a wave of enthusiasm and expectation.[31]

The old guard did not, however, disappear, and Koizumi decided to align with its nationalist elements even while targeting other elements representing vested interests, such as rural postmasters and pork-barrel construction interests. Even before he had assumed office, Koizumi had aligned himself with the right-wing nationalist LDP membership and their support groups such as the Bereaved Families Association (*Nihon Izokukai*).[32] He advocated constitutional revision, including of the war renouncing Article 9. Finally, he pledged to visit Yasukuni Shrine (a Shinto shrine dedicated to Japan's war dead, including fourteen A-class war criminals)[33] in an official capacity and did so every year. Both China and South Korea were alarmed at Koizumi's nationalism. Journals and magazines debated the depth of Koizumi's nationalism but even in this regard he seemed somehow in touch with a mood of apology fatigue, anger about China's perceived interference in Japan politics, and anxious about Japan being overshadowed by China regionally.

As promised, Koizumi formed a cabinet that gave key economic posts to advocates of radical economic change. More women were appointed than in any previous Cabinet, with Tanaka becoming the first woman to assume the power portfolio of foreign minister. In May 2001, it seemed as if Japan was on the road to serious reform. The public approval rating for Koizumi stood at 85.5 percent shortly after the start of his cabinet.[34] Because of the way he had won, Koizumi depended upon public opinion much more than his factionalist predecessors,[35] despite an image he later cultivated as being willing and able to defy public opinion. Because of the way he had won and the force of his headstrong personality, Koizumi's elevation to the post of prime minister was going to shake the political and economic system in Japan in unimagined ways. On top of this unpredictability came the dramatic terrorist attacks on the United States.

Koizumi's Response to 9/11

On September 10, 2001, no one could have envisaged the legislation and direction that Japanese politics would take over the next eight months. The events of 9/11 had a profound and unexpected effect on the Koizumi administration and Japan. Surprisingly, the hallmark of the Koizumi administration came in the area of increasing the scope of operations by Japan's constrained SDF. Koizumi's response to the terror attacks on the United States and his support for the war against terrorism have served to partially remold Japan's global image and highlights how the combination of a major event and a strong leader can transform domestic politics. By October 2002 the war on terrorism had seen one phase end with the overthrow of the Taliban government in Afghanistan, and the beginning of a second phase, regime change in Iraq. The third phase of normalization, stabilization, and democratization of both Iraq and Afghanistan remains problematic. This chapter concentrates on the actions of the Koizumi government in phase one, alludes to more recent phase two moves, and examines the role of opposition parties, such as the DPJ and the Japanese Communist Party (JCP), in representing and rallying public opinion against the unpopular Iraq War.

With the Bush administration determined to retaliate militarily for the attacks of 9/11, Koizumi was hard-pressed to find ways for Japan to contribute to the military operations within the confines of what Japanese public opinion would accept. For many officials and policy makers with poignant memories of the Gulf War, when Tokyo's thirteen-billion-dollar contribution to the U.S.-led coalition was deemed inadequate given Japan's economic primacy and global influence, the terror attacks offered chance for redemption. During the Gulf War, the reform-minded but weak Kaifu Toshiki government and a hawkish wing of LDP had pushed, but failed, in the face of overwhelming public opposition combined with opposition control of the upper house, to enact legislation allowing SDF personnel to provide noncombatant support to the multinational force arrayed against Iraq. As a result, Japan could only contribute money (thirteen billion dollars in all) and dispatch minesweepers after the fighting had ceased. However, with astronomically high public approval ratings then hovering around 80 percent, Koizumi was much better placed than Kaifu had been (not to mention his predecessor Mori, whose support rate was less than the inverse of Koizumi's support rate).[36]

Closely related to the issue of building public support were the limits set by Article 9 of Japan's war-renouncing constitution and the standing government interpretation thereof. This interpretation allows the SDF to defend Japan against enemy attacks but not to join bilateral or multinational collective-defense operations that involve using military force to defend others.

While Japan reacted with shock to the terrorist attacks on the World Trade Center and the Pentagon, and to the loss of more than twenty of its nationals in the Twin Towers, Koizumi immediately focused on the implications of the attacks for Japanese security and the U.S.–Japan alliance. Setting up an emergency task force in the prime minister's office within forty-five minutes of the attacks, he quickly decided upon a series of responses. A few hours after the attacks, Koizumi declared that the terrorist attacks signified "a challenge not only to the United States but also democracy," and he promised Japan's support for the quickly forming international coalition to fight terrorism. He also insisted on the need for Japan to quickly formulate "emergency defense legislation," and called for the Diet to convene in special session on September 27, in advance of its originally scheduled regular session.[37]

This was a bold step for Koizumi to take. He acted before consulting with the opposition. On the other hand, Koizumi bypassed his own party when formulating emergency legislation to permit SDF support for U.S. military operations in response to the 9/11 attacks. He first consulted with his coalition party partners, then with the opposition, and only then with the LDP's General Council and then the relevant committees of the LDP's Policy and Research Council (PARC).[38]

Conflicting opinions quickly surfaced. The May 1999 Law Concerning Measures to Ensure Peace and Security of Japan in Situations in Areas Surrounding Japan allowed the SDF to provide logistic support to U.S. forces if "a situation posing a serious threat to Japan's security" erupts in "areas surrounding Japan."[39] Several policy makers insisted the 1999 law was sufficient and could be applied to SDF support for U.S. operations in Afghanistan. "When the 1999 law was enacted, the government made it clear that (areas surrounding Japan) is not a geographic but a situational concept," said Iwaya Takeshi, an LDP Lower House member and ex-parliamentary vice minister for the Defense Agency.[40] Chief cabinet secretary Fukuda Yasuo, however, said he saw problems with stretching the law that far and instead suggested reinterpreting Article 9.[41] "As for the Defense Agency," Defense Agency director Nakatani Gen said, "we are trying to increase our options so that Japan's support will be visible."[42] Fukuda insisted "we will have to do more than we did in the Persian Gulf War."[43]

The DPJ was severely divided, with some advocating SDF provision of medical and refugee aid while other party members agreed with Fukuda, and some even suggested revising the interpretation of Article 9 to permit collective self-defense. Staunch defenders of Article 9 countered that the terrorist acts were not an act of war against the United States, but a crime and that the United States had not received approval from the UN to retaliate, making it different from the Gulf War. As such, they claimed Japan should act as a mediator between Afghanistan and the United States. Koizumi responded that Japan's planned support would be constitutional, but he refused to say at that point whether he would seek new legislation or invoke existing laws to enable SDF action.

Pressure to decide came during the week of September 16 when the United States asked the SDF to help guard its military installations in Japan. "As was the case so many years ago in the Gulf War, I'm sure they will want to be supportive, consistent with their capability and ability to be supportive," said U.S. secretary of state Collin Powell, the first top-level U.S. official to mention Japan with regards to the planned U.S. attack.[44] U.S. deputy secretary of state Richard L. Armitage also called on Japan to "show the flag" and play a visible role by deploying the SDF.[45] Politicians and talking heads argued vociferously as to what Armitage meant when he said "show the flag." This protracted discussion over Armitage's comments revolved around what he expected of Japan, an indication as to how strong American influence is and how reluctant Japanese public opinion was to get involved. Regardless of Armitage's comments, Koizumi promised, "we will fulfill our responsibility as a U.S. ally and we should not be isolated from the international community."[46]

On September 19, Koizumi unveiled a seven-point plan to ensure Japan would "show the flag." Koizumi announced plans to revise the SDF Law to allow troops to guard key public facilities in conjunction with police, such as the Diet building, the prime minister's official residence, nuclear power plants, and U.S. military bases around the country. The plan also called for the dispatch of MSDF ships and ASDF transports to provide noncombat, rear-area, logistic support, transporting fuel and other supplies to and from U.S. ships, providing intelligence and search and rescue support, and aiding refugees in areas well removed from combat zones. Another of the seven points suggested dispatching MSDF ships to gather information related to terrorist attacks and other points stipulated aid to Pakistan and India.[47]

The governing coalition, led by Koizumi's LDP, also announced that it was considering enacting emergency contingency legislation the following year that would temporarily exempt SDF troops from certain legal restraints in the event of an emergency.[48] Under the then current law, SDF members could have faced criminal charges if, for example, they had trespassed on private property without the prior permission of the owners in pursuit of fleeing suspects. It made no difference whether the suspects happened to be invading forces. The discharge of weapons was also severely restricted and SDF members could have been charged with gun violations. Although such contingency legislation had been studied by the Defense Agency since the late 1970s, enacting an emergency legal framework in the case of an armed attack on Japan was extremely difficult in light of the public's antimilitarist distrust of the state and Japan's war-renouncing constitution. Opponents, both foreign and domestic, declared any such legislation tantamount to unconstitutional war preparations.[49] Following the attacks in the United States, the legislative push gained previously unattainable momentum.

Koizumi used this dramatically altered international environment and strong initial public support to leverage the dispatching of the MSDF warship *Kurama* on September 21 to guard the USS *Kitty Hawk* as it embarked on its voyage to the Indian Ocean. The Self Defense Forces Law, however, does not permit MSDF ships to escort a U.S. ship in international waters. The government was able to dispatch MSDF ships to escort the USS *Kitty Hawk* by invoking Clause 5 of the Defense Agency Law, which permits the dispatch of the SDF to "conduct research and studies necessary for its duties."[50]

Koizumi also used the initial public support of his reaction to the 9/11 attacks to speed up the process of enacting a bill to permit the dispatch of the SDF to support U.S. military operations. He used the reversed normal process by consulting with the coalition partners, Komeito and the Conservative Party, before presenting the draft bill to the General Council and PARC of the LDP. This reversal of normal procedure sped up the process and reduced the leverage of internal LDP opponents of the bill. Komeito, which generally represents the pacifist mainstream in Japan, not least of all, the pacifist leaning lay Buddhist organization of *Soka Gakkai*, its main support group, expressed reservations about making an open-ended commitment to supporting U.S. forces in the Indian Ocean and to the SDF transporting weapons for U.S. forces or assisting U.S. forces preparing for an attack. According to Komeito leader Kanzaki Takenori, "the government should adopt a cautionary stance over the transport of arms and ammunition."[51] In response to these concerns the Koizumi cabinet agreed to a two-year time limit on the Indian Ocean deployment, and also agreed that SDF forces would not fuel or perform maintenance for U.S. aircraft or other weapons systems preparing for combat missions.[52]

Opposition party leaders claimed Koizumi was giving greater priority to speed than due process and called for proper legal procedures to be followed before embarking on such operations. DPJ and some LDP leaders such as Kato Koichi complained that the use of the SDF to guard the Imperial Palace, the Diet building, or the prime minister's official residence would give the impression that Japan was under martial law, and that, therefore, SDF personnel should not be used in this way.[53] Like Komeito, the DPJ also insisted SDF logistic support not include the transport of weapons or ammunition, and that prior Diet approval be obtained before dispatch.[54]

Ozawa Ichiro's Liberal Party argued that only explicit UN Security Council resolutions were sufficient to justify the dispatch of SDF units to faraway locales such as the Indian Ocean. The JCP claimed the deployment of SDF ships and troops would be unconstitutional regardless of UN sanction, and the Social Democratic Party (SDP) opposed all military retaliation. "SDF personnel never thought they would be assigned to lend logistic support to other forces in Afghanistan when they joined the SDF. It would constitute a violation of a contract, because they were assured that they would not have to die while serving their country," said Yoko Tajima, a member of SDP.[55] By contrast, Koizumi claimed "it will not do to say that we should not allow the SDF to go to dangerous places."[56]

Supporters of the new legislation argued that aiding refugees and providing medical aid in Pakistan and Afghanistan would be inherently dangerous and in wars where the enemy is not easily discernable it might become difficult to distinguish between the fighting front and rear. Many claimed for the SDF to be properly prepared, the conditions for rules of engagement (ROEs) with weapons must be eased to match UN standards for peacekeeping operations, allowing SDF soldiers to use force when perceived necessary to carry out their duties. Koizumi demurred, afraid that a drawn out battle in the Diet over an entirely new set of ROEs would prevent Japan from acting promptly and perhaps missing the battle once again.

In early October Koizumi presented three completed bills to opposition leaders. The first concerned the dispatch of SDF personnel. The bill Koizumi proposed enabled the SDF to provide rear-area, noncombatant, and humanitarian support to U.S. and multinational forces in the U.S.-led coalition in Afghanistan. The bill allowed troops to provide medical services, supplies, and other logistic support and permitted the SDF to engage in search-and-rescue and humanitarian aid operations. Although the bill limited SDF activities to noncombatant roles, it allowed Japanese troops to operate on foreign soil. The bill also eased restrictions on the use of weapons, allowing SDF personnel to protect themselves and also, "those who have come under their control," such as refugees and injured soldiers. Japanese troops would not be allowed to use weapons to defend U.S. or other coalition troops. Under the proposed law, the government would not have to obtain the Diet's approval before the dispatch of SDF personnel but provide post-operational reports upon the completion of SDF activities. The second bill allowed the SDF to protect its own facilities and U.S. bases in Japan and the third permitted the coast guard to open fire on suspicious ships in Japanese waters. Opposition parties, including the DPJ, were displeased.[57]

The DPJ demanded more control for the Diet, and sought an amendment that would ensure Diet approval prior to any SDF overseas dispatch under this law. Like Komeito during ruling party negotiations over the bill in mid-September, the DPJ also demanded that the bill be amended to prohibit SDF personnel from transporting weapons and ammunition for the coalition. Bowing somewhat to the DPJ, the ruling coalition approved amendments to the Anti-Terrorism Special Measures bill that forbade the transport of weapons and ammunition on foreign territory, although the bill did allow for the transport of weapons and ammunition in international airspace and waters. In subsequent practice, the SDF refrained from transporting weapons or ammunition for the United States, even in international waters or airspace. Koizumi also agreed to language obliging the government to obtain ex post facto approval within twenty days of an SDF dispatch or withdraw the deployed troops, thereby abandoning the original language in the bill that would have only provided ex post facto deployment reports. Not satisfied by this last provision, and having pushed for prior approval, the DPJ decided to oppose the bill.[58]

Shortly after talks broke down between Koizumi and DPJ leader Hatoyama Yukio, the Lower House passed, albeit without the support of the Democrats, the three bills and immediately sent them on to the Upper house. On October 26, a House of Councilors committee approved the three bills and on October 29, the SDF antiterrorism bill and the two other related bills won passage through the Diet, after speedy deliberations lasting only sixty-two hours.[59] No opposition party supported the bill despite Koizumi's diplomacy. As passed, the Anti-Terrorism Special Measures Law had a two-year time limit, during which the SDF would be allowed to provide logistical support to the U.S.-led force, engage in search and rescue operations, and provide refugee assistance. According to the legislation, operations would be limited to "noncombat areas," which would be defined by the government, and the SDF would be allowed to operate on foreign soil provided the host government provided its consent. Following the bill's passage, the government began mapping out a deployment plan so SDF units could be sent by the end of November.[60]

Following the passage of the bills, Japan and the United States held several security talks in Tokyo to discuss the details of SDF logistic support for the military coalition. The U.S. government informally requested Japan to transport fuel and other supplies from U.S. bases in Japan and Guam to Diego Garcia in the Indian Ocean. Bowing to domestic public opinion as expressed by the opposition parties, the Japanese government decided against transporting weapons or ammunition.[61] Before the bill was passed, the Japanese government had already begun discussing plans to transport supplies between U.S. military bases in Japan as part of its logistical support. The government also began considering a plan to transport supplies from U.S. bases in Japan to U.S. bases in Guam and elsewhere. The two governments agreed on November 1 that the Defense Agency's Joint Staff Council and the U.S. Pacific Command would coordinate the SDF's logistic support to the campaign. Japan and the United States also agreed to set up a bilateral coordination committee to discuss logistic support methods to help the Japanese government compile a basic plan and a section-chief-level working group to discuss the specifics of Japan's logistic support. It was decided the MSDF would be at the centerpiece of SDF operations, transporting food and fuel to Diego Garcia and refueling ships at sea.[62]

The government proceeded with caution, given that public opinion was becoming less supportive and thus increasingly uncertain about how the Diet would react and hoping to avoid further parliamentary setbacks or deliberations when approval was later required. The implementation plan required the director general of the Defense Agency to define a set of specific operational applications of the Cabinet-approved basic plan. After the prime minister's approval for the specific operations was received, the director general would issue an order to the SDF to execute the operations. The prime minister would then present the implementation plan to the Diet to seek its approval within twenty days after the Defense Agency issued the order to the SDF. Pending Diet approval, the operations would be carried out. The Japanese government decided to dispatch fifteen hundred SDF personnel overseas, including fourteen hundred crewmembers on six–seven maritime vessels. The remaining personnel included those working on ASDF planes ferrying humanitarian supplies to Pakistan. Seven-hundred crew members on three of the vessels left Japan on November 9 on an intelligence-gathering mission. The fleet included the *Kurama* and the supply vessel *Hanama*. The second fleet would be dispatched later in the month and would then join with the original three vessels to carry out their supply missions. The vessels' departure came more than six weeks after the government decided MSDF vessels could gather information to assist the U.S.-led coalition.[63]

In November and early December further legislation came before the Diet. On November 30, the Diet agreed to the deployment of the SDF. Even so, opposition was strong, causing a breakdown in DPJ party discipline for the first time in its history. "Within four weeks of the party voting against anti-terrorist bill, there was not even 1 mm of progress on how to secure civilian control (of the SDF)," complained one member of the DPJ who opposed the deployment plan. Thirteen members of the DPJ voted against the dispatch while fourteen others abstained from voting. In early December the DPJ reprimanded the twenty-seven party members who failed to follow the party line and vote for the SDF deployment plan. Among those reprimanded was DPJ vice president Yokomichi Takahiro who was handed a three-month suspension from party posts, along with the thirteen others who voted against the dispatch plan. Two of the fourteen who had abstained from the vote resigned from the party. Many of those disciplined, such as Yokomichi, were former members of the Japan Socialist Party, and thus had a core constituency opposed to the overseas deployment. This revolt also reflected the declining public support for the Indian Ocean dispatch by November—a trend that led to the cancellation of plans to dispatch an Aegis destroyer to join other Japanese warships there (see later). This outcome demonstrated how public opposition to overseas deployments that appeared connected to the use of force could split the DPJ.[64]

On December 4, the *Hamana*, one of the first three MSDF ships that had gone to the Indian Ocean, began supplying fuel to U.S. ships. The two other ships, the *Kurama* and the *Kirishima*, began supplying fuel shortly thereafter. ASDF C-130 cargo planes took off on December 3 to transport supplies to U.S. forces.[65]

On December 7, legislation concerning peacekeeping missions cleared a committee in the House of Councilors before heading to the full Diet for consideration. In the wake of discussions about Japan's involvement in Afghanistan, issues were raised about changing Japan's International Peace Cooperation Law. This 1992 law governs Japanese participation in such operations. The SDF's participation is governed by the so-called Five Principles.[66] These allow SDF personnel to use arms only for self-defense and also stipulate that the SDF may only be dispatched for PKO duty if a cease-fire is already in place. These Five Principles are such that SDF participation in UN peacekeeping operations conducted under the PKO law, "will never entail the possibility of the use of force or the dispatch of armed forces to foreign countries for the purpose of using force, or the deployment of troops overseas, banned by Article 9 of the Constitution."[67] In practice, the law prohibits SDF forces from participating in primary UN peacekeeping activities, or peacekeeping forces (or PKF, a term used only in Japan), and limits them to aspects of peacekeeping operations far removed from any hint of combat.

Since August 1995, the government had been reviewing the PKO law and the manner in which it has been implemented. In the past, debate has revolved around making international peace cooperation assignments a primary mission of the SDF, which would change the purpose of the SDF's existence. The new bill lifted the self-imposed ban on SDF participation in main peacekeeping operations. It eased restrictions on ROEs for SDF members on peacekeeping operations, allowing them to actively participate in monitoring truces and disarmament measures, patrol buffer zones, inspect the loading and unloading of weapons, and collect and dispose of abandoned arms. This new PKO bill enabled the SDF to protect "people under their control" consistent with the Counter-Terrorism Special Measures act passed in October. SDF troops were previously only allowed to use weapons to protect themselves.

During a visit to Washington, JDA director Nakatani agreed that the SDF would provide assistance to help remove the estimated ten million land mines in Afghanistan. Nakatani also explained that Japanese participation in the U.S.-led coalition was subject to two conditions: that military action is directly related to the 9/11 attacks and that military actions conform the UN Charter. The SDF is allowed to participate in the removal of land mines based on the 1992 PKO Law. During Nakatani's visit, the joint Theater Missile Defense System was also discussed: an indication as to Washington's next priority for the Japan–U.S. security alliance.[68]

Nakatani also elaborated on hopes that emergency legislation regarding the rights of private citizens during times of crises would be passed at the next Diet session in January. The legislation included amendments to the SDF Law to allow SDF to pass through private land, destroy buildings, and expropriate real estate and other assets, as well as revise laws under the jurisdiction of government departments other than the Defense Agency. Opposition parties have traditionally opposed legislation placing wartime restrictions on individual rights. The new legislation covered domestic measures against terrorism, including suicide attacks like those perpetrated on 9/11. The legislation Nakatani envisioned was the result of studies that began in 1977. In the past, due to such strong opposition, members of the LDP have not even tried to bring these legislative ideas to the table. "It goes without saying that the studies are conducted within the framework of the Constitution," explains the *Defense of Japan 2000* white paper. These moves prompted negative responses from Japan's neighbors.[69]

In the aftermath of 9/11, the Koizumi government reacted in a way that was undreamed of a decade earlier. With both speed and vision, Japan placed itself in a position as a global ally of the United States. The United States reacted to the moves made by Koizumi with delight. In conversations this author (Scott) had with a senior U.S. military officer in Japan, the lieutenant general was amazed at the speed and scope of Japan's new legislation. He remarked that the Japan of 2002 was certainly different than that of the Gulf War.

One should be cautious in analyzing these new moves. The nature of the arguments surrounding Japan's response to the terrorist attacks and the response that was eventually decided upon may not be indications that a more activist defense policy is gaining ground in Japan. The legislation, after all, had an expiration date. Koizumi committed Japan to a strengthened alliance with the United States at the most emotional time in U.S. history since the attacks on Pearl Harbor on December 7, 1941 (8 December Japan time). That Koizumi was at the helm of Japan's political ship was indeed fortunate. His charisma and personal appeal made his phenomena a high-value export item. The contrast, in short, between the bold and decisive Koizumi, and his inept predecessor, was huge.

Koizumi's words of support for the coalition came across loud and clear and the diplomatic, economic, and the military actions that followed his words gave credence to a new willingness to play a more active role in international security. In debating the new law to send troops to the Indian Ocean, however, Koizumi wound up strengthening the contradictions that have hampered Japan's defense policy for half a century. Instead of overturning the constitutional interpretation banning the exercise of the right of collective defense, Koizumi stretched the existing interpretation, thereby avoiding a potentially costly political battle. The Constitution bans the use of force to solve international disputes but there is no mention of the concept of "collective defense." The government argued that Japan cannot become party to the use of force but may, under the new stretched interpretation, support other nations whose troops use force. Koizumi himself used this reasoning to deflect opposition.[70]

A fundamental dilemma for Japan is how violent and extremist groups will both view and react to Japan being part of the coalition. The Japanese government has managed to skirt this fundamental issue by ignoring the more basic decision between involvement and noninvolvement. One theme of popular reaction during Japan's response to the attacks was that Japan could perform a plethora of other useful tasks to combat terrorism and, therefore, should not dispatch troops.[71] Little has changed in fundamental policy since the Gulf War.

What must be stressed is that Koizumi's actions in the wake of 9/11 and the Iraq War were dramatic but also constrained and cautious. In hindsight, with the Iraq War now longer than the Pacific War, with persistent sectarian violence, and with Japan's peacekeepers safely home having suffered no fatalities, Koizumi's ambitions, constrained by inter and intra-party rivalry and division and shaped by public opinion, ended up being not too overreaching. Deliberation, and the slow settling of both indigenous and exogenous forces, served Japan much better than a quick reactive command decision process.

Japanese troops have been sent overseas to support ongoing combat operations for the first time since 1945 and in so doing, Japan has set a legal precedent for its future role in overseas military operations. Nonetheless, no new principles for overall security policy emerged (such as recognizing the so-called right to "collective self-defense," or the right to conduct overseas combat operations in support of an ally) and contradictions between the nation's Constitution and its actions were left untouched. Even the innovative law authorizing SDF support for ongoing combat operations in areas far removed from Japan was set to expire in two years' time, returning the country to the status quo ante.

In this regard, Japan showed itself to be a complementary, cautious, and deliberative power. The Koizumi administration actively consulted China, Korea, and other Asian nations throughout this ordeal, and paid attention to public opinion much more than Koizumi's public persona would suggest, in order to avoid provoking a backlash.

This consideration reflects the continued importance of consensus norms in Japanese politics, especially on controversial defense issues. Although the ruling LDP/Komeito coalition had the votes to ram the Indian Ocean dispatch plan without the Democrats' vote, the desire to achieve as wide a consensus as possible provided the LDP with an additional reason to drop the Aegis dispatch. In 2003, Koizumi's willingness to accept DPJ amendments to the Emergency Legal Framework bill in order to ensure that party's support for the bill similarly reflects the importance of consensus norm. This consensus norm thus gives the Democrats greater leverage than their share of parliamentary seats would otherwise suggest.[86] Thus, the government's dispatch plan was modified as the Aegis was cut and the number of destroyers to be dispatched was reduced by one.[87]

Once settled, the Aegis dispatch issue did not remain settled more than six months. In early May 2002, as the first Indian Ocean dispatch plan approached expiration, Assistant Secretary of Defence Paul Wolfowitz asked a visiting nonpartisan delegation of Diet members specializing in security to push for the dispatch of an Aegis destroyer to augment the MSDF flotilla in the Indian Ocean supporting U.S. operations in Afghanistan. In response, the leader of the group Nukaga warned that because of a lack of public support, dispatching an Aegis under current conditions was "impossible."[88] Former Defense Agency director Kyuma, a member of the same defense delegation, told the Heritage Foundation that pushing the unpopular Aegis dispatch could endanger the enactment of the then pending Emergency Legal Framework bill.[89] Representatives from the other two ruling parties, Komeito and even the New Conservative Party, were also reluctant to back an unpopular Aegis dispatch.[90] Wolfowitz's even less popular idea of dispatching P-3C reconnaissance planes did not even meet with a reply. Thus, the Indian Ocean dispatch was extended for another six months without dispatching an Aegis destroyer or P-3C reconnaissance planes.

By November 2002, with the second dispatch plan approaching expiration, the issue of dispatching an Aegis destroyer and P-3C planes again resurfaced. This time the Koizumi administration pushed for the dispatch of an Aegis destroyer. Nonetheless, due to renewed opposition from within the LDP and Komeito, the third dispatch plan, extending the stationing of the MSDF flotilla, did not include the dispatch of an Aegis.[91]

However, less than a month later, Koizumi again resurrected the issue and quickly pushed through the Aegis dispatch. During a regular rotation in mid-December, an Aegis was dispatched, along with other MSDF ships, to replace ships on station in the Indian Ocean and Arabian Sea.[92] Opposition from within the LDP had not lessened, and Komeito remained firmly opposed. The weakening of Komeito, one of the major opponents of dispatch, appears to be the key reason for this policy reversal. In November a small number of DPJ members bolted from the main opposition party and joined the Conservative Party, the smallest of the three ruling coalition partners, and a party generally considered an appendage of the LDP.[93] These defecting DPJ members were believed to be seeking eventual (re) admission to the

LDP. This weakening of the DPJ (many observers saw this as the beginning of its collapse, just as the previous main opposition party, Shinshinto, had collapsed in 1997), like earlier discussions in fall 2001 regarding a potential DPJ–LDP compromise over the Anti-Terrorism Measures bill, reduced LDP dependence upon the Komeito. This increased Komeito's vulnerability and reduced their willingness to confront Koizumi over the Aegis issue. Thus, the eventual dispatch of an Aegis destroyer to the Indian Ocean reflected not a change in public opinion, but rather the temporary weakening of one of the main political forces giving voice to public opposition.

Despite the improved political environment for dispatch, the Koizumi cabinet limited the deployment in ways designed to minimize public opposition. Rather than justify the deployment on military grounds, chief cabinet secretary Fukuda emphasized that the Aegis dispatch was a way to enhance the amenities available for MSDF sailors. Because the living quarters on Aegis were supposedly plusher than those on other destroyers, sailors would "be thankful."[94] Moreover, the Japanese Aegis avoided any involvement in the March 2003 invasion of Iraq. After only eight months and the rotation of two Aegis destroyers into the Indian Ocean, no more Aegis destroyers were sent.[95]

Internal LDP Attitudes toward Public Opinion

Within the LDP one can find policy advisors who approach the issue of public opinion in a selective and even self-serving way. They advocate riding out public opposition to party policies while self-servingly citing public support to legitimate party policies and delegitimize opponents. One top security policy staffer at party headquarters cited public opinion polls supporting 1999 *Shuhen Yuji Ho*, or Surrounding Areas Emergency Law, to legitimate this law and discredit academics who wrote books opposing this law and the *Asahi Shimbun*, another opponent.[96] On the other hand, this staff expert argued that the best way to respond to public opposition to overseas dispatch of the SDF is to ride it out. The pernicious influence of a leftist media is cited as the reason for why so much of the Japanese public opposed the SDF dispatch to Iraq.[97] However, like similar public opposition to dispatching the SDF overseas to participate in noncombat peacekeeping operations, opposition to the Iraq dispatch would not have much political influence and would eventually evaporate, according to this expert.[98]

In other words, riding out public opposition will eventually pay off as the public, not the policy, changes. The party official also cited Korean president Roh Moo Hyun "as a model of leadership that Prime Minister Koizumi is following," because he is ignoring and riding out Korean public opinion opposing the dispatch of Korean troops to Iraq.[99] Reflective of this attitude is a remark by Prime Minister Koizumi during the debate over dispatching troops to Iraq, when he claimed that public opinion swings left and right, but that a politician's obligation is to maintain a consistent policy. This rather dismissive attitude toward public opinion suggests a reluctance to take

does have Iraq as an issue to criticize the Koizumi government. The JCP's position is clear and its regular use of dramatic posters garners sympathy. Nonetheless, this does not translate into support for the JCP among voters, because voters do not trust the JCP, having once adopted a revolutionary agenda in the early years of the Cold War, as a governing party.

The importance of the JCP in Japanese politics, society, and in the shaping of public of opinion is clear. There are few ways in Japan for citizens to actively be involved in reforming and shaping the public policy of the administrative state. The so-called electoral marketplace of majoritarian government is mired in an old-style model of representative democracy where voters have a small window of opportunity to exercise their influence on decision-makers. Japanese citizens are "enfranchised" but participation rates are falling, districts are gerrymandered, and a growing disconnect with policy-making is evident. Interparty competition has increased but there is insufficient intraparty competition, which would entail strengthening voting rights for party members, among other things. There is little "direct democracy" or "advocacy democracy." Citizens need access to government information, as well as revision of both administrative and judicial procedures to allow the incorporation of citizens to serve on advisory boards and have a voice at public hearings. The ombudsman system in Japan is still emerging, and only at the local level. Sweden, for example, established the first office of ombudsman in 1809. This office connects citizens to government. Other links are Consensus Conferences, which "are similar to citizens' juries but were developed specifically for the purpose of citizen participation on scientific and technical issues."[110] Japan has a limited number of citizen or consensus committees, no citizens' juries, and no new participatory initiatives.[111]

What this means is that the role of the JCP and other opposition parties is crucial. It opens the door to both alternative nongovernmental nonmainstream information and most importantly provides protest space. The discourse, language, and images produced by the JCP were powerful in reinforcing latent as well as deep continuities in Japanese politics. The JCP, the oldest political party in Japan by name, can trace its history of antiimperialism and antimilitarism back to the prewar period. While this lineage has a historical value for Japan, its prewar struggle (having been harassed by the government in the prewar period) is beyond the pale for the average voter. What resonates is not the use of the prewar Peace Preservation Laws for political repression, but the memory of 1945. It is here that the JCP fuses with a large segment of the NGO spectrum in forging a community (explored more in chapter six). This community is postmodern and post-Fordist. The traditional forms of social aggregation have been largely transformed as employment is restructured, the amount of casual and service labor increases, and the population becomes more flexible and floating. The JCP and the opposition thus form a political alliance with the new electronic-linked diaspora communities. Continuity of protest as well as the changing dynamic of information make the shaping of public opinion more problematic as well as dynamic.

CONCLUSION

The unintended casualty of 9/11 has been Japan's domestic reformist agenda. Koizumi was elected to begin to solve the twin crises of economic stagnation and political reform; however, 9/11 robbed him of time. Neither issue has been fully addressed. Although the economy began growing again under Koizumi, it is unclear whether this is the result of domestic reform, the clean-up of the bad-loan overhang at Japan's major banks, or the spillover effect of a booming China.

In any case, Koizumi has instead focused on taking the nation on an uncertain foreign policy course. In the short run Koizumi was extremely skilful at addressing almost all American defense requests in both phase one and phase two in the war on terror while maintaining fairly high support ratings. His approval ratings were so high in fact he could have conceivably pushed through a carefully articulated domestic reform program going beyond narrow and ultimately compromised initiatives such as postal reform. The skills he used to be chosen as prime minister would have worked wonders at the domestic political agenda level. The narrow window of opportunity was instead taken up with short-term emergency security legislation.

One can argue, therefore, that Koizumi's style was his substance. He managed to put a more attractive face to Japanese politics, placated the Americans, and amused some of the electorate. His most important pieces of legislation were security-related. Although American officials were extremely pleased and grateful for the show of support, even Koizumi could not really untie the Gordian knot of Japan's defense limitations or move Japan beyond the postwar Yoshida doctrine.

NOTES

1. Classic examples include Walter Lippmann, *The Phantom Public* (New York: Harcourt, Brace, 1925); Gabriel Almond, *The American People and Foreign Policy* (New York: Praeger, 1950); "Public Opinion and National Security," *Public Opinion Quarterly*, Vol. 20, No. 2 (Summer 1956), pp. 371–8; Thomas A. Bailey, *The Man in the Street: The Impact of American Public Opinion on Foreign Policy* (New York: Macmillan, 1948); Phillip E. Converse, "The Nature of Belief Systems in Mass Publics," in David Apter, ed., *Ideology and Discontent* (New York: Wiley, 1964), pp. 206–61; Michael Margolis and Gary Mauser, eds., *Manipulating Public Opinion: Essays on Public Opinion as a Dependent Variable* (Belmont, Calif.: Wadsworth, 1989); and Benjamin Ginsberg, *The Captive Public: How Mass Opinion Promotes State Power* (New York: Basic Books, 1986).
2. Miroslav Nincic, "A Sensible Public: New Perspectives on Popular Opinion and Foreign Policy," *Journal of Conflict Resolution*, Vol. 36, No. 4 (1992), pp. 772–89; "The United States, the Soviet Union, and the Politics of Opposites," *World Politics*, Vol. 40, No. 4 (July 1988), pp. 452–75; John E. Mueller, *War, Presidents and Public Opinion* (New York: Wiley, 1973); Sidney Verba, Richard A. Brody, Edwin B. Parker, Norman H. Nie, Nelson W. Polsby, Paul Ekman, and Gordon S. Black, "Public Opinion and the War

against War: Democracies' Responses to Operation Iraqi Freedom," *Foreign Policy Analysis*, Vol. 2, No. 2 (March 2006), pp. 137–56, esp. 149.

16. On these norms, see Arend Lijphart, *Patterns of Democracy: Government Forms and Performance in Thirty-Six Countries* (New Haven: Yale University Press, 1999), esp. chapter 3. Although the concept of consensus norms may seem unfamiliar to many American observers, the same consensual norms are embodied in American political institutions preventing simple majorities from changing the constitution, ratifying a treaty, recalling judges, or impeaching a president. Many of the rules of the U.S. Senate, most famously the filibuster, are based upon consensus norms mandating super-majorities.

17. Peter J. Katzenstein, *Cultural Norms and National Security: Police and Military in Postwar Japan* (Ithaca: Cornell University Press, 1996), p. 32; also see pp. 115–16.

18. Thomas P. Rohlen, "Order in Japanese Society: Attachment, Authority, and Routine," *Journal of Japanese Studies* Vol. 15, No. 1 (1989), p. 16.

19. Davis B. Bobrow, "Japan in the World: Opinion from Defeat to Success," *The Journal of Conflict Resolution*, Vol. 33, No. 4 (December 1989), p. 572.

20. Akio Watanabe, "Foreign Policy-Making, Japanese Style," *International Affairs*, Vol. 54, No. 1 (January 1978), p. 80.

21. T.J. Pempel, "Japanese Democracy and Political Culture: A Comparative Perspective," *PS: Political Science and Politics*, Vol. 25, No. 1 (March 1992), p. 11.

22. Ellis S. Krauss, "Conflict in the Diet: Toward Conflict Management in Parliamentary Politics," in Ellis S. Krauss, Thomas P. Rohlen, and Patricia G. Steinhoff, eds., *Conflict in Japan* (Honolulu: University of Hawaii Press, 1984), p. 263. Also see Lijphart, *Patterns of Democracy*, p. 108.

23. Watanabe, "Foreign Policy-Making, Japanese Style," p. 75.

24. Bobrow, "Japan in the World," p. 572.

25. Conversations with LDP politicians by one of the authors (Paul D. Scott) at the time confirmed the conventional wisdom that Hashimoto would be the next prime minister. Also see George Ehrhardt, "Factional Influence on the 2001 LDP Primaries: A Quantitative Analysis," *Japanese Journal of Political Science*, Vol. 7, No. 1 (April 2006), pp. 59–70, and James Conachy, "Koizumi's Election: A Turning Point in Japanese Politics," April 28, 2001, *World Socialist Web Site*, at http://www.wsws.org/articles/2001/apr2001/jap-a28_prn.shtml (accessed September 2007).

26. Ehrhardt, "Factional Influence on the 2001 LDP Primaries," pp. 60–2; Ikuo Kabashima and Gill Steel, "The Koizumi Revolution," *PS: Political Science and Politics*, Vol. 40, No. 1 (January 2007), pp. 79–80; and Conachy, "Koizumi's Election"; and Gregory E. Anderson, "Lionheart or Paper Tiger? A First-Term Koizumi Retrospective," *Asian Perspective*, No. 28 (March 2004), pp. 149–82.

27. Koizumi repeatedly promised "to destroy the LDP" (*Jiminto wo bukkawasu*). For the claim that this phrase was the defining image of Koizumi's tenure, see *Asahi Shimbun*, October 13, 2006 (international edition).

28. Conachy, "Koizumi's Election"; and Richard Katz, *Japanese Phoenix: The Long Road to Economic Revival* (Armonk, New York: M.E. Sharpe, 2003), pp. 13–14.

29. For more on this generally, see Katz, *Japanese Phoenix*.

30. Conachy, "Koizumi's Election."

31. Kabashima and Steel, "The Koizumi Revolution," p. 80, who report that the LDP sold around three million dollars worth of Koizumi paraphernalia in the aftermath of his election as prime minister. Also see Anderson, "Lionheart or Paper Tiger," p. 150.

32. For more on this organization, see its Japanese language website: http://www.nippon-izokukai.jp/index2.html.

33. For more on Yasukuni shrine, see John Nelson, "Social Memory as Ritual Practice: Commemorating Spirits of the Military Dead at Yasukuni Shinto Shrine," *Journal of Asian Studies*, Vol. 62, No. 2 (May 2003), pp. 445–67; and Tetsuya Takahashi, *Yasukuni Mondai* (The Yasukuni Problem) (Tokyo: Chikuma Shobo, 2005).

34. Koizumi's popularity would drop to 41.8 percent one year later in May 2002, recover to almost 70 percent after his visit to North Korea, and bounce between the mid-40s and mid-60s for the remainder of his term. In August 2006, prior to his departure, his popularity stood at 51.5 percent. See "Koizumi's Political Drama Drew Cheers, Boos," *Daily Yomiuri*, September 19, 2006, and Kabashima and Steel, "The Koizumi Revolution," pp. 79–84.

35. Kabashima and Steel, "The Koizumi Revolution," pp. 79–84.

36. Paul Midford, "Japan's Response to Terror: Sending the SDF to the Arabian Sea," *Asian Survey*, Vol. 43, No. 2 (March–April 2003), p. 337; Yukio Okamoto, "Mata Onaji Koto ni Naranai ka—Moshi Wangan Senso ga mo Ichido Okottara (Might the Same Thing Happen Again? What If the Gulf War Breaks Out Again?)," *Gaiko Forum*, No. 158 (September 2001), pp. 12–20; and Matsuura Koichiro, "Sono Toki, Gaimushou ha do Taio Shitaka (How Did the Foreign Ministry React at that Time)," *Gaiko Forum*, No. 158 (September 2001), pp. 21–7.

37. "Japan would Support Bush" *Japan Times*, September 13, 2001, and Midford, "Japan's Response to Terror," pp. 330–1.

38. "Statement by Prime Minister Junichiro Koizumi at the Press Conference," September 12, 2001, at http://www.kantei.go.jp/foreign/koizumispeech/2001/0912kaiken_e.html (accessed September 2007); David Leheny, "Tokyo Confronts Terror," *Policy Review*, No. 110 (December 2001/January 2002), at http://www.hoover.org/publications/policyreview/3462446.html (accessed September 2007); and Tomohito Shinoda, "Koizumi's Top-Down Leadership in the Anti-Terrorism Legislation: The Impact of Political Institutional Changes," *SAIS Review*, Vol. 23, No. 1 (Winter–Spring 2003), pp. 30–1.

39. *Defense of Japan*, 2000, pp. 117, 284–91.

40. "Japan must Avoid Treading Gulf War Path," *Japan Times*, September 20, 2001.

41. "Fukuda Hints at Change in Reading Article 9," *Japan Times*, September 14, 2001.

42. "Koizumi wants SDF to Support U.S. Action," *Japan Times*, September 18, 2001.

43. Ibid.

44. "Koizumi Seeks Law to Allow SDF to Back U.S. Retaliation," *Japan Times*, September 20, 2001.

45. "U.S. Asks Japan to Consider Providing Logistic Support," *Japan Times*, September 19, 2001.

81. "Shasetsu: Jieikan Haken Naze (Editorial: Why Dispatch SDF Forces?),"
    Yomiuri Shimbun, November 9, 2001.
82. "Under today's democratic politics, civilian control is assured, and the resurgence of pre-war militarism cannot occur." Ibid.
83. "Bei Shien no Iijisukan Haken Miokuri (Dispatch of Aegis Destroyer in Support of U.S. Postponed)," *Yomiuri Shimbun*, November 17, 2001.
84. "Yamasaki's Aegis Battle Lost to LDP 'Pacifists'," *Daily Yomiuri*, November 19, 2001.
85. "Kenshou Iijisukan no Haken Miokuri." Also see "Bei Shien No Iijisukan Haken."
86. Arendt Lijphart identifies the striving for broad super-majority coalitions as a characteristic of consensus democracy. See Lijphart, *Patterns of Democracy*, esp. chapters 3 and 6. On Japan as a consensus democracy, see Katzenstein, *Cultural Norms and National Security*, esp. 118–21; and Paul Midford, "Japan as a 'Normal' Democracy? Common Challenges with Other Advanced Industrial Democracies," *Journal of Policy Studies*, No. 15 (September 2003), pp. 73–83.
87. "Kensho Iijisukan no Haken Miokuri."
88. "'Iijisukan Haken ha Muri,' Chotoha Anpo Giin Dancho (Dispatch of Aegis Destroyer Impossible, According to Bipartisan Security Diet Members Group's Leader)," *Yomiuri Shimbun*, May 4, 2002.
89. "Iijisukan Haken 'Muzukashii' Bei no Shinpo de Kyuma Moto Boei Chokan (Dispatch of Aegis Destroyer 'Difficult,' According to Former Defense Minister Kyuma)," *Asahi Shimbun*, May 1, 2002. Also see *Asahi Shimbun*, April 24, 2002.
90. "Bei ga Iijisukan to P3C Haken o Yokyu, Yoto 3to Kanjicho ni (U.S. Requests Secretary Generals of 3 Parties of Ruling Coalition to Permit Dispatch of Aegis Destroyer and P3C)," *Asahi Shimbun*, April 30, 2002; and Tsutomu Ishiai, "US Makes Aegis Request Official," *Asahi Shimbun*, May 1, 2002.
91. "Iijisukan Haken Mondai, Ketsuron ha Miokuri (The Aegis Destroyer Dispatch Problem: Decision Postponed)," *Asahi Shimbun*, November 7, 2002.
92. "No Problem with Aegis Dispatch: Koizumi," *Japan Times*, December 6, 2002; "Iijisukan Haken, Komeito ha Hantai Kakunin 'Shincho ni Taio' (Komeito Opposed, Respond Carefully to Aegis Destroyer Dispatch)," *Asahi Shimbun*, December 4, 2002.
93. "Kumagai to Form 'New Party' with NCP and DPJ Defectors," *Japan Times*, December 25, 2002.
94. "Yotonai Chosei Tsukeba Nennai Haken mo Iijisukan Haken de Shusho (Prime Minister Announces if Ruling Parties Agree, Aegis Dispatch to Take Place by End of Year)," *Asahi Shimbun*, December 3, 2002
95. "Iijusukan, Indoyo Kara Tesshu he, Nihon Kinaki 'Kuhaku' Kaihi (Aegis Destroyer, Toward Withdrawing from the Indian Ocean, Need to Avoid 'Vacuum,'" *Asahi Shimbun*, July 3, 2003.
96. These opponents were dismissed as "anti-American" and "crazy." Tahara Shoichiro, host of the TV Asahi program "Sunday Project," was another target. Interview with a senior security expert in the LDP's Policy Analysis and Research Council (PARC), December 10, 2003.
97. This LDP security expert justified his conviction that Japan's media is excessively leftist by claiming that Japan's second largest daily, the *Asahi Shimbun*, still "celebrates the Russian revolution." He expressed a similar view about the then head of the Democratic Party of Japan, Kan Naoto, referring to

him as "essentially a Marxist." Ibid.

98. Ibid.

99. This comment was made before President Roh began directly and sharply criticizing Japan over its portrayal and handling of history. Had the interview been conducted even a year later, it is doubtful that Roh would have been held up as a model. Ibid.

100. Regarding the party's antimilitarist leaning tendencies, see Shunji Yanai, "Nihon no Kokusai Heiwa Kyoryoku o Kangaeru (Thinking about Japan International Peace Cooperation Bill)," *Gaiko Forum*, No. 78, p. 56; and the Research Institute for Peace and Security, *Asian Security 1991–92*, pp. 33, 115.

101. Based upon findings from Paul Midford, "From Up on High or From Below: Bringing the American Debate on Public Opinion and Foreign Policy to Japan," unpublished manuscript, Columbia University, July 1999, esp. p. 26.

102. "Coalition Leaders Split on SDF Bill," *Daily Yomiuri*, September 23, 2001.

103. Wada, "Tero Taisaku Tokubetsu Sochi ho o Meguru Seiji Katei."

104. See part 4, section 2, subsection iii of "The Anti-Terrorism Special Measures Law."

105. Ibid. Also based on Paul Midford's interview with an MSDF officer, January 17, 2002; and Midford, "Japan's Response to Terror," p. 332.

106. Christopher Hughes, *Japan's Reemergence as a "Normal" Military Power*, *Adelphi Paper* 368–9 (Oxford University Press, 2004), p. 127.

107. "Iijisukan Haken o Seifu Kettei, Kongetsu Chujun ni mo Indoyo ni (Government Decision on Aegis Destroyer, Dispatch to Indian Ocean Perhaps the Middle of This Month)," *Asahi Shimbun*, December 5, 2002. Also see "Iijisukan Haken Mondai, Ketsuron ha Miokuri"; "Yotonai Chosei"; and "Iijisukan Haken, Komeito ha."

108. For more on *Akahata*, visit their website (Japanese only) http://www.jcp.or.jp/akahata/. English translations of many *Akahata* articles are available at: http://www.japan-press.co.jp/ (accessed September 2007).

109. *Akahata*, April 18, 2004.

110. Christopher Ansell and Jane Grigrich, "Reforming the Administrative State," in Bruce E. Cain, Russell J. Dalton, and Susan E. Scarrow, eds., *Democracy Transformed? Expanding Political Opportunities in Advanced Industrial Democracies* (Cambridge: Oxford University Press, 2003), p. 180.

111. Ibid., pp. 182–7. Japan is now in the process of introducing a jury system.

and wide-ranging history of intellectual and public discourse in Japan. This trend remains strong today, particularly with the journals taken up in this study. Similarly, the history of the monthly intellectual journals as a forum for debate is quite long, with *Chuo Koron* (currently owned by the Yomiuri Newspaper Company) being the first of the still-existing journals to start publishing in 1887. Of the eight monthly journals surveyed, *Ronza*, published by the main rival of the center-right *Yomiuri Shimbun*, the center-left *Asahi Shimbun*, only recently began printing in March 1995 in what is a crowded but certainly not dull market. This section briefly reviews the history, philosophy, and current status of each journal based on interviews and written correspondence with the editorial leadership of each. After that, it takes a brief, comparative look at academic journals.

Chuo Koron

As mentioned earlier, *Chuo Koron* is the oldest of the eight journals surveyed.[2] Its predecessor, *Hanseikai Zasshi* (Magazine of the Hanseikai), began publication in 1887. Hanseikai, which can be translated as "the reflection society," and which served as the publisher of the magazine, was located within the grounds of the school affiliated with Kyoto's Nishi Honganji temple, the headquarters of Honganji School, a Jodo Shin sect of Buddhism. Hanseikai sought to debate and introduce to the readers of the magazine the direction in which Japan should be headed. In 1892, the name of the magazine changed from *Hanseikai Zasshi* to *Hansei Zasshi*, and in 1899, the name changed again to its current *Chuo Koron* after the publisher moved to Tokyo.

In July 1944, during World War II, the Army Intelligence Bureau directed Chuo Koron, Inc. (the company name change had taken place in 1914) to discontinue operations, and publishing stopped with that month's issue and the company dissolved on July 31. Following the end of the war and the occupation's canceling of wartime censorship, Chuo Koron, Inc. began publishing again in January 1946. The same month, it once again began publishing *Fujin Koron* (Wives' Forum), which first started in 1916 during the Taisho Democracy period (1912–25).

Most readers would probably agree that *Chuo Koron* has led the public debate on national issues during its 120-year history. Despite this success, *Chuo Koron*, like other monthly intellectual journals, has faced financial problems in the 1990s and was eventually bought by the Yomiuri Newspaper Co. in 1999. Its monthly sales are estimated at fifty-thousand copies.

Gendai

The next oldest journal is *Gendai*, published by Kodansha, Inc. *Gendai* began in 1920 during the time of Taisho Democracy, the era of political parties, a rejection of militarism following the end of World War I, and social freedoms. *Gendai* was the creation of Noma Kiyoshi, the president of Kodansha Publishing, which was founded some ten years before. In 1909,

Kodansha came into existence with the publishing of *Yuben* (Eloquence) hoping to "Broaden to the general public a great deal of knowledge," and since then has grown into a large publisher with some fifty types of magazines and book series.[3] *Yuben*, which became *Gendai* in 1920 as an attempt to improve its contents, continued as *Gendai* until 1946. *Gendai* reemerged in its present form in 1967, after incorporating the missions of the prewar journal *King* and the postwar journal *Nippon*.

According to the editorial office, currently one hundred thousand copies are printed each month, but many go to libraries and so the actual number of readers is unclear.[4] Despite the decline of nonfiction journals around the world, the editors of *Gendai* explain that they desire to be "the number 1 non-fiction journal in Japan."[5]

Bungei Shunju

The next oldest journal, following *Chuo Koron* and *Gendai*, is *Bungei Shunju*, created in 1923, the year of the great Tokyo earthquake. It is probably the most well known domestically and internationally of the Japanese monthly journals, with its sales reflecting this. On an average it prints 635,000 copies per month, and its March edition, which announces the prestigious Akutagawa Prize for literature, has even higher sales (in 2004, 1,185,000 copies were printed, the most ever).

According to its company history, shared with the author, it was founded by Kikuchi Kan, a best-selling author, as "a small literary magazine to showcase the works of a coterie of famous or promising authors."[6] At the same time, Kikuchi did not have long-term plans for it, content to see how it was received: "I founded this magazine whimsically and I have no definite plans for its future. If I can not collect enough articles, it may survive only one month. Or if it sells well and is prosperous, I may expand it and many newly written novels will appear and it can be a grand literary magazine."

While it started out as a literary magazine, it changed to a general magazine after the war. Its interviews and exposes, particularly on the illegal financial dealings of Prime Minister Tanaka Kakuei in the 1970s, which brought about his downfall, made *Bungei Shunju* a central voice in the public debate. At the same time, editors point out that they do not see the journal as having an influence on politics. Instead, "curiosity" is its driving force.[7]

Sekai

Sekai, or The World, is the next oldest of the monthly journals, having been established in 1946 following the end of World War II and in the years of the democratization reforms of the Allied Occupation. It is the farthest left of the journals surveyed. Unlike the offices of the other journals, despite repeated inquiries, *Sekai*'s chose not to share its history or other information in this study and as a result we are not able to provide a detailed description of the journal or of its sales here.

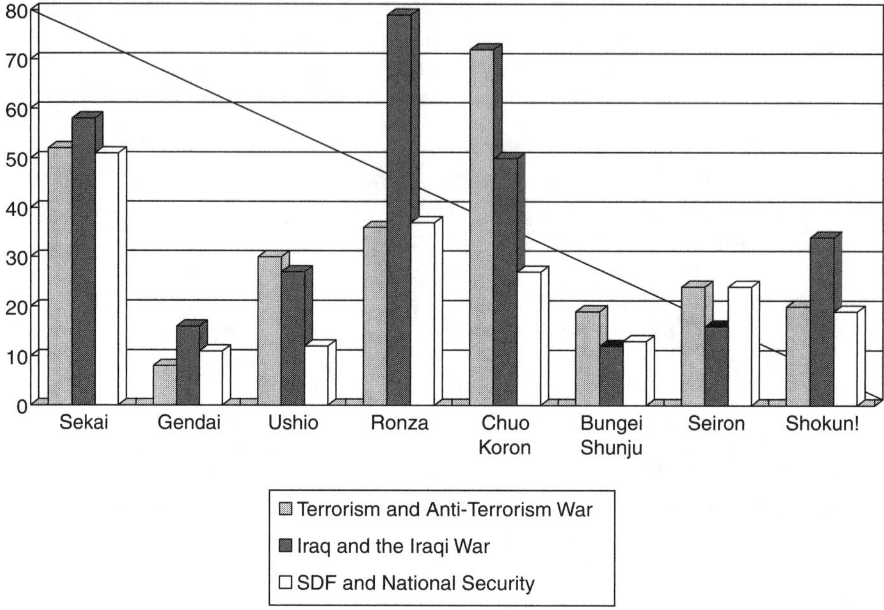

Figure 5.1 Number of articles placed in each journal on the three themes (between November 2001 and August 2004).

In addition to the monthly intellectual journals, articles appearing in academic journals are also looked at in this study. Admittedly, academic publications are not widely read among the general public, but they are read by almost all scholars of international affairs who in turn affect the public discourse in other forums such as symposiums, op-ed pieces, television appearances, and the earlier mentioned monthly journals by the wider use, or conversely, outright rejection, of the arguments of their colleagues. For this reason, the authors have introduced related discussions that appear in the academic journals *Kokusai Anzen Hosho* (International Security), published by the Japan Association for International Security (*Kokusai Anzen Hosho Gakkai*), and *Kokusaiho Gaiko Zasshi* (Journal of International Law and Diplomacy) of the International Law Association. Finally, the relevant articles by public intellectuals in an influential monthly journal called *Gaiko Forum* (Diplomatic Forum), published with the support of the Japanese Ministry of Foreign Affairs, are taken up.

Interpreting 9/11 in Japan

The 9/11 attacks on the Twin Towers of the World Trade Center in New York and the Pentagon in Washington, D.C., which took some three thousand lives, represented the reality of the threat of mass terror and shocked the entire world.

The incident also shocked Japan's intelligentsia and the following month, many articles and special editions began to appear in the monthlies and academic journals. Interpretations of 9/11 by Japanese intellectuals were various and numerous, but in general, they can be framed under three general categories.

The first interprets the events of 9/11 broadly on the scale of the history of civilization, arguing such positions as the "Clash of Civilizations," a view made popular almost a decade before 9/11 by American political scientist Samuel Huntington, or the "Decline of America." For example, critic Tachibana Takashi describes 9/11 as a conflict between Christianity and Islam and an extension of the history of the Crusades. "The 'Clash of Civilizations' is not a new issue," Tachibana wrote shortly after the attacks. "It has been going on for more than a thousand years. [9/11] is simply the latest manifestation of the result of this 1000-year conflict."[12] Conservative commentator Fukuda Kazuya, on the other hand, views 9/11 as the beginning of the decline of the United States, writing that as with the Roman Empire, "this was an incident in which, when civilization has to confront barbarians, the process by which it becomes barbarian itself begins."[13]

The second interpretation views the origins of 9/11 as poverty, oppression, and inequality, in other words, an incident that was born of the inherent contradictions of global society. The well-known peace scholar Sakamoto Yoshikazu, based on this interpretation, points out that "Many attribute the root of terrorism to poverty, but rather than poverty itself, I think the structure of social oppression, including poverty, and the acquiescence to this suppression are important factors."[14] Similarly, philosopher Takeda Seiji writes, "As long as a principle able to overcome the expansion of the inconsistencies of capitalism that is acceptable is not found, 'terrorism' will not stop and this will only lead to the repetition of new confrontations."[15]

Part of this debate views the pre-9/11 foreign policies of the United States as the problem. Critic Soejima Takahiko argues that the "United States of America has become too much the 'world empire' and the opposition and antagonism to this formed the background [to 9/11],"[16] and thinker Nishitani Osamu observes "the incident this time has shown that the very order [New World Order] that has produced the 'Clash of Civilization' has in fact historically and structurally gave rise to 'terrorism' and is only leading to the deepening of its radicalism. The [9/11] incident is clearly a result of America's policies after the Gulf War."[17]

The third interpretation is that the incident is not to be viewed in a historical sense or as a result of social contradictions, but as a crime, and one that must be punished.[18] Playwright and critic Yamazaki Masakazu pointed out that due to the lack of specific demands in the incident and the attempt to conceal their identities, the attacks were a "crime of self-indulgent pleasure" and thus "there was no choice but to first pass judgment on the crime. One can make allowances for their particular situation or consider the severity of the crime later, but to mix up the order and fall into an empty debate is not logical at all."[19] Similarly, Yamauchi Masayuki, a Middle East expert, points out that "Unlike states, terrorists can not be spoken or negotiated with on an equal basis."[20] Tanaka Akihiko, a scholar of international security, observed

of the use of force against terrorism, "There are those who say that the sending of aircraft carriers and bombers won't resolve the problem, but that to me is a ridiculous point. Of course poverty breeds crime, but it is certainly not all right to ignore crime while the issue of poverty is being solved."[32] Regarding the results of the war in Afghanistan, "On the military front, the military operations brought about results that completely refuted those questioning its effectiveness," wrote Tanaka Akihiko of Tokyo University.[33] These arguments are based on the view that the fight against terrorism is in fact a war, viewing 9/11 as a crime that must be dealt with by force. And diplomatic historian Iokibe Makoto of Kobe University (who was in the United States at the time on sabbatical at Harvard University) positively evaluated the response of the United States in the following way:

> if the U.S. under the leadership of President Bush did not stand up and fight and the terrible shock of the attacks, the world in the 21st century would have been forced to witness continued genocidal missions like the terrorist attacks. Fortunately, the U.S. after September 11 showed that when faced with a serious challenge it would respond even if it had to risk the ultimate sacrifice.[34]

Regarding the problem of legitimacy, Yamauchi Masayuki argued that legitimacy was preserved because the war in Afghanistan represented the construction of a tight net against terrorism and was "not a war against the people of Afghanistan but a strike against the Taliban."[35] Likewise, Aoi Chiyuki, who works on peace cooperation studies, wrote in the journal of the Japan International Security Studies Association, *Kokusai Anzen Hosho*, "the idea in international security of the 'domestic sources of international peace' has further taken root," thus positively evaluating the legitimacy of the war.[36]

Evaluations of the war in Afghanistan by Japanese observers are drawn from their interpretations of the events of 9/11 as well as being a reflection of the historic debate in postwar Japan between idealism and realism. However, the debate became much more complicated with the Iraq War, which followed shortly after.

EVALUATING THE IRAQ WAR

The United States, victorious in the Afghanistan War, turned its fire against Saddam Hussein's Iraq in March 2003. Earlier in 2002, President Bush accused Iraq, Iran, and North Korea of constituting an "axis of evil" during his State of the Union Address on January 19.[37] After that, in *The National Security Strategy of the United States of America*, the Bush administration announced that it would exercise the right of self-defense by acting preemptively against threats of weapons of mass destruction (WMD) and terrorism, advancing a hard-line policy that reserved the option of military action against Iraq.[38] It also stated that wars were best fought by coalitions of the willing.[39] On November 18, the UN Security Council adopted Resolution 1441, which demanded that Iraq provide immediate, unconditional, and unrestricted access to weapons inspection and mentioned that Iraq would "face serious consequences as a result of its continued violations of its obligations." Iraq accepted this resolution but did not appear to be complying.[40] As a result of Iraq's inadequate cooperation and the opposition from France and Germany to the adoption of a new resolution authorizing the use of force to make Iraq comply to supplement Resolution 1441, the United States, the United Kingdom, Australia, Spain, and other countries launched strikes on Iraq on March 20, 2003. On April 8, Baghdad fell and the Hussein regime collapsed.

As in the case of the Afghanistan War, Japanese academics in their public discourse questioned the effectiveness and the legitimacy of the Iraqi War. The issue of effectiveness in the Iraqi War mainly focused on the problem of WMD and the democratization of Iraq. As to its legitimacy, academics questioned whether preemptive action is acceptable, but deeper controversies existed than those of the Afghanistan War.

To begin, the authors examine the arguments critical of the Iraqi War, based on the question of efficacy. The academics of this position insisted that military action against Iraq would not lead to a solution of the problem of WMD and the democratization of Iraq. Like the intellectuals who believed that the cause of 9/11 was the fundamental contradictions of global society and argued that military action was not an effective solution to those problems, diplomatic historian Toyoshita Narahiko opinioned that "if we take a hard look at the question, 'who gave birth to Saddam Hussein in the first place,' we stand the risk of making another 'dictator' in the future."[41] Middle East expert Sakai Keiko observed that "we can say continuing the inspections may be more effective in the long run than a military attack even if it is a circuitous measure" and agued for the effectiveness of the weapons inspection.[42] Historian Matsumoto Kenichi questioned the motives of the war, saying that it is difficult to prove that WMD do not exist, and instead challenged "the U.S. and inspectors to prove the existence of WMD."[43]

Opinions regarding the legitimacy of military action were more severe than those seen at the time of the Afghanistan War. For example, international relations specialist Fujiwara Kiichi of Tokyo University, author of *Demokurashii no Teikoku* (Empire of Democracy), insisted that

> there is no international legitimacy when using farfetched arguments, such as the self-defense of the U.S. society or the emancipation of Iraq. The Iraqi war is clearly not an internationally authorized war in light of the fact that President Bush presented an ultimatum unilaterally while U.N. inspections were still going on…From an international relations perspective, the U.S. attack against Iraq is a war of aggression, plain and simple.[44]

In particular, on the issue of preemptive action, international law scholar Mogami Toshiki of International Christian University in Tokyo pointed out that "if such a move is accepted, preemptive attacks will occur legally all over

Still, it has to be mentioned that even among the conservatives who supported the war on terrorism, there were those who were critical of military action against Iraq. Most of these intellectuals did not doubt the legitimacy of the Iraqi War outright, but they criticized its effectiveness. For example, Nakanishi Hiroshi, a former student of the late Kosaka Masataka, one of Japan's most prominent scholars of international politics in the twentieth century, pointed out that "'the War on Terrorism' is a long-term war and we should fight against it quietly like during the Cold War" and viewed the policy of the Bush administration as that made in "haste."[61] Likewise Yamauchi Masayuki, introduced earlier, observed "It is too risky to change a containment policy into a plan for military action and a long occupation for Iraq and North Korea. It is not entirely certain that military action and its result will lead the U.S., which is fighting international terrorism, to victory in a long drawn out battle"[62] and insisted, in another article six months later, after the start of hostilities in Iraq that "it was necessary to give a full accounting and explain to the world" at the start of the conflict.[63] Moreover, Honma Nagayo, a senior scholar of U.S.–Japan relations and American political thought, questioned the prospects of the democratization of Iraq and had doubts about the democratization of Iraq:

> What should be done about a country that is neither totalitarian nor democratic and has little or no chance to construct a stable democratic state? Is it really appropriate to refer to the rebirth of Germany and Japan as democratic states after World War II as a precedent? More pressing, how realistic is the scenario that the democratization will proceed smoothly after the collapse of the Hussein administration?[64]

As mentioned earlier, the evaluations of the Iraqi War by Japanese academics were more complex than those of the Afghanistan War. In addition to interpretations about the effectiveness and the legitimacy of the military action, they contained various differences of opinion based on the views of the U.S.-as-empire theory and represented a crack among the conservatives. Whether the latter point was just academic or something more than that remains to be seen.

The Debate over Japan's Participation in the War on Terrorism

For Japanese policy-makers and for Japan's friends counting on it for support, the question of how Japan, which did not send personnel during the first Gulf War (1991) and was ridiculed by the international community, should commit itself following the 9/11 terrorist attacks was an important one. In the end, the Japanese government dispatched the Maritime SDF to the Indian Ocean to provide logistical support for the militaries of the United States and its allies in Afghanistan in December 2001 and dispatched the Air SDF and Ground SDF to Iraq in December 2003 for the sake of humanitarian relief and the reconstruction of Iraq. In this section, we examine the debate by intellectuals over Japan's participation in both wars, with a focus on the issue of dispatching the SDF.

As to the dispatch of the SDF in the Afghanistan War, viewpoints conflicted between critics who saw the issue in terms of the following question: "is it appropriate to justify Japan's military contribution for the U.S. revenging war under the cover of 'international solidarity' or 'humanitarian measure'?" (constitutional scholar Aikyo Koji[65]) and those, such as diplomatic historian Sakamoto Kazuya, who believed that it was important for Japan not only to act on behalf of the alliance but also for the sake of contributing to international security: "in this crisis, if Japan acts only to fulfill the duty of the Japan–U.S. security treaty, Japan–U.S. relations may be irreparably damaged."[66] When Japanese diplomats in Iraq were murdered in November 2003, the issue of dispatching the SDF to Iraq became more complicated and an even more heated debate emerged.

Most of the academics who criticized dispatching the SDF questioned not only the legitimacy of the Iraq War itself but also the legality of it domestically in Japan and whether the dispatch was in violation of the constitution. Critics of the legitimacy of Iraq War itself, such as political scientist Yamaguchi Jiro, saw the "essence of the SDF as a military participating in a faulty war,"[67] and Terashima Jitsuro described "the SDF as part of the occupational troops in Iraq centered the U.S. military, participating in wanton attacking, destroying, and killing."[68] Moreover, Tachibana Takashi wrote that he was alarmed that "in dispatching the troops to Iraq, I think there is a quiet threat of following in the footsteps of dispatching the troops to Siberia."[69] Similarly, international humanitarian law expert Koike Masayuki observed that "using the killings of the two Japanese diplomats as a stepping stone to dispatch the SDF to Iraq is the same as stepping all over the Constitution."[70] International law scholar Abe Koki argued that "in the decision to dispatch the SDF, which shook the core of the Constitution as the basic law of the state, the consideration paid to the U.S. government went beyond a normal alliance and put Japan in a subordinate situation."[71] These viewpoints are not especially new ones. From the perspective of academics who oppose the idea of military contributions, East Asian expert Tsuboi Yoshihara, for example, argued that "Japan has a policy not to follow the U.S. lead and has its own information and experience in non-military areas that the U.S. actually appreciates." This view was often seen in the discussions over the question of military contributions in Japan.[72]

On the other hand, diplomatic commentator Okamoto Yukio, a former senior official of the Ministry of Foreign Affairs and someone regularly tapped as an envoy and problem-solver for the prime minister's office on issues such as ministry reform, the Okinawa problem, and the issues of the Middle East, countered by asking: "is it acceptable to hesitate because of the potential risk? Just Japan won't dispatch forces? Is it better that other countries do? Is it right that we let someone other than Japan take the risk and we simply enjoy the benefits that Iraq doesn't become a collapsed state? These ideas aren't acceptable in international society."[73] Conservative international political scientist Nakanishi

Terumasa emphasized the dispatching of the SDF, pointing out that "in the incident of dying in the line of duty of counselor Oku Katsuhiko and secretary Inoue Masamori, all Japanese should pay attention that they were local representatives of the Japanese government and Japan...we should never forget that 'Hinomaru' [Japan's national flag] was soiled and trod on."[74] Moreover, Kitaoka Shinichi evaluated its effectiveness as "at first, Japan's decision to dispatch the SDF was effective in extending the morale of Coalition Powers" and pointed out that "if Japan decided not to dispatch the SDF, this would have shocked the U.S., Japan's only ally, and the coalition partners who would have been dissatisfied with Japan, although such a decision would not have did not violated the Japan–U.S. security treaty."[75] Similarly, as seen in military critic Kakiya Isao's argument, "if 'dispatching the troops' is abandoned or postponed indefinitely, the Japan–U.S. alliance may be fundamentally shaken," the effectiveness of dispatching the SDF was evaluated in light of the importance of the Japan–U.S. alliance.[76] In particular, this reflected the tension of the problem of North Korea's nuclear weapons development, and their opinions that "Japan dispatched the SDF to Iraq for the sake of strengthening the Japan–U.S. alliance and preventing having North Korea from possessing the capability to attack Japan with nuclear weapons" (political scientist Hara Osamu),[77] and "the most important agenda for Japan is to have the U.S. commitment in Asia. Japan should enter the Iraqi War for this purpose" (political scientist Kataoka Tetsuya).[78]

Of note, some of the academics who criticized the Iraq War actually supported the dispatch of the SDF. For example, Nakanishi Hiroshi pointed out that "now it is important as an ally and friend of the U.S. and that the U.S. not be isolated. Japan's action sends an important message that indicates the U.S. isn't isolated."[79] Similarly, Fujiwara Kiichi indicated understanding the SDF presence when he observed that he "would like to see a change in the U.S. military-led occupation. In creating a system by which other countries assist in the reconstruction process, it may be possible not to have to withdraw the SDF. Certainly this is a difficult task, but if we do not do so, Iraq will likely become a collapsed state more than ever."[80]

On the other hand, among younger commentators, one sees increasing calls for Japan to show a stronger independent identity. For example, national security expert Kamiya Matake explained "it is important that before one begins pointing out the importance [of the dispatch of the SDF to Iraq] to Iraq's reconstruction or the Japan–U.S. alliance, the most important issue is how this relates to the future national image that Japan wishes to portray itself."[81] U.S. expert Furukawa Katsuhisa said that "discussions in Japan are too focused on U.S. actions, and a view of positive 'homelandism' which discusses mid and long term policy toward Iraq in light of own national interest seems too weak."[82] Scholar of European diplomacy Watanabe Hirotaka also discussed that

> in it [dispatching the SDF to Iraq], it cannot be denied that there was as an incomplete level of discussion. Rather than full debate on the issue of attacking Iraq and the question of cooperating in the attacks, it was more of a result

of implementing "appropriate cooperation" for a while. The gap between explaining to the public and the international significance of the actions was consciously confused.[83]

Moreover Ikeuchi Satoshi mentioned that "we should ask what reason caused such a deadlock in foreign policy which Japan can't help deciding the dispatch without enough legal basis and preparation in such time rather than whether or not the SDF should be dispatched" and suggested the necessity of reviewing Japanese diplomacy itself.[84]

Finally, international relations scholar Watanabe Akio noted "in the present world, the most dangerous threat against our safety is international terrorism. In this context, [the dispatch of the SDF to Iraq] was not for the 'sake of the helpless people' of Iraq but an action of significance to prevent a disaster from befalling us."[85]

As mentioned earlier, the discussion over Japan's participation centered on the dispatch of the SDF followed by the problem of interpreting the Constitution and represents events to come as Japan implements military contribution. On the other hand, there was a wide-ranging debate going beyond the traditional "theological argument" over the interpretation of the Constitution as indicated by intellectuals who were critical of the Iraq War, but showed an understanding of the need to dispatch the SDF, and younger scholars calling for Japan's diplomatic posture to be strengthened.

CONCLUSION

As seen from the earlier discussion, the opinions of Japanese intellectuals after the events of 9/11 are based first on the respective interpretations of 9/11, and can be divided based on the appraisal of the validity and legitimacy of each issue.

When 9/11 was interpreted as being part of the broader history of civilization or due to the society's structural contradictions, the utility of the use of force in the war on terrorism and the Iraq War is challenged. On the other hand, when 9/11 is interpreted as a crime that needs to be dealt with by action, then the effectiveness of the use of force is viewed highly. Similarly, depending on how flexible one is when interpreting international law and constitutional limitations, the question of legitimacy changes.

Two characteristics regarding the debate of Japanese intellectuals on the post-9/11 world need to be pointed out. First, the debate on 9/11, the Afghanistan War, the Iraq War, and Japan's participation is also a discussion of America itself. This is seen by the fact that in the discussions on the Iraq problem, the description of the American empire would appear. The second characteristic is the fact that the conservatives split on the issue of the Iraq War. The conservatives are generally pro-American, and showed understanding with regard to the war on terrorism, but they split on the evaluation of both the utility and legitimacy of the Iraq War. It can be said that their split dramatically symbolized just how difficult the issue of the Iraq War was in Japan.

Often the debate by Japan's postwar intellectuals was between idealism and realism, a domestic version of the Cold War. However, in the post-9/11 debate, Japanese observers took sides on the questions of utility and legitimacy, and a free-flowing varied discussion less tied down by ideology was seen. This suggests that Japan's intellectual community is entering a new stage now, in this interpretation, what is being called the century of the war on terrorism. The debate is becoming more nuanced, and may be of more relevance to policy makers, political leaders, and the public as a whole as Japan makes its way in this post, post–Cold War environment.

NOTES

1. The journal of the Japan Association of International Relations (Nihon Kokusai Seiji Gakkai), *Kokusai Seiji*, did not carry any special issues on 9/11, the war on terrorism, or the Iraq War during the time that this study took place. The issue of the Peace Studies Association of Japan (Nihon Heiwa Gakkai), *Heiwa Kenkyu*, published once a year is slow in getting to press and thus the issues currently available include no coverage of these topics.
2. Correspondence with *Chuo Koron* senior representatives, August 3, 2004. Also see the homepage of *Chuo Koron* at http://www.chuko.co.jp/ad/ck (accessed August 2004).
3. Correspondence with *Gendai* representatives, December 1, 2004.
4. Correspondence with *Gendai* representatives, November 26, 2004.
5. Correspondence with *Gendai* representatives, December 2, 2004.
6. Kikuchi Kan, "From the Editor," *Bungei Shunju*, Vol. 1, No. 1 (January 1923).
7. Correspondence with *Bungei Shunju* representatives, August 6, 2004.
8. Correspondence with *Ushio* representatives, November 25, 2004.
9. Correspondence with representatives of *Bungei Shunju*, August 16, 2004. Also see the homepage of *Bungei Shunju* at http://www.bunshun.co.jp/ company/frontline01.htm (accessed December 2004).
10. Correspondence with editor of *Seiron*, December 12, 2004.
11. Correspondence with editor of *Ronza*, August 11, 2004.
12. Tachibana Takashi, "Jibaku Tero no Kenkyu (A Study of Terrorist Bombers)," *Bungei Shunju*, Vol. 79, No. 13 (November 2001), p. 110. Tachibana (1940–) is most famous for his expose of then prime minister Tanaka Kakuei (1972–4), which led to Tanaka's resignation. After graduating from Tokyo University, Tachibana entered Bungei Shunju, Ltd., and later began his writing career after leaving the company.
13. Fukuda Kazuya, "'Hakenkoku Amerika' Sono Shuen no Hajimari (The Beginning of the End of 'Hegemon America')," *Seiron*, No. 351 (November 2001), p. 38. After graduating from Keio University's graduate school, Fukuda (1960–) has been active as a conservative commentator.
14. Sakamoto Yoshikazu, "Tero to 'Bunmei' no Seijigaku (The Political Science of Terrorism and 'Civilization')," *Sekai*, No. 697 (January 2002), p. 59. Sakamoto (1927–) is professor emeritus of Tokyo University, his alma mater. His works include *Gunshuku no Seijigaku* (The Politics of Disarmament) (Tokyo: Iwanami Shoten, 1982).
15. Takeda Seiji, "Jiyu to Byodo no Anchinomii (The Antinomy of Freedom and Equality)," *Ronza*, No. 92 (January 2003), p. 41. Takeda (1947–) began his

career as a literary writer and is currently a professor of philosophy at Meiji Gakuin University.

16. Soejima Takahiko, "Daijiken o Tokiakasu 'Buroobakku Riron' no Kyokun (Explaining the [9/11] Incident: The Lessons of the 'Blowback Theory')," *Seiron*, No. 351 (November 2001), p. 50. Following his graduation from Waseda University, Soejima (1953–) worked as a bank employee before beginning a career as a writer. Currently he is an associate professor at Tokoha Gakuen University.

17. Nishitani Osamu, "Kore ha 'Senso' de ha Nai (This is Not a 'War')," *Sekai*, No. 694 (November 2001), p. 34. Nishitani (1950–) is a graduate of Tokyo University and currently a professor at Tokyo University of Foreign Studies, specializing in political culture. His works include *Sensoron* (Theory of War).

18. For the sake of disclosure, the authors of this chapter fall into this group.

19. Yamazaki Masakazu, "Terrorizumu ha Hanzai de Shikanai (Terrorism is a Crime, Pure and Simple)," *Chuo Koron*, Vol. 116, No. 11 (November 2001), p. 34. Yamazaki (1934–) is a graduate of Kyoto University and has been a professor at Osaka University and a well-known playwright. His many works include *Individualism and the Japanese* (Tokyo: The Japan Echo, Inc., 1994).

20. Yamauchi Masayuki, "'Hirakareta Shakai' no 'Teki' (The 'Enemy' of 'Open Society')," *Shokun!*, Vol. 33, No. 11 (November 2001), p. 65. A graduate of Hokkaido University, Yamauchi (1947–) is currently a professor at Tokyo University. His works include *Bunmeiron to Shite no Isuramu* (Islam as Civilization) (Tokyo: Kadokawa Shoten, 2002).

21. Tanaka Akihiko, "Tero to no 'Senso' de Nihon ha Nani wo Nasu Beki Ka (What Should Japan Do in the 'War' on Terrorism)," *Chuo Koron*, Vol. 116, No. 11 (November 2001), p. 105. Tanaka (1954–) received his doctorate at the Massachusetts Institute of Technology and is currently a professor at Tokyo University. His works include *Anzen Hosho* (Security) (Tokyo: Yomiuri Shimbunsha, 1997), p. 282.

22. U.S. Government, *President's Remarks at National Day of Prayer and Remembrance, September 14, 2003* http://www.whitehouse.gov/news/releases/2001/09/20010914-2.html (accessed June 21, 2004).

23. Sakai Keiko, "'Seigi'to 'Seigi' no Tatakai ni Suru Na (Don't Make This into a Fight between [Two Views of] 'Justice')," *Chuo Koron*, Vol. 116, No. 11 (November 2001), pp. 94–5. Sakai is a senior fellow at the Institute of Developing Economies (*Ajia Keizai Kenkyusho*) in Tokyo. Her book, *Iraku to Amerika* (Iraq and America), won the 2003 Asia Pacific Award (Ajia Taiheiyo Sho), sponsored by the Asia Affairs Council of the Mainichi Shimbun.

24. United Nations, Security Council, Resolution 1368 (2001), September 12, 2001, http://ops-dds-ny.un.org/doc/UNDOC/GEN/N01/533/82/PDF/N0153382.pdf?OpenElement (accessed June 21, 2004).

25. Miyata Osamu, "Isuramu Kagekiha no Taibei Zouo no Yoin ha Nani ka (What are the Reasons behind the Islamic Extremists' Attacks on America?)," *Sekai*, No. 694 (November 2001), p. 61. Miyata (1955–) received his master's degree at the University of California at Los Angeles, having studied at Keio University. Currently he is a professor at Shizuoka Prefectural University. His books include *Chuto Seiji Kozo no Bunseki* (An Analysis of the Structure of Middle Eastern Politics) (Tokyo: Gakubun Sha, 1996), p. 283 .

26. Kato Shuichi, "Bunmei no 'Shototsu' kara 'Taiwa' he (From the 'Clash' of Civilization to 'Dialogue')," *Ushio*, No. 516 (February 2002), p. 97. Born in

1919, Kato has been a well-known commentator since graduating from the medical department of Tokyo University.

27. Katayama Yoshio, "9/11 Jiken ga Imi Suru Mono (What the 9/11 Incident Means)," *Kokusai Anzen Hosho*, Vol. 30, Nos. 1 & 2 (September 2002), p. 65. Katayama (1956–) received his doctorate at Aberdeen University and after serving as an associate professor in Auckland University has been the head of research at the National Institute of Defense Studies. His area of focus is security studies, and his writings include *Seiji to Shimin no Genzai* (Contemporary Politics and Citizens) (Kyoto: Horitsu Bunka Sha, 1995).

28. Matsui Yoshiro, "Beikoku no Buryoku Koshi ha Seito Na No Ka (Was the Use of Force by the U.S. Legitimate?)," *Sekai*, No. 695 (December 2001), pp. 42, 46. After graduating from Kyoto University, Matsui (1941–) worked as a professor at Nagoya University. His works include *Kokusaiho kara Sekai o Miru* (Looking at the World from the Perspective of International Law) (Tokyo: Toshindo, 2004).

29. Terashima Jitsuro, "21 Seiki Nihon Gaiko no Kosoryoku Iraku Senso o Koete (The Power of Japan's Diplomatic Thinking in the 20th–21st Century: Beyond the Iraq War)," *Ronza*, No. 104 (January 2004), p. 23. Terashima (1947–) is a regular commentator on Asahi Television programs. After graduating from Waseda University's graduate program, he entered Mitsui Bussan. He currently serves as director of Mitsui's Global Strategic Studies Institute, and as a professor of his alma mater.

30. Matsuda Takeo, "Kokusai Terorizumu to Jieiken (International Terrorism and the Right of Self-Defense)," *Kokusaiho Gaiko Zasshi*, Vol. 101, No. 3 (November 2002), p. 4. Matsuda (1946–) is a professor of Osaka City University and is a graduate of Nagoya University's graduate program. His works include *Kokusaiho* (International Law) (Tokyo: Yuhikaku, 2002).

31. Asada Masahiko, "Doji Tahatsu Tero Jiken to Kokusaiho (The Simultaneous Terrorist Attacks and International Law)," *Kokusai Anzen Hosho*, Vol. 30, Nos. 1 & 2 (September 2002), p. 79. Asada, a graduate of Kyoto University, is currently a professor at his alma mater. His coauthored books include *Tairyo Hakai Heiki Fukakusan no Kokusai Seijigaku* (The International Politics of Non-Proliferation of Weapons of Mass Destruction) (Tokyo: Yushindo Kobun Sha, 2000), p. 285.

32. Yamazaki Masakazu, "Bunmei Tai Hanbunmei (Civilization versus Those against Civilization)," *Ushio*, No. 515 (January 2002), p. 78.

33. Tanaka Akihiko, "Beikoku, Iraku Kogeki no Mittsu no Shinario (3 Scenarios of a U.S. Attack on Iraq)," *Chuo Koron*, Vol. 117, No. 1 (October 2002), p. 52.

34. Iokibe Makoto, "Kyoki to Hakai wo Koete (Going beyond Madness and Destruction)," *Ronza*, No. 79 (December 2001), p. 19. Born in 1943, Iokibe graduated from Kyoto University before joining the faculty of Hiroshima University. In 1981, he moved to Kobe University. He has been a member of several governmental advisory panels. His works include *Beikoku no Nihon Senryo Seisaku* (U.S. Occupation Policy for Japan). He became the eighth president of the National Defense Academy on August 1, 2006.

35. Yamauchi Masayuki, "Posuto Tariban to Yuurashia Seijigaku (Post Taliban and the Politics of Eurasia)," *Chuo Koron*, Vol. 117, No. 1 (January 2002), pp. 43–4.

36. Aoi Chiyuki, "9.11 Go no Gunji Kodo to Kokuren Taisei (Military Actions Following 9/11 and the United Nations System)," *Kokusai Anzen*

Hosho, Vol. 30, Nos. 1 & 2 (September 2002), p. 88. Aoi received her PhD at Columbia University. After serving as a researcher at the United Nations University, she is now an associate professor at Aoyama Gakuin University.

37. U.S. Government, *The President's State of the Union Address*, January 19, 2002, http://www.whitehouse.gov/news/releases/2002/01/20020129-11.html (accessed June 21, 2004).

38. See U.S. Government, *The National Security Strategy of the United States of America*, September, 2002, p. 6.

39. See U.S. Government, Department of Defense, *Annual Report to the President and the Congress 2002*, August 15, 2002, p. 30.

40. United Nations, Security Council, *Resolution 1441 (2002)*, November 18, 2002, http://ods-dds-ny.un.org/doc/UNDOC/GEN/N02/682/26/PDF/N0268226.pdf?OpenElement (accessed June 21, 2004).

41. Toyoshita Narahiko, "'Atarashii Senso' to 'Furui Domei' ('The New War' and 'the Old Alliance')," *Sekai*, No. 697 (January 2002), p. 70. Born in 1945, Toyoshita has been a professor at Kyoto University, Ritsumeikan University, and is now at Kansai Gakuin University.

42. Sakai Keiko, "Fusein to Amerika no Sakuso Shita Kankei (Complicated Relations between Hussein and the U.S.)," *Ushio*, No. 531 (May 2003), p. 78.

43. Matsumoto Kenichi, "Beikoku Tsuizui ha Honto ni Kokueki ka (Is Going Along With the U.S. Really in the National Interest?)," *Ronza*, No. 102 (November 2003), p. 36. After graduating from Tokyo University, Matsumoto (1936–) has been a historian and critic, and currently is a professor at Reitaku University.

44. Fujiwara Kiichi, "Teikoku no Senso ha Owaranai (The Empire's Never-Ending War)," *Sekai*, No. 713 (May 2003), p. 59. Fujiwara (1956–) is a specialist in international relations. After completing from graduate school at Tokyo University, he worked as an associate professor at Chiba University before taking up a position at his alma mater.

45. Mogami Toshiki, "Kokuren Heiwa Taisei ga Shuen Suru Mae ni (Before the End of the UN Peace System)," *Sekai*, No. 711 (March 2003), p. 60. A graduate of Tokyo University, Mogami (1950–) is a professor at International Christian University. His works include *Jindoteki Kainyu* (Humanitarian Intervention) (Tokyo: Iwanami Shinsho, 2001), p. 286.

46. Nishibe Susumu, "Amerika Senryaku ni Haramareru Kyoki" (Madness Fraught in the U.S. Strategy)," *Seiron*, No. 369 (April 2003), p. 67. After working as a professor at Tokyo University, his alma mater, Nishibe (1939–) has been active as a conservative commentator.

47. Fukuda Kazuya, "Teikoku no Kage no Moto de (Under the Shadow of the Empire)," *Shokun!*, Vol. 35, No. 6 (June 2003), p. 30.

48. Okamoto Atsuhisa, "Chijo wo Oi Tsukusu 'Anzen no Sensei' ('The Tyranny of Safety' on the Ground)," *Ronza*, No. 96 (May 2003), p. 70. Okamoto (1959–) is a specialist on constitutional law. After completing graduate school at Senshu University, he has worked as a professor at Hiroshima University and currently is at Kobe Gakuin University.

49. Kobayashi Masaya, "'Han Tero' Sekai Senso no Kakudai ni Koshite (Resisting Expansion of the Global War on 'Terrorism')," *Ronza*, No. 97 (June 2003), p. 79. Kobayashi, born in 1963, graduated from Tokyo University and currently is an associate professor at Chiba University. His field is political

theory, and his works include *Seijiteki Onko Shugiron* (Political Opportunism) (Tokyo: Tokyo Daigaku Shuppankai, 2000).

50. Kitaoka Shinichi, "Nichi Bei Anpo wo Kijiku ni Shita 'Kokuren Jushi' he (Toward Making the Japan–U.S. Alliance Rooted More in the 'UN-First School')," *Chuo Koron*, Vol. 118, No. 5 (May 2003), pp. 58–60. Kitaoka (1948–) completed graduate school at Tokyo University and after working at Rikkyo University became a professor at his alma mater. His specialty is Japanese political and diplomatic history, and his works include *Nichibei Kankei no Riarizumu* (Realism in the Japan–U.S. Relationship) (Tokyo: Chuko Sosho, 1995). He completed his time as deputy representative of Japan to the United Nations in September 2006 and has since returned to Tokyo University.

51. Murata Koji, "Kyocho Sareta 'Iraku no Sekinin' 'Kita Chosen' (The Emphasized 'Responsibility of Iraq' and 'North Korea')," *Ronza*, No. 102 (November 2003), p. 44. Murata (1964–) studied at the George Washington University prior to completing graduate school at Kobe University. He has worked as an associate professor at Hiroshima and Doshisha Universities. His books include *Daitoryo no Zasetsu* (Frustration of a President) (Tokyo: Yuhikaku, 1998), p. 287.

52. Ikeuchi Satoshi, "Iraku 'Tai Tero' Senso ni Fusenpai ha Yurusarenai (We Cannot Lose in the Iraqi 'Anti-Terror' War)," *Ronza*, Vol. 36, No. 101 (January 2004), p. 57. Born in 1973, Ikeuchi studied at Tokyo University and then moved to Egypt to study Arabic language and culture before returning to his alma mater to earn his master's degree. After working as a researcher at the Institute of Developing Economies for several years, Ikeuchi moved to the International Research Center for Japanese Studies as an associate professor in 2004.

53. Yokota Yozo, "Kokuren Kensho no 'Hatten Teki Kaishaku' he (Toward a 'Progressive Interpretation' of the UN Charter)," *Chuo Koron*, Vol. 118, No. 6 (June 2003), p. 63. [A full English language translation of the article appears as "The UN Charter and the Attack on Iraq," *Japan Echo*, Vol. 30, No. 4 (August 2003), pp. 31–3.] Born in 1940, Yokota completed graduate studies at Tokyo University and currently is a professor at Chuo University. His numerous works include *Kokusai Kiko no Ho Kozo* (The Structure of the Law of International Organizations) (Tokyo: Kokusai Shoin, 2001), p. 288.

54. Shikata Toshiyuki, "Fusein ha Korosanai (Hussein Cannot be Killed)," *Shokun*, Vol. 34, No. 2 (November 2002), p. 73; and Mayama Akira, "Buryoku Kogeki no Hassei to Jieiken Koshi (The [U.S.] Armed Attack and the Use of the Right of Self-Defense)," *Kokusai Anzen Hosho*, Vol. 31, No. 4 (March 2001), p. 23. Shikata (1936–) is a graduate of the National Defense Academy, and earned his PhD at Kyoto University. He served as the commander, Northern Headquarters, Ground Self-Defense Forces. Currently he is a professor at Teikyo University, specializing in security studies. Mayama (1957–), a specialist in international law, did his graduate work at Kyoto University. After working as an associate professor at Konan University, he has been a professor at the National Defense Academy.

55. Morimoto Satoshi, "'Iraku no Jiyu' Sakusen no Kyokun to Imiai (Lessons and Implications of Operation 'Iraqi Freedom')," *Gaiko Foramu*, Vol. 16, No. 7 (July 2003), p. 42. Born in 1941, Morimoto graduated from the National Defense Academy and served in the Air Self-Defense Force before joining the

Foreign Ministry. After heading the National Security Policy Division of the Informational Analysis Bureau in MOFA, he retired. Since then, he has been a researcher at the Nomura Research Institute and a professor at Takushoku University. His writings include *Anzen Hoshoron* (On Security) (Tokyo: PHP Kenkyusho, 2000).

56. Jinbo Ken, "'Sensei Kodo' o Seitoka Suru Beikoku no Ronri (The U.S. Logic that Legitimizes 'Preemptive Action')," *Chuo Koron*, Vol. 118, No. 4 (April 2003), pp. 121–2.

57. Yoshizaki Tomonori, "Kokusai Chitsujo to Beikoku no Sensei Kogeki Ron (International Order and U.S. Policy on Preemptive Strikes)," *Kokusai Anzen Hosho*, Vol. 31, No. 4 (March 2004), pp. 10–11. Born in 1962, Yoshizaki did his graduate work at Keio University after which he entered the National Institute for Defense Studies. As a senior researcher, he has focused on European security issues.

58. See U.S. Government, *Remarks by the President from the* USS Abraham Lincoln *at Sea off the Coast of San Diego, California*, May 1, 2003, http://www.whitehouse.gov/news/releases/2003/05/iraq/20030501-15.html (accessed May 2004).

59. Kitaoka Shinichi, "Aratamete Toku 'Jieitai Iraku Haken' no Imi (Talking Anew the Meaning of 'Dispatching the SDF to Iraq')," *Chuo Koron*, Vol. 119, No. 2 (February 2004), p. 110.

60. Agawa Naoyuki, "Soredemo Watashi ha Shin Bei wo Tsuranuku (I Will Still Always be Pro-U.S.)," *Bungei Shunju*, Vol. 80, No. 13 (October 2002), p. 268. Agawa (1951–) entered the Sony Corporation after studying at Keio and Georgetown Universities. While at Sony, he passed the bar as a lawyer. He subsequently became a professor at Keio University, teaching American Constitutional Law and history. Among his works is *Umi no Yujo* (Friendship Across the Sea) (Tokyo: Chuko Shinsho, 2001), p. 289. He completed his time as minister for public affairs at the Embassy of Japan in Washington, D.C., in March 2006 and has since returned to Keio University.

61. Nakanishi Hiroshi, "'Kyofu to no Senso' no Jidai (The Era of 'the War against Terror')," *Chuo Koron*, Vol. 119, No. 6 (June 2004), p. 47. After graduating from Kyoto University, Nakanishi (1962–) studied at the University of Chicago. Currently he is a professor at Kyoto University. Among his writings is *Kokusai Seiji to wa Nani ka* (What is International Relations?) (Tokyo: Chuo Koronsha, 2003).

62 Yamauchi Masayuki, "Kita Chosen to Iraku no Akumu (The Nightmare of North Korea and Iraq)," *Chuo Koron*, Vol. 117, No. 1 (November 2002), pp. 66–67.

63. Yamauchi Masayuki, "Dai 2 ji Wangan Senso to Iraku no Saisei (The Second Gulf War and the Revival of Iraq)," *Gaiko Foramu*, Vol. 16, No. 5 (May 2003), p. 13.

64. Honma Nagayo, "Amerika wo Do Rikai Suru ka (How Should We Understand the U.S.?)," *Gaiko Foramu*, Vol. 16, No. 2 (February 2003), p. 17. Born in 1929, Honma graduated from Tokyo University, upon which he studied at Amherst College and Columbia University. He worked as a professor at Tokyo University, where he is now professor emeritus. Among his recent works is *Shiso to Shite no Amerika* (America as an Ideology) (Tokyo: Chuko Sosho, 1996).

65. Aikyo Koji, "Bei Gun Shien ha 'Kenpo no Wakunai' de ha Nai (Supporting of the U.S. Military is Not 'Within the [Boundaries of the] Constitution')," *Sekai*, No. 695 (December 2001), p. 55. Aikyo (1956–) is an associate professor

at Nagoya University. After doing graduate work at Waseda University, he worked as an associate professor at Shinshu University. His field is the history of British constitutional thought, and his coauthored works include *Gurobaru Anpo Taisei ga Ugokidasu* (The Global Security System Moves) (Tokyo: Nihon Hyoron Sha, 1998), p. 290.

66. Sakamoto Kazuya, "Domei no Haba o Hiroge 'Seiryoku Kinko' de Kyoryoku o (Expanding the Range of the Alliance and Cooperating by the 'Balance of Power')," *Ronza*, No. 93 (February 2003), p. 58. Sakamoto (1956–) finished graduate school at Kyoto University and continued his studies at Ohio State University. He is currently a professor at Osaka University. His specialty is diplomatic history, and his writings include *Nichibei Domei no Kizuna* (The Bonds of the Japan–U.S. Alliance) (Tokyo: Yuhikaku, 2000).

67. Yamaguchi Jiro, "Taigi Naki Senryo he no Katan ha Yurusarenai (Having a Part in an Occupation Not Justified is Unacceptable)," *Sekai*, No. 726 (May 2004), p. 85. After graduating from Tokyo University, Yamaguchi (1958–) has worked as a professor at Hokkaido University. His field is policy studies, and a recent work of his is *Sengo Seiji no Hakai* (The Collapse of Postwar Politics) (Tokyo: Iwanami Shinsho, 2004), p. 291.

68. Terashima Jitsuro, "Busshu Tandoku Haken Shugi no Hatan to Nippon (The Collapse of Bush's Unilateral Hegemonism and Japan)," *Ronza*, No. 97 (June 2004), p. 53.

69. Tachibana Takashi, "Iraku Shuppei no Taigi wo To (On the Legitimacy of Dispatching Troops to Iraq)," *Gendai*, Vol. 38, No. 3 (March 2004), pp. 42–3. The reference to Siberia has to do with the prewar dispatching of Imperial Army troops to that region in 1918 as part of an Allied intervention there during the Communist revolution. After the Japanese government agreed to dispatch the troops, the Army took advantage, according to the late Edwin O. Reischauer, and his collaborator Albert M. Craig of "its 'autonomy of command' and sent in many times the number of troops originally agreed on and kept them there long after the other Allies [including the U.S.] had withdrawn. This action was enormously expensive and enormously unpopular within Japan. It contributed to the declining prestige of the military, and the troops were finally withdrawn in 1922 with nothing to show for their efforts." See Edwin O. Reischauer and Albert M. Craig, *Japan: Tradition and Transformation* (Tokyo: Charles E. Tuttle, Co., 1978), p. 235.

70. Koike Masayuki, "'Fukko Jindo Shien' ga Dekiru Joko de ha Nai (This is Not a Situation in Which We Can Provide 'Reconstruction and Humanitarian relief')," *Sekai*, No. 723 (February 2004), p. 85. After studying at Helsinki University, Koike (1951–) entered the Foreign Ministry and currently is a professor at the Japanese Red Cross's Nursing College. He specializes in international law, and his writings include *Kokusai Jindoho* (International Humanitarian Law) (Tokyo: Asahi Sensho, 2002).

71. Abe Koki, "Hahei ha 'Fu Seigi' he no Katan de Aru (Dispatching Troops is Playing a Part in the 'Injustice')," *Sekai*, No. 721 (December 2003), p. 49. Abe (1958–) completed graduate school at Waseda University and currently is a professor at Kanagawa University. His specialty is constitutional law and his works include *Jinken no Kokusaika* (The Internationalization of Human Rights) (Tokyo: Gendai Jinbun Sha, 1998).

72. Tsuboi Yoshiharu, "Tai Tero Ajia Kokusai Kyoryoku Taisei no Kochiku wo (Construct an Anti-Terrorist, Asian International Cooperative System),"

Sekai, No. 695 (December 2001), p. 58. Tsuboi (1948–) earned his PhD in Paris. After working as a professor at Hokkaido University, he joined the faculty of Waseda University. He specializes in Vietnamese studies, with one of his books titled *Betonamu Gendai Seiji* (Contemporary Politics in Vietnam).

73. Okamoto Yukio, "Wangan Senso no Yona Kakon wo Nokosanai Tameni (In Order Not to Leave Problems like those After the Gulf War)," *Chuo Koron*, Vol. 118, No. 11 (November 2003), p. 110. After graduating from Hitotsubashi University, Okamoto (1945–) joined the Foreign Ministry. He served as director of the North American Division. After retiring, he established the consulting firm Okamoto Associates.

74. Nakanishi Terumasa, "Koizumi Shusho yo 'Rekishi no Chosen' wo Ukete Tate (Prime Minister Koizumi, Stand Up and Accept 'the History Challenge')," *Shokun*, Vol. 36, No. 2 (February 2004), p. 48. Nakanishi (1947–) studied at Cambridge University and after working as a professor at Shizuoka Prefectural University, joined the faculty at Kyoto University. His books include the *Daiei Teikoku Suiboshi* (History of the Decline of the British Empire) (Tokyo: PHP Bunko, 2004), p. 293.

75. Kitaoka Shinichi, "Aratamete Toku 'Jieitai Iraku Haken' no Imiai," pp. 112–13.

76. Kakiya Isao, "Jieitai ga Iraku ni Ikanakattara Do Naru ka (What Would Happen if the SDF Doesn't go to Iraq?)," *Seiron*, No. 380 (February 2004), p. 104. Kakiya (1938–) entered the Ground Self-Defense Forces after graduating from the National Defense Academy. After completing graduate school at Osaka University, he became a professor at the Academy. Currently, he is a commentator.

77. Hara Osamu, "Jieitai Iraku Haken ha Tai Kita Chosen Seisaku de Aru (Dispatching the SDF is a Policy Toward North Korea)," *Seiron*, No. 384 (June 2004), p. 91. Hara received his PhD at the University of Hawaii and is currently a lecturer at Hiroshima Women's College. His field is the international relations of the Asia–Pacific.

78. Kataoka Tetsuya, "Waga Jieitai no 'Tai Iraku Senso' Sansen Ron no Settoku Ryoku (Persuasion of the Theory of Joining our SDF into 'the Iraqi War')," *Seiron*, No. 366 (January 2003), p. 282. Born in 1933, Kataoka completed graduate school at the University of Chicago. He worked as a professor of political science at Tsukuba University before becoming a researcher at the Hoover Institute of Stanford University.

79. Nakanishi Hiroshi, "Kokusai Seiji kara Mita 'Jieitai Iraku Haken' no Imi (The Significance of 'Dispatching the SDF to Iraq' from the View of International Politics)," *Ushio*, No. 541 (March 2003), p. 159.

80. Fujiwara Kiichi, "Iraku Wahei to Nippon no Yakuwari (Peace in Iraq and the Role of Japan)," *Ushio*, No. 544 (June 2004), p. 160.

81. Kamiya Matake, "Naze Jieitai o Iraku ni Haken Suru no ka (Why Dispatch the SDF to Iraq?)," *Gaiko Foramu*, Vol. 117, No. 3 (March 2004), pp. 26–7. Born in 1961, Kamiya graduated from Tokyo University. After completing graduating school at Columbia University, he has worked as a professor at the National Defense Academy. His field is international security studies, and nuclear issues in particular.

82. Furukawa Katsuhisa, "Fusein ha Naze Saidai no Kyoi ka (Why is Hussein the Biggest Threat?)," *Ronza*, No. 93 (February 2003), p. 75. Furukawa (1966–)

studied at the Kennedy School of Government at Harvard, and worked as a researcher at the Council on Foreign Relations before becoming a researcher at the Washington office of the Monterey Institute of International Studies. His field is security policy.

83. Watanabe Hirotaka, "Nichi Bei Domei to Sekai Anzen Hosho no Kishimi (The Japan–U.S. Alliance and Creak of World Security)," *Chuo Koron*, Vol. 118, No. 2 (February 2003), p. 97. Watanabe (1954–) earned his PhD in Paris and worked as a visiting researcher at the George Washington University. His specialty is French political and diplomatic history, and his works include *Yooroppa Kokusai Kankeishi* (The International Relations History of Europe) (Tokyo: Yuhikaku, 2002).

84. Ikeuchi Satoshi, "Iraku Kokumin no Niizu wo Shirukoto ga Senketsu da (Knowing the Needs of the Iraqi People is Top Priority)," *Chuo Koron*, Vol. 119, No. 2 (February 2004), pp. 128–9.

85. Watanabe Akio, "'Senso' wa Omoku, 'Jindo Shien' ha Karui to Iu Sakkaku (The Illusion that Regards 'War' as Serious and 'Humanitarian Assistance' as Light)," *Chuo Koron*, Vol. 119, No. 2 (February 2004), p. 41. Watanabe (1932–), a graduate of Tokyo University, worked as a professor at his alma mater before becoming president of the Research Institute for Peace and Security. He served as a member of the Defense Advisory Panel during the Hosokawa Morihiro cabinet. His numerous writings include *Ajia Taiheiyo no Kokusai Kankei to Nihon* (The International Relations of the Asia–Pacific and Japan) (Tokyo: Tokyo Daigaku Shuppankai, 1992).

CHAPTER 6

Japanese Civil Society, NGOs, and Spatialized Politics: Mobilizing Public Opinion and the War in Iraq

Paul D. Scott

INTRODUCTION

Japan in the postwar period has won respect for its economic growth but not trust for its intentions. In nominal terms, Japan's percentage of the world's GDP outstrips any other nation in the region, and the new triad of power—aid, trade, and investment—should put it in a strong potential leadership role, but in fact Japan has few followers. Doubts linger as those in policy-making positions as well as those at the fringes of policy-making send out mixed and conflicting signals regarding its intentions and values. Public policy does not exist without a public, and the debate over the nature and values of the public at large cannot be easily categorized although they are easily stereotyped.

There were two direct consequences of the terror attacks of 9/11 on far-away Japan: the testing of Japan's new leadership under crisis and the public's response to the lifting of limits on Japan's expansion of its military role. Prime Minister Koizumi Junichiro's quick responses to the needs of Washington were clear and unambiguous. Japan would not repeat its Gulf War passivity but would play an active and assertive role by "showing the (Japanese) flag" and supporting the coalition of the willing. Japan as a latecomer to global politics would, at the turn of the twenty-first century, once again seek outside certification that it had arrived to play an enlarged role. Koizumi would view the charged post-9/11 climate to meld and mold a new engaged Japan. The American government was overjoyed with the response. Japan's power would be certified. The relevant question concerning this chapter is how Koizumi's vision would interact with Japan's civil society.

The Koizumi administration was steering the state and the Self-Defense Forces into untested waters. To implement this new agenda, he would have to both confront and engage public opinion and civil society, as well as factions within his own party, coalition partners, and the opposition parties (see chapters one and five for more on public opinion, and chapter four for political parties).

In this latter debate, the role of the nongovernmental organization (NGO) community in responding to the actions and policies of the Japanese government is a key indicator of the shape of Japan's postwar civil society and is the subject of this chapter. The chapter, organized into six sections, attempts to demonstrate that Japan's civil society is not well organized, borders on the atomistic, and yet despite or perhaps because of this, it helps to form and articulate public opinion, and thereby exert a passive influence over public policy.

Postwar Japan has developed a set of values that on the surface have been largely incorporated and partially internalized by its society and somewhat reflected in the polity. The previous sentence is cautionary in the extreme. It would be facile to say that Japanese society and politics has fully accepted the judgment of the International Military Tribunal for the Far East (IMTFE—or the Tokyo War Crimes Trial), the American-authored constitution and its clauses on equal rights and the much debated Article 9 no-war clause. Even former prime minister Sato Eisaku's much touted three non-nuclear principles that earned him a Nobel Peace Prize is not a cause of celebration. There are many stable bridges still intact that lead back to the wartime and prewar periods. There is more than a cottage industry in recreating the wartime period in glorious terms. The dividing line of August 15, 1945, is more dotted than demarcated. It is true, however, that international violence and war are publicly taboo.[1] Peace museums, both public and private, are numerous, the best well known being those in Hiroshima, Nagasaki, Osaka, Kyoto, and Okinawa. Human rights and peace education is part of the public school curriculum. This is not to say that all of these values have been wholly internalized or fully accepted. There are vocal and sometimes violent actions against those who rally in support of pacifism and what some may even consider the re-gendering or feminization of Japanese society. This battle between what we may call a reinvented *Shin Dai Nippon shugi* (New Big Japanism) and an older *Sho Nippon shugi* (Small Japanism) has been waged since the Meiji period.[2] Simply put, the former is more hierarchical, centralized, industrialized, and militarized, while the latter is more egalitarian, communal, agricultural, and pacifist.

These conflicting features of postwar society have allowed space for peace (or antiwar) NGOs to operate as the messages that they play are simple and direct and are not alien or imposed.[3] Opposition to Koizumi's visits to Yasukuni Shrine is as much a local reaction as an international one. On a more recent controversy, Defense Minister Kyuma Fumio's remarks in the summer of 2007 that appeared to justify the U.S. dropping of atomic bombs on Hiroshima and Nagasaki was a statement that caused his abrupt resignation. In an odd way, both historical revisionists as well as antiwar pacifists were outraged.[4] This issue clearly indicates that Japan has not fully stepped out of the postwar period. Outrage also indicates that civil society actors are ready to voice their opinions and are capable of articulating wider public opinion. This competition for support does not imply a level playing field as more statist forces, the prime minister's office, and the newly created Ministry of Defense use their power to guide and steer Japan away from overt antiwar sentiment.

This fractured domestic sentiment is where the Koizumi administration's promotion of policies that were seen as threatening to abruptly change the course of postwar Japan's constitutional restraints created a mobilization of civil society groups both opposed and in favor of where he wanted to go. By no means does this imply that all anti-Koizumi groups spoke with a unified voice, however.

It is also important to note that Koizumi's sharp break with the past also motivated right-wing factions as well, groups that demanded more nationalistic policies. Manifestations of right-wing civil society, such as the Society for History Textbook Reform (*Atarashii Rekishi Kyokasho Tsukurukai*),[5] and the *Nippon Izokukai* (The Japan Society of War-Bereaved),[6] echo prewar values and narratives and have powerful allies among elected politicians and right-wing pressure groups.

The very nature of NGOs is often contra-authoritarian. Individualism coupled with a distrust of authority are hallmarks. Cross-cutting themes are evident but this does not lead to long-lasting horizontal integration.

A traditional view of Japan has been that due to hierarchy and status consciousness, and time restraints, informal voluntary organizations were not part of the Japanese landscape. However, recent research demonstrates otherwise: between the early 1960s and the mid-1990s, there was a literal explosion in informal voluntary organizations. Between 1960 and 1991 the number of interest groups in Japan tripled, while internally these organizations moved toward "greater participation and pluralization." During this period business associations increased almost 300 percent, labor associations, 325 percent, political associations by nearly 500 percent, and academic associations by nearly 600 percent. "Other associations," which include "civic associations along with foundations and quasi-official bodies," increased 411 percent over this period.[7] Other research reinforces this finding. For example, the Japanese newspaper *Asahi Shimbun* found that the number of Japanese belonging to consumer cooperatives more than quadrupled between 1970 and 1995, growing from 12.7 to 45.2 million people.[8] Despite the rapid growth in civic organization in Japan between the 1960s and the early 1990s, the number of interest groups per one hundred thousand people remained much lower in Japan than in the United States: 29.2 for Japan versus 35.5 for the United States (although the Japanese number was almost three times the level found in South Korea).[9] Although Japanese civil society has developed rapidly in the postwar era, it has not yet caught up with the density of civil society found in the United States.

The January 1995 Hanshin-Awaji earthquake in Kobe made almost everyone rethink the concept of Japan's volunteerism and informal organizations as a myriad of groups quickly formed.[10] Japanese society has shown an ability to mobilize and organize quickly. The run-up to the Iraq War can thus be seen as a test of the reaction of these groups to a global call to protest as well as a barometer of Japan's postwar identity as a peace-loving society and nation.

CIVIL SOCIETY

The question as to whether or not Japan has an active civil society is critical. As someone who has worked with political parties and NGOs in Afghanistan, Pakistan, Cambodia, Singapore, Malaysia, and Timor Leste, I can attest that the discussion over civil society space has been intense. For example, are religious organizations members of civil society? Should NGOs work with the government and political parties? Yet, despite these internal debates, it is clear that the wider that civil society groups can operate, the deeper the roots of democratic norms can grow. In this context, it is interesting to note that civil society in Japan was promoted and encouraged by Allied Occupation authorities. All prewar and wartime limits on the rights of association, speech, and assembly were revoked. Workers, housewives, and student organizations were quickly formed. Parent teacher associations (PTAs) also grew.[11] By the time of the first postwar election, Japanese civil society was active and vibrant. This does not mean that it was unrestrained, criticism of the occupation and General Douglas A. MacArthur was censored,[12] and more importantly the newly energized civil society was, at times, a tool used by the occupation to help destroy the old system. Civil society existed during the occupation to the extent that it did not hinder changeable occupation goals. It would not be allowed to totally reshape the new society. In many ways, GHQ's cancellation of the February 1, 1947, General Strike was a harbinger of a whole series of reversals.[13] Civil society in Japan suddenly found itself under attack by those forces that felt that democratization was going too far. This betrayal was keenly felt by the left-wing.

Yet, despite Japan re-centralizing, re-industrializing, and re-militarizing, civil society groups remained active and vocal. The 1950s in Japan can be seen as a decade where politics had taken a confrontational mode. Civil society groups were mobilized, organized, and highly ideological. The Bikini Atomic test and the deaths of the members of the fishing boat Lucky Dragon No.5 sparked a protest campaign that garnered fifty million signatures.[14] The movement was initiated by housewives from Suginami-ku in Tokyo. The antinuclear movement is perhaps one of the best organized and deep-rooted in Japan; led by The Japan Council against Atomic and Hydrogen Bombs (*Gensuikyo*), it is but one example of grassroots mobilization. Organized September 1955 *Gensuikyo* is an umbrella organization with offices in all forty-seven prefectures of Japan (including Okinawa, then under U.S. administration). According to its website, "There are also some 50 national organizations (such as trade unions, women, youth/students, religious, lawyers organizations) and individuals that share the same goals."[15]

According to the Asia Democracy Index 2005, 69.35 percent of those polled strongly agreed with the statement, "Civil association and political organizations can freely organize, mobilize, and advocate their view."[16] A further 63.99 percent strongly agreed to the statement, "Civil society organizations effectively promote the public interest." These findings, part of a larger study indexing democratization in sixteen countries in Asia, saw Japan scoring the highest percentages identifying a positive role for civil society.[17]

One standard definition of civil society is as follows:

> Civil society refers to the arena of uncoerced collective action around shared interests, purposes and values. In theory, its institutional forms are distinct from those of the state, family and market, though in practice, the boundaries between state, civil society, family and market are often complex, blurred and negotiated. Civil society commonly embraces a diversity of spaces, actors and institutional forms, varying in their degree of formality, autonomy and power. Civil societies are often populated by organizations such as registered charities, development-oriented NGOs, community groups, women's organizations, faith-based organizations, professional associations, trade unions, self-help groups, social movements, business associations, coalitions, and advocacy groups.[18]

The Japan Center for International Exchange (JCIE), an organization created in 1970, proclaims, "For more than three decades, JCIE has been promoting the development of a vibrant civil society in Japan, Asia Pacific, and around the world by creating collaborative networks of civil society organizations worldwide and encouraging cooperation on common challenges."[19] Although more of a public relations blurb for JCIE than an objective analysis, it suggests the existence of a regionalized civil society in which Japan must play some sort of role. Networks of relationships and associations based on the freedom of civil society in Japan help create social capital that interacts and overlaps with a variety of both public and private institutions. Civil society shapes, frames, and highlights public opinion and is either proactive or reactive to public policy formation and implementation.[20]

Don Eberly of the Civil Society Project claims civil society is a "third sector" made up of associations "that operate neither on the principle of coercion, nor entirely on the principle of rational self-interest."[21] Civil society is based on voluntary participation. Civil society includes businesses, charities, families, self-help groups, some religious establishments, trade associations, Boy and Girl Scout troops, bowling leagues, sports and martial arts clubs, adult education classes, clubs, and an infinite variety of other kinds of associations, of which there are many in Japan. "No one is coerced into joining them, and they have no coercive power to force their desires on the unwilling."[22] As such, civil society is the primary locomotive for creating social capital, defined as features of social organization that promote trust, norms, and networks that can improve the efficiency of society. According to Putnam, "the more we connect with other people the more we trust them and vice versa."[23] Voluntary associations that bring people together for various reasons are the most important building blocks of social capital. This social capital will have political inputs.

Information Technology and the Deterritorialized State

The explosive growth of NGOs cannot be separated from the revolution in information and communication technologies (ICT) nor from the changing structure of opinion articulation in emerging postmodern societies. There is no doubt that ICTs have been indispensable tools for a wide range of democracy-enhancing activities. While there is undoubtedly a digital divide that can easily be viewed on a comparative regional basis, worldwide Japan places in the first rank of nations in usage.[24] The triple "C" challenges of cost, compatibility, and connectivity have largely been overcome as a combination of mobile phone technology as well as intense broadband competition has created a digitally connected Japan. While language barriers continue to hinder Japan from transmitting, receiving, and sharing information, as compared to English language or English-conversant societies, Japan internally is highly interconnected. In fact it is safe to say that the age of English language Internet dominance is a relic of the past. The effect of this ICT revolution on politics is just beginning to be understood and analyzed. What is certain is that the spatial dimensions of politics have been fundamentally transformed from a two-dimensional paradigm with fixed nodes to one that is "multidimensional, shifting, and contingent."[25]

Information and communication technologies both respond to and help create new power relations, reinforcing and enhancing the established and entrenched economic elites, while also providing access for those in the diaspora communities to connect and interact. The term "diaspora" is from the Greek *diaspeirein*. The term has traditionally been intimately linked to the Jewish dispersal outside Israel after the destruction of the Second Temple. It is now being applied to a growing list of migratory non-sedentary groups. The contemporary debate on diaspora encompasses anthropology, sociology, human geography, migration, language, culture, race, multiculturalism, traditional history, postcolonialism, political economy, globalization, antiglobalization, and communication. In this sense, we can use it when discussing public opinion formation and social movements.

Diaspora communities need not have a sense of homeland at the center of their teleology. The chant "Next Year in Jerusalem" is a yearning for such a physical space. This physicality, however, is not necessary since the discourse revolves around the twin concepts of an "imagined community" and the "deterritorialized state." A simple dialectic can be constructed between older static spatial dimensions and newer and fluid modalities.

Information technology has compressed space and time and expanded contact. Information, gossip, rumor, and belief overlap and interlock across an almost infinite number of nodal information points. In a widely read *New Yorker* article, Lt. Col. David Kilcullen, an Australian counterinsurgency specialist, remarked, "If bin Laden didn't have access to global media, satellite communications, and the Internet, he'd just be a cranky guy in a cave."[26]

The blog has become a source of public wisdom often displaying acumen and insight that can trump the higher profile "news and entertainment" global media.[27] A globalization from below has been made possible. This should not be confused with "globalization from above." Accompanying the flat scripted blog is the multidimensional personal video that is sent out into cyber-community. These videos are accessed on a variety of websites. The most notable is Youtube. com, called the "Invention of the Year" in 2006 by *Time* magazine. All major servers have video sites. These sites have become an outlet for an endless array of voices to be seen and heard. While Vietnam has often been categorized as the first rock-n-roll war, Iraq is certainly the first Internet-blogged, video music "youtubed" war. The men and women in the armed forces are technologically savvy and are fluent in the use of ipods, video cams, and computer editing. This has given the war in Iraq an exposure way beyond the confines of government–military control. Soldiers are recording their war in a way that has never been done before. This living history is visual with the oral narrative being the music of the generation that is fighting. What is most fascinating in these narratives is the blend of violence and patriotism. Flag, uniform, weapons, and yes, explosions, dominate. The Iraqis themselves are largely absent except as bystanders or enemy or target. These videos record experience but are not antiwar. But they have consequences, such as inflaming opinion in Iraq, when a member of the U.S. military sang "Hadji Girl" on Youtube.com.

Conversely, the "other" in this war has not been passive and silent as pro-insurgent and anti-American and anti-coalition information competes and challenges. The war in Iraq has made all sides technologically savvy in the battleground over information and the shaping of public opinion.

This is important as we look at public opinion in Japan. The video bytes of Youtube.com show a young and resourceful and energetic warrior class doing their duty. The gap between the youth of Japan and America could not be wider; the gulf between the civil societies could not be deeper.

A look at the growth and development of the NGO community in Japan, particularly over the last decade following the Kobe earthquake and the increasingly interconnected society that email and the Internet has made possible, supports the idea of diaspora communities being formed. We are struggling to understand as well as deal with these new human geographic landscapes. Identities are being challenged, shaped, and reformed.

"Globalization-from-below" is carried out mainly by organizations that do not have strong links with governments or large corporations. Some of these organizations, such as Amnesty International, Transparency International, and Greenpeace, actually monitor the performance of governments on human rights, corruption, and environmental protection. Others like the International Committee for the Red Cross and Doctors without Borders act as global relief agencies. Academic, professional associations, religious groups, and peace networks participate in globalization-from-below because they develop communication links between members in various parts of the world. In the battle over public opinion, the linked diaspora communities play a vital role as communicators and facilitators of "alternative" information and powerful uncensored images. Unlike the global corporation, the commodities are not-for-profit symbolic goods and services.

The 1990s witnessed the growth and development of NGOs as both bridge actors on the international scene as well as independent forces with their own unique agendas. The 1990s also saw a rising debate in political science over the scope and activities of the state itself. One unanticipated consequence of 9/11 was that it forcefully and dramatically brought the state back as the central and decisive force in international politics. War-making on a global scale is something that only the central state can maintain. In the rubble of the twin towers, the role of NGOs was temporarily diminished. The war in Iraq has reenergized NGOs (not including right-wing social society) in both forging public opinion and challenging politicians.

How has Japanese politics made use of ICT? The June 2000 general elections in Japan can be said to be the first "web" election in that country.[28] Japanese mainstream political actors quickly learned how to use the Internet by setting up websites and individual home pages, taking their cue from their American political counterparts. The monthly printed newsletter soon became an electronic, interactive, and many, mostly younger, lawmakers now send them out regularly. (The most well known was the Koizumi mail magazine that initially attracted much attention and subscribers.) This phenomenon extended from the national level right down to the city council level.[29] One could make a cognitive leap in asserting that the Democratic Party of Japan's issuing of a well-publicized political "Manifesto" in the 2004 Upper House elections was successful because of the ability and ease of disseminating this political platform across electronic space.[30]

Outside the well-funded mainstream political actors, other players also began making use of ICT. Beneath the radar, so to speak, the various actors in society began connecting. This would serve to enlarge "protest space." The growth and development of NGOs was particularly explosive in the 1990s. Nongovernmental organizations filled a gap in the relationship between the civil society and the government. In fact, governments ceded some political functions to the amorphous NGO community. This was particularly true in Japan during the Koizumi years as he sought to streamline the government and download more and more of its functions onto the private sector and civil society led by nonprofit organizations (NPOs).

Along these lines, one definition of NGOs is instructive:

> Non-profit distributing organizations, which are institutionally independent from the state (while operating within its legal framework), channeling social development, aid to the poor, from donors who are largely situated in the developed countries. In this context, they can also be referred to as Non-Governmental Development Organizations (NGDOs)...or Popular Development Agencies (PDAs).[31]

This definition allocates to the NGO a social and distributive function in a variety of politico-economic realms. The NGOs were outside government yet they also sought ways to influence government. In Japan, the definition of NGO's as well as NPOs fit snugly into this supportive function.

NGOs, Community-based Organizations, and Civil Society in Japan

Looking at the acronyms for International Organizations (IOs) muddies the waters when we attempt to separate an organization that works for, gets funding from, and supports government policy from those who advocate, and finally those whose function is to protest and advocate. To oversimplify, organizations, whether NGOs, NPOs, PDAs, and even NGDOs or Quasi-Autonomous Non-Governmental Organizations (QUANGOs), have in common the role of providing access to information. If one were only to examine the role of NPOs or registered NGOs in Japan, the conclusion likely reached, especially when compared to the United States, would be that their effect on public opinion is limited and that the organizations are largely nonpolitical. However, as discussed later, if one were to expand the definition of NGOs to community-based organizations (CBOs), then an entirely different picture emerges. And finally, expanding consideration of CBOs to university organizations as well as political action groups presents us with a dynamic picture of an active and vibrant civil society in Japan, rich with social capital.[32]

In light of the findings presented earlier, one finding of this chapter is that regarding the experience in Iraq, Japanese civil society witnessed a shift in focus among groups that were primarily humanitarian and environmental as they crossed overly into the political protest realm. The rallies against the war in Iraq, which occurred in Tokyo, Osaka, Kyoto, and Okinawa, for example, cut across functional specialization.

Hashimoto Michio, president of the Overseas Environmental Cooperation Center, has identified four types of NGOs in Japan: those that primarily engage in development, advocacy, fundraising, and education. Development NGOs focus on agricultural development and sustainability, refugee support, medical assistance, and other humanitarian needs. Advocacy NGOs conduct policy research and use this to critique government policies and advocate alternative policies. Fundraising NGOs specialize in collecting donations for other NGOs that specialize in implementing projects out in the field. Educational NGOs specialize in developing and implementing educational programs in such areas as environment and development.[33]

Sato Taishitaro, president of the Japan Wildlife Research Center, divides environmental NGOs into biting dogs, barking dogs, and working dogs. According to Sato, "Biting dogs are good at biting governments or industries concerning environmental policies. Barking dogs bark from a safe distance, issuing warnings and appealing to the middle-class majority. Working dogs devote themselves to basic study and research."[34]

The following figures help to describe the current legal, financial, and staffing situation of Japanese NGOs. Of the NGOs, 10 percent have legal status,

90 percent do not. There are currently 250 NGOs with an annual budget of 1 million yen (US\$ 8,700). Of these 40 percent have an annual budget of between 10 million (US\$ 86,000) and 50 million yen (US\$ 435,000). More than 100 million yen (US\$ 860,000) is the annual budget of 13 percent NGOs. Like their Western counterparts, NGOs derive their income from a number of sources: donations, membership fees, and income-generating activities account for 66 percent, subsidies from governmental bodies 14 percent, grants from private foundations 4 percent, and contract funds from government and UN agencies, 5 percent. The remaining 10 percent is from other sources. There are about 1,200 paid staff members working in NGOs, of which 25 percent work on a part-time basis. About 280,000 people around the country are individual supporting or sustaining members of NGOs. About 5,900 companies and corporations support 80 NGOs, of which over 50 are supported by less than 10 companies. Only 7 NGOs are supported by more than 100 companies. About 100 NGOs are supported by about 4,500 NPOs, such as churches, temples, labor unions, and junior chambers.[35]

In Japan companies can deduct donations up to 0.125 percent of their capital plus 1.25 percent of their annual profit. This is called the general ceiling. When a donation is made to government-operated organizations or those specially registered by the government, no limitation is imposed. If the donation goes to organizations authorized by the government as a "special public interest promotion organization," the ceiling is twice that of the general ceiling. In the case of individuals a tax exemption is allowed only when their donation goes to the government-owned or government-authorized organizations or one that is specially registered. The ceiling is 25 percent of an individual's income. Japanese NGOs lacked the political clout to get more favorable tax treatment in a society that generally was not disposed to NGOs.[36]

The unfavorable standards of Japanese law hinder the formation of Japanese NGOs. For example, before a Japanese NGO can be registered, "the founders must obtain authorization from each concerned agency of the central government." It generally takes two–three years to obtain tax-exempt status. Consequently, many would-be Japanese volunteer organizations choose not to apply for registration as an NGO, preferring to remain in an undefined status even though this means forgoing the advantages of tax-exempt status when seeking donations from companies and individuals.[37]

The main activities of Japanese implementation NGOs can be divided into those who specialized in overseas projects versus domestic projects. Overseas work includes education, medical and health services, vocational training, environmental protection, rural development, relief and emergency assistance for refugees, fair trade, while domestic projects include development education, global citizenship education, advocacy, protecting human rights of foreigners in Japan. One can further divide the NGO community into those that work to a certain extent with the government, and those that are either adversarial or at least keep a distance.[38]

The Ministry of Foreign Affairs as well as other government-related trade and labor organizations view the NGOs and the more formally structured NPOs as working hand-in-hand with government. This perception is seen in the following MOFA description of its relations with NGOs who operate in the international sphere:

Japanese NGOs for International Cooperation:...include those non-governmental and non-profit organizations that address such global issues as development, the economy, human rights, humanitarian concerns, and the environment. Today, more than 400 Japanese NGOs are engaged in international cooperation activities. First emerging in the 1960s, NGOs increased in number and quality in the late 70s and early 80s, mainly through providing assistance to Indochinese refugees. Recent cooperative activities of Japanese NGOs in Kosovo and Afghanistan are the proof of their steady growth.

International Cooperation NGOs and Japanese Government: NGOs have become an indispensable part of today's international community. Their mobility and flexibility are vital in providing grassroots-level assistance and emergency humanitarian relief. The Japanese government believes collaboration with NGOs is crucial in gaining public understanding and support for its Official Development Assistance (ODA) programs. NGOs provide a channel through which people can lend a hand directly to international cooperation activities. Partnership between NGOs and the government assumes two forms: collaboration and support. Working with them in ODA policy-making and project implementation, the government benefits much from their knowledge and human resources, and in return, provides them with financial and other forms of support...

Collaboration, Support, and Close Dialogue: By evaluating and discussing ODA programs that are implemented jointly by MOFA and NGOs, both parties have come to understand each other better and thus are able to work out ideal cooperation schemes. Another example of collaboration is Japan Platform, which was established in 2000. This system is intended to help the government, the business community, and NGOs cooperate to provide emergency humanitarian relief more effectively and quickly. The NGO Project Subsidy and the Grant Assistance for Grassroots Projects, both introduced in 1989, have been the main pillars of the governmental NGO support schemes... While NGO international cooperation activities continue to expand, increased expertise and organizational skills have not necessarily followed. In addressing this issue, MOFA introduced Capacity Building Support for NGOs in fiscal 1999, which consists of various programs such as the NGO Advisors, the NGO Study Groups, and the NGO Researchers. None of the collaborative and supportive efforts by MOFA can succeed without close communication with NGOs. MOFA continues to deepen the dialogue with NGOs through NGO-MOFA Regular Meetings, NGO-Embassy Meetings, among others.[39]

This conception would not view the NGO community as adversarial or even antigovernment, but rather, as supportive of government activities and even of its public relations efforts; almost an extension of government. Trade, aid, and investment, what this author calls the new triad of Japanese power, is reflected in mainstream orientations toward both NGOs and their more corporate-driven NPOs. Listing 250 NGOs with budgets of over one million yen understates that, since there are over 26,000 NGOs operating in Japan today. Even this number is highly suspect as it represents only those organizations that are approved under the strict standards of Japanese law.[40] As a result the number excludes most community-based organizations as well as those who want to keep as far away from government association as possible. It is these groups, mostly operating beneath the government bureaucratic radar, that play a significant role in shaping public opinion. The NGOs at this level are small scale (often only one or two members), operating on a shoestring and are understaffed. It is here that the "biting, barking, working" dog analogy by Sato is instructive (although demeaning).[41]

In Japan, the NGO community began their relationship with government in a highly charged acrimonious and emotional battle. The distrust of government and the business community forged during the great pollution, antiwar, and environmental protests of the 1960s and 1970s[42] still lingers. This is why the information provided by the Ministry of Foreign Affairs as well as JANIC, the Japan NGO Center for International Cooperation, on the NGO community focuses on aide, development, and humanitarian assistance, ignoring the so-called barking dogs. Japanese NGOs remain for the large part, "pure but poor."

THE WAR IN IRAQ AND JAPAN'S NGOS

The literature devoted to the "NGO community" in Japan is overwhelmingly developmental, environmental, and poverty alleviation-based. By NGO Community, the author is referring to a loose and floating base of organizations whose base is electronic not personal. Although the government and the large business community has sought to co-opt and expropriate the NGO community, as far as the war in Iraq and public opinion is concerned, the pure but poor community was empowered and reacted in ways that mirror NGOs in other advanced industrial countries.

On the other hand, right-wing informal organizations such as *Nihon Izokukai* and the Committee for Creating New History Textbooks (see the earlier discussion) did not mobilize to support the government position in favor of the war. They saw little connection between their nationalist causes and backing the Japanese government's support for the U.S. invasion of Iraq (see the discussion about how the Iraq War divided the Japanese conservatives in chapter five by Eldridge and Chijiwa). This disinterest demonstrates both the ambivalence of right-wing civil society toward the United States and its disinterest in promoting a larger overseas military role for Japan as a part of a larger nationalist agenda. For these reasons, right-wing civil society sat on the sidelines.

This section concentrates on non-right-wing civil society and their antiwar activities. In fact, this floating community is well grounded in organizations that not only share information, knowledge, and experience but also establish regional branches. The famous antiwar group Women in Black has a Japan chapter that is very active. They were out spreading their message and providing information at all antiwar rallies that the author observed.

On the other hand, in doing this research, the author attempted to contact many antiwar NGOs in Japan. In some instances, email messages were not returned, sites were described as "under construction," or *kojichu*, and telephone contact was impossible. One of the most famous NGOs in Japan, Peace Winds Japan, was inaccessible. Also, many organizations mostly formed in direct reaction to 9/11, the war in Afghanistan, and the Iraq War were not forthcoming. A short list of contacted groups includes: Act and Unite Kyoto,[43] Act and Unite Osaka, "Block the Road to War!"[44] Peace Walk Kyoto,[45] and Women in Black (Japan chapter).[46]

Act and Unite Kyoto may be typical. It was established on March 6, 2003, or two weeks prior to the formation of Act and Unite Osaka Group. The main office is at Kyoto University, a traditional bastion of radical left-wing student movements, with a forty-person subcommittee and a core group of about ten people. The members are a conglomeration of housewives, college students, part-time workers, and business people. Their motto and main goal is to stop the war in Iraq. Their major activities are demonstrations and the dissemination of materials. They joined with other groups in Tokyo and went to Nagoya's Komaki Airbase in March 2003, when the war broke out, to protest. Importantly, two individuals, who would form Act and Unite, went to Washington, D.C., and joined the protests in February 2003 that attracted an estimated five hundred thousand. Upon their return to Japan, the two students shared their experiences and lessons learned.[47] Act and Unite is also linked to International ANSWER (Act Now to Stop War and End Racism) United. This organization is funded by a five-hundred-yen monthly membership fee plus donations and the proceeds from selling pins.

Peace Walk Kyoto also mirrors the structure and function of Act and Unite. Completely voluntary, the membership is made up of NGO workers, students, housewives, unemployed and part-timers (and non-regular workers known as *freeters*), as well as labor union members. One activity was to develop an email list. Peace Walk was formed after the 9/11 Parade for Peace, which was organized by the Kyoto YMCA.[48]

After the war started, a new organization composing over fifty-three hundred Japanese citizens from eleven cities formed to file a lawsuit to stop the dispatch of the SDF to Iraq in 2004.[49] Community-based activism was widespread in Japan in the run-up to the war in Iraq. Several dozen demonstrations were held every week throughout Japan.[50] Japanese volunteered as human shields. After hostilities commenced, NGOs and community-based organizations received, collected, and collated information on the human cost of the war.

In April 2004, in a high-profile and emotional case that received widespread media exposure, three Japanese nationals were kidnapped in Iraq. Imai Noriaki, eighteen, Koriyama Soichiro, thirty-two, and Takato Nahoko, thirty-four, were later released unharmed.[51] The reaction of the Japanese government in this matter was to hold the three responsible for financial costs incurred. The three vowed to return to Iraq. Koriyama is a freelance photojournalist working with *Shukan Asahi*, Imai was in Iraq supporting NGO medical services, and Takato was engaged in NGO activities to aide Iraqi children.

The role of all three hostages was linked in that they were volunteers and/or freelancers whose need to "do something" outweighed the considerable risks. All three, upon their return to Japan, spoke at a variety of venues. The NGOs and community-based organizations were deeply supportive, although the government and ruling party were quite critical, as were some commentators on television.[52] The Japanese government did not escape criticism, as the government's decision to hold Japanese nationals financially responsible was criticized as a blatant attempt of coercion and control. U.S. Secretary of State Colin Powell's praise of the released Japanese hostages presented a jarringly different position from that of the Japanese government spokesmen. According to Powell, "I'm pleased that these Japanese citizens were willing to put themselves at risk for a greater good, for a better purpose. And the Japanese people should be very proud that they have citizens like this willing to do that."[53]

The NGOs provided alternative information, information that although sometimes relatively old, nonetheless had the potential to influence policy. For example, Peace Depot, a Yokohama-based NGO,[54] and its director Umebayashi Hiromichi, a well-known observer of U.S. forces in Japan, uncovered U.S. documents in September 2007 suggesting that Maritime Self-Defense Forces ships had refueled the *USS Kitty Hawk* aircraft carrier in the Gulf of Oman in February 2003, just before the *Kitty Hawk* headed for the Persian Gulf to participate in Operation Southern Watch, an operation involved in destroying Iraqi air defenses. This, the group claimed, violated the pledge made by the Koizumi cabinet at the time that the MSDF mission in the Indian Ocean would not support any military action involving Iraq. This information threatened to undermine efforts by the LDP-led coalition government to renew the MSDF mission during the fall of 2007.[55]

Beyond providing alternative information, the NGOs humanized the Iraqi people at a time of dangerous objectification. Posters and materials of women and children, hospitals and schools were all visible reminders of the potential costs of war.

Also in April 2004, a rally was held in Osaka protesting the war and demanding the withdrawal of both U.S. and Japanese forces from Iraq. The thirty participants in the rally carried signs criticizing the siege of Fallujah, and used their bullhorn to demand "Don't kill the children of Fallujah!" and called on the SDF "Not to Die for Koizumi."[56] The rally also conducted a signature drive for a petition opposing the U.S. presence in Iraq, and tried to deliver the petition to U.S. president George Bush via the consulate staff.[57]

The influence of the antiwar NGO community has been acknowledged in a backhanded way by the SDF. The leaking of internal documents in June 2007 revealed that the SDF's Intelligence Unit Corp or IUC had very meticulously conducted surveillance of anti-Iraq War and anti-Iraq dispatch demonstrations and other activities by antiwar NGOs. Internal documents leaked to the JCP revealed graphs of demonstrations tracked by week and region, with several dozen demonstrations per week nationwide being tracked from December 2002 through the end of February 2003, the period covered by the leaked documents. The sponsors, numbers, organizers, and other information about each demonstration were recorded, along with pictures. The fact that the SDF paid such close attention to the antiwar NGO community attests to a belief (or fear of) in their potential to influence on public opinion and policy.[58] The ability of the antiwar movement to spread its message, seep into the mainstream business, professional communities, and even local governments, and have a politically secure base is a testament that Japan is hardly a passive player in the mass movements associated with those who were against the waging of war in Iraq.[59]

CONCLUSION

Although not an organized party like the Japanese Communist Party, which is also active in protest movements, the war in Iraq impelled NGOs in Japan to take on a larger political protest and function as a source of alternative information. Deeply antimilitarist and even pacifist, they find their support among large segments of the population who are horrified by state-sanctioned violence. Membership is not merely the young but cross-cuts across age and gender.

The NGO community and civil society in Japan are well informed about the human cost of the wars in Afghanistan and Iraq. Their strength is that their antiwar message resonates in a Japan that both suffered in war and inflicted untold suffering itself. They have framed an antiwar policy that is part and parcel of Japan's postwar identity. While the NGO community lacks central control, it has still managed to stage a large number of well-attended protests throughout Japan, serve as a source of alternative information, and act as sources of advocacy. While the Koizumi government enunciated one consistent policy, the NGOs did not remain silent.

The antiwar NGO community, small and often disorganized though it was, helped to articulate if not mobilize public opinion. Although its organizational shortcomings make it easy to dismiss, their antiwar message found deep resonance in Japanese public opinion. Although it is hard to directly measure their influence, the anti-Iraq War NGO message was, at least in its general outlines, supported by the vast majority of the Japanese public. Opposition to the Iraq War ranged from just under 60 percent to over 75 percent and tended to grow overtime (see chapter one by Midford for more detail). Thus, there exists a clear correlation between the views articulated by the antiwar NGOs and the majority of public opinion, even though evidence of a causal relationship remains thin. On the other hand, government and conservative efforts to sell the virtues of the Iraq War failed miserably. Although the antiwar NGO community failed to prevent the SDF from being dispatched to Iraq, they arguably had some influence in articulating public skepticism about this mission and ensuring that what was originally promoted as a security mission in support of the U.S. military was eventually transformed into a largely humanitarian mission aimed at purifying water and rebuilding schools. Ironically, the SDF ended up limiting its operations to some of the same humanitarian roles that NGO activists and former hostages Koriyama and Takato had gone to Iraq to engage in (i.e., providing medical services and helping Iraqi children).

The NGOs were successful in spreading their message because they were voicing a message that the Japanese public was not deaf to. People could join a march, buy a pin or poster, listen to music, and feel that they were part of not only a nationwide movement but also part of a worldwide expression. This feeling of commonality, of solidarity with many citizens around the world opposed to the war, cannot be underestimated. Globalism, combined and fused with a particular Japanese pattern of the present, helped to create a multitude of voices that the government could ignore only at its own risk.

The antiwar NGO community is by its nature a very loose network that lacks a single leader or a single umbrella organization. Lacking resources and staffed mostly by volunteers, a major segment of Japanese civil society was able to put enough sandals on the ground to make the government take notice. The spying by the SDF attests to the fact that the movement could not be ignored. The movement also had the support of the Japanese Communist Party as well as politicians from other major parties. Public opinion voiced by civil society was a constraining factor in policy formation that could not be lightly dismissed

Notes

1. The debate over domestic violence, and spousal and child abuse is only now beginning to receive attention.
2. Two recent works dealing with the concept of small Japanism are: Ide Sonroku, *Ishibashi Tanzan to Shokoku Shugi* (Ishibashi Tanzan and Small Countryism) (Tokyo: Iwanami Booklet, No. 510, 2000); and Akira Tanaka, *Shokoku Shugi Nippon no Kindai wo Yominaosu* (Rereading Modern Small Japanism) (Tokyo: Iwanami Shinsho, 1999).
3. By contrast, Greenpeace's anti-whaling message is alien, force-fed, moralized, and at times appears to be imposing, and too openly confrontational. Not surprisingly, therefore, this message has never caught on and Greenpeace has never established a strong foothold in Japan. Regarding their relatively modest presence, see http://www.greenpeace.or.jp/index_en_html (accessed September 2007).
4. "Nagasaki, Tokyo de koki kodo Kyuma Boeisho 'Shoganai' hatsugen"; and "Ogosoka ni Tsutsushinde Moraitai, Shusho ga Kyuma Boeisho ni," *Asahi Shimbun*, July 2, 2007.
5. The website of the Society for History Textbook Reform is available only in Japanese: http://www.tsukurukai.com/ (accessed September 2007).
6. The Japanese-only website of the Japan Society of War-Bereaved is available at http://www.nippon-izokukai.jp/index2.html (accessed September 2007).

7. Yutaka Tsujinaka, "Interest Group Structure and Regime Change in Japan," Maryland/Tsukuba Papers on U.S.–Japan Relations, November 1996, pp. 12–13, 21, 37; and Tsujinaka Yutaka, *Rieki Shudan* (Interest Groups) (Tokyo: Tokyo Daigaku Shuppankai, 1986), as cited by Susan Pharr, "Officials' Misconduct and Public Distrust: Japan and the Trilateral Democracies," in Susan Pharr and Robert Putnam, eds., *Disaffected Democracies: What's Troubling the Trilateral Countries* (Princeton: Princeton University, 2000), pp. 183–4. Tsujinaka in turn used statistics for nongovernmental, non-profit organizations and associations compiled by the Management and Coordination Agency, Bureau of Statistics, *Census on Establishments*, selected years.

8. Asahi Shimbun, *Japanese Almanac* (Tokyo: Asahi Shimbun, 1999), 195; and Pharr, "Officials' Misconduct and Public Distrust," p. 184.

9. Tsujinaka, "Interest Group Structure and Regime Change in Japan," pp. 12–13, as cited by Pharr, "Officials' Misconduct and Public Distrust," p. 183.

10. Ironically, some of the "civil society" groups that mobilized to provide disaster relief were organized crime gangs, or *Yakuza gumi*.

11. Jacob van Staaveren, "The Growth of Parent–Teacher Associations in Japan (A Prefectural View)," *Peabody Journal of Education*, Vol. 27, No. 3 (November 1949), pp. 162–66.

12. For a recent discussion of GHQ censorship of Japanese film in the late 1940s, see Rachel Hutchinson, "Kurosawa Akira's *One Wonderful Sunday*: Censorship, Context and 'Counter-Discursive' Film," *Japan Forum*, Vol. 19, No. 3 (Fall 2007), pp. 369–89. For a first-hand account, see Akira Kurosawa, *Something Like an Autobiography*, translated by Audie Bock (New York: Vintage, 1983), pp. 145–7.

13. On GHQ's cancellation of the planned general strike and its significance, see John W. Dower, *Embracing Defeat: Japan in the Wake of World War II* (New York: W.W. Norton & Company, 1999), pp. 268–70.

14. See www.japan-press.co.jp/2003/2324/i.html (accessed September 2007). The Japan Press Service is the Communist Party-affiliated website and publishing house.

15. For the website of this organization, see http://www10.plala.or.jp/antiatom/html/e/discription_gensuikyo.htm (accessed September 2007).

16. *Asia Democracy Index 2005*, published by the Alliance for Reform and Democracy in Asia, p. 91. Paul D. Scott serves as the Project Director.

17. Ibid., p. 97.

18. See http://pages.britishlibrary.net/blwww3/3way/civilsoc.htm (accessed February 2007; as of September 2007, the link is down, effective March 2007).

19. See www.jcie.or.jp/thinknet/civilsociety.html (accessed September 2007).

20. For a recent study on social capital in Japan, see Yuko Nishide, "Social Capital and Civil Society in Japan" Doctoral Dissertation, School of International Public Policy, Osaka University, 2007.

21. See www.civilsocietyproject.org/pages/index.php?pID=965 (accessed September 2007).

22. See http://www.cato.org/pubs/handbook/hb105-2.html (accessed September 2007).

23. Robert D. Putnam, "Tuning In, Tuning Out: The Strange Disappearance of Social Capital in America," *PS: Politics and Political Science*, Vol. 28, No. 4 (1995), p. 665.

24. Japan falls far behind the United States, Finland, Iceland, Sweden, Canada, and Singapore as far as Internet users as percent of population is concerned but nonetheless is still above France and Italy. The trend is upward in Japan in the case of people with Internet access at home. These figures must be balanced with statistics on the percentage of the population accessing the Internet via cell phones. In Japan people are connected and the amount and quality of information available at both the mobile and fixed station levels is increasing. For more, see Nielsen/NetRatings at http://www.nielsen-netratings.com/ (accessed September 2007).

25. Gillian Rose, "Feminism and Geography: The Limits of Geographical Knowledge," in Jayne Rodgers, ed., *Spatializing International Politics: Analyzing Activism on the Internet* (New York: Routledge, 2003), p. 11.

26. George Packer, "Knowing the Enemy: Can Social Scientists Redefine the 'War on Terror'?" *The New Yorker*, December 18, 2006.

27. The case of candidate Bush's Texas Air National Guard records and the way it was reported on America's CBS is an obvious case in point. The blogs were correct. In another case, soon after the second round presidential debates in the United States, there was widespread speculation that the president was wired to get help from advisors. A still photo apparently showed a small boxy shape between Bush's shoulders. Soon bloggers began to muse about this on various websites. There is even one website, www.isbushwired.com (accessed September 2007), solely devoted to this matter.

28. Leslie M. Tkach-Kawasaki, "Clicking for Votes: Assessing Japanese Political Campaigns on the Web," in K.C. Ho, Randolph Kluver, and Kenneth C.C. Yang, eds., *Asia.com: Asia Encounters the Internet* (London: RoutledgeCurzon, 2003), pp. 159–74.

29. Based on personal communication between the author and Miyamoto Takashi, city council member in Neyagawa, Osaka. Miyamoto's monthly political newsletter also provides a question and answer section. The questions that are asked are highly specific and patron–client oriented, i.e., concerning narrow questions about pension, employment, spousal abuse, and home help care (*kaigo*). Miyamoto was a volunteer in the 1992 William J. Clinton–Albert A. Gore, Jr., campaign, came back to Japan, and successfully ran as an unknown twenty-eight-year old.

30. For the English version of the current manifesto, see http://www.dpj.or.jp/english/manifesto4/index.html (accessed September 2007).

31. Fletcher Tembo, *Participation, Negotiation and Poverty: Encouraging the Power of Images: Designing Pro-Poor Development Programmes*, King's SOAS Studies in Development Geography (London: Ashgate, 2003), p. xiv.

32. For an overview of the political economy of internationally active NGOs generally, see Alexander Cooley and James Ron, "The NGO Scramble: Organizational Insecurity and the Political Economy of Transnational Action," *International Security*, Vol. 27, No. 1 (Summer 2002), pp. 5–39.

33. Michio Hashimoto, Kokusai Kankyo Seisaku Kenyukai, "Kankyo Mondai ni kansuru Seisaku, Seron Keisei ni Okeru Kokusaiteki na Minkan Soshiki no Yakuwari ni Kansura Chosa (Research on the Role of International Private Organizations in Establishing Policies, Public Opinion on Environmental

Issues)," Working Paper of the Study Group on International Environmental Policies, n.d., cited by Atsushi Yamakoshi, "The Changing Face of NGOs in Japan," as accessed at http://www.gdrc.org/ngo/jpngo-face.html, in September 2007.

34. Yamakoshi, "The Changing Face of NGOs in Japan." For a similar description of the non-profit sector in the United States, see Lester M. Salamon, *America's Nonprofit Sector: A Primer* (New York: The Foundation Center, 1992), p. 6.

35. See Yamakoshi, "The Changing Face of NGOs in Japan," which cites JANIC 2001. The Japan Center for NGO International Cooperation. (JANIC) is a nonprofit, nonpartisan networking NGO founded in 1987 by a group of NGO leaders who saw the need to better coordinate activities in Japanese society and facilitate communication with overseas groups (for more, see http://www.janic.org/en/en-index.html, accessed September 2007). According to the latter website, "JANIC aims to: foster closer relations among Japanese NGOs engaged in international cooperation; provide services for NGOs' sound development; encourage networking among domestic and international NGOs and related organizations; encourage dialogue between NGOs and other sectors of society; deepen Japanese public understanding of and support for NGO activities and international cooperation; and conduct research on NGOs and international cooperation."

36. On the politics behind the new law on nonprofits, see Robert Pekkanen, "The Politics of Regulating the Non-Profit Sector," in Stephen P. Osborne, ed., *The Voluntary and Non-Profit Sector in Japan: The Challenge of Change* (London: RoutledgeCurzon, 2003), pp. 53–75, esp. 55–6, 61, 63. For an early and more liberal proposal, see NIRA, *Shimin Koeki Katsudo Kiban Seibi ni Kansuru Chosa Kenkyu* (Research Report on the Support System for Citizens' Public Interest Activities) (Tokyo: National Institute for Research Advancement, 1994). In the United States, NGOs are defined by their tax-exempt status. The tax code distinguishes tax-exempt groups as corporations organized under an act of Congress—501(c)(1); title-holding companies—501(c)(2); and religious, charitable, educational, or similar organizations meeting the criteria for 501(c)(3). See Yamakoshi, "The Changing Face of NGOs in Japan."

37. By way of contrast, American NGOs can apply at the state level. The examination period for obtaining tax-exempt status usually lasts only a few months. See Yamakoshi, "The Changing Face of NGOs in Japan."

38. Ibid.

39. The Ministry of Foreign Affairs, "Partnership with Japanese NGOs under ODA," accessed at http://www.mofa.go.jp/policy/oda/category/ngo/partnership.html (accessed September 2007).

40. There are 26,089 registered Public Interest Legal Persons (PILPs) in Japan, versus 1,140,000 VNPOs registered as legal entities. Given that the American population is about 2.5 times larger than Japan's population, these numbers clearly show that the United States has a far denser network of registered nonprofits. See Robert Pekkanen and Karla Simon, "The Legal Framework for Voluntary and Non-Profit Activity," in Osborne, ed., *The Voluntary and Non-Profit Sector in Japan*, p. 97.

41. See Yamakoshi, "The Changing Face of NGOs in Japan."

42. On this period, see Thomas R.H. Havens, *Fire Across the Sea: The Vietnam War and Japan 1965–1975* (Princeton: Princeton University Press, 1987); and

George Packard, *Protest in Tokyo: The Security Treaty Crisis of 1960* (Princeton: Princeton University Press, 1966); Steven Reed, "Environmental Politics: Some Reflections on the Japanese Case," *Comparative Politics*, Vol. 13 (April 1981), pp. 260–1; Ellis S. Krauss, Thomas P. Rohlen, and Patricia G. Steinhoff, *Conflict in Japan* (Honolulu: University of Hawaii Press, 1984).

43. Kyoto Act and Unite has a web page that as of July 2007 had not been updated for four years: http://kyoto.cool.ne.jp/act_and_unite/index3.html. This page also lists another site, http://www.act-unite.org/, and several other links that were no longer valid as of the earlier mentioned date.

44. The Japanese language website of this organization, known as *Tomeyo senso e no michi!*, was updated as recently as May 1, 2007: http://www.geocities.jp/kansaihyakuman. As of July 30, 2007, this site had been accessed 39591 times.

45. Peace Walk Kyoto has a dated web page focusing on a prewar demonstration, accessed July 30, 2006: http://pwkyoto.com/pw2/2003.02.16.htm.

46. The Japan chapter of Women in Black maintains two websites: http://www1.jca.apc.org/fem/wib/ and http://home.interlink.or.jp/%7Ereflect/WIBTokyo/home.html (both accessed in September 2007).

47. For more details see http://kyoto.cool.ne.jp/act_and_unite/index3.html.

48. Regarding Peace Walk Kyoto, see http://pwkyoto.com/pw2/2003.03.15.htm (accessed September 2007). For more recent antiwar NGO activities related to the Kyoto YMCA, see http://www.kyotoymca.or.jp/hq/kyoto_seinen/2005/ky_20050809.html (accessed September 2007).

49. For the English version, see "The Law Suit to Stop Dispatching Self Defense Force to Iraq," at http://www.haheisashidome.jp/english/ and http://www.haheisashidome.jp/ for the Japanese (both accessed September 2007). The Nagoya chapter appears especially active, with two separate websites in Japanese: http://blog.goo.ne.jp/harumi-s_2005/e/efd5a9e498cbcd8653feb13ee15d2b0f and http://list.jca.apc.org/public/aml/2005-June/002092.html (both accessed September 2007).

50. This data comes from the SDF's Intelligence Unit Corp, or IUC, which kept meticulous track of antiwar and anti-dispatch demonstrations. Its research was later leaked to the JCP's party newspaper (*Akahata*), and the IUC's documents were put on line.

51. For a profile of Imai, see http://news.bbc.co.uk/1/hi/programmes/panorama/4627777.stm (accessed September 2007).

52. For an account that mistakenly projects the government's hostility toward the three hostages onto the broader Japanese public, see Norimitsu Onishi, "For Japanese Hostages, Release Only Adds to Stress," *The New York Times*, April 22, 2004.

53. Ibid.

54. For more on Peace Depot, see its website at http://www.peacedepot.org/e-news/whatspd/whatspd.html#pagetop. Strikingly, Peace Depot appears to have received at least an unofficial and quasi-endorsement from one member of the governing LDP party, Kono Taro, who put Peace Depot's URL link in his own web page where he presents information about the Japan chapter of the Parliamentary Network for Nuclear Disarmament (PNND). Kono, who is widely regarded as knowledgeable if outspoken on security issues, is the secretary general of PNND Japan, and represents a district near Yokohama, where Peace Depot is located. See http://www.konotaro.org/policy/pnnd.html (accessed September 2007).

55. Reiji Yoshida, "MSDF Fuel was Used in Iraq War, Group Charges," *Japan Times*, September 21, 2007. For more on Umebayashi, and his role in uncovering information about the involvement of U.S. Forces Japan (USFJ) in operations related to U.S. homeland missile defense, see Umebayashi Hiromichi (translated and introduced by Richard Tanter), "The Covert Expansion of the U.S.–Japan Security Treaty: Missile Defence Response to the July 5, 2006, North Korean Missile Test by U.S. Naval Vessels Home-Ported at Yokosuka," *Japan Focus*, No. 2484 (available at http://www.japanfocus.org/products/details/2484, accessed September 2007); and "The Role of NGOs in Japan and the World," Wade L. Huntley, Kazumi Mizumoto, and Mitsuru Kurosawa, eds., *Nuclear Disarmament in the Twenty-First Century* (Hiroshima: Hiroshima Peace Institute, 2004), pp. 338–53.

56. Brian Covert, "Japan Protestors Demand U.S. Withdrawal from Iraq," *Indymedia*, April 17, 2004 (available at http://sf.indymedia.org/news/2004/04/1690548.php and accessed September 2007).

57. The petition read: PETITION IN SOLIDARITY WITH IRAQI CITIZENS FACING THE U.S.-LED OCCUPATION, TO: President George Bush and The U.S. Consular (*sic*) General Osaka-Kobe, 15 April 2004.

    As the Iraqi people resist U.S.-led occupation force escalated attacks which are terrorizing entire populations of Iraqi towns and neighborhoods, we urgently demand a stop to fighting and an immediate withdrawal of troops. According to reports in Fallujah alone, hundreds of Iraqis have been killed and hundreds more injured since attacks began on Sunday, April 4. Although the Geneva Convention prohibits holding civilian communities under siege, Fallujah and Adaamiya are currently under siege and surrounded by occupation forces. THIS IS IN VIOLATION OF THE GENEVA CONVENTION. In the many towns and cities now under attack, hospitals, mosques and ambulances trying to transport the injured are being bombed and fired at by occupation forces. The indiscriminate killing of civilians, the refusal to provide people with security, electricity, and a decent medical infrastructure appear to characterize the "freedom" that occupation authorities have brought to Iraq. In solidarity with Iraqi civilians facing the gruesome manifestations of the occupation, we urge the United States to: 1) Put an immediate end to the siege of Fallujah and Adaamiya. The surrounding of these cities is in contravention to the Geneva Convention; 2) Put an immediate end to the massacre of civilians in Iraqi cities and neighborhoods; 3) Give immediate access to humanitarian and medical aid organizations seeking to provide assistance to Iraqi people who are living under attack; 4) Put an immediate end to the U.S.-led occupation of Iraq.

58. "GSDF Kept Files on Peace Groups," *Asahi Shimbun*, June 7, 2007; "Editorial: SDF Monitors Civilians," *Asahi Shimbun*, June 8, 2007; Chisaki Watanabe, "Japan's Defense Official Defends Monitoring Civic Groups, Individuals Opposed to Iraq Dispatch," *Daily Yomiuri*, June 8, 2007.

59. The author notes that one could not walk into any local government office in the Kansai region (i.e., the Osaka, Kyoto, Kobe region) without seeing anti-Iraq War posters as well as posters defending Article Nine of the Constitution. Similarly, many small and medium cities in Japan declare themselves to be "non-nuclear." These declarations, which are directed against weapons of mass destruction and not nuclear energy, are visible manifestations of a public consensus based on historical experience.

CHAPTER 7

Public Opinion in a Base Community: Okinawa and the War on Terrorism

Robert D. Eldridge

Introduction: The Day after 9/11 in Okinawa

Like those in most parts of the world, newspapers in Okinawa condemned the terrorist attacks on New York and Washington, D.C., which claimed 2996 victims from some 80 countries. "The terrorist attacks were an act of violence against the international community," the *Ryukyu Shimpo*, one of Okinawa's two dailies, observed, "and can not be forgiven no matter what the political reason," the *Shimpo* editorialized.[1] Similarly, the *Okinawa Taimusu* (Times), after pointing out that "many Japanese were killed," condemned the "indiscriminate attacks" as "unjustifiable, no matter what the political situation. We strongly oppose the view that the problems and various contradictions in society should be solved by indiscriminate terrorism."[2]

At the same time, there was an immediate sense of urgency, if not anxiety, about what all this meant for Okinawa. Although more than ten thousand miles from the sites of the attacks on America's East Coast, the residents of Okinawa prefecture were concerned about their homeland becoming a target as well. This was because Okinawa, Japan's southernmost prefecture, is home to thirty-eight exclusive-use U.S. military bases under the arrangements of the U.S.–Japan security treaty, facilities that provide the logistical backbone and fighting force of America's forward presence and deployment capabilities in the region.[3] U.S. bases, first built in 1945 during the Battle of Okinawa and expanded in the decade afterward, currently cover approximately twenty-three thousand hectares, or 19 percent of the main island of Okinawa, giving rise to the expression of *kichi no naka no Okinawa*, or "Okinawa, an island inside the bases."[4]

Two related incidents in the early morning of September 12 near these bases in Okinawa added to the anxiety of both the American and Okinawan sides. When an unmarked car belonging to a reporter of the *Ryukyu Shimpo* stopped on Route 330 alongside Camp Foster in Kitanakagusuku Village, with two cameramen, an armed Marine guard ordered the occupants (according to the reporter's version of events) to put their hands up and poked his gun inside the window.[5] A short time after that, the same reporter proceeded to enter a gate area at nearby Futenma Air Station and was stopped, told to put his hands up, and to get out of the car. Another guard looked around in the car and took a camera from a cameraman and told the newspaper team to turn over the film. When questioned about what right the military guard had to ask for it, the camera was returned but then taken again when the guard discovered it was a digital camera. The guard proceeded to take out the data card and go inside the base. The reporter was told to do a U-turn and exit immediately. He returned forty minutes later to request the card be returned, which eventually was done. *Ryukyu Shimpo* chief editor Miyara Takenori described the incident as "an infringement on the rights of the press and lamentable," and explained that the "manner in which the guards [protect the bases right now] is a legitimate subject to cover."[6] U.S. military public affairs officials later described to the author the incident as irresponsible and provocative behavior by the journalist.[7]

Adding to this sense of tension was the interview in the same day's newspaper with a center-left academic specialist on military affairs, Maeda Tetsuo, of Tokyo International University, who is regularly quoted in the Okinawan press.[8] When asked about whether bases in Okinawa would be a target of a terrorist attack, Maeda responded that "All military bases that U.S forces have abroad may be a target. Bases in Saudi Arabia were attacked [in the past], and in the 1980s, bases in West Germany were also targets. We have to plan for a possible attack on Okinawa. Japan is no longer a sacred place (*seiiki*, i.e., invulnerable, in this case, to attack)."[9]

When U.S. commanders informed base workers not to come into work on the thirteenth and instead wait at home, the anxiety spread. Labor unions called upon the Defense Facilities Administration Agency (*Boei Shisetsucho*), which is in charge of managing U.S. facilities in Japan and worker contracts, to develop measures to protect base workers.[10] The subsequent initiating of strict car and ID checks paralyzed traffic around the gate areas. This was true at other bases on the mainland, such as Yokosuka and Yokota.

Members of the business community were also concerned, particularly in light of the already poorly performing economy. China Yoji, president of the Association of Prefectural Business Owners (*Kenkeieisha Kyokai*), described the situation as "terrible, something not heard of during the Cold War. This may impact the ability to promote relocating companies to Okinawa."[11]

With these concerns in mind, Oyakawa Seiichi, director general of the Executive Office of the governor, called upon the community liaison office of the Okinawa area coordinator (the highest-ranking U.S. military officer in Okinawa—Marine Corps Lt. Gen. Wallace C. Gregson) at Camp Butler, the U.S. consulate general, Naha (located in Urasoe City), and the Okinawa liaison office of the Foreign Ministry in Naha to "report as quickly as possible to the prefecture any information relating to terrorism against U.S. bases in the prefecture in the future."[12] Oyakawa's request was made after the Okinawa Prefectural Government (OPG), discovering that it had been left out of the information loop, expressed its dissatisfaction to the press on September 12.[13] While the U.S. government had informed its Embassy in Tokyo and the Japanese police about a terrorist threat against U.S. bases in Japan, including Okinawa, in advance, "no such information was presented to the prefecture."[14] Using the opportunity, Oyakawa also requested reassurance that the "lives and human rights of the people of the prefecture are not disturbed in any way in the future."

This latter issue was precisely what many in the prefectural leadership and the local communities that host U.S. bases were worried about. Miyagi Tokujitsu, mayor of the town of Kadena, which hosts Kadena Air Base, the largest U.S. Air Force base in East Asia, stated the following in a press interview: "With such a base here, [Kadena] is certainly a target for countries and groups [opposed to the U.S.] and the people of this area are full of concern...An unimaginable thing happened [in the U.S.], and it is very alarming."[15] Mayor Hentona Tomokazu of neighboring Chatan, the site of a rape incident a few months before in its shopping mall/entertainment district of Mihama involving an American serviceman, echoed this feeling: "The fear of communities hosting the bases is huge. I hope the Foreign Ministry provides information in great detail and helps to do away with our fears."[16] Farther north in Kin, which was the site of the 1995 tragic abduction and rape of a twelve-year-old schoolgirl by three U.S. servicemen, Mayor Yoshida Katsuhiro stated that he was "quite concerned, having heard that U.S. facilities around the world were targets of attacks. The very intense guarding [of Camp Hansen] is probably necessary to prevent any possible extended damage. However, the sight of U.S. military personnel with rifles in their hands is something that I wish would be limited as it is upsetting to residents."[17] Finally, Nakasone Masakazu of Okinawa City, who condemned the attacks as "inhumane" and "unpardonable," was more philosophical, or perhaps better put, practical, about the high defense alert: "at this point it is probably a necessary measure. I only hope that in order to stabilize the lives of the residents here, normality returns as quickly as possible."[18]

Unfortunately, as events covered in this chapter show, the pre-9/11 "normality" would not return to Okinawa or to the rest of the world for a long time. Indeed, as Okinawa has been host to an abnormally large U.S. military presence since 1945—far larger than any other prefecture hosting bases in Japan—one might argue whether there ever was a normal situation there. In any case, clearly a new, tense situation has emerged in the post-9/11 environment and in the war on terrorism. How Okinawa viewed this situation is the subject of this study.

The purpose of this study is to examine the implications the events of 9/11 and the subsequent war on terrorism has had on Okinawa, Japan's forty-seventh prefecture, home to some fifty thousand U.S. personnel and their dependents, and the site of occasionally explosive incidents, the most infamous being the 1995 rape of the schoolgirl, which led to large, island-wide protests calling for the reduction or elimination of the bases, revision of the Status of Forces Agreement, and a crackdown on discipline among U.S. personnel stationed in Okinawa. When then-Okinawa governor Ota Masahide announced his decision to not cooperate with the central government on the forced leasing of land within the prefecture for military use and Okinawa went ahead and initiated a prefecture-wide referendum on the bases and SOFA, the so-called Okinawa problem became a subject of national and international attention, and thus the most important issue on the national and bilateral agenda at the time.[19]

Because of this large presence and the high dependency of the U.S.–Japan alliance on Okinawa's cooperation in hosting of these vital facilities, understanding Okinawan views on issues affecting both the alliance and Okinawa's relations with the central government has been important, a dynamic captured in the now famous quote by U.S. ambassador Armin H. Meyer in a 1970 telegram to Washington: "As Okinawa goes, so goes Japan."[20] Okinawan views, desiring reversion, exercised an important influence on both the Japanese government's efforts to call for the return of Okinawa and on the U.S. government's decision to revert the Ryukyu Islands to Japan. Similarly, having experienced a horrific battle (in which one-third of the local population was killed) followed by twenty-seven years of occupation/ administration by a foreign power (the United States), Okinawan opposition to training exercises and base construction in the post-reversion period has greatly influenced bilateral alliance affairs in the 1970s, 1980s, and 1990s. Most well known perhaps was the bilateral recognition of the need to "reduce the burden in Okinawa" leading to the creation of the Special Action Committee on Okinawa (SACO) in November 1995 after the rape incident. Local opposition, on the other hand, likewise has delayed the implementation of the central piece of SACO's many recommendations, the return of Marine Corps Air Station Futenma, conditioned on relocation within the prefecture.[21] In light of the history mentioned earlier, it goes without saying that Okinawan opinion needs to be watched quite closely because the views and actions of the 1.3 million people of the prefecture literally impact the 130 million people of Japan and the bilateral relationship, not to mention regional security.

This chapter examines how public opinion in Okinawa developed following 9/11 and local interactions with the bases during the 2001–2003 period, providing wherever relevant historic and other comparisons to understand where the Okinawa public stood at that time in relation to its own history and to other parts of the country. The former comparison is meant for those readers interested in Okinawa itself; the latter as to where Okinawa, with its unique situation, stands in relation to other views in Japan as a whole, particularly for those interested in security perceptions.

The discussion relies primarily on articles and editorials appearing in the two main dailies, the *Ryukyu Shimpo* and the *Okinawa Taimusu*, which control an amazing 98 percent of the local market, as well as interviews by the author with local observers and key players in events covered, and respective public opinion polls. He does not employ the visual media (local television stations) or radio coverage in his analysis, instead relying on the written media, opinion polls, interviews, and correspondence.[22] Following this introduction, the author looks at the history of the local media and their dual role as both reflectors of opinion as well as sometimes the self-appointed creators of that opinion. Next, the chapter examines the debate in Okinawa after 9/11 and the war on terrorism. Finally, the concluding section will attempt to summarize the issues discussed in the chapter.

The *Ryukyu Shimpo* and *Okinawa Taimusu*: Opinion Reflectors or Opinion Creators?

Before we continue, it is necessary to introduce the history of the local media, specifically the *Shimpo* and the *Taimusu*, and discuss the criticism that exists regarding their reporting of news (an issue that is not limited to Okinawa as the media wars in the United States over media fairness and responsibility in the past few years have shown).

The *Shimpo* dates its history to September 1893, when three men in their twenties—Sho Jun, the fourth son of the last king of the Ryukyus, Sho Tai, Takamine Chokyo, the first Okinawan to study at prefectural expense in mainland Japan (Keio University), and Ota Chofu, also of Keio—came together to establish the first newspaper in the prefecture. Continuing as the *Ryukyu Shimpo* until 1940, it merged with the *Okinawa Asahi Shimbun* to form the *Okinawa Shimpo* as a prowar propaganda organ of the Japanese military.[23] The *Okinawa Shimpo* was discontinued in May 1945, and some of the former staff of the *Ryukyu Shimpo* joined together to establish the *Uruma Shimpo* in July that year after the Battle of Okinawa under the leadership of U.S. occupation authorities in Ishikawa, where one of the relocation camps was located. The *Uruma Shimpo* was renamed the *Ryukyu Shimpo* on September 8, 1951 (the day the Treaty of Peace with Japan was signed in San Francisco), and continues to this day with this name.[24] It was located in the business and administrative center of Naha in Izumisaki, a less than five-minute walk to the Okinawa Prefectural Government and Okinawa Prefectural Assembly buildings, until the spring of 2005 when it moved to Ameku in northern Naha City into a brand new building. According to representatives of the *Shimpo*, currently approximately 220,000 copies are sold everyday. Some cynics in Okinawa say the *Shimpo*'s anti-base stories helped to pay for the new headquarters building.

The *Okinawa Taimusu*, whose sales reach approximately 190,000 copies a day, had already made the move to the same area in 2002. The *Taimusu* came into being in July 1948, following the easing of restrictions on newspapers.[25] It drew on former staff of the *Okinawa Shimpo* and the *Okinawa Asahi Shimbun*. The *Okinawa Taimusu* began to attract more readers due to its pro-reversion stance, which was in contrast to the pro-U.S. occupation position of the *Uruma Shimpo* and later *Ryukyu Shimpo*. By the early 1950s, circulation reached 30,000 for the *Taimusu* compared to the *Shimpo*'s 5000.[26] In September 1953, following the U.S. decision to return the Amami Islands and the death of pro-American *Shimpo* president Matayoshi Kowa, the new president, Oyadomari Seihaku, decided to move the editorial policy closer to the anti-base stance of the more popular *Taimusu*.[27] Neither, it can be said, has departed from this stance since.[28]

Editorial staffs from both newspapers meet everyday after the papers come out to compare notes and comment on each other's stories and editorials, a practice not seen in Tokyo, for example. On the one hand, in addition to the more common fear of collusion or duopoly, such meetings can encourage an intense level of competition in an effort to distinguish oneself and outdo the other. With one newspaper focusing on one issue, such as the SOFA, the other might choose to concentrate its attention on another issue. Along these lines, it can also theoretically encourage the sensationalism of stories.

Equally of concern is another problem—conscious or unconscious conformity. The fact that most observers of Okinawa, local readers, and even workers at the respective newspapers are unable to clearly state the differences in the newspapers suggests that the dynamics of conformity or collusion (along the lines of an anti-base, anti-central government stance) may be at play. Indeed, as one senior writer of the *Taimusu* told the author, "it takes a lot of courage to make any differences clear."[29]

Okinawa has a wide range of ideological views, from conservatives to communist, as well as Ryukyuan nationalists who call for Okinawa's independence. Historically, they have been lumped into two generic groups—the conservatives (*hoshukei*) and the reformists (*kakushinkei*).[30] With two clearly divided groups, one would expect, for example, the existence of at least two newspapers, one with a strong conservative bent and the other with progressive (liberal) leanings.

But one can also argue that much of Okinawa possesses a shared sense of history and a common identity, which is so strong that it mitigates dramatic shifts in popular perceptions, much like a reef brings relative tranquility to what otherwise would be a rough shoreline. This does not mean that elections in Okinawa are not bitterly contested or that some issues are not divisive, but it does suggest that Okinawans have a stronger sense of shared identity among themselves than they do with their mainland compatriots.[31] The editorial policies thus reflect this worldview, as suggested by the title of the book *Okinawa: Datsuwa no Jidai* (Okinawa: The Age of Leaving Japan) published in 1992 at the time of the twentieth anniversary of the reversion of Okinawa to Japan by the then-deputy chief editor of the *Ryukyu Shimpo*.[32] As seen in the name they give themselves, *uchinanchu*, to distinguish themselves from the mainlanders (*yamatonchu*), Okinawans do not always feel a part of Japan, if they ever did. Miki Ken's book was a call to reject Japan.

As mentioned earlier, the two dailies currently control approximately 98 percent of the local market, which means the remaining 2 percent is divided between the five mainland newspapers—the *Asahi Shimbun, Mainichi Shimbun, Yomiuri Shimbun, Sankei Shimbun,* and *Nihon Keizai*

Shimbun.[33] Mainland newspapers are expensive (at least two thousand yen more per month when subscribing, making it almost twice the price as the local papers) and do not come until later in the day (after the first flights from the mainland arrive), and have no local coverage. Although the "Newspaper Sales Code (*Shimbun Hanbai Yoryo*)" of the Japan Newspaper Publishers and Editors Association (*Nihon Shimbun Kyokai*) states that "Newspapers are able to fulfill their roles only when they are delivered to readers. In order to ensure that readers can read newspapers equally at any time and in any place, we are determined to maintain the home delivery system and to deliver newspapers swiftly and without fail," it has yet to be fully realized in Okinawa and isolated populated islands.[34] Protected from competition geographically, Okinawa's media, critics argue, has been able to promote its pacifist stance as urged on by the local labor unions, without readers having an affordable or practical alternative. This criticism, that the local media is inherently biased or free to pursue its bias against the bases and central government as well as those promoting coexistence/cooperation with either of the two, became all the more intense as national attention began to focus on Okinawa following the 1995 rape incident and Governor Ota's decision not to cooperate with the forced leasing of land.[35]

The October 1996 issue of *Bungei Shunju,* one of Japan's leading intellectual monthly journals, published an expose on the composition of the so-called Hitotsubo Anti-war Landowners, finding that some of the editorial board of the *Ryukyu Shimpo* and in the executive management of the *Okinawa Taimusu* were members of this group.[36] "The opinions of both newspapers are clearly anti-base. They are free to have that opinion," the writer observes, "but when the leadership of newspapers representing free journalism is involved in such 'movements,' a problem exists. For example, just think what would happen if the editors of the *Yomiuri Shimbun* or the *Asahi Shimbun* were found to be involved in the Narita movements [violently opposing the extension of the airport runway for some 30 years]."[37] In response, one of the editors of the *Shimpo* is reported to have stated that his membership in the organization exercises no influence over the editorials:

> The Hitotusubo Anti-war Landowners Association is not a political movement. To me, it is a question of lifestyle (*seikatsu no mondai*) and a conscientious movement (*ryoshin no undo*). But this does not mean that it has any influence on what appears in our pages. Editorials are written in light of the existence of conflicting opinions in the background, and [we show] which is the more influential. In order to do this, a discussion of the facts minus subjectivity is essential. When I write about the base problem, there is nothing that is influencing me.[38]

A member of the leadership of the *Taimusu* was more forthcoming. After mentioning that "As a journalist, I felt it especially important to purchase land [and become a member of the association]," the then-advisor to the *Taimusu* stated somewhat inconsistently that "The coverage of the *Okinawa Taimusu* is not biased. This is because the basis of the coverage of the

Okinawa Taimusu which began in the postwar has been an anti-war stance (*senso hantai*)."[39]

Another note of criticism had to do with the local reporters' real or imagined close contacts with Governor Ota, a former professor of journalism at Ryukyu University elected in November 1990, who was said to be a mentor to many of them.[40] Similarly, the connections between the labor unions, whose members include reporters and camera staff, and the then reformist prefectural administration, elected due to the support of these same unions, was too close for comfort for many.

The criticism only got worse. In April 1997, as the Diet debated the passing of a bill simplifying the procedures for land-leasing (which would give the central government strengthened power to pursue eminent domain and violently opposed in Okinawa and the Diet), former deputy managing editor at the Jiji Press with thirty years of experience in the newspaper business, Professor Takubo Tadae of Kyorin University, set off a fire storm in Okinawa when he stated that "To be perfectly frank, the two newspapers in Okinawa are not normal newspapers" at a session of the Special Committee on the Use of Land Relating to the Implementation of the Japan–U.S. Security Treaty.[41] His comment was followed by that of the controversial nationalist Nishimura Shingo, then with New Frontier Party (*Shinshinto*), who, as a member of the committee, commented in the same session that "When you have a situation in which two dailies, whose leadership is dominated by the anti-war landowners, controlling 99 percent (sic) of the readership, this can only be called mind control."[42] Shortly after this, the conservative *Sankei Shimbun* leveled in with its own critical story on the top page of its April 12 evening edition questioning the objectivity of the local press.[43]

It goes without saying that these comments prompted local responses, such as editorials by the *Ryukyu Shimpo* (April 12), and letters to the editor in both newspapers that month criticizing the lack of understanding of Okinawan history and sensitivity. "In this day and age," then editor-in-chief Miki Ken wrote subsequently

> To say that one or two newspapers exercise "mind control" is to say that the people of Okinawa prefecture are stupid. There is nothing worse than saying that the people of the prefecture are being controlled. If we are a newspaper that has ignored the voices of the people and tried to control them, we would be rejected by the readers and no longer exist as a newspaper. If, however, someone says that we are protecting the rights and interests of the people of the prefecture based on their own voices, then we will just have to live with that "criticism."[44]

In short, Okinawan media representatives insist that they faithfully report on the "situation in Okinawa, *as seen from the perspective of the people of the prefecture*."[45] When examining opinion polls, however, they have been shown to underestimate (or overestimate, depending on one's view) the position of residents on certain issues, which suggests that they can get ahead of themselves in the coverage and editorializing and thus may not necessarily always reflect the "perspective of the people."[46]

A typical edition of the *Ryukyu Shimpo* is twenty-four–twenty-six pages in length for the morning edition and eight pages for the evening edition. Regarding the morning edition, the top page is a mixture of local, national, and international news. Page two is almost entirely local news, and sometimes national when it affects Okinawa directly (such as base issues). Page three is international and page four is the op-ed and commentary page, including a section for letters to the editor. Pages six–eight are set aside for economic and business news, followed by several pages of pure advertising. The latter half of the paper is usually dedicated to culture, living, people, education, and other social issues, with occasional base-related or election/politics-related stories appearing. Younger staff in various locations throughout the prefecture and in Tokyo (near the Diet) handle the reporting, with senior staff taking on the interpretation and editorials (and these are usually done with one person taking the lead as the person designated to write it[47]).

The tone of both editorials and articles, as alluded to earlier, is generally critical of both the U.S. military and the Japanese central government, which is seen as responsible for the current "oppressive" situation in Okinawa with the bases.[48] This constant criticism has frustrated and continues to challenge public affairs officials of both the U.S. military and Japanese government as they feel their side of the story is not presented adequately or even accurately.[49] Media representatives on the other hand resent the stonewalling that they feel they get when asking questions, the answers that are incomplete, and the general lack of professionalism of those with whom they come into contact, especially among the younger officers and local staff.

It is in this tense atmosphere that reporters and the respective public affairs officials work, and which forms the prism by which the news is covered and reported to the prefecture's readers. With the proliferation of domestic and international travel to and from Okinawa, Internet use, and study in mainland Japan and abroad, local residents are less dependent than they were in the past on the local media's views of local, national, and world affairs.[50] Nevertheless, because of the still overwhelmingly large number of readers that the two newspapers, whose editorial stance and coverage differ only slightly, possess, it would not be incorrect to say that they set the tone and contents (level of understanding) of the debate in Okinawa, more so than the mainland-affiliated local television stations, which have less in depth and systematic reporting, and thus for better or worse public opinion in Okinawa is affected by the articles and editorials appearing in the local press.[51]

THE DEBATE IN OKINAWA AFTER 9/11 AND THE WAR ON TERRORISM

This section, introducing the local commentary after 9/11, is based on an examination of the contents of all of the editorials and articles appearing in the local press in the three years after the terrorist attacks, and includes public opinion polls where available. The following issues are looked at: general commentary after 9/11, commentary on Japan's response to events (including Prime Minister Koizumi Junichiro's September 24, 2001, trip to the United States and the Diet passage of the antiterrorism special measures bills), commentary on the military action in Afghanistan by the United States and its allies (and the dispatch of the SDF), commentary on the economic situation in Okinawa as a result of the terrorist attacks, and commentary on the war in Iraq and Japan's participation.

Commentary in the Aftermath of 9/11

As discussed earlier, although there was a fair showing of condemnation for the indiscriminate terrorist attacks in the editorials in Okinawa, there was an equal if not greater expression of concern about the impact events would have on Okinawa. There were also allusions to U.S. policies as being the root cause of the attack.

The *Okinawa Taimusu*, for example, in its September 13 editorial, after condemning the attacks, used the remaining space to introduce its interpretations of events leading up to the attacks:

> It has to be said that there is a limit to American strategy which uses its power to force its views. In particular, this is true in its anti-terror policies…It is probably not a coincidence that the target of the terrorists was the World Trade Center and the Pentagon. The World Trade Center is not only a symbol of America's wealth, but also a symbol of globalization. The Pentagon, which is the nickname of the U.S. Department of Defense, is as its title suggests, the building symbolizing America's military power. This act of terrorism is believed to have been undertaken by a group close to radical Islamists who oppose U.S. "hegemony." Residents living in the Palestinian Autonomous Area cheered the attacks. On the one hand, you have innocent residents in New York who met tragic circumstances, crying, and on the other we have seen innocent residents [in Palestine] standing on tops of cars cheering. This contrasting sight is sad. Without thinking calmly about why such a scene has emerged, an effective anti-terrorism policy cannot be made. In order to do away with terrorism, it is necessary to listen to the voices of the people who welcomed the news of the attacks.

Continuing, the *Taimusu* also alluded to the bases in Okinawa and the implications for the prefecture.

> It is said that U.S. bases in Okinawa have gone on high alert due to the terrorist attacks [Stateside]. Whether one likes the bases or not, because they are located here, there is a chance that Okinawa will be drawn into an unpredictable situation. It is not something taking place away from its shores. The attacks in the U.S. will become with all probability the "beginning of a change" in the Japan–U.S. alliance. It will be very unfortunate for Okinawa if there is a return to the Cold War-like days of choosing friends and enemies.

The *Shimpo* on the other hand, in the editorial of the same day, called for solidarity and an international response, but in a way to caution against actions that could worsen the situation:

> International society, together, should make anew its commitment to fight against all forms of terrorism and search for the legal (*gohoteki*) means that are effective to deter terrorism . . . However, it is probably impossible to prevent or eliminate terrorism by strengthening military power and traditional security thinking seen to date. In fact, such actions might actually have the opposite effect of escalating the tragedy . . . If international society as a whole does not make serious efforts to overcome the poverty that provides the breeding ground for terrorism and avoid the frictions and clashes of religion, ethnicity, and civilization, then the "chain of hatred" can not be broken.

In this vein, the *Shimpo* was concerned when U.S. president George W. Bush labeled the attacks as "acts of war" in his press conference on the morning of September 12 in the Cabinet Room and stated that the "country would use all its resources to conquer this enemy."[52] Describing the anticipated U.S. response as a "retaliation (*hofuku*)" (a word that the president did not use[53]), the *Shimpo* "call[ed] for a cautious response by the United States."[54] "The history of conflicts (*funso no rekishi*) shows that retaliation is not a solution to problems." While introducing the opinion that the background to the terrorist attacks was the result of American unilateralism, it at the same time (somewhat paradoxically) called on the United States "as the sole superpower in the world to exercise leadership and show how international society should live in the post–Cold War era . . . and to work toward bringing peace toward regions experiencing conflict." Unfortunately, it did not give details on how to do this.

The *Taimusu* also used the word retaliation when discussing the possible response, editorializing that "we can not permit just any and all retaliatory measures. The idea that an illegal action [terrorism] should be met with another illegal action is dangerous. If this is permitted, the foundation of international society will be shaken and a dangerous situation in which hatred and animosity fills the air will likely be the result."[55] After expressing concern about possible injuries among "innocent civilians, especially those of women and children" as a result of "retaliatory military attacks," the *Taimusu* ended the editorial by stating that "International society is faced with the question of how to respond to international terrorism and a crisis it has never faced on this scale." Unfortunately, like the *Shimpo*, it did not offer an answer.

Commentary on Japan's Response

It was a week in the case of the *Shimpo* and ten days for the *Taimusu* before local editorials appeared on the response the Japanese government should take. (Indeed, commentary about concern over the economic impact appeared earlier in the *Taimusu* than about the proper response of Japan.) In both cases the commentary urged caution.

On the eve of Prime Minister Koizumi's September 19 announcement of a seven-point package, including the unprecedented dispatch of the SDF, to support the United States in its efforts to deal with international terrorism, the *Shimpo* had the following editorial. "Lending support, of course, is to be expected," it observed, "but the constitutional debate to date is also important...What is necessary is a calm discussion on what the limits are."[56] The *Shimpo*'s suggestion was for Japan to think about the way it "can contribute to avoiding the clash of civilizations." Just how it could do so was left unspecified.

The *Taimusu*, which has a close working relationship with the center-left *Asahi Shimbun*, had its own editorial a couple of days later, calling for the protection of the constitution's peace clause:

> The contents [of the statement] had the danger of going beyond the basic stance [of the government] that "it would do as much as it could within the confines allowed by the constitution." The constitutional restraints, which prevent the exercise of the right of collective self-defense and form the government's interpretation, are significant and we must not allow them to be done away with step by step.[57]

Both the *Taimusu*'s comments and those of the *Shimpo*, which had a similar editorial the next day, hinted that Koizumi's decision to introduce the package outlining its support of the United States and to seek an "honored place in international society (*kokusai shakai de meiyo aru chii*)" was made in response to Deputy Secretary of State Richard L. Armitage's reported request to Japanese ambassador Yanai Shunji for Japan "to show the flag."[58]

The *Shimpo*'s editorial went on to warn, in what would be one of the central themes of the local press' antiwar stance, of civilian causalities.

> If the civilian population is affected in Afghanistan and other countries which are the targets of attack in the American-led "retaliatory war," this would mean that [the United States] has itself fallen to the same moral level as those that committed the surprise attack on the World Trade Center...If many citizens are killed or injured in the country targeted for strikes by America's use of force, this would clearly be against the spirit of [the Japanese] constitution and would likely allow [Japan] to occupy a place of honor in international society.

Apparently, the local press equates intentional and indiscriminate killing in the terrorist attacks with unintentional victims of the conflict in Afghanistan.

Continuing on the controversy of the reported Show the Flag comment, the *Shimpo* in its September 25 editorial observed that "responding to an American official's request, the Japanese government is ignoring the constitutional restrictions and the history of the debate on the constitution built up over the years…We are very scared," it continued, "with the 'leaning to the right' of the Koizumi administration, which seems to permit just about anything in the name of support America in the War on Terrorism…Where is it written that in order to secure an honored place in international society, the SDF must be sent?"[59]

The *Shimpo* continued with this argument in its editorial on Koizumi's September 25 trip to Washington and New York, which appeared in the September 27 edition. "We hear that the prime minister is obsessed with the need to realize the phrase appearing in the preamble of the Constitution 'an honored place in international society.' But there must be other ways than sending the SDF in which an honored place in international society can be actualized in the spirit of the constitution."[60] If there is, it was not introduced in the editorial.

In a similar vein, the *Taimusu* editorial of September 28 described (without specifics) the "setting forth of detailed policies to realize Article 9's spirit of the non-use of force and the preamble's spirit of international cooperation" as "extremely important."[61] It went on to argue that the "treating of Article 9 as some bothersome thing and going ahead whenever one feels like it with exercising the right of collective self-defense is most dangerous (*ichiban kiken*)."

There were several points of criticism over the legislation introduced and being discussed in the Diet in the fall of 2001, in addition to the fundamental question of dispatch of the SDF. One had to do with the view that the legislation was "vague (*aimai*)," something to which even the prime minister admitted. A second issue, which became the target of local editorials, was on the question of whether Diet approval was necessary prior to the dispatch of SDF forces. The Democratic Party of Japan (*Minshuto*) had introduced an amendment making prior approval (*jizen shonin*) necessary. The ruling parties (Liberal Democratic Party, Komeito, and Conservative Party) opposed the amendment because of delays that could emerge in a crisis situation with such a requirement.

To this, the *Okinawa Taimusu* argued "what is more important [than responding to a crisis quickly] is the full implementation of civilian control over the dispatch of the SDF in time of conflict."[62] The *Shimpo*'s editorial was amazingly similar: "'approval of the dispatch of SDF after the fact' completely does away with 'civilian control' and amounts to the Diet surrendering on its own its role."[63] Based on the two newspapers' commentary, the *Shimpo* and the *Taimusu* both seem to define civilian control as that which is exercised by the Diet. In fact, however, when the concept or practice of civilian control is mentioned in the literature or professional settings, it usually means the management of military affairs by a civilian or non-uniformed representative who is directly above the military organization he or she is charged to manage. In Japan's case, not only is this condition met by the existence of a prime minister, a civilian and democratically elected member of the Diet (which in turns designates the prime minister by a resolution), but it is also realized by the presence of a civilian director of the Defense Agency (now Ministry, effective January 9, 2007).[64] (Indeed, as per Article 66 of the postwar constitution, all members of the cabinet must be civilians, or *bunmin*.) In other words, civilian control of the SDF and the Diet's exercise of a possible veto power over the prime minister's decision to dispatch the SDF (or use it as a foreign policy tool) can be said to be two separate things. The local press, however, tended to blend the two issues viewing civilian control as a larger process that involves the full participation of the Diet.

Commentary on the War in Afghanistan

The Diet's approval of the legislation came a little more than a week after the United States and Britain launched strikes against Taliban regime structures and Al Qaeda training camps on October 7. The *Shimpo* lamented the turn of events as "unfortunate (*zannen*)."[65] The *Taimusu* questioned whether there was an international consensus for the strikes in the first place.[66]

Introducing occasional letters from readers, the editorials in Okinawa focused on four issues: (i) the lack of convincing debate for the air strikes; (ii) the fact that retaliation will only invite reprisals; (iii) the need to avoid civilian casualties; and (iv) the fear of having U.S. bases in the prefecture. Of these, the latter two issues had the most impact on the Okinawa debate.[67] The first of these is discussed in the following paragraphs. The second is discussed in a later section following this one.

First, the concern over civilian casualties was based on Okinawa's own tragic war history, when more civilians died than those of both the Japanese Imperial Army forces and the U.S. invading forces combined. Caught up in the almost three-month battle, and having been subjected to bombing runs for six months prior to the April 1, 1945, invasion of the main island of Okinawa, the people of the prefecture, being the only Japanese civilians to have experienced a land battle in World War II, were particularly sensitive to the devastation that can be caused when fighting takes place in areas heavily populated by non-combatants. That history and the stories of survivors have been retold in countless books and documentaries over the years, including the writings of former governor Ota Masahide.[68] It has also been remembered in the memorial of the Princess Lilies (Himeyuri) Girls High School and more recently with the construction of the Cornerstone of Peace (*Heiwa no Ishiji*) and Peace Memorial Museum in Mabuni, the site of the last organized fighting of the Battle of Okinawa, in which the names of all those killed, including foreign and Japanese troops as well as civilians, are listed on dozens of walls.[69] Raising awareness of "peace," in other words, the horror of war, has been a particularly strong mission of many in Okinawa, especially during the Ota administration.

Along these lines, academic/activist Arasaki Moriteru, one of those asked to regularly comment in the local press, co-organized a rally attended by some ninety people (from thirty-three organizations) on September 22 against the likely U.S. strikes. The day before, the anti-base group called

Okinawa Kara Kichi wo Nakushi Sekai no Heiwa wo Motomeru Shimin Renrakukai (Citizen's Liaison Council Demanding the Removal of U.S. Bases and World Peace) that he coheads began a sit-in in front of the prefectural government building. The group subsequently submitted a petition criticizing the lack of disclosure regarding the movements of U.S. forces (such as the visit of a nuclear-powered submarine to Okinawa in September) to the base affairs office and Foreign Ministry's liaison office on the twenty-fifth of that month.[70]

Many guest speakers from Afghanistan and those involved in NGO/NPO work came to Okinawa to speak. Photo exhibits were also held over the coming weeks and months about the bombing and its effects on the local population in Afghanistan. These events were it was widely covered by the press. (A search of the pre-9/11 editorials shows no discussion of the repressive Taliban regime, however, and the amount of internal destruction the regime brought to Afghanistan, including of its own cultural heritage sites and violence against foreigners and its own citizens.) Symbolic of the new attention Afghanistan was receiving then and after, the first Okinawa Peace Prize (*Okinawa Heiwasho*), awarded by the OPG, was granted in July 2002 to a medical services and humanitarian relief organization called Peshawar Kai, based in Fukuoka with local staffs in Afghanistan and Pakistan.[71]

As seen from the low turnout of the above rally, not all residents of the prefecture were so strongly opposed to military action against the terrorists. In a poll of the mayors of thirty-two cities, towns, and villages in the prefecture, 65.6 percent expressed support for the U.S. military strikes.[72] This, by chance, was the same percentage as a national poll conducted a few days before that by the *Nihon Seron Chosakai* (Japanese Public Opinion Council).[73]

Similarly, on the eve of the war, some 84.4 percent of respondents in Okinawa thought Japan should extend its cooperation to the United States. However, it should be noted, no one, according to the poll organizers at the *Shimpo*, answered that Japan should participate in combat operations. This was in line with the answers to a subsequent question—should Japan be able exercise the right of collective self-defense (presumably through reinterpretation or revision)? Some 59.4 percent expressed their opposition to it, with only 9.4 percent expressing support. National polls, however, showed much greater support for exercising the right of collective self-defense, suggesting a huge difference in views on that very important issue. Still, 53.1 percent stated their support of revising the SDF Law (*Jieitaiho*) to permit the SDF to guard U.S. bases in Japan. Considering Okinawa's historic distrust of Japan's military, in this case the predecessor to the current SDF, the Japanese Imperial Army, the level of support is not insignificant.[74]

Part of this has to do with the general increase in support for the SDF over the years, as is discussed in the next part. Another reason was simple realism. Namely, 75 percent of the respondents felt a sense of fear that Okinawa would become a target with U.S. bases concentrated there. Thus, the respondents may have viewed the efforts of the SDF to strengthen the level of force protection of U.S. bases in a more positive light based out of necessity. (At the same time, as seen later, some thought the heavy SDF/police presence was overkill.)

"Dangerous Okinawa"

The view that Okinawa was vulnerable to attack was held not only among many Okinawans, but also among people in mainland Japan. In particular, the organizers of group travel tours such as class trips were concerned about air travel and their safety in Okinawa. The timing could not have been worse. Many of the high-school and middle-school class trips to Okinawa begin in the fall. The delays in air travel and the images of a locked-down but still vulnerable Okinawa was enough to discourage vacation travelers and the schools from sending their students. With Okinawa heavily dependent on tourism, and the number of travelers to Okinawa increasing every year (in the year 2000, the number of students visiting Okinawa on class trips reached three hundred thousand), any drop off could have a serious effect.[75]

The first of many editorials on the issue of tourism (as many as on the war on terrorism itself) began to appear a week after the attacks and was captured in political cartoons as well.[76] Recognizing the need for action to be taken, the *Shimpo* called for an active campaign to bring visitors to the prefecture, much like New York did with a forty-million-dollar campaign of its own.[77] This became all the more important when it was discovered in the latter half of September that air travel to Okinawa had by then already dropped off 16 percentage points. In the meantime, on September 26, representatives of the Okinawa Convention Bureau departed for all parts of Japan to speak with travel agencies and school boards and tell them that "Okinawa is safe." This message—a declaration that Okinawa was in fact safe—was subsequently passed as a resolution in the Prefectural Assembly on October 15. In the meantime, the hotel industry asked people living in the prefecture to stay at a local hotel once in a while to support the industry. Organizations and associations in other parts of Japan, which have different types of exchange relations with their Okinawa counterparts, organized trips to the prefecture to show their concern, in other words to show the flag, for Okinawa's plight, particularly to express their thanks for Okinawan residents who had traveled to their areas in the past when their own areas had been affected by some problem or natural disaster.[78]

These efforts did not stop the cancellations, however, which not only impacted the tourist industry including the hotels that cater to travelers, but also the associated businesses, and Okinawa as a whole. In late October, figures released showed a rise in unemployment to 9.4 percent (nationally 5.3 percent), a rise of 0.2 percentage points, during the month of September alone. Almost everyday, editorials focused on the tourism crisis and/or the worsening economy. A response by the central government was called for.

Okinawans tended to view the bases as the root of this evil, and described the tightened security around the bases as "leading to the lowering of Okinawa's image as a tourist destination and the crisis with cancellations."[79]

A local survey of those involved in the tourism industry (hotels, gift shops, marine sports, rental car offices) conducted in November showed that 59 percent of respondents believed that "the bases being concentrated [in Okinawa] was the reason" that tourism dropped off, and 54 percent said that it was "impossible" for "bases (*kichi*)" and "tourism (*kanko*)" to coexist.[80] Only 11 percent said that the drop off was likely due to a fear of flying.[81]

Eventually, as the shock of the hijackings and crashing of the planes into the Twin Towers and Pentagon faded from memory, domestic and international travel began to pick up and tourists going to Okinawa would hit record numbers again. But for those several months after 9/11, an inherently weak prefectural economy in a poorly performing national economy hit with the worldwide impact of terrorism made the situation appear extremely desperate for Okinawans—something they did not want to see repeated again.

Commentary on the War in Iraq

This would be one of the reasons, but obviously not the only reason, why Okinawans would oppose the invasion by the United States and its coalition partners of Iraq less than a year after Okinawa began to recover economically. Like the situation in Afghanistan, Okinawans were also concerned about civilian casualties, particularly as the ground war was much more intense than that in Afghanistan a year and half before.

But even before the Iraq War actually began, Okinawans, like many of their Japanese compatriots (and indeed many in the world), were not satisfied with the reasons for going to war in Iraq, did not believe the Bush administration had made a credible case, and thought that the UN weapons inspectors should have been given more time to conduct their search for Saddam Hussein's weapons of mass destruction. For example, according to a telephone poll conducted by the *Shimpo* in mid-March on the eve of the start of hostilities with more than one thousand people locally, 92 percent of the respondents said that inspections should continue.[82] Only 7 percent said that the inspections were unsuccessful and thus military action was unavoidable. Similarly, 90 percent of respondents voiced their opposition to a possible war, with only 8 percent in favor.

Symbolic of this strong opposition to the war, peace activists and labor unions (forming the "Stop the Attack on Iraq! Prefectural People's Committee against War," or *Sutoppu Iraku Kogeki! Senso wo Yurusanai Okinawa Kenmin Taikai*) organized a demonstration at Yogi Park in Naha, a traditional gathering point for anti-base and other protests. Unlike the lead up to the Afghan War with its small turnout, this rally was attended by some fifty-five hundred people, according to organizers.

Likewise, in light of this opposition, 63 percent of the respondents in the poll mentioned earlier stated that Japan "should not cooperate" if asked to do so by the United States, and only 4 percent believed it should do so. Moreover, only 30 percent said Japan could cooperate even with a UN resolution. From another perspective, 50 percent of respondents stated that Japan's diplomacy should be focused on avoiding war.

When tensions build internationally, Okinawans tend to feel that the so-called Okinawa problem gets less attention on the national agenda, and that any plans to reduce the burden, through, for example, base consolidations and troop reductions, get shelved. "In the constantly changing situation with the Iraq War and the Korean Peninsula issue, the interest of the people of the country in Okinawa's base problem gets less and less."[83]

For Okinawa, with its heavy concentration of U.S. bases, this had several of the same serious consequences. While the fear of flying following the terrorist hijackings had generally abated, the view of Okinawa as *kiken*, or dangerous, continued (or got stronger). Moreover, in the post-9/11 environment with strengthened force protection measures in place, frictions emerged over information disclosure and access to sites near bases (popular with tourists) to watch the U.S. military in action. Nevertheless, due to the tourist promotion campaigns put into place since the 9/11 attacks, 2003 actually saw the highest number of visitors ever, with 5,850,000 tourists coming.[84]

Like most observers in Japan and around the world, opinion of the U.S.-led handling of the occupation and administration of Iraq since the initial invasion has been quite critical in Okinawa. Moreover, a great deal of criticism emerged over the government's decision to dispatch the Ground Self Defense Forces to Iraq to help in the reconstruction efforts. As the situation in Iraq deteriorated, local editorials called for the government to withdraw the SDF.[85] Since the transfer of sovereignty to Iraqi authorities at the end of June 2004, there was less commentary in the press, and following the SDF departure in the summer of 2006, very little coverage is now given.

Conclusion

As this study has shown, many unresolved problems, such as Futenma Air Station relocation and Okinawan desires for the revision of the Status of Forces Agreement, were on the agenda of Okinawa–U.S.–Japan relationship when the 9/11 attacks occurred. Numerous base issues, such as the construction of a new Urban Warfare training facility within Camp Hansen (that came to light a few months after the 9/11 attacks) and the U.S. global posture review that led to the "Roadmap for Implementation" agreement in May 2006 are also gradually complicating the local political scene and public opinion, further muddied by a helicopter crash in August 2004 and its aftermath. These concerns, as well as the overall criticism of American foreign policy during the Bush administration, showed themselves at the time of the July 12 (2004) Upper House elections in which two progressive candidates won in Okinawa.

Summarizing public opinion as introduced in the newspapers, in their articles and editorials, and in public opinion polls, we see the following trends.

First, Okinawans were sympathetic to the United States in its time of national crisis with the 9/11 terrorist attacks and several commentators and local leaders and citizens actually expressed support for the U.S. military campaign in Afghanistan, like their mainland compatriots. Likewise, there was support for Japan to cooperate in some way, although only a small percentage expressed actual support in revising the interpretation of the right of collective self-defense. Mainland Japanese on the other hand voiced stronger support for reinterpretation or constitutional revision. All of this suggests that Okinawans, while aware of the need for Japan to play a larger role, desire that it be a purely nonmilitary one.

Second, and similarly, Okinawans retain a deep distrust of anything military. While support of the SDF has clearly grown over the years, it is support for an SDF not close by (in Okinawa) and one that is not being dispatched abroad. This suggests the need for the SDF to undertake expanded public relations efforts if they wish to foster greater support for their activities, which includes disaster relief. Likewise, Okinawans retain a fear of having U.S. military bases in the prefecture, which could make Okinawa a target of attack. They also consider the bases a huge inconvenience during times of crisis as the potential for tourism to drop off increases (this was true after the 9/11 attacks, but not so much after the start of the Iraq War).

Third, Okinawan newspaper editorials are often critical, making broad and sweeping suggestions without the specifics to realize them. Actual policy recommendations they are not. They are not policy recommendations and generally follow a "peace-at-any-cost" school of thought.

Finally, a word needs to be said on the need for systematic studies on public opinion in Okinawa. The polls done to date have been superficial and haphazard at best, with little or no efforts at coordination and systematizing the information. Each newspaper does its own thing, at its own time. This, of course, is fine, but when academics and other interested individuals are attempting to discover, through public polling information, where Okinawa has been, where it is now, and where it is going, there is a surprising lack of reliable data to be had.

Notes

1. "Shasetsu (Editorial): Beichusu Doji Tero Kokusai Shakai ni taisuru Bokyo Nikumu Aku Umu Dojo Nakusu Doryoku wo (The Terrorist Attacks in the U.S. were Violence against International Society: Efforts Must be Made To Rid World of Hatred)," *Ryukyu Shimpo*, September 13, 2001.
2. "Shasetsu (Editorial): Beikoku he no Doji Tero Zoaku no Rensa wo Yuryo Suru (Terrorist Attacks in U.S. Concern about Cycle of Hatred)," *Okinawa Taimusu*, September 13, 2001.
3. The bilateral security treaty was first signed on September 8, 1951, and went into effect on April 28, 1952. It was revised as the Treaty of Mutual Cooperation and Security, signed on January 19, 1960, and has continued to this day. When administrative rights over Okinawa were returned to Japan on May 15, 1972, U.S. facilities there came under the Status of Forces Agreement of January 1960 (officially known as the Agreement Under Article VI of the Treaty of Mutual Cooperation and Security, Facilities and Areas and the

Status of United States Armed Forces in Japan Between the United States of America and Japan).

4. For more on the history of Okinawa following its return to Japan in 1972, see Robert D. Eldridge, *Post-Reversion Okinawa and U.S.–Japan Relations: A Preliminary Survey of Local Politics and the Bases, 1972–2002* (Osaka: Center for International Security Studies and Policy, 2004), available at http://www2.osipp.osaka-u.ac.jp/~cissp/CISSP_En/top_e.htm.

5. "Raifuruju de Honshi Kisha Ikaku, Deetakaado Ubau Beigun Heishi (U.S. Soldier Threatens Reporter from Ryukyu Shimpo with Rifle, Steals Data Card)," *Ryukyu Shimpo*, September 13, 2001. Interviews by author with reporter mentioned in incident between September 2001 and August 2004.

6. According to the reporter, editor Miyara lodged no formal complaint, but a representative of the U.S. Marine Corps did visit the *Shimpo*'s office to discuss the contents of the story. The conversation ended with both sides insisting on their respective version of events.

7. Author's conversations with public affairs and community relations officials of the U.S. Marine Corps familiar with events, both in Okinawa and during a visit by one of these individuals to the author's university for a roundtable the author organized on "Crisis Management and Public Relations" October 19, 2001 (for highlights of the roundtable, see http://www.osipp.osaka-u.ac.jp/newsletter/97-00NL/NL21PDF/NL21-3.pdf). Apparently there were similar incidents with the crews of other news agencies (*Okinawa Times*, Okinawa Television, etc.), but not widely reported. Despite this, there was no subsequent follow-up on discussing proper procedures for covering the bases in this tense situation—a missed opportunity to build better, or at least more professional, relations between the two sides.

8. Even a cursory glance at back editions of the Okinawan press will show that it limits, for reasons unclear, the number of experts whose comments it introduces in its pages to a few regulars, and due to their regular appearance, one almost knows what they will say without reading the article/interview.

9. "Shudanteki Jieiken wo Yonin, Okinawa Kichi mo Shugeki Taisho ni (Recognize Right of Collective Self-Defense, Okinawan Bases a Target for Attack)," *Ryukyu Shimpo*, September 13, 2001.

10. "Kichi Jugyoin ni Jitaku Taiki Shiji, Tero Jiken Taio de Beigun (U.S. Military Directs Base Workers to Wait at Home in Response to Terror Incident)," *Ryukyu Shimpo*, September 13, 2001. The DFAA was disbanded in September 2007, with its responsibilities assumed by the Defense Ministry.

11. "Keiki he no Eikyo wo Kenen Bei Chusu Doji Tero Ken Keizaikai Hankyo (Fearing the Impact on the Economy Prefectural Business Communities Reactions to the Terrorist Attacks)," *Ryukyu Shimpo*, September 13, 2001.

12. "Tero Joho no Jizen Teikyo wo, Ken Yongunchoseikan Jimusho ni Yosei (Prefecture Requests Okinawa Area Coordinator's Office to Relay Terror Information in Advance)," *Ryukyu Shimpo*, September 15, 2001.

13. "Kichi Jugyoin ni Jitaku Taiki Shiji."

14. The then-U.S. consul general in Okinawa was in the United States at the time of the attacks. (The author attended a meeting with him in Hawaii shortly after the attacks and was told this directly.) His absence may explain the failure for the information to be relayed by the U.S. side, but more likely, it may have been systematic in nature (i.e., that informing the OPG was not the responsibility of U.S. authorities). In any case, the Okinawa liaison office

of the Foreign Ministry or the Defense Facilities Administration Agency's Naha Office would most likely have been the channel of such information. If the OPG's assertion that it was not informed is true, then it appears that MOFA or the DFAA may be to blame.

15. "Jumin ni Fuan to Kincho, Kichi Shozai no Shichoson (Fear and Anxiety among Residents in Cities, Towns, and Villages Hosting Bases)," *Ryukyu Shimpo*, September 13, 2001. Kadena Air Base covers approximately 83 percent of the town of Kadena, alone, not to mention neighboring communities such as Chatan and Okinawa City.

16. Ibid.

17. Ibid.

18. Ibid.

19. For more on this, see Robert D. Eldridge, "The 1996 Okinawa Referendum on U.S. Base Reductions: One Question, Several Answers," *Asian Survey*, Vol. 37, No. 10 (October 1997), pp. 879–904. The crash of a Marine Corps CH-53D helicopter on a routine training mission in mid-August 2004 highlighted the issue once again.

20. Armin H. Meyer, *Assignment Tokyo: An Ambassador's Journal* (Indianapolis: The Bobbs-Merrill Company, 1974), p. 27. Meyer was ambassador to Japan during the reversion negotiations and completion of the reversion agreement. For a thoughtful essay on Okinawa's complicated relations with the central government over the years, see Sheila A. Smith, "A Place Apart: Okinawa and Japan's Postwar Peace," in Akira Iriye and Robert A. Wampler, eds., *Partnership: The United States and Japan, 1951–2001* (Tokyo: Kodansha, 2001), pp. 179–98. Also see Eldridge, *Post-Reversion Okinawa and U.S.–Japan Relations*.

21. For more on the opposition to the relocation of Futenma, currently the site of a sit-in demonstration that has been going on since the middle of 2004, see Robert D. Eldridge, "Okinawa and the Nago Heliport Problem in the U.S.–Japan Relationship," *Asia–Pacific Review*, Vol. 7, No. 1 (May 2000), pp. 137–56.

22. At the time of the publication of this book in 2008, the author has visited Okinawa a total of eighty times. This study, as will be seen, does not include or separately analyze demographics (age, gender, education, career, income, dependency on bases, geographical location, relative proximity to base, etc.). A fuller study would be necessary for that. Some important characteristics of Okinawa that must be kept in mind when discussing the prefecture include the fact that the southern and central areas are the more prosperous, and also the more populated, and include the heavier concentration of military bases (and thus noise pollution, fear of accidents, trouble with rowdy young U.S. personnel, etc.). Communities hosting bases generally have a different worldview than those that do not. However, the dynamics are more complicated in that while closeness sometimes breeds friction, it also creates a cycle of dependency with the landowners, business owners, and base workers (of which there are currently eight thousand). Another dynamic includes a general feeling held by people in the north that they are the "dumping ground" for unwanted projects much of the time; witness the Futenma relocation plan to build the facility in Henoko, off of Nago City's eastern shore.

23. As part of the prewar and wartime censorship, the Japanese government saw to it that each prefecture would have only one newspaper necessitating

the three newspapers (*Ryukyu Shimpo, Okinawa Nippo,* and *Okinawa Asahi Shimbun*) that existed at the time in Okinawa to merge into one. For more, see Ryukyu Shimpo Hyakunenshi Kanko Iinkai, ed., *Ryukyu Shimpo Hyakunenshi* (One Hundred Years of the Ryukyu Shimpo) (Naha: Ryukyu Shimposha, 1993), pp. 139–40, and for a short online history, *Ryukyu Shimpo 110 Nen no Rekishi: Okinawa no Ima Tsutaetsuzuke* (The 110-Year History of the Ryukyu Shimpo: Continuing to Report on Okinawa Today), available at http://www.ryukyushimpo.co.jp/special/kiseki/kiseki.html. Also see Makuta Satoshi, *Sengo Okinawa no Shimbunjin* (Postwar Okinawa Newspaper Personalities) (Naha: Okinawa Taimusu sha, 1999).

24. The name change and its timing was significant. It was symbolic and meant to show that foreign control was ending with the signing of the peace treaty. In fact, the United States would continue to administer the islands as part of Article 3 of the treaty, until May 15, 1972. For more on the formation of Article 3, see Robert D. Eldridge, *The Origins of the Bilateral Okinawa Problem: Okinawa in Postwar U.S.–Japan Relations, 1945–1952* (New York: Garland, 2001).

25. Takamine Choko, *Shimbun 50 Nen* (50 Years of Newspapers) (Naha: Okinawa Taimusu, 1973), pp. 359–73. Takamine was the first president of the *Okinawa Taimusu.* Around this time, a number of newspapers began to spring up—the *Okinawa Mainichi Shimbun* (in August 1948), the *Ryukyu Nippo* (in September 1949), and the *Okinawa Herald Shimbun* (in October 1949). U.S. authorities were concerned that media organizations' concentration in Naha "could lead to the reemergence of militarist ideas." As a result, U.S. occupation authorities assigned each newspaper different areas of circulation. The *Uruma Shimpo,* which had close ties and was most dependent on the military, was assigned the area from Naha to central Okinawa. The *Taimusu* was assigned the area south of Naha. The *Herald* was given the rest of central Okinawa, and the *Okinawa Mainichi,* which was also dependent on the military for printing presses, ink, and paper, was assigned the northern part of Okinawa. See Mark Hollstein, "Framing Security: A Trilateral Discourse Analysis of Ideology in Newspaper Reports about the United States Military in Okinawa" (Unpublished PhD dissertation, University of Hawaii, 2000), p. 124; and Okinawa Furii Jaanarisuto Kaigi, ed., *Okinawa no Shimbun ga Tsubureru Hi* (The Day Newspapers in Okinawa are Gone) (Naha: Gekkan Okinawasha, 1994). For a thoughtful article comparing Japanese (Okinawan-included) press and the U.S. press on Okinawa-related issues, see Reimei Okamura, "U.S.–Japan Relations and the Media in the Information Age: Coverage of the American Bases Issues in Okinawa," *The Japanese Journal of American Studies,* No. 9 (1998), pp. 5–27.

26. M. Toguchi, "Taimusu-Shimpo no Shito (The Times–Shimpo Struggle)," in Okinawa Furii Jaanarisuto Kyogi, ed., *Okinawa no Shimbun,* pp. 293–316.

27. Hollstein, "Framing Security," p. 127.

28. For more on the Okinawa Taimusu, see Okinawa Taimusu Shashi Henshu Iinkai, ed., *Shimbun 30 Nen: Okinawa Taimusu Ga Ikita Okinawa Sengoshi* (30 Years of the Newspaper: The Postwar History of Okinawa that the Okinawa Times Has Lived) (Naha: Okinawa Taimusu, 1979).

29. Correspondence with senior writer of *Taimusu,* August 2004.

30. In recent years, the reformists have had trouble working together on common policies, particularly on the base problems. The die-hards are seen as

unrealistic by some of their colleagues who have called in recent years for a middle road between the two positions (immediate withdrawal and acceptance of the bases). For more, see Eldridge, *Post-Reversion Okinawa and U.S.–Japan Relations.*

31. Two recent books deal with such themes. See Glenn D. Hook and Richard Siddle, eds., *Japan and Okinawa: Structure and Subjectivity* (London: Routledge Curzon, 2003); and Laura Hein and Mark Selden, eds., *Islands of Discontent: Okinawan Responses to Japanese and American Power* (Lanham: Rowman & Littlefield, 2003).

32. See the book by the then deputy chief editor of the Ryukyu Shimpo, Miki Ken, *Okinawa: Datsuwa no Jidai* (Okinawa: The Age of Leaving Japan) (Naha: Niraisha, 1992).

33. According to statistics as of June 2004, the *Nikkei* sells 3938 copies per month, the *Asahi* 1735 copies, the *Yomiuri Shimbun* 532, the *Mainichi Shimbun* 407, and the *Sankei* 284, for a total of 6946.

34. See the homepage of the association at http://www.pressnet.or.jp/english/index.htm (accessed August 2004).

35. For more on this standoff, see Eldridge, *Post-Reversion Okinawa and U.S.–Japan Relations.* Also see Eldridge, "The 1996 Okinawa Referendum on U.S. Base Reductions."

36. Aso Iku, "Tettei Chosa Beigun Kichi no Hitotsubo Jinushi 3000 Nin (Investigation: The 3000 Hitotsubo Anti-War Landowners of U.S. Bases)," *Bungei Shunju*, October 1996, pp. 118–29. While not the subject of this study, one could argue that if such membership impairs accurate coverage of the news, then this would be in violation of "The Canons of Journalism (*Shimbun Rinri Yoryo*)" as adopted by the Nihon Shimbun Kyokai, which reads, "Newspapers are the first chroniclers of history, and the mission of reporters lies in the constant pursuit. Reporting must be accurate and fair, and should never be swayed by the reporter's personal conviction or bias." See http://www.pressnet.or.jp/english/index.htm (accessed August 2004). For the comments of the media leadership implicated, see Aso, "Tettei Chosa," pp. 125–6. The "Hitotsubo Anti-War Landowners," or *Hitotsubo Hansen Jinushikai*, is an organization of supporters of the original antiwar landowners, created by the president of the latter group, Hirayasu Tsuneji. Supporters purchase a small parcel of Hirayasu's land, about 3.3 square metres or one *tsubo* in Japanese measurements, for about ten thousand yen. By increasing the number of people owning land, no matter how small, organizers hoped the leasing process would become more complicated for the central government. Eventually, several thousand people would join from both within and outside Okinawa, dwarfing the number of original antiwar landowners (and exposing the movement to criticism that it was made up of outside agitators). For more, see Eldridge, *Post-Reversion Okinawa and U.S.-Japan Relations*, p. 67.

37. Aso, "Tettei Chosa," p. 125.

38. Ibid., pp. 125–6. Another editor from the same newspaper interviewed declined to comment, Aso writes.

39. Ibid., p. 126.

40. Formerly a national university (Kokuritsu Daigaku) until April 2004 when administrative reforms made it an independent body, Ryukyu University, or *Ryudai*, is considered (some would say, considers itself) the best of the half-dozen colleges in Okinawa, from which many—but not all—of the local

reporters have graduated. It was built in 1950 during the U.S. occupation of Okinawa, making it the first university Okinawa ever had.

41. This intriguing discussion and attended by witnesses of all backgrounds and opinions can be found at the Japanese Diet's committee meetings page, http://kokai.ndl.go.jp/cgi-bin/KENSAKU/swk_list.cgi?SESSION=13782&SAVED_RID=3&MODE=1&DTOTAL=1&DMY=13922 (accessed August 2004). Takubo had recently published an essay criticizing the editorial stances of the local newspapers entitled "'Okinawa no kokoro' to Nichibei Anpo ('Okinawa's Heart' and the Japan–U.S. Alliance)," in the July 1996 issue of center-right monthly journal *Seiron* (pp. 74–83). An English-language version appeared as "The Okinawan Threat to the Security Treaty," *Japan Echo*, Vol. 23, No. 3 (Autumn 1996), pp. 46–52. While this opinion is from a self-identified conservative commentator, it has to be pointed out that reporters from mainland newspapers and television of all political walks of life have said similar things off the record to this author. Due to professional considerations, they do not say so publicly.

42. A month later, Nishimura set off another firestorm when he traveled by boat to and landed on the Senkaku Islands, which are claimed by both Japan and China. Nishimura has also called for Japan to possess nuclear weapons.

43. "Hodo Shisei Towareru Jimotoshi (Local Newspapers' Stance on Reporting Being Questioned)," *Sankei Shimbun*, April 12, 1997, evening edition. The Sankei Newspaper Company (Sankei Shimbunsha) is also the publisher of *Seiron*, the journal cited in note 41 in which Takubo published his article critical of the Okinawan media.

44. Kamada Satoshi, "'Hankichi' no Shimen Zukuri ni Nozomu Kisha Oni (The Reporting Devils Who Create the 'Anti-Base' Newspaper)," *Ushio*, No. 469 (March 1998), p. 146. Despite the title, the article was quite favorable to the *Shimpo*. *Ushio*, published with the support of religious organization Soka Gakkai, has historically taken an anti-base attitude in line with the traditional stance of its political party, *Komeito*.

45. This quote is borrowed from numerous conversations by the author with representatives of all generations of the local media. The italics are the author's.

46. In a dinner conversation with a senior director for a local television station (part of the Television Asahi network), the director said that the media in Okinawa reports "especially for Okinawa (Okinawa no tame ni toku ni yatte iru)," but "is objective." When asked to explain the apparent inconsistency, the director responded that he did not think it was inconsistent.

47. According to a senior member of the editorial board of one of the newspapers, this leads to inconsistency in the quality of the editorials. It also has the danger of personal views being introduced intentionally or unintentionally.

48. This interpretation is based on numerous conversations with U.S. government and military representatives and officials of the Japanese government. Also see Hollstein, "Framing Security," pp. 127–40. The same can be said for local coverage of the Self-Defense Forces.

49. Curiously, little or no effort is made to seek correction of stories. Some public affairs officials have resigned themselves to what they believe is the fact that they will never get a fair deal. Others follow the policy (short-sighted in this writer's opinion) not to comment on any story because by commenting it will be interpreted as verifying that the story is in fact true, something frowned

upon with particularly sensitive stories. The less-than-accurate translations of the stories done by of the public affairs office of the U.S. military no doubt adds to the sense of frustration. The *Shimpo* and the *Taimusu* provided a weekly summary in English of some of the more important stories, although the *Taimusu*, beginning in January 2004, stopped carrying the translations due to the "physical incapacity of our editor…for the next few weeks." In fact, the homepage has yet to be updated, and in effect has been done away with it. The *Shimpo*, similarly, dramatically cut down its coverage of English stories to a few per week and then ended it as well. Apparently both companies feel that it is not economically viable to continue to carry the English-language versions.

50. Clearly this suggests that there is a case for creating in the future a comprehensive survey on what the sources of information and news are for the people of the prefecture, and throughout Japan as a whole, when studying public opinion.

51. While not the subject of this chapter, the producer of a news show for the Ryukyu Asahi Broadcasting Company once said to the director who was interviewing the author on the results of the 2002 gubernatorial election in Okinawa and the question of the so-called fifteen-year time limit on the Futenma relocation, "make him say [this]." I politely declined and told them the interview was over unless the producer left. The director, originally from mainland Japan, has since departed the company, and Okinawa, in fact.

52. "Remarks by the President in Photo Opportunity with the National Security Team (September 12, 2001)," http://www.whitehouse.gov/news/releases/2001/09/20010912-4.html (accessed August 2004).

53. President Bush described responses as an "assault on terrorism" (September 15 radio address) and later "War on Terrorism." Retaliation has an emotional connotation, striking back one time out of anger. Few would probably disagree that the U.S. efforts are a sustained campaign of various political, diplomatic, and military intelligence, financial components to eliminate the terrorist organizations and the networks that support them.

54. "Shasetsu (Editorial): Tero he no Hofuku Shincho na Mikiwame wo Daiichi ni (Retaliating Against Terrorism Cautious Ascertainment Should be First [Priority])," *Ryukyu Shimpo*, September 14, 2001.

55. "Shasetsu (Editorial): Bei Doji Tero to Hofuku Sochi Bunmeikan no Tairitsu ni Suru Na (The Terrorist Attacks in the U.S. and Retaliatory Measures. Do not Make this a Clash of Civilizations)," *Okinawa Taimusu*, September 15, 2001.

56. "Shasetsu (Editorial): Bei Taitero Senso Shien Akumade Kenpo no Wakunai de Nihon no Yakuwari to Genkai Mikawame Yo (Support for the War on Terrorism Has to be Done with the Confines of the Constitution Realize the Limits of Japan's Role)," *Okinawa Taimusu*, September 18, 2001.

57. "Shasetsu (Editorial): Tero to Taibei Shiensaku Isogutomu, Shincho de Are (The Faster [the Government is to Develop] Policies to Support U.S. [in War on] on Terrorism, the More Careful [the Government] Should Be)," *Okinawa Taimusu*, September 21, 2001.

58. Ibid., and "Shasetsu (Editorial): Beidaitoryo Enzetsu 'Buryoku Hofuku' Kyocho ni Kowasa Junpo to Hakuai Seishin Shimesu Beki (Scared of U.S. President's Speech Emphasizing 'Military Retaliation' [U.S. Must Show] Law-Abiding and Benevolent Spirit)," *Ryukyu Shimpo*, September 22, 2001. For more on the impact of the "Show the Flag" debate on Japanese policy-making, see Chijiwa Yasuaki, "Insights into Japan–U.S. Relations on the Eve

of the Iraqi War: Dilemmas over 'Showing the Flag',"*Asian Survey*, Vol. 45, No. 6 (November–December 2005), pp. 843–64.

59. "Shasetsu (Editorial): Jieitai Haken Kenpo no Seiyaku Koeru Kodo Koizumi Seiken no Ukeisha wo Ayugu (The Dispatch of the SDF Goes Beyond Constitutional Restrictions Fearing Koizumi Administration's Shift to Right)," *Ryukyu Shimpo*, September 25, 2001.

60. "Shasetsu (Editorial): Rinji Kokkai Kuni no Shinro Amaranai Rongi wo Tero Taio (Special Session of Diet Make Sure the Debate Does Not Mess up Country's Future)," *Ryukyu Shimpo*, September 27, 2001.

61. "Shasetsu (Editorial): Shoshin Hyomei Enzetsu Kokkai ga Yakuwari wo Hatasuban (Prime Minister's Speech Diet's Turn to Act)," *Okinawa Taimusu*, September 28, 2001.

62. "Shasetsu (Editorial): Tero Taisaku Hoan Kaketsu Gimon no Kaisho ni Mada Toi (Draft Bill on Counter Terror Measures Still a Long Way Before Concerns Resolved)," *Okinawa Taimusu*, October 17, 2001.

63. "Shasetsu (Editorial): Tero Hoan Seiritsu 'Bunmin Tosei' Hoki Shisei (Passage of Draft Bill on Terrorism Appear to Surrender of 'Civilian Control')," *Ryukyu Shimpo*, October 18, 2001.

64. For a recent detailed study on the evolution of Japanese democratic and civilian control, see Tani (Musashi), Katsuhiko, "Reisengo Nihon no Anzen Hosho Seisaku no Rippo Katei ni Okeru Shibirian Kontororu no Kenkyu (A Study of Civilian Control in the Legislative Process for Japanese Security Policy in the Post Cold War)," Doctoral Dissertation, Osaka School of International Public Policy, Osaka University, 2007.

65. "Shasetsu (Editorial): Afugan Kubaku Ippan Shimin wo Makikomuna Kokuren Shudo de Soki Sento Shusoku," *Ryukyu Shimpo*, October 9, 2001.

66. "Shasetsu (Editorial): Beiei ga Afugan Kogeki Saki no Mitooshi ha Aru no ka (The U.S.–British Strikes on Afghanistan. Are There Any Prospects for the Future?)," *Okinawa Taimusu*, October 9, 2001.

67. Ibid., and "Shasetsu (Editorial): Afugan Kubaku Ippan Shimin wo Makikomuna (Do Not Entangle Civilians in the Bombing of Afghanistan)," *Ryukyu Shimpo*, October 9, 2001.

68. See, e.g., Ota Masahide, *The Battle of Okinawa: The Typhoon of Steel and Bombs* (Tokyo: Kume Publishing, 1984).

69. The Cornerstone of Peace was completed in 1995 in time for the fiftieth anniversary of the end of the Battle of Okinawa. The Prefecture Peace Memorial Museum opened in 2000.

70. For more on Arasaki and the group's activities, see Arasaki Moriteru, *Aratana Shiso wa Tsukureruka: 9–11 to Heiwa Undo* (Is New Thinking Possible? 9–11 and the Peace Movement) (Tokyo: Gaifusha, 2004). This is the tenth in a series of books that Arasaki publishes every three years representing a collection of essays during that time.

71. The awarding of the peace prize by a conservative governor seen as "welcoming U.S. bases" set off criticism within the prefecture who challenged Inamine's qualifications. See, e.g., Ibid, pp. 137–41. Apparently some of the committee members wanted to award the prize to the "One-Feet (*sic*) Movement" headed by Nakamura Fumiko, which has sought to document the battle of Okinawa and Okinawa's postwar history by having people contribute money to purchase one foot of film.

72. "Shasetsu (Editorial): Shucho Ankeeto Kichi wo Daeru ga Yue no Fuan (Survey of Mayors With the Bases Fear Looms Large)," *Ryukyu Shimpo*, October 5,

2001. The governor was also asked to respond to the survey, but declined, something that the Shimpo editorial writers "could not understand" and felt was "unfortunate."

73. Ibid., and "Beidoji Tero Zenkoku Yoron Chosa Hofuku Kogeki Shiji 66% Hansu ha Iryo Nanmin Shien Nozumu Kenpo Kaishaku Henko 49 Yonin (National Public Opinion on Terrorist Attacks in U.S. 66% Supports Retaliatory Strikes Half Desire Medical Assistance for Refugees 49% See Need for Constitutional Revision)," *Okinawa Taimusu*, October 3, 2001.

74. As is introduced in the next part, Okinawan support toward the SDF has been gradually increasing over the years and is close to 70 percent today.

75. One of the reasons that so many students are brought to Okinawa is as part of "peace study (*heiwa gakushu*)" tours. Hiroshima and Nagasaki are also regular destinations. The figures used for "visitors" to Okinawa cited by the prefecture actually include regular travelers, including Okinawans returning from business or other trips. The figures, in other words, are generally highly misleading. In this case, however, the discussion concerned school trips.

76. "Shasetsu (Editorial): Kanko Kyanseru Taisaku no Kyogi ga Isogareru (Immediate Discussion on Tourist Cancellations Necessary)," *Okinawa Taimusu*, September 20, 2001.

77. "Shasetsu (Editorial): Kanko no Kiki Yuchi Doryoku Igai Te ha Nai (The Tourism Crisis There is no Choice but to Lure Tourists)," *Ryukyu Shimpo*, October 4, 2001.

78. The *Shimpo* recognized this effort and expressed its thanks in an editorial in early 2002. "Shasetsu (Editorial): Akarui Kizashi 'Yujo Kanko' no Arigatasa (A Promising Prospect Appreciating 'Friendship Tourism')," *Ryukyu Shimpo*, January 27, 2002.

79. "Shasetsu (Editorial): Kichi Keibi Kaijo he Ososugiru Kurai Da (Removing the Tight Base Security Way Too Late)," *Ryukyu Shimpo*, February 15, 2002.

80. "Shasetsu (Editorial): Kankokyaku Gekigen Genin ha 'Beigun Kichi'ni (Reason Why Tourist Numbers have Dropped Off Dramatically is Bases)," *Ryukyu Shimpo*, December 9, 2001.

81. This appears to be an usually low figure that underestimates the fear of flying that the 9/11 hijackings had on people who had been relatively comfortable flying in the past. A poll taken in the United States of nearly five thousand people after the attacks showed that some 64 percent were afraid of flying. It also does not take into consideration the overall hassles involved with flying. People simply switched to driving or to taking trains when possible, or changed their travel destinations.

82. "Iraq Kogeki 'Hantai' ga 90%, Ryukyu Shimpo Kennai Yoron Chosa (90% 'Oppose' Attacks on Iraq, Ryukyu Shimpo Public Opinion [Shows])," *Ryukyu Shimpo*, March 17, 2003.

83. "Shasetsu (Editorial): Boei Mondai Yoron Chosa Yowai Okinawa no Joho Hashinryoku (Public Opinion Poll on Defense Issues Low Ability to Relay Information about Okinawa)," *Ryukyu Shimpo*, March 31, 2003.

84. Although the figure is said to represent tourists, it is already very much inflated as it actually includes all travelers, including those living in the prefecture who are returning from a trip outside the prefecture.

85. "Shasetsu (Editorial): Iraku Chian Akka Saisho Kara Giron Yarinaose (Public Order in Iraq Worsens Start Over Again from Scratch)," *Ryukyu Shimpo*, June 28, 2004.

Conclusions

Robert D. Eldridge and Paul Midford

Japanese mass opinion has been gradually evolving away from seemingly inflexible pacifism and toward views best described as cautious defensive realism. As discussed throughout this book, Japanese, both mass and elite, are increasingly willing to distinguish justifiable wars for the sake of national defense against an imminent threat, moving away from the tendency to see all wars as equally unjustified. However, at the same time, Japanese continue to view the use of force for purposes other than territorial defense as being both groundless and ineffective. Japanese are skeptical about the utility of military force for promoting democracy along the lines of the U.S. "neocons," rooting out terrorism, or preventing the proliferation of weapons of mass destruction. Contrary to some views of Japanese nationalism, economic stagnation over the years has apparently discouraged, rather than encouraged, a greater appetite for an expansive foreign policy. To be sure, overseas dispatches of the Self-Defense Forces for humanitarian and reconstruction missions, including to a limited extent the Iraq dispatch, enjoy reasonably consistent public support, although those dispatches that appear to have even a slight implication of involvement in combat quickly lose support. Ironically, this pattern reflects the public's belief that nonmilitary solutions have the highest utility for conflict resolution and suppressing terrorism. Finally, commentary about the impact of the North Korean threat in radically altering mass opinion toward security issues notwithstanding, concern about North Korea has not translated into sudden or significant change in Japanese opinion toward security. Notably, while the rhetoric of Japanese leaders regarding North Korea has been hawkish, public opinion tends to favor a negotiated settlement with that reclusive country. Although some American politicians like to proclaim that 9/11 changed everything, there is little evidence that 9/11, the ensuing war on terrorism, or even the North Korean threat has brought radical change to Japanese public opinion. Rather, as Midford argues in chapter one, Japanese public opinion continues a gradual and long-term evolution toward a defensive realist position, recognizing military force as necessary for national defense but not useful for much else.

Weston concludes in chapter two through her survey of the three largest mainstream newspapers that the Japanese government more than before has a clearer mandate to move ahead with homeland security. While there is Japanese public support for a "country strong against danger" and "safe for its citizens," she further maintains Japanese citizens are less supportive of Japan's involvement in U.S.-led military actions against terrorism. Clearly, further improvement of Japanese homeland security infrastructure is also needed, namely, tighter immigration controls, increased information gathering (while respecting civil rights), deeper cooperation among various related ministries/agencies, as well as quicker crisis management. Along with the enhancement of Japanese government efforts against terrorism, she argues the U.S.–Japan alliance has also become stronger. However, this deepening of alliance ties has costs as well as advantages. While benefiting from U.S. protection, Japan's expansion of SDF domestic and international parameters could be perceived as a military threat by other regional actors. Japan's support for the U.S. war on terrorism could also make Japan a future target for a terrorist attack, thereby entrapping Japan. Finally, the alliance, while facing varying degrees of positive to negative support regarding their respective homeland security policies, must struggle to comprehend the new security paradigm that includes global terrorism and a post-9/11 world.

In chapter three, Hollstein sought to establish whether "insider" *kisha* club reporters would prefer the themes he identifies as part of the ruling Liberal Democratic Party's "Normal Nation Frame," which justifies an expanded role for the SDF, over those of the opposition's "Antimilitarism Frame," which favors a restricted role for the SDF. He also looked at television and newspaper reports from non-*kisha* club media to test whether such "outsider" media would be more critical of government arguments. He found that the two insider newspapers, the *Asahi Shimbun* and the *Yomiuri Shimbun*, did indeed provide more space for positive reports about the dispatch than negative ones, while outsider newspaper *Nikkan Sports* provided mostly neutral discussion of the issue. However, important differences in how the two insider papers covered the story suggest that these newspapers were not simply parroting government positions as a result of *kisha* club membership. He found even more diversity in the television reports analyzed. Insider NHK, Japan's public television network, did tend to emphasize government positions and Normal Nation Frame themes while the outsider program, TV Asahi's *News Station,* provided the most critical reporting on the SDF dispatch. However, the insider program, TBS's *News Forest,* provided more time to critics of the government than to proponents of the SDF dispatch to Iraq. Therefore, *kisha* club membership did not appear to be the defining element in how the TV news was framed. Nevertheless, criticism of the SDF dispatch in all the media tended to lack ideological clarity. Antimilitarism themes were suggested rather than articulated while Normal Nation Frames tended to be better supported with clear ideological rationales. Therefore, while the *kisha* clubs may not be homogenizing news in favor of government positions, the government does appear to be better at using the media to explain its positions than the opposition.

Midford and Scott find that politicians, even when they bravely proclaim to lead rather than follow public opinion, are in fact highly sensitive to public opinion. Former prime minister Koizumi, the epitome of such a politician, nonetheless carefully crafted his policies for dispatching the SDF to the Indian Ocean and Iraq to support the U.S. war on terrorism to avoid provoking an opposing opinion majority that the opposition parties could exploit. Despite his desire to expand SDF operations into areas risking combat, and to contribute to security and stabilization missions, Koizumi watered down his proposals to appeal to a public that has only supported noncombat deployments of the SDF overseas in areas far removed from the danger of combat. The clearest case of Koizumi defying public opinion, when he dispatched an advanced Aegis destroyer to the Indian Ocean in late 2002, came only after the main opposition party, the DPJ, had been temporarily weakened by the defection of a number of Diet members to the ruling side. Even on the issue where Koizumi did more to establish his reputation as a headstrong, buck-public-opinion politician than any other, namely, his controversial visits to Yasukuni Shrine, the prime minister in fact showed great sensitivity to public opinion. He commissioned repeated private polls before paying his most controversial visit on August 15, 2006, to confirm there would not be a sharp public backlash, and to help him modulate his message justifying this visit.[1] Less bold and skilled politicians, most notably Koizumi's immediate successors, Abe Shinzo and Fukuda Yasuo, appear to be even more constrained by public opinion than was the daring Koizumi.

Chapter five by Eldridge and Chijiwa explored the opinions on the 9/11 terrorist attacks and the war on terrorism expressed by Japanese intellectuals suggesting that the initial interpretation of 9/11 became a prism for evaluating events afterward, such as the Afghanistan War, the Iraq War, and Japan's participation in both. The chapter discovered a more sophisticated debate than the traditional bipolar idealism versus realism that dominated much of Japan's postwar intellectual and political atmosphere. In the post-9/11 debate, Japanese observers took sides on the questions of utility and legitimacy, and a free-flowing and varied discussion was seen, suggesting that Japan's intellectual community has entered a new stage from ideologically motivated to policy relevant. Specifically, two characteristics regarding the debate of Japanese intellectuals should be noted. First, the debate on 9/11, the Afghanistan War, the Iraq War, and Japan's participation was also a discussion of America itself as seen when in the discussions on the Iraq problem, the description of the "American Empire" would appear. The second characteristic was the fact that the conservatives split on the issue of the Iraq War. The generally pro-American conservatives showed understanding with regard to the war on terrorism, but they were divided on the evaluation of both the utility and legitimacy of the Iraq War. This split symbolized just how difficult the issue of the Iraq War was in Japan, as it was throughout much of the world and among America's traditional allies.

In chapter six Scott showed that Japan's NGOs demonstrated an ability and capacity to mobilize and respond to an impending war in Iraq. This should come as no surprise as the antiwar movement is one part of a key divide in Japanese political culture. The debate over remilitarization and recentralization has been a dominant theme in Japanese politics in the post-war period. The crisis over Iraq was an opportunity for all political forces in Japan to take part in the shaping of policy. A "left of center" loose coalition was arranged against "right of center" forces. The NGOs, many of them small antiwar groups, raised their voices to the debate. Some observers argue that Koizumi was taking Japan into uncharted waters as he expanded the mission of the SDF and enacted a series of legislative measures. Japan's civil society has demonstrated that it can help to constrain some of the government's actions. (If this leads the government to be less-than-candid when explaining its policies, NGOs, alone or in conjunction with the media, can again play an important role by uncovering this fact, as seen in recent disclosures of MSDF refueling U.S. naval vessels destined for Iraq.) While NGOs remain relatively weak and uncoordinated, in times of crisis they can help form and articulate public opinion. Neither civil society nor the NGOs should be underestimated as a force in shaping Japan's political culture now and in the future.

In chapter seven on public opinion in the base community most directly affected by the war on terrorism, Okinawa, Eldridge shows how the two local newspapers, whose readership represents 98 percent of the local market, try to portray themselves as reflectors or interpreters of public opinion in the prefecture, but more often than not they are able to create or frame public opinion in their own anti-base image. Three trends were found in the press in particular and among the public in general following 9/11. First, Okinawans were sympathetic to the United States in its time of national crisis with the 9/11 terrorist attacks and several actually expressed support for the U.S. military campaign in Afghanistan, like their mainland compatriots. Likewise, there was strong support for Japan to cooperate in some way, although only a small percentage expressed actual support in revising the interpretation of the right of collective self-defense. All of this suggests that Okinawans, while aware of the need for Japan to play a larger role, desire that it be a purely nonmilitary one. Second, and similarly, Okinawans retain a deep distrust of anything military. Likewise, Okinawans retain a fear of having U.S. military bases in the prefecture, which could make Okinawa a target of attack. Third, Okinawan newspaper editorials are often critical, making broad and sweeping suggestions without the specifics to realize them. Actual policy recommendations they are not. They generally follow the "peace-at-any-cost" school of thought, when the world is not as simple as that.

Post-Koizumi Japan

In the immediate post-Koizumi period, public opinion is likely to grow in influence for at least three reasons. First, Koizumi's immediate successor as the LDP's twenty-first president and Japan's eighty-ninth (and youngest) prime minister, Abe Shinzo, and his successor, Fukuda Yasuo, who took office on September 25, 2007, clearly lacks the innate political skills to influence, mold, or defy public opinion that Koizumi had. Second, the commitment of the LDP to pushing constitutional reform, including revision of the war-renouncing Article 9, in the short run can only increase the influence of public opinion. This is because any constitutional revision requires not only the approval of two-thirds of both houses of the Diet, but also an absolute majority of votes cast in a national referendum. Given that the LDP has not won a majority of votes cast in a Lower House election since 1963, the prospect of winning the majority of votes in a national plebiscite, as well as two-thirds of both houses of the Diet, is indeed a daunting hurdle. Consequently, the LDP is likely to be especially cautious about getting out in front of public opinion in the short run for fear of derailing support for constitutional reform.

Third, the crushing defeat the LDP suffered in the July 2007 Upper House election, which left the opposition DPJ, along with the Social Democrats and JCP, in control of that chamber will make it difficult for the LDP to promote new overseas deployments of the SDF for years to come, even under its latest leader Fukuda Yasuo. Indeed, one result of the election was to make *Komeito*, the LDP's coalition partner, even more cautious about such initiatives. Post election polls among Upper House members show a large shift against constitutional reform, and especially against reform of Article 9.[3]

We find that mass opinion, while subject to some degree of elite molding, is nonetheless an important policy influence in democratic Japan. Although the events of 9/11 and the subsequent war on terrorism shook Japan, and although ruling political elites, led by then prime minister Koizumi Junichiro, sought to expand Japan's military role overseas, public opinion set limits that prevented Japan's military role from exceeding incremental and slow expansion. Most importantly, public opinion prevented this slow and incremental expansion from approaching direct involvement in combat. Consequently, Japanese participation in joint combat operations with U.S. military forces in areas far removed from Japanese shores remains a distant prospect.[4] Japan, in short, is not close to becoming a "Britain of Asia," a call reflected in the October 2000 report "The United States and Japan: Advancing Toward a Mature Relationship," by the bipartisan study group cochaired by Richard L. Armitage and Joseph Nye. Rather, Japan today is more comparable to the Germany of the early 1990s.[5] Nonetheless, unlike Germany in the 1990s, Japan's international military role is unlikely to expand dramatically during the remainder of this decade, indeed, overseas operations of the SDF are contracting. Consequently, those US and Japanese elites hoping that Japan emerges as the Britain of Asia, an ally loyally joining the United States in joint combat operations in far-flung corners of the world, will be disappointed.

On the other hand, much more important changes occurred domestically, as public opinion increasingly accepted an expansion of the state's role in preparing for attacks on Japan from terrorists or more conventional threats. Politicians with lesser skills than Koizumi possesses will have limited success molding, ignoring, or defying public opinion or changing the channel to another issue. In contrast to Koizumi's ability to shift from the Iraq deployment to postal privatization in 2005, Abe's attempt to change the channel from pension and other economic issues toward Japan's international security role and constitutional revision failed miserably, and may have pushed the debate backward rather than forward.

Overall, elites have some leeway to lead during short-term contingencies and then to "educate" the public. After attempting to educate, elites need to listen, and then incorporate public opinion into policy-making. Otherwise they risk pursuing unsustainable, if not politically counterproductive, policies. Political developments in the immediate post-Koizumi period of late 2006 and 2007, such as the temporary suspension of the MSDF mission to the Indian Ocean, demonstrate that sending the SDF overseas without a clear mandate from the public can undermine the long-term viability of overseas SDF deployments.

Notes

1. "Seifu, Kyokumitsu ni Yoron Chosa (Government Conducted Public Opinion Surveys in Secret)," *Yomiuri Shimbun*, August 16, 2006.
2. At the time of the completion of this manuscript, Fukuda Yasuo had just been elected twenty-second president of the LDP, and the ninetieth prime minister, on September 23 and 25 (2007) respectively, after Abe had served only one year.
3. "Sanin Kaikenha 3 Bun no 2 Wareru (Division in Upper House)," *Asahi Shimbun*, August 7, 2007; and "Sanin Sameru Kaiken Detsu (Upper House Cool to Revision)," ibid. For an insightful article on the role of the Upper House after the 2007 elections, see Machidori Satoshi, "Rethinking the Role of the Upper House," *Japan Echo*, Vol. 35, No. 2 (April 2008), pp. 18–22.
4. Japan has been debating a change in constitutional interpretation to allow the so-called right of collective defense, or the right to assist an ally under attack. In some areas, such as missile defense, where the destination of a launched missile is in doubt, or even when it might be clearly targeting the United States or its ally, constitutional interpretation is likely to be reinterpreted to allow Japanese missile defense assets to intercept such a missile (assuming this would be technically feasible). However, when it comes to joint combat operations with U.S. forces in areas far from Japan, the public opinion barrier remains formidable. Indeed, it is striking that both Koizumi and his successor Abe have been calling for a constitutional reinterpretation for several years, yet have failed to realize this vow, other than seeing the LDP to approve a new draft constitution and developing legislation to permit the holding of a national referendum necessary to vote on constitutional change (a bill for this was enacted in May 2007). Overall, less than a third of Japanese support lifting the ban on the exercise of collective self-defense. See "Kempo ni tsuite Yoron Chosa (Public Opinion Poll on Constitution)," *Yomiuri Shimbun*, April 8, 2005.
5. Daniel M. Kliman also draws a comparison between Japan and Germany, although he sees Japan moving toward overseas participation in combat operations in fairly short order, paralleling the German experience of the 1990s. See *Japan's Security Strategy in the Post-9/11 World: Embracing a New Realpolitik* (Washington: CSIS, 2006), p. 39.

BIBLIOGRAPHY

Abe, Koki. "Hahei ha 'Fu Seigi' he no Katan de Aru (Dispatching Troops is Playing a Part in the 'Injustice')," *Sekai*, No. 721 (December 2003), pp. 49–56.

Abe, Shinzo. *Utsukushii Kuni he* (Toward a Beautiful Japan) (Tokyo: Bungei Shunju, 2006).

Agawa Naoyuki, "Soredemo Watashi ha Shin Bei wo Tsuranuku (I Will Still Always be Pro-U.S.)," *Bungei Shunju*, Vol. 80, No. 13 (October 2002), pp. 262–8.

Aikyo Koji, "Bei Gun Shien ha 'Kenpo no Wakunai' de ha Nai (Supporting of the U.S. Military is Not 'Within the [Boundaries of the] Constitution')," *Sekai*, No. 695 (December 2001), pp. 48–55.

Akhavan-Majid, Roya. "The Press as an Elite Power in Japan," *Journalism Quarterly*, Vol. 67, No. 4 (1990), pp. 1006–14.

Albig, William. *Public Opinion* (New York: McGraw-Hill, 1939).

Almond, Gabriel. *The American People and Foreign Policy* (New York: Praeger, 1950).

———. "Public Opinion and National Security," *Public Opinion Quarterly*, Vol. 20, No. 2 (1956), pp. 371–8.

Altman, Kristin Kyoko. "Television and Political Turmoil: Japan's Summer of 1993," in Susan J. Pharr and Ellis S. Krauss, eds., *Media and Politics in Japan* (Honolulu: University of Hawaii Press, 1996), pp. 165–86.

Anderson, Gregory E. "Lionheart or Paper Tiger? A First-Term Koizumi Retrospective," *Asian Perspective*, No. 28 (March 2004), pp. 149–82.

Ansell, Christopher, and Jane Grigrich, "Reforming the Administrative State," in Bruce E. Cain, Russell J. Dalton, and Susan E. Scarrow, eds. *Democracy Transformed? Expanding Political Opportunities in Advanced Industrial Democracies* (Cambridge: Oxford University Press, 2003).

Aoi, Chiyuki. "9.11 Go no Gunji Kodo to Kokuren Taisei (Military Actions Following 9/11 and the United Nations System)," *Kokusai Anzen Hosho*, Vol. 30, Nos. 1 & 2 (September 2002), pp. 86–102.

Arai, Naoyuki. *Sengo Journalism Danmen* (A View of Postwar Journalism) (Tokyo: Soshisha, 1984).

Arasaki, Moriteru. *Aratana Shiso wa Tsukureruka: 9–11 to Heiwa Undo* (Is a New View Possible? 9–11 and the Peace Movement) (Tokyo: Gaifusha, 2004).

Asada, Masahiko. "Doji Tahatsu Tero Jiken to Kokusaiho (The Simultaneous Terrorist Attacks and International Law)," *Kokusai Anzen Hosho*, Vol. 30, Nos. 1 & 2 (September 2002), pp. 68–85.

Aso, Iku. "Tettei Chosa Beigun Kichi no Hitotsubo Jinushi 3000 Nin (Investigation: The 3000 Hitotsubo Anti-War Landowners of U.S. Bases)," *Bungei Shunju*, October 1996, pp. 118–29.

Bailey, Thomas A. *The Man in the Street: The Impact of American Public Opinion on Foreign Policy* (New York: Macmillan, 1948).

Berger, Thomas U. "From Sword to Chrysanthemum: Japan's Culture of Anti-Militarism," *International Security*, Vol. 17, No. 4 (Spring 1993), pp. 119–50.

———. *Cultures of Antimilitarism: National Security in Germany and Japan* (Baltimore: Johns Hopkins University Press, 1998).

———. "Alliance Politics and Japan's Postwar Culture of Antimilitarism," in Michael J. Green and Patrick Cronin, eds., *The U.S.–Japan Alliance: Past, Present, and Future* (New York: Council on Foreign Relations Press, 1999), pp. 189–207.

Blumler, Jay G., and Denis McQuail. *Television in Politics: Its Uses and Influence* (London: Faber and Faber, 1968).

Bobrow, Davis B. "Japan in the World: Opinion from Defeat to Success," *The Journal of Conflict Resolution*, Vol. 33, No. 4 (December 1989), pp. 571–604.

Boei Nenkan Kankokai, ed. *Boei Nenkan 2001 Nenban* (The Year in Defense, 2001 Edition) (Tokyo: Boei Nenkan Kankokai, 2002).

Bowman, Karlyn H. *America after 9/11: Public Opinion on the War on Terrorism and the War with Iraq* (Washington, D.C.: American Enterprise Institute, 2003).

Boyd, J. Patrick, and Richard J. Samuels. *Nine Lives? The Politics of Constitutional Reform in Japan, Policy Studies #19* (East–West Center Washington, 2005).

Calder, Kent. "The Broken Dialogue Revisited," *Gaiko Forum*, Vol. 2, No. 1 (Spring 2003), pp. 19–26.

Cappella, Joseph N., and Kathleen Hall Jamieson. *Spiral of Cynicism: The Press and the Public Good* (New York: Oxford University Press, 1997).

Chan, Steve, and William Safran, "Public Opinion as a Constraint against War: Democracies' Responses to Operation Iraqi Freedom," *Foreign Policy Analysis*, Vol. 2, No. 2 (March 2006), pp. 137–56.

Chidiwa, Yasuaki. "Insights into Japan–U.S. Relations on the Eve of the Iraq War: Dilemmas over 'Showing the Flag,'" *Asian Survey*, Vol. 45, No. 6 (November/December 2005), pp. 843–64.

Chino, Kyoko. "Henka Suru Nihon no Kokurenkan (Changing Views in Japan of the United Nations)," *Kokusai Mondai*, No. 523 (October 2003), pp. 43–56.

Cohen, Bernard C. "The Relationship between Public Opinion and Foreign Policy Maker," in Melvin Small, ed. *Public Opinion and Historians* (Detroit: Wayne State University, 1970).

Converse, Phillip E. "The Nature of Belief Systems in Mass Publics," in David Apter, ed., *Ideology and Discontent* (New York: Wiley, 1964), pp. 206–61.

Council on Security and Defense Capabilities, *The Council on Security and Defense Capabilities Report—Japan's Vision for Future Security and Defense Capabilities*, Tokyo, http://www.kantei.go.jp/jp/singi/ampobouei/dai13/13siryoupdf (2004).

Curtis, Gerald. *The Logic of Japanese Politics: Leaders, Institutions, and the Limits of Change* (New York: Columbia University Press, 1999).

Dower, John W. *Embracing Defeat: Japan in the Wake of World War II* (New York: W.W. Norton & Company, 1999).

Drezner, Daniel W. "Mind the Gap," *The National Interest*, No. 87 (January/February 2007), pp. 47–53.

Ehrhardt, George. "Factional Influence on the 2001 LDP Primaries: A Quantitative Analysis," *Japanese Journal of Political Science*, Vol. 7, No. 1 (April 2006), pp. 59–70.

Eldridge, Robert D. "The 1996 Okinawa Referendum on U.S. Base Reductions: One Question, Several Answers," *Asian Survey*, Vol. 37, No. 10 (October 1997), pp. 879–904.

———. "Okinawa and the Nago Heliport Problem in the U.S.–Japan Relationship," *Asia–Pacific Review*, Vol. 7, No. 1 (May 2000), pp. 137–56.

———. *The Origins of the Bilateral Okinawa Problem: Okinawa in Postwar U.S.–Japan Relations, 1945–1952* (New York: Garland, 2001).

———. *Post-Reversion Okinawa and U.S.–Japan Relations: A Preliminary Survey of Local Politics and the Bases, 1972–2002* (Osaka: Center for International Security Studies and Policy, 2004).

———. "Prospects for Constitutional Revision in Japan," *International Public Policy Studies*, Vol. 10, No. 1 (September 2005), pp. 17–38.

———. "My One Year with the Marines: Reflections on Bridging the Gap between Academics and the Military," *International Public Policy Studies*, Vol. 10, No. 2 (March 2006), pp. 162–80.

Ellings, Richard J., and Aaron L. Friedberg, eds., *Asian Aftershocks: Strategic Asia 2002–03* (Seattle: The National Bureau of Asian Research, 2002).

Entman, Robert M. "Framing: Toward Clarification of a Fractured Paradigm," *Journal of Communication*, Vol. 43, No. 4 (Winter 1993), pp. 52–8.

Entman, Robert M. *Projection of Power: Framing News, Public Opinion and Foreign Policy* (Chicago: The University of Chicago Press), pp. 1–28.

Fallows, James. *Breaking the News: How the Media Undermine American Democracy* (New York: Pantheon Books, 1996).

Farley, Maggie. "Japan's Press and the Politics of Scandal," in Susan J. Pharr and Ellis S. Krauss, eds., *Media and Politics in Japan* (Honolulu: University of Hawaii Press, 1996), pp. 133–63.

Feldman, Ofer. *Politics and the News Media in Japan* (Ann Arbor: University of Michigan Press, 1993).

Foreign Press Center. *Japan's Mass Media* (Tokyo: Foreign Press Center, 1997).

Foyle, Douglas C. "Leading the Public to War? The Influence of American Public Opinion on the Bush Administration's Decision to Go to War in Iraq," *International Journal of Public Opinion Research*, Vol. 16 (2004), pp. 269–94.

Freeman, Laurie Anne. *Closing the Shop: Information Cartels and Japan's Mass Media* (Princeton, New Jersey: Princeton University Press, 2000).

Fujita, Hiroshi. "Public Journalism: Controversies Over the Media's Role in 1990s America," *The Japanese Journal of American Studies*, No. 9 (1998), pp. 29–52.

Fujiwara, Kiichi. "Teikoku no Senso ha Owaranai (The Empire's Never-Ending War)," *Sekai*, No. 713 (May 2003), pp. 59–66.

———. "Iraku Wahei to Nippon no Yakuwari (Peace in Iraq and the Role of Japan)," *Ushio*, No. 544 (June 2004), pp. 158–61.

Fukuda, Kazuya. "'Hakenkoku Amerika' Sono Shuen no Hajimari (The Beginning of the End of 'Hegemon America')," *Seiron*, No. 351 (November 2001), pp. 31–9.

———. "Teikoku no Kage no Moto de (Under the Shadow of the Empire)," *Shokun*, Vol. 35, No. 6 (June 2003), pp. 22–30.

Furukawa, Katsuhisa. "Fusein ha Naze Saidai no Kyoi ka (Why is Hussein the Biggest Threat?), *Ronza*, No. 93 (February 2003), pp. 70–5.

Garon, Sheldon. *Molding Japanese Minds: The State in Everyday Life* (Princeton: Princeton University Press, 1997).

Gaubatz, Kurt T. *Elections and War: The Electoral Incentive in the Democratic Politics of War and Peace* (Stanford: Stanford University Press, 1999).

Gershman, John. "Democracy and the Making of Foreign Policy," *Foreign Policy in Focus*, February 2006, www.fpif.org.

Ginsberg, Benjamin. *The Captive Public: How Mass Opinion Promotes State Power* (New York: Basic Books, 1986).

Goldberg, Bernard. *Bias: A CBS Insider Exposes How the Media Distort the News* (New York: Perennial, 2003).

Gotoda, Masaharu. "Kaigai Hahei no Boron wo Haisu (Stopping the Debate on Sending the SDF Abroad)," *Gekkan Asahi* (December 1990), pp. 40–6.

Graber, Doris A. *Media Power in Politics*, 4th Ed. (Washington, D.C.: Congressional Quarterly Press, 2000).

Green, Michael J. *Japan's Reluctant Realism.* (New York: Palgrave Macmillan, 2001).

Green, Michael J. "The Iraq War and Asia: Assessing the Legacy," The Washington Quarterly, Vol. 31, No. 2 (Spring 2008), 181–200.

Green, Michael, and Patrick Cronin, eds., *The U.S.–Japan Alliance: Past, Present and Future* (New York: Council on Foreign Relations Press, 1999).

Gregson, Wallace C., James North, and Robert D. Eldridge, "Jindo Shien to Kyuen Katsudo he no Taio: Kaijo Kyoten ni Yoru Nichibei Kyodo Haken no Shorai Koso (Responses to Humanitarian Assistance and Disaster Relief: A Future Vision for U.S.–Japan Combined Sea-based Deployments)," *Securitarian*, Nos. 557–9 (April–June 2005), pp. 56–57, 54–55, and 54–55 respectively.

Halberstam, David. *The Powers That Be* (Urbana: University of Illinois Press, 2000).

Hara Osamu, "Jieitai Iraku Haken ha Tai Kita Chosen Seisaku de Aru (Dispatching the SDF is a Policy toward North Korea)," *Seiron*, No. 384 (June 2004), pp. 84–95.

Havens, Thomas R.H. *Fire Across the Sea: The Vietnam War and Japan 1965–1975* (Princeton: Princeton University Press, 1987).

Hein, Laura, and Mark Selden, eds. *Islands of Discontent: Okinawan Responses to Japanese and American Power* (Lanham: Rowman & Littlefield, 2003).

Hellman, Donald. *Japanese Foreign Policy and Domestic Politics* (Berkeley: University of California Press, 1969).

Herzog, Peter J. *Japan's Pseudo-Democracy* (Sandgate: Japan Library, 1993).

Hess, Stephen, and Marvin Kalb, eds. *The Media and the War on Terrorism* (Washington, D.C.: Brookings Institution, 2003).

Hollstein, Mark. "Framing Security: A Trilateral Discourse Analysis of Ideology in Newspaper Reports about the United States Military in Okinawa" (Unpublished PhD Dissertation, University of Hawaii, 2000).

Holsti, Ole R. "Public Opinion and Foreign Policy: Challenges to the Almond–Lippmann Consensus," *International Studies Quarterly*, Vol. 36, No. 4 (December 1992), pp. 440–5.

Honma, Nagayo. "Amerika wo Do Rikai Suru ka (How Should We Understand the U.S.?)," *Gaiko Forum*, Vol. 16, No. 2 (February 2003), pp. 12–17.

Hook, Glenn D. *Militarisation and Demilitarisation in Contemporary Japan* (New York: Routledge, 1996).

Hook, Glenn D., and Richard Siddle, eds. *Japan and Okinawa: Structure and Subjectivity* (London: Routledge Curzon, 2003).

Hosaka, Hiroshi. "Sengo Okinawa Jaanarizumu no Jiko Keisei: Heiwa no Jiko Ninshiki wo Toshite (The Self-Fashioning Process of Okinawan Journalism after World War II by Looking at Views of Peace)," in Teruya Yoshihiko and Yamazato Katsunori, eds., *Sengo Okinawa to Amerika: Ibunka Sesshoku no 50 Nen* (Postwar Okinawa and America: Fifty Years of Cross-Cultural Contact) (Naha: Okinawa Taimususha, 1995), pp. 272–301.

Hughes, Christopher. *Japan's Reemergence as a "Normal" Military Power, Adelphi Paper* 368–9 (Oxford University Press, 2004).

Hutchinson, Rachel. "Kurosawa Akira's *One Wonderful Sunday*: Censorship, Context and 'Counter-discursive' Film," *Japan Forum*, Vol. 19, No. 3 (Fall 2007), pp. 369–9.

Ide, Sonroku. *Ishibashi Tanzan to Shokoku Shugi* (Ishibashi Tanzan and Small Countryism) (Tokyo: Iwanami Booklet, No. 510, 2000).

Iijima, Isao. *Koizumi Kantei no Hiroku* (A Secret History of Prime Minister Koizumi's Office) (Tokyo: Nihon Keizai Shimbunsha, 2006).

Ikeuchi, Satoshi. "Iraku 'Tai Tero' Senso ni Fusenpai ha Yurusarenai (We Cannot Lose in the Iraqi 'Anti-Terror' War)," *Ronza*, Vol. 36, No. 101 (January 2004), pp. 54–62.

———. "Iraku Kokumin no Niizu o Shirukoto ga Senketsu da (Knowing the Needs of the Iraqi People is Top Priority)," *Chuo Koron*, Vol. 119, No. 2 (February 2004), pp. 118–29.

Iokibe, Makoto, ed. *Yoron Chosa ni Miru Nichibei Kankei: Yomiuri-Gyarappu Kyodo Chosa 22 Nen* (The U.S.–Japan Relationship as Seen From Public Opinion Polls: 22 Years of Yomiuri–Gallup Joint Polling) (Tokyo: Yomiuri Shimbunsha, 2000).

———. "Kyoki to Hakai wo Koete (Going beyond Madness and Destruction)," *Ronza*, No. 79 (December 2001), pp. 16–25.

Iyengar, Shanto. *Is Anyone Responsible? How Television Frames Political Issues* (Chicago: University of Chicago Press, 1991).

———. "Agenda Setting and Beyond: Television News and the Strength of Political Issues," in William H. Riker, ed., *Agenda Formation* (Ann Arbor: University of Michigan Press, 1993).

Japan Defense Agency. *Defense of Japan 2006* (Tokyo: Japan Defense Agency, 2006).

Jeffords, Susan, and Lauren Rabinovitz, eds. *Seeing Through the Media: The Persian Gulf War* (Newark: Rutgers University Press, 1994).

Jentleson, Bruce W. "The Pretty Prudent Public: Post Post-Vietnam American Opinion on the Use of Military Force," *International Studies Quarterly*, Vol. 36, No. 1 (March 1992), pp. 49–74.

Jervis, Robert. "Hypothesis on Misperception," *World Politics*, Vol. 20, No. 3 (April 1968), pp. 454–79.

———. "Cooperation under the Security Dilemma," *World Politics*, Vol. 30, No. 3 (January 1978), pp. 167–214.

Jinbo Ken, "'Sensei Kodo' wo Seitoka Suru Beikoku no Ronri (The U.S. Logic that Legitimizes 'Preemptive Action')," *Chuo Koron*, Vol. 118, No. 4 (April 2003), pp. 116–27.

Johnson, Chalmers. *Japan: Who Governs? In The Rise of the Developmental State* (New York: W.W. Norton & Company, 1995).

Johnson, Stephen, Helle C. Dale, and Patrick Cronin. *Strengthening U.S. Public Diplomacy Requires Organization, Coordination, and Strategy* (Heritage Foundation Backgrounder No. 1875, August 5, 2005).

Kabashima, Ikuo, and Gill Steel. "The Koizumi Revolution," *PS: Political Science and Politics*, Vol. 40, No. 1 (January 2007), pp. 79–84.

Kakiya, Isao. "Jieitai ga Iraku ni Ikanakattara Do Naru ka (What Would Happen if the SDF Doesn't go to Iraq?)," *Seiron*, No. 380 (February 2004), pp. 100–108.

Kaku, Kensuke, and Maruyama Hitoshi. *Seiji Henyo no Paasupekutibu: Nyuu Poritikusu no Seijigaku* (Perspectives on Political Change: The Political Science of New Politics), Vol. II. (Kyoto: Minerva, 2005).

Kamiya, Matake. "Naze Jieitai wo Iraku ni Haken Suru no ka (Why Dispatch the SDF to Iraq?)," *Gaiko Forum*, Vol. 117, No. 3 (March 2004), pp. 24–9.

Kataoka, Tetsuya. "Waga Jieitai no 'Tai Iraku Senso' Sansen Ron no Settokuryoku (Persuasion of the Theory of Joining our SDF into 'the Iraqi War')," *Seiron*, No. 366 (January 2003), pp. 282–91.

Katayama, Yoshio. "9/11 Jiken ga Imi Suru Mono (What the 9/11 Incident Means)," *Kokusai Anzen Hosho*, Vol. 30, Nos. 1 & 2 (September 2002), pp. 51–67.

Kato, Shuichi. "Bunmei no 'Shototsu' kara 'Taiwa' he (From the 'Clash' of Civilization to 'Dialogue')," *Ushio*, No. 516 (February 2002), pp. 96–103.

Katz, Richard. *Japanese Phoenix: The Long Road to Economic Revival* (Armonk, New York: M.E. Sharpe, 2003).

Katzenstein, Peter J. *Cultural Norms and National Security: Police and Military in Postwar Japan* (Ithaca: Cornell University Press, 1996).

———. "Same War—Different Views: Germany, Japan, and Counter-terrorism," *International Organization*, Vol. 57, No. 4 (Fall 2003), pp. 731–60.

Kawakami, Kazuhisa. *Joho Sosa no Torikku: Sono Rekishi to Hoho* (The Trick of Information Manipulation: Its History and Methodology) (Tokyo: Kodansha, 1994).

———. *Media no Shinka to Kenryoku* (Media: Its Evolution to Power) (Tokyo: NTT Shuppan, 1997).

Keddell, Joseph P., Jr. *The Politics of Defense in Japan: Managing Internal and External Pressures* (New York: M.E. Sharpe, 1993).

Kiehl, William P. "Can Humpty Dumpty be Saved?" *American Diplomacy*, October 2003, AmericanDiplomacy.org .

"*Kisha* Club Guidelines," Nihon Shimbun Kyokai (The Japan Editors and Publishers Association), http://www.pressnet.or.jp/english/index.htm (March 2, 2006).

Kitaoka Shinichi, "Nichi Bei Anpo wo Kijiku ni Shita 'Kokuren Jyushi' he (Toward Making the Japan–U.S. Alliance Rooted More in the 'UN-First School')," *Chuo Koron*, Vol. 118, No. 5 (May 2003), pp. 56–61.

———. "Aratamete Toku 'Jieitai Iraku Haken' no Imi (Talking Anew the Means of 'Dispatching the SDF to Iraq')," *Chuo Koron*, Vol. 119, No. 2 (February 2004), pp. 108–16.

Kobayashi, Masaya. "'Han Tero' Sekai Senso no Kakudai ni Koshite (Resisting Expansion of the Global War on 'Terrorism')," *Ronza*, No. 97 (June 2003), pp. 76–81.

Koike Masayuki, "'Fukko Jindo Shien' ga Dekiru Jyokyo de ha Nai (This is Not a Situation in Which We Can Provide 'Reconstruction and Humanitarian Relief')," *Sekai*, No. 723 (February 2004), pp. 82–5.

Kojima, Akira. "The Abiding Strength of Soft Power," *Gaiko Forum*, Vol. 2, No. 1 (Spring 2003), pp. 3–10.

Kono, Takeshi. "Kokumin no Taigai Ishiki ni Oyobosu Masu Media no Eikyo (Impact of Mass Media on Japanese People's Sense of Trust toward U.S.)," Nihon Seiji Gakkai, ed., *Gakunen Seijigaku, 2005 II: Shimin Shakai ni Okeru Seisaku Katei to Seisaku Joho* (The Annals of the Japanese Political Science Association, 2005 II: The Policy Process and Information in Civil Society) (Tokyo: Kibokusha, 2005), pp. 69–86.

Krauss, Ellis. "Changing Television News in Japan," *The Journal of Asian Studies*, Vol. 57, No. 3 (August 1998), pp. 663–92.

———. *Broadcasting Politics in Japan: NHK and Television News* (Ithaca, NY: Cornell University Press, 2000).

Krauss, Ellis S., Thomas P. Rohlen, and Patricia G. Steinhoff. *Conflict in Japan* (Honolulu: University of Hawaii Press, 1984).

Kurosawa, Akira. *Something Like an Autobiography*, translated by Audie Bock (New York: Vintage, 1983).

Kusano, Atsushi. *Terebi Hodo no Tadashii Mikata* (The Proper Way to View Television News) (Tokyo: PHP Shinsho, 2000).

Kushner, Barak, and Sato Masaharu, "Digesting Postwar Japanese Media," *Diplomatic History*, Vol. 29, No. 1 (January 2005), pp. 27–48.

Ladd, Everett Carll, and Karlyn H. Bowman. *Public Opinion in America and Japan: How We See Each Other and Ourselves* (Washington, D.C.: The American Enterprise Institute Press, 1996).

LaMay, Craig L. *Democratic Enterprise: Sustaining Media and Civil Society* (Washington, D.C.: The Aspen Institute, 2003).

Lang, Kurt, and Gladys Engel Lang. *Politics and Television* (Chicago: Quadrangle Books, 1968).

Leheny, David. "Tokyo Confronts Terror," *Policy Review*, No. 110 (December 2001/ January 2002), pp. 37–47.

Lijphart, Arendt. *Patterns of Democracy: Government Forms and Performance in Thirty-Six Countries* (New Haven: Yale University Press, 2000).

Lippmann, Walter. *Public Opinion* (New York: Free Press, 1965, reprint of 1922 ed.).

————. *The Phantom Public* (New York: Harcourt, Brace, 1925).

Luther, Catherine A. *Press Images, National Identity, and Foreign Policy: A Case Study of U.S.-Japan Relations from 1955–1995* (New York: Routledge, 2001).

Machidori, Satoshi. "Rethinking the Role of the Upper House," *Japan Echo*, Vol. 35, No. 2 (April 2008), 18–22.

Makuta, Satoshi. *Sengo Okinawa no Shimbunjin* (Postwar Okinawa Newspaper Personalities) (Naha: Okinawa Taimusu sha, 1999).

Mansfield Center for Pacific Affairs, ed. *Summary of Conference and Research Creating Images: American and Japanese Television News Coverage of the Other* (Missoula, Montana: The Mansfield Center for Pacific Affairs, March 5 & 6, 1994).

Mansfield Center for Pacific Affairs and Dentsu Institute for Human Studies, eds. *Japanese and American Media: Coverage of Friction between Two Nations* (Missoula, Montana: The Mansfield Center for Pacific Affairs, 1994).

Margolis, Michael, and Gary Mauser, eds. *Manipulating Public Opinion: Essays on Public Opinion as a Dependent Variable* (Belmont, Calif.: Wadsworth, 1989).

Matsuda, Takeo. "Kokusai Terorizumu to Jieiken (International Terrorism and the Right of Self-Defense)," *Kokusaiho Gaiko Zasshi*, Vol. 101, No. 3 (November 2002), pp. 407–26.

Matsui, Yoshiro. "Beikoku no Buryoku Koshi ha Seito Na No Ka (Was the Use of Force by the U.S. Legitimate?)," *Sekai*, No. 695 (December 2001), pp. 40–7.

Matsumoto, Kenichi. "Beikoku Tsuizui ha Honto ni Kokueki ka (Is Going Along With the U.S. Really in the National Interest?)," *Ronza*, No. 102 (November 2003), pp. 34–41.

May, Earnest R. "The News Media and Diplomacy," in Gordon A. Craig and Francis L. Lowewenheim, eds., *The Diplomats, 1939–1979* (Princeton: Princeton University Press, 1994), pp. 665–700.

Mayama, Akira. "Buryoku Kogeki no Hassei to Jieiken Koushi (The [U.S.] Armed Attack and the Use of the Right of Self-Defense)," *Kokusai Anzen Hosho*, Vol. 31, No. 4 (March 2001), pp. 17–27.

McCargo, Duncan. "The Political Role of the Japanese Media," *Pacific Review*, Vol. 9, No. 2 (1996), pp. 251–64.

Mearshaeimer, John. "Back to the Future: Instability in Europe after the Cold War," *International Security*, No. 15 (Summer 1990), pp. 5–56.

Mendel, Douglas H., Jr. *The Japanese People and Foreign Policy: A Study of Public Opinion in Post-Treaty Japan* (Westport: Greenwood, 1971).

Meyer, Armin H. *Assignment Tokyo: An Ambassador's Journal* (Indianapolis: The Bobbs-Merrill Company, 1974).

Midford, Paul. "The Logic of Reassurance and Japan's Grand Strategy," *Security Studies*, Vol. 11, No. 3 (Spring 2002), pp. 1–43.

———. "Japan as a 'Normal' Democracy? Common Challenges with Other Advanced Industrial Democracies," *Journal of Policy Studies*, No. 15 (September 2003), pp. 73–83.

———. "Japan's Navy: Politics and Paradox, 1971–2000," book Review in *International Relations of the Asia-Pacific*, Vol. 3, No. 2 (2003), pp. 293–6.

———. "Japan's Response to Terror: Sending the SDF to the Arabian Sea," *Asian Survey*, Vol. 43, No. 2 (March–April 2003).

———. "Japanese Public Opinion and the War on Terrorism: Implications for Japan's Security Strategy," Policy Study #27 (East–West Center Washington Office, 2006).

Miki Ken. *Okinawa: Datsuwa no Jidai* (Okinawa: The Age of Leaving Japan) (Naha: Niraisha, 1992).

Mikuriya, Takashi. *Nihirizumu no Saisho: Koizumi Junichiroron* (The Nihilist Prime Minister: On Koizumi Junichiro) (Tokyo: PHP Shinsho, 2006).

Ministry of Foreign Affairs, *Anzen Hosho ni Kansuru Seron Chosa*, http://www. mofa.go.jp/mofaj/gaiko/ah_choosa/ah_choosa.html (2002).

Ministry of Foreign Affairs, *Bei Dooji Tahatsu Tero Jiken Kokusaiteki na Torikumi*, http://www.mofa.go.jp/mofaj/area/usa/terro0109/k_torikumi.html (2001).

Ministry of Foreign Affairs, Headquarters for Promotion of Measures against Transnational Organized Crime and Other Relative Issues and International Terrorism, *Action Plan for Prevention of Terrorism*, http://www.mofa.go.jp/ policy/terrorism/action.pdf (2004).

Ministry of Foreign Affairs, Japan's International Counter-Terrorism Cooperation, http://www.mofa.go.jp/policy/terrorism/cooperation.html (2005).

Ministry of Foreign Affairs, Public Relations Division, *Beikoku ni okeru tai Nichi Seron Chosa ni Tsuite*, http://www.mofa.go.jp/mofaj/area/usa/yoron03/ pdfs/2003_1.pdf (2003).

Ministry of Foreign Affairs, Public Relations Division, *Nicchu Kankei ni Kansuru Seron Chosa, Chosa Kekka*, http://www.mofa.go.jp/mofaj/area/china/yoron_k. html (2003).

Ministry of Foreign Affairs, *Saikin no Beikoku Josei to Nichibei Kankei* http://www. mofa.go.jp/mofaj/area/usa/kankei.html (2003).

Miura, Shumon, and Yamazaki, Masakazu. "Chuo Koron no Rekishi wo Kataru: Rondan no 'Chuo' wo Hashiritsuzuketa 120 Nen (Talking about the History of Chuo Koron: 120 Years of Leading the Public Debate)," *Chuo Koron*, Vol. 121, No. 4 (April 2006), pp. 166–78.

Miyashita, Akitoshi. "Where do Norms Come From? Foundations of Japan's Postwar Pacifism," *International Relations of the Asia-Pacific*, Vol. 7 (2007), pp. 99–120.

Miyata, Osamu. "Isuramu Kagekiha no Taibei Zouo no Yoin ha Nani ka (What are the Reasons behind the Islamic Extremists' Attacks on America?)," *Sekai*, No. 694 (November 2001), pp. 57–62.

Mizukoshi, Hideaki. "Terrorists, Terrorism and Japan's Counter-Terrorism Policy," *Gaiko Forum*, Vol. 3, No. 2 (Summer 2003), pp. 53–63.

Mogami, Toshiki. "Kokuren Heiwa Taisei ga Shuen Suru Mae ni (Before the End of the UN Peace System)," *Sekai*, No. 711 (March 2003), pp. 51–62.

Morgan, Peter. "LDP on the Way to Extinction?" *Japan Weekly HSBC*, July 16, 2004, pp. 1–5.

Morimoto Satoshi, "'Iraku no Jiyu' Sakusen no Kyokun to Imiai (Lessons and Implications of Operation 'Iraqi Freedom')," *Gaiko Forum*, Vol. 16, No. 7 (July 2003), pp. 38–43.

Moromizato, Michihiro. "Okinawa Jaanarizumu ni Miru Anpo to Kenpo (The U.S.–Japan Security Treaty and the Constitution as Seen in Okinawan Journalism)," in Kan Hideki and Ishida Masaharu, eds., *21 Seiki no Anzen Hosho to Nichibei Anpo Taisei* (21st Century Security and the Japan–U.S. Security Treaty System) (Kyoto: Minerva, 2005), pp. 316–41.

Mueller, John E. *War, Presidents and Public Opinion* (New York: Wiley, 1973).

Murata, Koji. "Kyocho Sareta 'Iraku no Sekinin' 'Kita Chosen' (The Emphasized 'Responsibility of Iraq' and 'North Korea')," *Ronza*, No. 102 (November 2003), pp. 42–9.

Nakamura, Tamotsu. "Fukkigo 20 Nenkan no Taibeikoku ni Kansuru Ishiki no Henka (Changes in Views of the United States in the 20 Years following Reversion)," in Teruya Yoshihiko and Yamazato Katsunori, eds., *Sengo Okinawa to Amerika: Ibunka Sesshoku no 50 Nen* (Postwar Okinawa and America: Fifty Years of Cross-Cultural Contact) (Naha: Okinawa Taimususha, 1995), pp. 252–71.

Nakanishi, Hiroshi. "Kokusai Seiji kara Mita 'Jieitai Iraku Haken' no Imi (The Significance of 'Dispatching the SDF to Iraq' from the View of International Politics)," *Ushio*, No. 541 (March 2003), pp. 158–63.

———, "'Kyofu to no Senso' no Jidai (The Era of 'the War against Terror')," *Chuo Koron*, Vol. 119, No. 6 (June 2004), pp. 45–53.

———. "Democracy and Foreign Policy: An Age Old Dilemma," *Gaiko Forum*, Vol. 4, No. 4 (Winter 2005), pp. 3–11.

Nakanishi, Terumasa. "Koizumi Shusho yo 'Rekishi no Chosen' wo Ukete Tate (Prime Minister Koizumi, Stand Up and Accept 'the History Challenge')," *Shokun!*, Vol. 36, No. 2 (February 2004), pp. 44–56.

National Police Agency (Keisatsucho), *Keisatsuho no Ichibu o Kaisei Suru Horitsu No Gaiyo* http://www.npa.go.jp/seisaku/soumu5/gaiyou.pdf (2004).

Nelson, John. "Social Memory as Ritual Practice: Commemorating Spirits of the Military Dead at Yasukuni Shinto Shrine," *Journal of Asian Studies*, Vol. 62, No. 2 (May 2003), pp. 443–468.

Nelson, Thomas E. "Media to Seiji (Media and Politics)," in Kawata Junichi and Araki Yoshinobu, eds., *Seiji Shinrigaku* (Political Psychology) (Tokyo: Kitaju Shuppan, 2003), pp. 74–86.

Nihon Hoso Kyokai, ed. *Broadcasting in Japan: Twentieth Century Journey from Radio to Multimedia* (Tokyo: NHK, 2002).

Ninic, Miroslav. "A Sensible Public: New Perspectives on Popular Opinion and Foreign Policy," *Journal of Conflict Resolution*, Vol. 36, No. 4, pp. 772–89.

———. "The United States, the Soviet Union, and the Politics of Opposites," *World Politics* Vol. 40, No. 4 (July 1988), pp. 452–75.

NIRA, *Shimin Koeki Katsudo Kiban Seibi ni Kansuru Chosa Kenkyu* (Research Report on the Support System for Citizens' Public Interest Activities) (Tokyo: National Institute for Research Advancement, 1994).

Nishibe, Susumu. "Amerika Senryaku ni Haramareru Kyoki (Madness Fraught in the U.S. Strategy)," *Seiron*, No. 369 (April 2003), pp. 64–77.

Nishide, Yuko. "Social Capital and Civil Society in Japan." (Doctoral Dissertation, School of International Public Policy, Osaka University, 2007).

Nishitani, Makiko. "Kokusai Yoron to Kokunai Yoron no Renkan: Beikoku no Wangan Kiki-Senso ni Taisuru Gaiko Seisaku wo Jirei to Shite (The Relationship between Domestic Opinion and International Public Opinion: The Case of America's Foreign Policy at the Time of the Gulf Crisis and War)," *Kokusai Seiji*, No. 128 (October 2001), pp. 115–29.

Nishitani, Osamu. "Kore ha 'Senso' de ha Nai (This is Not a 'War')," *Sekai*, No. 694 (November 2001), pp. 32–9.

Noelle-Neumann, Elisabeth. *The Spiral of Silence: Public Opinion, Our Social Skin* (Chicago: University of Chicago Press, 1984).

———. "The Effect of Mass Media on Opinion Formation," in David Demers and K. Viswanath, eds., *Mass Media, Social Control, and Social Change: A Macrosocial Perspective* (Ames: Iowa University Press, 1999).

Norris, Pippa, Montague Kern, and Marion Just, eds. *Framing Terrorism: The News Media, the Government, and the Public* (New York: Routledge, 2003).

Okada Naoyuki, Sato Takumi, Nishihira Shigeki, and Miyatake Michiko. *Yoron Kenkyu to Seron Chosa* (Opinion Research and Public Opinion Polls) (Tokyo: Shinyosha, 2007).

Okamoto, Atsuhisa. "Chijo wo Oi Tsukusu 'Anzen no Sensei' ('The Tyranny of Safety' on the Ground)," *Ronza*, No. 96 (May 2003), pp. 70–1.

Okamoto, Yukio. "Wangan Senso no Yona Kakon wo Nokosanai Tameni (In Order Not to Leave Problems like those After the Gulf War)," *Chuo Koron*, Vol. 118, No. 11 (November 2003), pp. 102–12.

Okamura, Reimei. "U.S.–Japan Relations and the Media in the Information Age: Coverage of the American Base Issues in Okinawa," *The Japanese Journal of American Studies*, No. 9 (1998), pp. 5–28.

Okinawa Furii Jaanarisuto Kaigi, ed. *Okinawa no Shimbun ga Tsubureru Hi* (The Day Newspapers in Okinawa are Gone) (Naha: Gekkan Okinawasha, 1994).

Okinawa Taimusu Shashi Henshu Iinkai, ed. *Shimbun 30 Nen: Okinawa Taimusu ga Ikita Okinawa Sengoshi* (30 Years of the Newspaper: The Postwar History of Okinawa that the Okinawa Times Has Lived) (Naha: Okinawa Taimusu, 1979).

Ota Masahide, *The Battle of Okinawa: The Typhoon of Steel and Bombs* (Tokyo: Kume Publishing, 1984).

Otake, Hideo. *Koizumi Junichiro Populizumu no Kenkyu: Sono Senryaku to Shuho* (Research into the Populism of Koizumi Junichiro: Its Strategy and Methods) (Tokyo: Toyo Keizai Shinposha, 2006).

Packard, George. *Protest in Tokyo: The Security Treaty Crisis of 1960* (Princeton: Princeton University Press, 1966).

Packer, George. "Knowing the Enemy: Can Social Scientists Redefine the 'War on Terror'?" *The New Yorker*, December 18, 2006.

Page, Benjamin I., and Robert Y. Shapiro, *The Rational Public: Fifty Years of Trends in Americans' Policy Preferences* (Chicago: Chicago University Press, 1992).

Pekkanen, Robert. "The Politics of Regulating the Non-Profit Sector," in Stephen P. Osborne, ed., *The Voluntary and Non-Profit Sector in Japan: The Challenge of Change* (London: RoutledgeCurzon, 2003).

Pekkanen, Robert, and Ellis S. Krauss, "Japan's 'Coalition of the Willing' on Security Policies," *Orbis*, Vol. 49, No. 3 (Summer 2005).

Pekkanen, Robert, and Karla Simon, "The Legal Framework for Voluntary and Non-profit activity," in Stephen P. Osborne, ed., *The Voluntary and Non-Profit Sector in Japan: The Challenge of Change* (London: RoutledgeCurzon, 2003).

Pempel, T.J. "Japanese Democracy and Political Culture: A Comparative Perspective," *PS: Political Science and Politics*, Vol. 25, No. 1 (March 1992).

Peterson, Peter G., et al. *Finding America's Voice: A Strategy for Reinvigorating U.S. Public Diplomacy: Report of an Independent Task Force Sponsored by the Council on Foreign Relations* (New York: Council on Foreign Relations, 2003).

Peterson, Sophia. "Events, Mass Opinion, and Elite Attitudes," in Richard L. Merritt, Communication in International Politics, ed., *Communication in International Politics* (Urbana: University of Illinois Press, 1972), pp. 252–71.

Pew Research Center for the People and the Press, *A Year After Iraq War: Mistrust of America in Europe Ever Higher, Muslim Anger Persists* (March 2004).

Pharr, Susan J. "Public Trust and Democracy in Japan," in Joseph S. Nye, Jr., Philip D. Zelikow, and David C. King, eds., *Why People Don't Trust Government* (Cambridge: Harvard University Press, 1997).

Pharr, Susan J., and Ellis S. Krauss, eds. *Media and Politics in Japan* (Honolulu: University of Hawaii Press, 1996).

Pharr, Susan J., and Robert Putnam, eds. *Disaffected Democracies: What's Troubling the Trilateral Countries* (Princeton: Princeton University, 2000).

Price, Vincent, David Tewksbury, and Elizabeth Powers. "Switching Trains of Thought: The Impact of News Frames on Readers' Cognitive Responses," *Communication Research*, Vol. 24, No. 5 (October 1997), pp. 481–506.

Prime Minister's Office. *Anti-Terrorism Special Measures Bill, Outline of the Basic Plan Regarding Measures Based on the Anti-Terrorism Special Measures Law*, http://www.kantei.go.jp/foreign/policy/2001/anti-terrorism/1116keikakus_e.html (2001).

———. *Emergency Response Measures*, http://www.kantei.go.jp/foreign/koizumispeech/2001/1008taiuo_e.html (2001).

———. *Establishment of the Emergency Anti-Terrorism Headquarters*, http://www.kantei.go.jp/foreignpolicy/2001/anti_terrorism/1008taisakuhonbu_e.html (2001).

———. *Kuni to Kokumin no Anzen he no Kyoi oyobi Kore ni taisuru Taio ni tsuite*, http://www.kantei.go.jp/jp/singi/anpohouei/dai3/3aryou.pdf (2004).

———. *NBC Tero Taisaku ni Kansuru Hosaku no Suishin Jokyo*, http://www.kantei.go.jp/jp/kikikanri/nbc/2001/0416suisin.html (2001).

———. "Public Opinion Survey on Diplomacy" (Tokyo: Foreign Press Center, March 1987).

———. *The Outline of the Basic Plan Regarding Response Measures based on the Law concerning the Special Measures on Humanitarian and Reconstruction Assistance in Iraq*, http://www.kantei.go.jp/foreignpolicy/2003/031209housin_e.html (2003).

Putnam, Robert D. "Tuning In, Tuning Out: The Strange Disappearance of Social Capital in America," *PS: Politics and Political Science*, Vol. 28, No. 4 (1995), pp. 664–83.

Pyle, Kenneth B. *Japan Rising: The Resurgence of Japanese Power and Purpose* (New York: Public Affairs, 2007).

Reed, Steven. "Environmental Politics: Some Reflections on the Japanese Case," *Comparative Politics*, Vol. 13 (April 1981), pp. 260–71.

Reischauer, Edwin O., and Albert M. Craig. *Japan: Tradition and Transformation* (Tokyo: Charles E. Tuttle, Co., 1978).

Research Institute for Peace and Security, *Asian Security, 1991–1992* (London: Brassey's, 1992).

Reston, James. *The Artillery of the Press: Its Influence on American Foreign Policy* (New York: Harper and Row, 1967).

Richman, Alvin. "Public Opinion and Foreign Affairs: The Mediating Influence of Educational Level," in Melvin Small, ed. *Public Opinion and Historians* (Detroit: Wayne State University, 1970).

Rohlen, Thomas P. "Order in Japanese Society: Attachment, Authority, and Routine," *Journal of Japanese Studies*, Vol. 15, No. 1 (1989), pp. 5–26.

Ron, James. "The NGO Scramble: Organizational Insecurity and the Political Economy of Transnational Action," *International Security*, Vol. 27, No. 1 (Summer 2002), pp. 5–39.

Rose, Gillian. "Feminism and Geography: The Limits of Geographical Knowledge," in Jayne Rodgers, ed., *Spatializing International Politics: Analyzing Activism on the Internet* (New York: Routledge, 2003).

Rosenau, James N. *Public Opinion and Foreign Policy: An Operational Formulation* (New York: Random House, 1961).

Ryukyu Shimpo Hyakunenshi Kanko Iinkai, ed. *Ryukyu Shimpo Hyakunenshi* (One Hundred Years of the Ryukyu Shimpo) (Naha: Ryukyu Shimposha, 1993).

Sakai, Keiko. "'Seigi' to 'Seigi' no Tatakai ni Suru Na (Don't Make This into a Fight between [Two Views of] 'Justice')," *Chuo Koron*, Vol. 116, No. 11 (November 2001), pp. 92–5.

———. "Fusein to Amerika no Sakuso Shita Kankei (Complicated Relations between Hussein and the U.S.)," *Ushio*, No. 531 (May 2003), pp. 76–83.

Sakamoto, Kazuya. "Domei no Haba wo Hiroge 'Seiryoku Kinko' de Kyoryoku wo (Expanding the Range of the Alliance and Cooperating by the 'Balance of Power')," *Ronza*, No. 93 (February 2003), pp. 53–65.

Sakamoto, Yoshikazu. "Tero to 'Bunmei' no Seijigaku (The Political Science of Terrorism and 'Civilization')," *Sekai*, No. 697 (January 2002), pp. 56–9.

Salamon, Lester M. *America's Nonprofit Sector: A Primer* (New York: The Foundation Center, 1992).

Sano, Shinichi. *Koizumi Seiken: Hijo no Saigetsu* (The Koizumi Administration: Heartless Years) (Tokyo: Bunshun Bunko, 2006).

Sato, Takumi, ed. *Sengo Yoron no Media Shakaigaku* (The Media Science of Postwar Public Opinion) (Tokyo: Kashiwa Shobo, 2003).

Seko, Hiroshige. *Profeshonaru Koho Senryaku* (Professional Communications Strategies) (Tokyo: Goma Books, 2005).

Shepard, Alicia C. *Narrowing the Gap: Military, Media, and the Iraq War* (Chicago: Robert R. McCormick Tribune Foundation, 2004).

Shigemura, Toshimitsu. *Gaiko Haiboku: Niccho Shuno Kaidan to Nichibei Domei no Shinjitsu* (Diplomatic Loss: The Truth behind the Japan–North Korea Summit and the U.S.–Japan Alliance) (Tokyo: Kodansha, 2005).

Shikata, Toshiyuki. "Fusein ha Korosanai (Hussein Cannot be Killed)," *Shokun*, Vol. 34, No. 2 (November 2002), pp. 72–79.

Shimizu, Masato. *Kantei Shudo: Koizumi Junichiro no Kakumei* (Leadership of the Prime Minister's Office: Koizumi Junichiro's Revolution) (Tokyo: Nihon Keizai Shimbunsha, 2005).

Shinoda, Tomohito. *Kantei no Kenryoku* (Power of the Prime Minister's Office) (Tokyo: Chikuma Shobo, 1996).

————. "Koizumi's Top-Down Leadership in the Anti-Terrorism Legislation: The Impact of Political Institutional Changes," *SAIS Review*, Vol. 23, No. 1 (Winter–Spring 2003), pp. 19–34.

————. *Koizumi Diplomacy: Japan's Kantei Approach to Foreign and Defense Affairs* (Seattle: University of Washington Press, 2007).

Shister, Neil. *A Matter of Degree: The Role of Journalists as Activists in Journalism Business and Policy* (Washington, D.C.: The Aspen Institute, 2004).

Small, Melvin, ed. *Public Opinion and Historians* (Detroit: Wayne State University, 1970).

Smith, Sheila A. "The Evolution of Military Cooperation in the U.S.–Japan Alliance," in Michael J. Green and Patrick Cronin, eds., *The U.S.–Japan Alliance: Past, Present, and Future* (New York: Council on Foreign Relations Press, 1999), pp. 69–93.

————. "A Place Apart: Okinawa and Japan's Postwar Peace," in Akira Iriye and Robert A. Wampler, eds., *Partnership: The United States and Japan, 1951–2001* (Tokyo: Kodansha, 2001), pp. 179–98.

Snyder, Jack. *Myths of Empire: Domestic Politics and International Ambition* (Ithaca: Cornell University Press, 1991).

Soejima, Takahiko. "Daijiken wo Tokiakasu 'Buroobakku Riron' no Kyokun (Explaining the [9/11] Incident: The Lessons of the 'Blowback Theory')," *Seiron*, No. 351 (November 2001), pp. 50–61.

Stimson, James A. *Public Opinion in America: Moods, Cycles, and Swings* (Boulder: Westview Press, 1999).

Stockwin, J.A.A. *Governing Japan* (London: Blackwell, 1999).

————. "Koizumi and Blair as Political Leaders: A View from the United Kingdom," *International House of Japan Bulletin*, Vol. 27, No. 1 (2007), pp. 1–14.

Suwa, Tetsuji, Morinaga Takuro, et al. *Shasetsu Taiketsu: Goban Shobu* (The Clash of Editorials among the Big Five) (Tokyo: Chuo Koron Shinsha, 2007).

Tachibana, Takashi. "Jibaku Tero no Kenkyu (A Study of Terrorist Bombers)," *Bungei Shunju*, Vol. 79, No. 13 (November 2001), pp. 94–111.

Tachibana, Takashi, "Iraku Shuppei no Taigi wo Tou (On the Legitimacy of Dispatching Troops to Iraq)," *Gendai*, Vol. 38, No. 3 (March 2004), pp. 28–43.

Takahashi, Tetsuya. *Yasukuni Mondai* (The Yasukuni Problem) (Tokyo: Chikuma Shobo, 2005).

Takamine, Choko, *Shimbun 50 Nen* (50 Years of Newspapers) (Naha: Okinawa Taimusu, 1973).

Takase, Junichi. *Joho to Seiji* (Information and Politics) (Tokyo: Shinhyoron, 1999).

————. *Akusesu: Nihon Seijiron* (Japanese Politics) (Tokyo: Nihon Keizai Hyoronsha, 2003).

————. *Buki to Shite no "Kotoba Seiji": Furieki Bunpai Jidai no Seiji Shuho* ("Word Politics" as a Weapon: Political Methods in the Age of Non-Profit Distribution) (Tokyo: Kodansha, 2005).

Takashima, Hatsuhisa. "What are the Media Telling Us?" *Gaiko Forum*, Vol. 4, No. 4 (Winter 2005), pp. 12–23.

Takasugi, Tadaaki. "Reisengo no Amerika no Tainichi Yoron to Nichibei Domei: Anzen Hosho ni Kansuru Yoron wo Megutte (American Public Opinion in the Post–Cold War and the Japan–U.S. Alliance with a Focus on Public Opinion on Security Issues)," in Sato Seizaburo, ed., *Shinsenryaku no Mosaku: Reisengo no America* (U.S. Foreign and Defense Policies After the Cold War) (Tokyo: Kokusai Mondai Kenkyusho, 1994), pp. 169–97.

Takeda, Seiji. "Jiyu to Byodo no Anchinomii (The Antinomy of Freedom and Equality)," *Ronza*, No. 92 (January 2003), pp. 40–7.

Takeda, Yasuhiro. "Redefining Japan's National Security," *Business Times*, August 27, 1994, p. 1.

Takemura, Masayoshi. *Chisakutomo Kirari to Hikaru Koku Nihon* (A Small But Bright and Shining Japan) (Tokyo: Kobunsha, 1994).

Takenaka, Harukata. *Shusho Shihai: Nihon Seiji no Hensen* (Control by the Prime Minister: The Evolution of Japanese Politics) (Tokyo: Chuko Shinsho, 2006).

Takenaka, Heizo. *Kozo Kaikaku no Shinjitsu* (The Truth behind Structural Reform) (Tokyo: Nihon Keizai Shimbunsha, 2006).

Takubo, Tadae. "'Okinawa no kokoro' to Nichibei Anpo ('Okinawa's Heart' and the Japan–U.S. Alliance)," *Seiron*, No. 287 (July 1996), pp. 74–83.

———, "The Okinawan Threat to the Security Treaty," *Japan Echo*, Vol. 23, No. 3 (Autumn 1996), pp. 46–52.

Tamura, Shigeru. *Deeta no Wana: Seron ha Ko Shite Tsukureru* (The Data Trap: This is How Public Opinion is Created) (Tokyo: Shueisha, 2006).

Tanaka, Aiji, "Yoron to Media (Public Opinion and Media)," in Kume Ikuo et al. eds., *Seiji Gaku* (Political Science: Scope and Theory) (Tokyo: Yuhikaku, 2003), pp. 421–40.

Tanaka, Akihiko. *Waado Poritikusu: Gurobarizeeshon no Naka no Nihon Gaiko* (Word Politics: Japanese Diplomacy amid Globalization) (Tokyo: Chikuma Shobo, 2000).

———. "Tero to no 'Senso' de Nihon ha Nani wo Nasu Beki Ka (What Should Japan Do in the 'War' on Terrorism)," *Chuo Koron*, Vol. 116, No. 11 (November 2001), pp. 104–107.

———. "Beikoku, Iraku Kogeki no Mittsu no Shinario (3 Scenarios of a U.S. Attack on Iraq)," *Chuo Koron*, Vol. 117, No. 1 (October 2002), pp. 49–57.

———. "Asian Opinions: A Mixed Bag for Japan," *Japan Echo*, Vol. 34, No. 3 (June 2007), pp. 31–4.

Tanaka, Akira. *Shokokushugi Nippon no Kindai wo Yominaosu* (Rereading Modern Small Japanism) (Tokyo: Iwanami Shinsho, 1999).

Tani (Musashi), Katsuhiko. "Reisengo Nihon no Anzen Hosho Seisaku no Rippo Katei ni Okeru Shibirian Kontororu no Kenkyu (A Study of Civilian Control in the Legislative Process for Japanese Security Policy in the Post Cold War)," (Doctoral Dissertation, Osaka School of International Public Policy, Osaka University, 2007).

Taniguchi, Masaki. "Masu Media (Mass Media)," in Fukuda Yuhiro and Fukuda Masaki, eds., *Demokurashii no Seijigaku* (The Politics of Democracy) (Tokyo: Tokyo Daigaku Shuppankai, 2002), pp. 269–86.

Tanioka, Ichiro. *"Shakai Chosa" no Uso: Resaachi Riterashii no Susume* (The Lie of "Social Research": Recommending Research Literacy) (Tokyo: Bunshu Shinsho, 2000).

Tasei, Yasuhiro, and Clay Chandler. *Media to Seiji: Nichibei Media Daiarogu* (Media and Politics: A Dialogue between Japanese and American Members of the Media) (Tokyo: Akashi Shoten, 1999).

Task Force on Foreign Relations for the Prime Minister, *Basic Strategies for Japan's Foreign Policy in the 21st Century New Era, New Vision, New Diplomacy*, http://www.kantei.go.jp/foreign/policy/2002/1128tf_e.html (2002).

Tasker, Peter. *The Japanese: A Major Exploration of Modern Japan* (New York: E.P. Dutton, 1988).

Tembo, Fletcher. *Participation, Negotiation and Poverty: Encouraging the Power of Images: Designing Pro-Poor Development Programmes.* King's SOAS Studies in Development Geography (London: Ashgate, 2003).

Terashima, Jitsuro. "21 Seiki Nihon Gaiko no Kosoryoku Iraku Senso o Koete (The Power of Japan's Diplomatic Thinking in the 20th Century: Beyond the Iraq War)," *Ronza*, No. 104 (January 2004), pp. 20–7.

———. "Busshu Tandoku Haken Shugi no Hatan to Nippon (The Collapse of Bush's Unilateral Hegemonism and Japan)," *Ronza*, No. 97 (June 2004), pp. 52–5.

Thayer, Nathaniel. "Competition and Conformity: An Inquiry into the Structure of a Japanese Newspaper," in Ezra F. Vogel, ed., *Modern Japanese Organization and Decision-making* (Berkeley: University of California Press, 1975), pp. 284–303.

Thayne, David. *Danko* (Lion Heart) (Tokyo: Sanshusha, 2001).

Thomas, Helen. *Watchdogs of Democracy? The Waning Washington Press Corps and How it Has Failed the Public* (New York: Simon and Schuster, 2006).

Tkach-Kawasaki, Leslie M. "Clicking for Votes: Assessing Japanese Political Campaigns on the Web," in K.C. Ho, Randolph Kluver, and Kenneth C.C. Yang, eds., *Asia.com: Asia Encounters the Internet* (London: RoutledgeCurzon, 2003).

Toguchi, M. "Taimusu-Shimpo no Shito (The Times-Shimpo Struggle)," in Okinawa Furii Jaanarisuto Kyogi, ed., *Okinawa no Shimbun* (Naha: Okinawa Times, 1994), pp. 293–316.

Tomisek, Steven J. "Homeland Security—The New Role for Defense," *Strategic Forum*, No. 189 (2002), p. 4.

Toyoshita, Narahiko. "'Atarashii Senso' to 'Furui Domei' ('The New War' and 'the Old Alliance')," *Sekai*, No. 697 (January 2002), pp. 66–73.

Tsuboi, Yoshiharu. "Tai Tero Ajia Kokusai Kyoryoku Taisei no Kochiku o (Construct an Anti-Terrorist, Asian International Cooperative System)," *Sekai*, No. 695 (December 2001), pp. 56–61.

Tsujinaka,Yutaka. *Rieki Shudan* (Interest Groups) (Tokyo: Tokyo Daigaku Shuppankai, 1986).

———. "Interest Group Structure and Regime Change in Japan," *Maryland/Tsukuba Papers on U.S.–Japan Relations*, November 1996.

Tsuruta, Tomohisa."Shugiinsen Yoron Chosa ni Miru Kokumin Ishiki (Public Opinion as Seen in the Results of Public Opinion Polls at the Time of the Lower House Election)," *Choken Kwaatarii* (Yomiuri Shimbun Chosa Kenkyu Honbu Quarterly), No. 10 (Winter 2003), pp. 31–47.

Uchigawa, Yoshimi, and Tsujimura Akira, eds. *Joho to Seiji* (Information and Politics) (Tokyo: Tokyo Daigaku Shuppankai, 1974).

Uesugi, Takashi. *Koizumi no Shori, Media no Haiboku* (Koizumi's Victory, Media's Defeat) (Tokyo: Sosoha, 2006).

Umebayashi, Hiromichi. "The Role of NGOs in Japan and the World," in Wade L. Huntley, Kazumi Mizumoto, and Mitsuru Kurosawa, eds., *Nuclear Disarmament in the Twenty-First Century* (Hiroshima: Hiroshima Peace Institute, 2004), pp. 338–53.

United Nations, Office on Drugs and Crime, 2004, Conventions against Terrorism, Vienna, Austria, http://www.unodc.org/unodc/terrorism_conventions.html.

United Nations, Security Council, *Resolution 1441 (2002)*, November 18, 2002.

Uozumi, Akira. *Kanryo to Media* (The Bureaucracy and the Media) (Tokyo: Kadokawa Shoten, 2007).

U.S. Government, Department of Defense. *Annual Report to the President and the Congress 2002*, August 15, 2002.

———. *President's Remarks at National Day of Prayer and Remembrance, September 4, 2003*, http://www.whitehouse.gov/news/releases/2001/09/20010914-2.html.

U.S. Government. *Remarks by the President from the USS Abraham Lincoln at Sea off the Coast of San Diego, California*, May 1, 2003, http://www.whitehouse.gov/news/releases/2003/05/iraq/20030501-15.html.

———. *The National Security Strategy of the United States of America*, September 2002.

———. *The President's State of the Union Address*, January 19, 2002, http://www.whitehouse.gov/news/releases/2002/01/20020129-11.html.

Utagawa, Reizo, and Kawakami Takashi, "Hanseiki ni Miru Amerika no Tainichi Paasepushon to Japan Porishii no Henka (Changes in Japan Policy and in America's Perceptions of Japan over the Past 50 Years)," in Sato Seizaburo, ed., *Shinsennryaku no Mosaku: Reisengo no America* (U.S. Foreign and Defense Policies after the Cold War; *literally* Searching for a New Strategy: America After the Cold War) (Tokyo: Kokusai Mondai Kenkyusho, 1994), pp. 199–259.

Valkenbury, Patti M., Holli A. Semetko, and Claes H. De Vreese, "The Effects of News Frames on Readers' Thoughts and Recall," *Communication Research*, Vol. 26, No. 5 (October 1999), pp. 550–69.

Van Evera, Stephen. *Causes of War* (Ithaca: Cornell University Press, 1999).

Verba, Sidney, Richard A. Brody, Edwin B. Parker, Norman H. Nie, Nelson W. Polsby, Paul Ekman, and Gordon S. Black. "Public Opinion and the War in Vietnam," *American Political Science Review*, Vol. 61, No. 2 (June 1967), pp. 317–33.

Vosse, Wilhelm. "The Emergence of a Civil Society in Japan," *Japanstudien*, Band 11 (1999), pp. 31–53.

Walt, Stephan W. *Origins of Alliance* (Ithaca: Cornell University Press, 1987).

———. "Identity and Threat Perception—an Experimental Analysis," Paper Presented Before the American Political Science Association, August 2001 (http://www.soc.penn.edu/"rousseau/APSA2001id.PDF).

Watanabe, Akio, "Japanese Public Opinion and Foreign Affairs: 1964–73," in Robert Scalapino, ed., *Foreign Policy of Modern Japan* (Berkeley: University off California Press, 1977), pp. 105–45.

———. "Foreign Policy-Making, Japanese Style," *International Affairs*, Vol. 54, No. 1 (January 1978), pp. 75–88.

———. "'Senso' ha Omoku, 'Jindo Shien' ha Karui to Iu Sakkaku (The Illusion that Regards 'War' as Serious and 'Humanitarian Assistance' as Light)," *Chuo Koron*, Vol. 119, No. 2 (February 2004), pp. 38–41.

Watanabe, Hirotaka, "Nichi Bei Domei to Sekai Anzen Hosho no Kishimi (The Japan–U.S. Alliance and Creak of World Security)," *Chuo Koron*, Vol. 118, No. 2 (February 2003), pp. 96–103.

Watanabe, Tsuneo. "Seiji to Shidoryoku oyobi Media no Yakuwari (Politics, Leadership, and the Role of the Media)," *Choken Kwaatarii* (Yomiuri Shimbun Chosa Kenkyu Honbu Quarterly), No. 10 (Winter 2003), pp. 4–30.

Weinstein, Martin. *Japan's Postwar Defense Policy, 1947–1968* (New York: Columbia University Press, 1971).

Weston, Stephanie. "The U.S.–Japan Alliance in the New Post Cold War," *Japanese Studies*, Vol. 24, No. 1 (May 2004), pp. 45–59.

Wildes, Harry Emerson. *Social Currents in Japan with Special Reference to the Press* (Chicago: University of Chicago Press, 1927).

van Wolferen, Karl. *The Enigma of Japanese Power* (New York: Alfred A. Knopf, 1989).

Woolley, Peter J. *Japan's Navy: Politics and Paradox, 1971–2000* (Boulder: Lynne Rienner, 2000).

Yamaguchi, Jiro. "Taigi Naki Senryo he no Katan ha Yurusarenai (Having a Part in an Occupation Not Justified is Unacceptable)," *Sekai*, No. 726 (May 2004), pp. 82–7.

Yamakoshi, Atsushi. "The Changing Face of NGOs in Japan" (http://www.gdrc. org/ngo/jpngo-face.html).

Yamamoto, Taketoshi, ed. *Shimbun, Zasshi, Shuppan* (Newspapers, Magazines, Publishing) (Kyoto: Minerva, 2005).

Yamauchi, Masayuki. "'Hirakareta Shakai' no 'Teki' (The 'Enemy' of 'Open Society')," *Shokun*, Vol. 33, No. 11 (November 2001), pp. 56–66.

———. "Posuto Tariban to Yuurashia Seijigaku (Post Taliban and the Politics of Eurasia)," *Chuo Koron*, Vol. 117, No. 1 (January 2002), pp. 42–5.

———. "Kita Chosen to Iraku no Akumu (The Nightmare of North Korea and Iraq)," *Chuo Koron*, Vol. 117, No. 1 (November 2002), pp. 64–7.

———. "Dai 2 ji Wangan Senso to Iraku no Saisei (The Second Gulf War and the Revival of Iraq)," *Gaiko Forum*, Vol. 16, No. 5 (May 2003), pp. 12–17.

Yamazaki, Masakazu. "Terorizumu ha Hanzai de Shikanai (Terrorism is a Crime, Pure and Simple)," *Chuo Koron*, Vol. 116, No. 11 (November 2001), pp. 32–42.

———. "Bunmei Tai Hanbunmei (Civilization versus Those against Civilization)," *Ushio*, No. 515 (January 2002), pp. 76–85.

Yanai, Shunji. "Nihon no Kokusai Heiwa Kyoryokuho wo Kangaeru (Thinking about Japan's International Peace Cooperation Bill)," *Gaiko Forum*, Vol. 78, No. 36 (1993), pp. 35–61.

Yokota, Yozo. "Kokuren Kensho no 'Hatten Teki Kaishaku' e (Toward a 'Progressive Interpretation' of the U.N. Charter)," *Chuo Koron*, Vol. 118, No. 6 (June 2003), pp. 58–63.

———. "The UN Charter and the Attack on Iraq," *Japan Echo*, Vol. 30, No. 4 (August 2003), pp. 31–3.

Yomiuri Shimbun Seijibu, ed. *Gaiko wo Kenka ni Shita Otoko: Koizumi Gaiko 2000 Nichi no Shinjitsu* (The Man Who Made Diplomacy a Fight: The Truth Behind the 2000 Days of Koizumi Diplomacy) (Tokyo: Shinchosha, 2006).

Yomiuri Shimbunsha, ed. *Kempo Kaisei: Yomiuri Shian 2004 Nen* (Constitutional Revision: The 2004 Yomiuri Draft) (Tokyo: Chuo Koronsha, 2004).

Yomiuri Shimbunsha Chosa Kenkyu Honbu, ed. *Teigen Hodo: Yomiuri Shimbun no Chosen* (Policy Recommendations and News: The Challenge Facing the Yomiuri Newspaper) (Tokyo: Chuo Koronsha, 2002).

Yomiuri Shimbunsha Yoron Chosabu, ed. *Nihon no Yoron* (Japanese Public Opinion) (Tokyo: Kobundo, 2002).

Yoshida, Reiji. "Koizumi's Career Could be Biggest Casualty of Iraq Dispatch," *Japan Times*, February 12, 2004.

Yoshizaki, Tomonori. "Kokusai Chitsujo to Beikoku no Sensei Kogeki Ron (International Order and U.S. Policy on Preemptive Strikes)," *Kokusai Anzen Hosho*, Vol. 31, No. 4 (March 2004), pp. 1–15.

Zelizer, Barbie, and Stuart Allan, eds. *Journalism after September 11* (New York: Routledge, 2002).

Zhang, Yumei. *Pacific Asia: The Politics of Development* (New York: Routledge, 2003).

NEWSPAPERS

Asahi Shimbun
Daily Yomiuri
Der Spiegel
Japan Times
Mainichi Shimbun
Okinawa Taimusu
Ryukyu Shimpo
Yomiuri Shimbun

WEBSITES

In addition to the respective websites for the newspapers mentioned under the previous heading, the contributors in their respective chapters have utilized the websites of several organizations. Please consult each chapter for those websites.

INDEX